JOURNAL FOR THE STUDY OF THE NEW TESTAMENT SUPPLEMENT SERIES

97

Executive Editor
Stanley E. Porter

Editorial Board
Richard Bauckham, David Catchpole, R. Alan Culpepper,
Joanna Dewey, James D.G. Dunn, Craig A. Evans, Robert Fowler,
Robert Jewett, Elizabeth Struthers Malbon, Dan O. Via

JSOT Press
Sheffield

Prophet, Son, Messiah

Narrative Form and Function in Mark 14–16

Edwin K. Broadhead

Journal for the Study of the New Testament
Supplement Series 97

Copyright © 1994 Sheffield Academic Press

Published by JSOT Press
JSOT Press is an imprint of
Sheffield Academic Press Ltd
343 Fulwood Road
Sheffield S10 3BP
England

Typeset by Sheffield Academic Press
and
Printed on acid-free paper in Great Britain
by Bookcraft
Midsomer Norton, Somerset

British Library Cataloguing in Publication Data

A catalogue record for this book is available
from the British Library

ISBN 1-85075-476-4

To

LOUISE GRAHAM BROADHEAD
1927–1989

Parent,
Friend,
Faithful witness

With much love

CONTENTS

Preface	9
Abbreviations	10

Chapter 1
INTRODUCTION — 11
    Passion Story and Gospel Story — 11
    A Methodological Proposal — 15
    Narrative Analysis and Passion Narrative — 27

Chapter 2
MARK 14.1-42: THE PREPARATION AND BETRAYAL — 29
    Mark 14.1-11: The Anointing Scene — 29
    Mark 14.12-26: The Passover Meal — 50
    Mark 14.26-32a: The Prophecy of Betrayal — 73
    Mark 14.32-42: Gethsemane — 88
    Conclusion — 109

Chapter 3
MARK 14.43–15.15: THE ARREST AND TRIAL — 112
    Mark 14.43-53a: Betrayal, Arrest, Abandonment — 112
    Mark 14.53-65: The First Trial — 128
    Mark 14.66-72: The Trial of Peter — 146
    Mark 15.1-15: The Trial before Pilate — 161
    Conclusion — 177

Chapter 4
MARK 15.16–16.8: THE DEATH OF JESUS — 181
    Mark 15.16-20: Abuse and Mockery — 181
    Mark 15.20c-37: The Death Scene — 194
    Mark 15.38-47: Signs of Hope — 217
    Mark 16.1-8: The Resurrection Promise — 232
    Conclusion — 254

Chapter 5
CONCLUSION 259
    Narrative Form and Function in Mark 14–16 259
    The Characterization of Jesus in Mark 14–16 267
    The Role of the Passion Story in the Gospel of Mark 273
    The Nature and Purpose of the Gospel of Mark 281
    The Gospel Genre 284
    The Composition of the Gospel Tradition 286
    Theses 292
    Concluding Thoughts 295

Appendix
SAYINGS TRADITIONS IN THE PASSION NARRATIVE 297

Bibliography 299
Index of References 308
Index of Authors 322

PREFACE

This study of the passion story is part of a larger concern for the Gospel of Mark and its images of Jesus. This study also partakes in a more personal concern for the demands of discipleship and the sense of calling embodied in this tradition. The completion of this text fulfills a long-cherished personal and academic dream. Thanks are due to many who have encouraged and sustained this work. Professor Frank Stagg has provided an inspiring model of teaching ministry throughout my academic career. Professor Hans Weder has accompanied this study with much grace and encouragement. Professor Peter Stuhlmacher and Mrs Stuhlmacher served as frequent hosts, and he has supported this work with his interest and his kindness. Professor Eduard Schweizer read a preliminary draft and provided both critique and encouragement. Various institutions have contributed to this study. I am grateful to the Theological Faculty of the University of Zürich for their acceptance as a doctoral candidate and for the Dr theol. awarded on the basis of this research. The Baptist Theological Seminary in Rüschlikon proved a gracious host. It supplied an ample library and a quiet corner in which to pursue my work. More personally, I am grateful to my parents, Dempsey and Louise Broadhead, and to my sister, Janet Tidmore, for their unfailing support and encouragement. Loretta Reynolds, my spouse and co-minister, has supported this project from its inception to its completion. I am grateful to her for the love and encouragement which have sustained my dreams for this task. This text is dedicated to my mother. Though her journey ended before the completion of this work, I am sustained by her enduring encouragement and her undying love.

Abbreviations

ATANT	Abhandlungen zur Theologie des Alten und Neuen Testaments
Bib	*Biblica*
BJRL	*Bulletin of the John Rylands Library*
BL	*Bibel und Leben*
EKKNT	Evangelish-Katholischer Kommentar zum Neuen Testament
ETL	*Ephemerides theologicae lovanienses*
EvT	*Evangelische Theologie*
ExpTim	*Expository Times*
HTKNT	Herders theologischer Kommentar zum Neuen Testament
HTR	*Harvard Theological Review*
IEJ	*Israel Exploration Journal*
JBL	*Journal of Biblical Literature*
JR	*Journal of Religion*
JSNT	*Journal for the Study of the New Testament*
JSOT	*Journal for the Study of the Old Testament*
JTS	*Journal of Theological Studies*
LB	*Linguistica Biblica*
NICNT	New International Commentary on the New Testament
NovT	*Novum Testamentum*
NovTSup	*Novum Testamentum*, Supplements
NTS	*New Testament Studies*
OTNT	Ökumenischer Taschenbuchkommentar zum Neuen Testament
RAC	*Reallexikon für Antike und Christentum*
RevExp	*Review and Expositor*
RSR	*Recherches de science religieuse*
SANT	Studien zum Alten und Neuen Testament
SBB	Stuttgarter biblische Beiträge
SE	*Studia Evangelica*
SPIB	Scripta pontificii instituti biblici
TBü	Theologische Bücherei
TDNT	G. Kittel and G. Friedrich (eds.), *Theological Dictionary of the New Testament*
TLZ	*Theologische Literaturzeitung*
WMANT	Wissenschaftliche Monographien zum Alten und Neuen Testament
ZNW	*Zeitschrift für die neutestamentliche Wissenschaft*
ZTK	*Zeitschrift für Theologie und Kirche*

Chapter 1

INTRODUCTION

The Gospel of Mark does not receive its primary identity from the historical details which echo through its stories. The preaching of an 'Easter kerygma' does not determine its shape and function. Its pattern is not sketched from the parameters of a fixed, independent passion tradition. It is not primarily a biographical sketch or an eschatological program. Its construction is not determined by anti-Peter polemic. Its identity is not controlled by an aretalogical agenda, nor by the correction of such an agenda. It is not a monolithic apology for the death of Jesus.

The keys to the identity of this Gospel lie elsewhere. They are to be found in a more complicated web of strategies and a more complex perception of early Christian proclamation.

Passion Story and Gospel Story

The nature and the purpose of the Gospel of Mark are most clearly unveiled in the strategy which guides this narrative. Formally the Gospel presents itself as a unified narrative text which must be interpreted in the context of its own distinct world-view. Materially the content of this narrative is christological, centering on the identity and mission of Jesus as the messiah. Functionally the narrative defines proclamation as its central, comprehensive task. Thus, narrative analysis unveils the Gospel of Mark as a narrative account of Jesus' messianic life, death and resurrection shaped by and for the task of proclamation. Nowhere is this more evident than in the account of Jesus' death in Mark 14–16.

Typically the story of Jesus' death is identified as the central component of the gospel message. Indeed, various lines of thought see in the passion story the whole of the gospel. Paul repeats such a tradition in 1 Cor. 15.3-7: Jesus died for our sins, was buried, was raised, was seen by witnesses. This singular focus on the passion story is also prevalent in modern thought, where the Gospels are frequently seen as passion narratives with extensive introductions or as scattered tradition gathered around and focused by the story of Jesus' death.[1]

1. This position has dominated through a century of research. In 1892 Martin Kähler (*The So-Called Historical Jesus and the Historic, Biblical Christ* [trans. and ed. C.E. Braaten; Philadelphia: Fortress Press, 1964 (1892)]) suggested that 'Somewhat provocatively, one could call the Gospels passion narratives with extensive introductions'. His analysis was primarily a theological position which sought to negotiate a path between the reductionism of the Life-of-Jesus research and a simple biblicism. Kähler sought an 'invulnerable area' upon which faith could stand, and he found this in the dogmatic or christological authority of the Bible. For Kähler the key to faith was not the *historische Jesu* reconstructed through the Life-of-Jesus research, but rather the *geschichtlichte, biblische Christus*, the Christ of the whole Bible. Thus, Kähler's description of the Gospels as passion narratives was primarily a theological position.

Kähler's contention that the passion story provides the ideological foundation for the Gospels was given new application by the form critics. Karl Ludwig Schmidt (*Der Rahmen der Geschichte Jesu: Literarkritische Untersuchungen zur ältesten Jesusüberlieferung* [Darmstadt: Wissenschaftliche Buchgesellschaft, 1964 (1919)]), Martin Dibelius (*From Tradition to Gospel* [trans. B. Woolf; New York: Charles Scribner's Sons, 1966 (1919)]), Rudolf Bultmann (*The History of the Synoptic Tradition* [trans. J. Marsh; Oxford: Basil Blackwell, 1963 (1921)]; *Theology of the New Testament* [trans. Kendrick Grobel; New York: Charles Scribner's Sons, 1951 (1948)]), and Vincent Taylor (*The Formation of the Gospel Tradition* [London: MacMillan, 1933]) each argued that an early, connected, pre-Markan narrative of the death of Jesus was the first and most important block of Christian tradition. For each of them, this primary tradition provided the framework for the development of the Gospel genre. In this manner the form critics transformed Kähler's maxim from a theological position into a historical premise: the passion story provides both the ideological center and the traditional base for the Gospel tradition.

When redaction criticism developed out of form criticism, the idea of a fixed pre-Markan passion narrative was taken over as a foundational presupposition. Attention was then given to changes which the Evangelists may have made in this primary tradition. This approach may be seen in the formative work of Willi Marxsen (*Introduction to the New Testament: An Approach to its Problems* [trans. G. Buswell; Philadelphia: Fortress Press, 1968 (1963)]; *Mark the Evangelist: Studies on the Redaction History of the Gospel* [trans. J. Boyce, *et al.*; Nashville: Abingdon Press, 1969 (1956)]), Hans Conzelmann ('Historie und Theologie in den synoptischen Passionsberichten', in F. Viering [ed.], *Zur Bedeutung des Todes Jesu: Exegetische Beiträge* [Gütersloh: Gerd Mohn, 2nd edn, 1967]) and Günther Bornkamm (*Jesus of Nazareth* [trans. I. McLusky and F. McLusky; London: Hodder & Stoughton, 1960 (1956)]). In suceeding generations the idea of a pre-Markan passion account which provided the

1. Introduction

Some recent views have seen in the Gospel of Mark a corrective pattern in which passion theology is employed to moderate or refocus traditions of wonder, power or glory. While these scholars disagree on what it is that Mark resists, they agree that Mark's real concern is the cross of Jesus. The various forms of this model argue that the Evangelist has consciously employed passion Christology to realign other traditions about Jesus.[1]

A closer look at the Gospels reveals extensive material reflecting various types of tradition. Indeed the largest percentage of the Gospels is not focused on the death of Jesus, but on his life and ministry. Attempts at reconstruction confirm that a variety of material circulated in the early church as independent stories of Jesus' words and deeds. It is likely that early collections of material were drawn mostly from the life of Jesus: miracle stories, parables, controversies, sayings. These traditions carried significant weight within the memory of the early church. While the passion story is crucial, the Gospel tradition is built primarily upon the story of Jesus' life and ministry.

Alongside this phenomenon of what the Gospels contain is the equally important characteristic of how the Gospels relate the various traditions of the Jesus event. Closer analysis demonstrates a reciprocal relationship between the stories of Jesus' life and the scenes of his death in the Gospel of Mark. The passion narrative casts an interpretive frame around the entirety of the Jesus story, but the reverse is also true: the events of Jesus' life provide the sole interpretive context for the story of his death. Jesus is properly understood only in view of

---

primal stock of Christian tradition and the central element in the composition of the Gospels became a widely-held, seldom-questioned presupposition. The most radical expression of this position is found in the work of Rudolf Pesch (*Das Markusevangelium* [HTKNT; Freiburg: Herder, 3rd edn, 1980]). For Pesch the pre-Markan passion tradition begins at Mk 8.27 and continues through the rest of the Gospel. For Pesch this tradition is both extensive and dominant: it provides 'the distinctive ground stock for the Markan presentation... which fundamentally determines the construction of the entire Gospel and especially its second half' (*Markusevangelium*, II, p. 1). What Kähler suggested on theological grounds is restated as a historical certainty in the work of Pesch: the Gospel message centers in the death of Jesus, the Gospel of Mark is a passion narrative.

1. More moderate forms of corrective Christology are offered by J. Schreiber, E. Schweizer, U. Luz, L. Keck, K. Kertelge, D.-A. Koch, G. Schille, J. Kingsbury, W. Kelber, B. Mack. More radical proposals of corrective Christology are held by T. Weeden, N. Perrin, E. Trocmé, P. Achtemeier.

his destiny as the One Crucified, yet the Crucified One is none other than Jesus the Nazarene (Mk 16.6).

What then is the proper place of the passion story in the midst of the various gospel traditions? While recent narrative studies have given topical attention to the interrelation between passion story and Gospel story,[1] a more detailed analysis is in order. What role does the death of Jesus play in the story of his life, in the formation of the Gospels, in the shaping of Christian theology, in the saving work of

---

1. See W. Kelber (ed.), *The Passion in Mark: Studies on Mark 14–16* (Philadelphia: Fortress Press, 1976). The linguistic unity of the Gospel of Mark has been affirmed through a series of studies: J.C. Hawkins, *Horae Synopticae: Contributions to the Study of the Synoptic Problem* (Oxford: Clarendon Press, 1899); C. H. Turner, 'Marcan Usage: Notes, Critical and Exegetical, on the Second Gospel', in *JTS*: 25 (1923–24), pp. 377-86; 26 (1924–25), pp. 12-20, 145-56, 225-40, 337-46; 27 (1925–26), pp. 58-62; 28 (1926–27), pp. 9-30, 349-62; 29 (1927–28), pp. 275-89, 346-61; M. Zerwick, *Untersuchungen zum Markus-Stil: Ein Beitrag zur stilistischen Durcharbeitung des Neuen Testaments* (SPIB; Rome: Pontifical Biblical Institute, 1937); J.C. Doudna, *The Greek of the Gospel of Mark* (JBLMS, 12; Philadelphia: Society of Biblical Literature, 1961); F. Neirynck, *Duality in Mark: Contributions to the Study of the Markan Redaction* (ETL 31; Leuven: Leuven University Press, 1972); E.J. Pryke, *Redactional Style in the Markan Gospel: A Study of Syntax and Vocabulary as Guides to Redaction in Mark* (Cambridge: Cambridge University Press, 1978); P. Dschulnigg, *Sprache, Redaktion und Intention des Markus-Evangeliums: Eigentumlichkeiten der Sprache des Markus-Evangeliums und ihre Bedeutung fur die Redaktionskritik* (SBB; Stuttgart: Verlag Katholisches Bibelwerk, 1986).

A few scholars have argued for the passion narrative as a Markan creation. Different forms of this theory are proposed by J. Schreiber, *Die Markuspassion: Wege zur Erforschung der Leidensgeschichte Jesu* (Hamburg: Furche Verlag, 1969); E. Linnemann, *Studien zur Passionsgeschichte* (Göttingen: Vandenhoeck & Ruprecht, 1970); L. Schenke, *Studien zur Passionsgeschichte des Markus: Tradition und Redaktion in Markus 14.1-42* (Würzburg: Echter Verlag, 1971); Wolfgang Schenk, *Der Passionsbericht nach Markus: Untersuchung zur Überlieferungsgeschichte der Passionstraditionen* (Gütersloh: Gerd Mohn, 1974); D. Dormeyer, *Die Passion Jesu als Verhaltensmodell: Literarische und theologische Analyse der Traditions- und Redaktionsgeschichte der Markuspassion* (Münster: Aschendorff, 1974); H.C. Kee, *Community of the New Age: Studies in Mark's Gospel* (Philadelphia: Westminster Press, 1977); B. Mack, *A Myth of Innocence: Mark and Christian Origins* (Philadelphia: Fortress Press, 1998); *Mark and Christian Origins: A Myth of Innocence* (Philadelphia: Fortress Press, 1988); E. Trocmé, *The Formation of the Gospel according to Mark* (trans. P. Gaughan; London: SPCK, 1975 [1963]); P.J. Achtemeier, *Mark* (Proclamation Commentaries; Philadelphia: Fortress Press, 1975).

1. Introduction

God? This study will address these questions by examining the narrative strategy of the story of Jesus' death in Mark 14–16. Particular attention will be given to the content and the process used to characterize Jesus in this material. This narrative strategy and its portrait of Jesus will be subjected to ongoing comparison with the story of Jesus' words and deeds in Mark 1–13.

A critical analysis of the narrative patterns and strategies of Mark 14–16 reveals a carefully crafted text which is intimately linked to the larger Gospel story. Through these intratextual links the passion account both shapes and is shaped by the larger portrait of Jesus. This analysis will show that the passion story is one component in an intricate, extensive, paradoxical portrait of Jesus created through a complex intratextual strategy of reciprocity.

The implications of this narrative strategy are inescapable. In view of the conscious reciprocity at work in the passion story, the question of the nature and purpose of the Gospel of Mark is reopened. Previous assumptions about its author and about authorial intention must be reconsidered. In view of the narrative strategy at work in Mark 14–16, new light is shed upon the history and development of the Gospel tradition. The purposes and strategies of an early Christian community come into view, and fundamental questions about the form and function of the Gospel genre re-emerge. Ultimately this investigation seeks to uncover the narratological strategy which shapes Mark 14–16. In doing so, it touches upon the theological strategies which guided the first presentation of the gospel as a Gospel.

A Methodological Proposal

This investigation will analyze the contribution of the passion narrative to the characterization of Jesus in the Gospel of Mark. This analysis will employ a methodological approach designed to highlight the unique narrative identity and christological focus of this Gospel. Thus, this investigation will provide a formalistic analysis set within a broad *traditionsgeschichtliche* context. This methodology operates around three poles: synchronic analysis, comparative analysis, narrative analysis.[1]

---

1. For a more detailed discussion of methodology, see E. Broadhead, *Teaching with Authority: Miracles and Christology in the Gospel of Mark* (Sheffield: JSOT Press, 1992), pp. 26-55.

Synchronic Analysis of Texts

Synchronic analysis views a text as a systematic whole which is limited to a single relational axis or plane. The significance of the text is found in relationships created by organizational patterns within the common framework. Relationships based on a span between different genetic, evolutionary or historical phases are excluded. The text is thus seen as an autonomous system which addresses a singular frame of reference. Such synchronic analysis lies at the base of all formalist and structuralist methodologies. Synchronic analysis has been advanced through the fields of linguistics, semiotics and literature.

Linguistics. The application of synchronic methods of analysis to narrative material received its impetus from a Swiss linguist, Ferdinand de Saussure, and from a Russian folklorist, Vladimir Propp. The initiative provided by Saussure was taken up and advanced by various groups. Russian formalists investigated the components of the literary work and the linguistic means by which the literary work was accomplished. A group of linguists who became known as the Prague School studied the role of phonology in structuralist linguistics. The structural linguistics of the Copenhagen School, under the influence of Louis Hjelmslev, sought to establish a deductive system of formal logic which would describe both a given text and the language system upon which the text was founded. A Russian member of the Prague School, Roman Jakobson, linked the Russian, Czechoslovakian and French schools. Jakobson believed that poetic language has an autotelic nature and that the poetic function is a self-generated element; he thus sought to find the meaning of a work by investigating the means of production of the work. Claude Lévi-Strauss advocated the use of linguistics in anthropological study and in other social sciences. Lévi-Strauss applied the principles of structural linguistics to the analysis of myths, seeking the underlying structure which guides the relation of the individual elements. Noam Chomsky sought to describe the grammar which lies behind a language and serves as the generative base for all grammatical expressions of that language. A few scholars have attempted to extend Chomsky's work directly into the field of literature.[1]

---

1. See Broadhead, *Teaching with Authority*, pp. 26-29 for a fuller discussion.

1. *Introduction*

Semiotics. While Chomsky and his followers pursued the systematic base which regulates linguistic and even literary production, others have followed a more indirect route from linguistics to literature. Building upon the work of Ferdinand de Saussure and C.S. Peirce, a number of scholars attempt to move from the linguistic base to a broader theory of semiotics—the study of signs. This semiotic theory is then used to interpret literary texts, as well as other systems.[1]

Literature. Having developed from structural linguistics through semiotics, synchronic analysis advances in the science of narratology to direct treatment of narrative texts from a synchronic perspective.[2] It is in the realm of narratology that synchronic analysis has exerted its greatest influence upon biblical studies.[3]

This investigation will apply a formalistic type of synchronic analysis to the passion narrative in the Gospel of Mark. The basic components in this analysis will be drawn from the grammatical categories of the host language. The foundational level of linguistic grammar is the simple sentence, composed of substantives and predicates. Transferring these linguistic categories into narrative terms, basic units of text will be analyzed as narrative sentences composed of agents and actions. These sentences will be understood in narrative terms as motifs. In this manner a taxonomy of each story may be constructed by noting various motifs and their pattern of employment. The synchronic analysis of each unit of the passion narrative will

---

1. L. Marin, *Semiotik der Passionsgeschichte: Die Zeichensprache der Ortsgaben und Personnamen* (trans. S. Virgils; Munich: Chr. Kaiser Verlag, 1976 [1971]), seeks to apply semiotic theory to the passion story. He gives particular attention to the naming of places and persons in the passion account. Building on the work of Erhardt Güttgemanns, Marin believes this information provides 'speech signs' (*Zeichensprache*) which guide the reading and interpretation of the passion. In particular, Marin investigates the way in which these speech signs help to transform contradictory, disjunctive elements to create a narrative equilibrium (pp. 1-2). Thus, Marin employs a semiotic system to describe the operations of the text of the passion narrative.

2. Representative of this science are the works of Roland Barthes, A.J. Greimas, Claude Bremond, Tzvetan Todorov, Gerard Genette, Seymour Chatman. For further discussion see Broadhead, *Teaching with Authority*, pp. 30-31.

3. See, for example, the works of Dan Via, Daniel Patte, R. Alan Culpepper, Norman Petersen, Robert Tannehill, Mary Ann Tolbert, Elisabeth Struthers Malbon.

consist of a narrative morphology and of a narrative syntax. The morphology describes the various motifs which compose the story, the manner of their construction, and their order of presentation. The narrative syntax gives attention to patterns of interrelationship constructed among the various motifs in each pericope. The result is a formal grammatical description of the contents and the dynamics of each story.[1]

Comparative Analysis of Texts
A type of diachronic analysis will also be employed. The formalistic analysis of the passion narrative will be set within a broad *traditionsgeschichtliche* (history of traditions) context. While historical critics have generally understood diachronic analysis along the lines of an archaeological or genealogical model and used it to expose strata or layers beneath the Gospel narratives,[2] this investigation will offer an alternative to the traditional use of historical-critical findings. Diachronic analysis will not be used here to establish the evolution of a tradition through various historical contexts; it will be used to suggest a field of possible literary contexts in which a text may operate.

While synchronic analysis investigates the operation of narrative elements within the same system, the diachronic analysis will be concerned with comparative analysis of narrative elements as they work within different systems. The various forms of a story will be viewed not in terms of priority and dependence, but in phenomenological terms. Each version will be seen as an alternate expression of a story. This phenomenological description and comparison requires a crossing over from the temporal world of the present narrative to the temporal world of another system. It is in this sense that the term

---

1. The descriptive nature of this grammar avoids the problems inherent in attempts to define deep structures and generative bases which underlie the linguistic performance. The formal nature of this grammar avoids problems inherent in the ideas that the substance of a text lies in the purposes of its author (the intentional fallacy) or in the response of its reader (the affective fallacy).

2. Source criticism looks for more ancient sources, and it usually values these more than the text at hand. Form criticism seeks to isolate the original shape of the tradition, to trace its subsequent development, then to describe the sociological environment(s) in which traditions operated. Redaction criticism points to the theological intent of the author behind the text. In each of these the key to interpretation tends to lie outside the text.

'diachronic' is applied. This crossing of time may involve comparison with systems that are historically earlier, some that are later, and some that share the same historical era. Undated texts also retain their importance. This comparative, diachronic analysis is not controlled by the question of historical relationships between the two versions of the same story. Setting aside for the moment the question of historical lineage, each variation will be viewed as one of several possible forms of the story.

The primary goal of this type of diachronic analysis is not genetic, but descriptive and comparative. This comparative look at the operation of other systems provides a helpful backdrop against which to highlight the distinctiveness of the text at hand. Different options may be shown for the construction of such a text, giving focus to which options the present text realizes and how it chooses to do so. Thus, diachronic analysis can be used to define a precise *literary* context within which to interpret the present text, highlighting both its similarities and its uniqueness.

In the investigation which follows, the synchronic focus on the morphology and syntax operative within individual passages will be supplemented by a comparative analysis focusing various accounts which serve as co-texts for the passage at hand. These co-texts will provide a field of comparison against which to evaluate the narrative strategy of the text under consideration. In this manner the formalistic description of each text is set within a broad *traditionsgeschichtliche* context of interpretation. A summary statement will provide a final description of the narrative strategy and identity at work in each text, giving particular attention to the portrait of Jesus sketched through this process.

Narrative Analysis of Texts
The larger narrative system provides the key to this analysis. Although each element has its own history of development and use, the presence of the unit within a narrative structure provides its true identity. The joining of narrative units into a narrative system brings them under the control of a new and distinct environment which defines its own codes. This relationship is reciprocal: the system shapes the units and the units shape the system. Thus, the central concern of narrative criticism is not for the isolated components nor the historical author, but the resulting literary creation. Ultimately

narrative elements are analyzed in terms of their participation in narrative systems. These systems form a type of narrative world and serve as the source and means for articulation of narrative significance. Various aspects of this narrative world require further description.

Significance and Meaning. The fundamental presupposition of this analysis may be stated thus: narratives articulate a field of signification to which readers may assign meaning.[1] The significance of the text will be pursued by applying Saussure's linguistic distinction between signifier and signified to the level of the narrative.

The grammar of a narrative creates an associative bond between its compositional elements and the concepts which it articulates. The narrative signifiers are the components of the narrative with their patterns of morphology and syntax. The narrative signified is the concept with which these elements are associated—the narrative signification or narrative significance. Through this association of narrative signifiers and narrative significance, the narrative itself becomes the sign. In Saussurian terms the narrative elements are signifiers, narrative concepts are the signified, the narrative is the

---

1. This distinction between significance and meaning stands in direct contrast to the proposal of E.D. Hirsch. For Hirsch (*Validity in Interpretation* [New Haven: Yale University Press, 1967], pp. 24-67, and *The Aims of Interpretation* [Chicago: University of Chicago Press, 1976], pp. 1-13), 'meaning' is the whole of the intrinsic verbal meaning of the text. 'Significance' is this textual meaning as related to some context beyond itself.

This technical distinction of significance and meaning also relates to the German use of *Sinn* and *Bedeutung*. *Sinn* refers to sense and significance, while *Bedeutung* refers to meaning and reference. The text has its *Sinn* within itself, while its *Bedeutung* grows from its relationship to readers. This distinction was put forth by Gottlob Frege in an article entitled 'Ueber Sinn und Bedeutung', translated as 'On Sense and Reference' by M. Black, in P. Geach and M. Black (eds.), *Translations from the Philosophical Writings of Gottlob Frege* (Oxford: Basil Blackwell, 1970), pp. 56-78. On this relationship, see P. Ricoeur, *Interpretation Theory: Discourse and the Surplus of Meaning* (Fort Worth: Texas Christian University, 1976), pp. 19-22. Ricoeur explains that 'Whereas the sense is immanent to the discourse, and objective in the sense of ideal, the reference expresses the movement in which language transcends itself' (p. 20). See also P. Ricoeur, 'Structure, Word, Event', *Philosophy Today* 12 (1968), pp. 114-29. See also H.-G. Gadamer, *Truth and Method* (trans. and ed. G. Barden and J. Cumming; London: Sheed & Ward, 1975 [1960]), pp. 372-74. See also B. Russell, *An Inquiry into Meaning and Truth* (London: George Allen & Unwin, 1940), pp. 170-203.

sign. As with linguistic signs, narrative signs are arbitrary—nothing in the genre or the mind of the redactor need explain their motivation. Likewise, narrative signs are linear—they operate across the synchronic plane of their narrative world.

Delineation of narrative significance thus involves an objective and formalistic process—as objective and formalistic as delineation of linguistic signs. The formal operation of the elements of a narrative and the manner in which they generate narrative concepts may be stated in descriptive and programmatic language. Descriptive narrative grammars may be written as clearly as descriptive linguistic grammars. Narrative significance is the inherent, formal conceptual pattern of a narrative text. Thus, delineation of the inherent significance of a narrative is an objective, formalistic process. In contrast, the 'meaning' of a text is an external, subjective association. To interpret the sign and then to assign meaning to it involves a process largely external to the world of the text. Narratives articulate fields of significance to which a reader may variously assign meaning.[1]

Morphosis and Metamorphosis. This analysis will give attention to the manner in which significance is created, preserved and transmitted within the operations of the narrative. The narrative system provides

---

1. Such a programmatic statement raises the issue of the origin of meaning. Is meaning found inherently within narrative structures in a formalistic and mechanical way, or is meaning altogether the creation of the human mind? Literary criticism, philosophy, psychology and anthropology answer the question in a number of ways. In the context of this methodology, meaning is best understood to emerge from the interaction of reader and narrative in the performance of the text. Neither reader nor text is ultimately determinative of meaning, and neither is dispensable to the process. Codes engrained in the reader clash with codes inherent to the text, and the negotiation of meaning is begun. While description of that process may be pursued, it is sufficient in this context to contend that humans do find meaning in the confrontation of reader and text. Formalistic narrative analysis seeks to demonstrate not meaning, but the formal significance of a text. This is accomplished by investigating both the form and the function of the textual elements in order to demonstrate what the text presents and how the text presents it. The reader's assignment of 'meaning' to this formal narrative significance may take a variety of forms and belongs largely to another field of inquiry.

This does not mean, however, that the text may mean anything, that there are as many meanings as there are readers, or that all readings of the text are equal. Various interpretations may be critiqued, ranked or discarded according to the manner in which they engage the process of signification set forth by the narrative.

the host environment in which agent, action, motif and genre collaborate to create a world. This creative process involves not only compositional patterns, but also the series of transformations and interactions orchestrated between narrative elements. This dynamic process of structuration generates new forms, new relations, new significance. This self-generative process which occurs within the narrative system will be labeled 'morphosis', the process of literary formation.

This analysis will also give attention to the manner in which old elements, old processes, old meanings are employed within a new narrative framework. No literary form can be understood apart from its system of use, and traditional literary forms may be redefined by a different system of use. Likewise, the change in systems may effect narrative operations such as characterization. Narrative analysis must give close attention to the process in which traditional material is re-employed in new narrative settings. This promises to be a most productive direction for research, offering hope of clarifying the orientation of a Gospel over against, or in sympathy with, its sources, parallels, and descendants. Using diachronic analysis to provide a comparative base, the movement of elements into a particular system can be studied. This process will be labeled 'metamorphosis', the process of literary transformation.

Narrative Grammar. The outcome of this methodological approach is a descriptive narrative grammar for New Testament material. This investigation will focus the grammar of the passion narrative in the Gospel of Mark. The aim of the grammar is descriptive—to focus what the narrative does and how it does it—so the approach is necessarily inductive. Moving from the inductive grammar of the *koine* Greek of the New Testament, a grammatical description of the narrative will be constructed on the base of the sentence model. Agents and actions will be analyzed, then restated in the form of narrative sentences. These narrative sentences will be analyzed, and motifs will be defined. The thematic manipulation of motifs into genre units will be observed. Ultimately the various elements will be considered in terms of their operation within a meaningful narrative system. The operations of both the local system (the passion account) and the extended system (the Gospel of Mark) will be observed. This narrative grammar will give attention to both narrative form (morphology)

1. Introduction

and to the narrative interaction of form units (syntax). The ultimate goal of this grammar is a description of the formal narrative strategy by which the passion account in Mark 14–16 operates. This formal narrative strategy articulates the significance of the narrative and engages the reader in a dialogical quest for meaning.

The Narrative World. The concept of a narrative world provides the key to this investigation. For the purpose of analysis the narrative may be viewed as a closed environment. The narrative elements operate within this world to name, to define, to describe, to affirm, to negate. In addition to sponsoring the interaction of narrative elements, the narrative world also facilitates the interaction of various narrative voices. The narrative generates the voice of an implied author. Through textual operations this voice addresses an implied reader. A second conversation is sponsored through the narrative process. The text creates an image of a narrator. This narrative voice may or may not distinguish itself from the voice of the implied author. The narrator speaks in and through the text to the narratee. These voices are narrative constructs whose existence and reference points lie within the dynamics of the text and within the created world of the narrative.[1]

Narrative elements and voices (signifiers) generate points of reference (signified) and create a narrative world-view (sign). Through this process of signification the narrative offers the reader a biased and pointed view of reality. This narrative sign serves as the catalyst and guide which may stimulate various reader responses to the text.

The narrative places before the reader this textual world of portraits and persuasion and polemic. Reader and text engage in a mutual process of confrontation, dialogue, persuasion, rejection and affirmation. Readers interpret texts, and texts interpret readers. Ultimately the reader may chose his/her response to the text, but the choice is not wholly undetermined, nor is it without consequence. This narrative world offers seductive persuasion and powerful sanction to its readers. The text thus provides a narrative sign which engages the

---

1. For theoretical descriptions of the narrative voices, see G. Genette, *Narrative Discourse: An Essay in Method* (trans. J. Lewin; Ithaca, NY: Cornell University Press, 1980); S. Chatman, *Story and Discourse* (Ithaca, NY: Cornell University Press, 1978). For application of the voices to biblical texts, see R.A. Culpepper, *Anatomy of the Fourth Gospel* (Philadelphia: Fortress Press, 1983).

reader in the construction of meaning. Both reader and text then participate in the dynamics, the dialogue, the negotiation from which meaning emerges.

History and Hermeneutics. While the narrative generates an autonomous, self-referential world, its existence cannot be abstracted from the real world of writers and actors and readers. The narrative world has intimate connections both to history and to hermeneutics.

The image of an implied author lives within the narrative world. This author is a literary construct which may or may not have parallels outside the world of the text. The implied author is a self-referential narrative element. At the same time, the image of the implied author is a shadow image; this specter images some form of connection to an actual, historical author or authors. The actual author may be a mirror of the implied author, he/she may be the opposite of the implied author, he/she may be some mixture of the image of the implied author. Nonetheless the text implies a connection between authors outside of texts and images of authors inside texts.

In the same manner the text creates a literary image of reality which is a self-referential construction. Truth and falsehood, courage and cowardice, virtue and vice are each defined within the frame of the narrative. This narrative world carries its own values, rewards, sanctions—its own reality. At the same time the reality of the narrative world implies an intimate connection to some historical reality. In the mind of readers the story does not exist unto itself; it says something about somebody, about some time, about some place. The text itself imagines a real history by the way in which it constructs the world of the narrative. Indeed, the reader's desire to see the text as a story about something is encouraged by the text itself. Thus, the narrative suggests to the reader intimate connections between the reality of the text and the authors and histories which lie outside the text.

On the one hand the narrative world images intimate connections with real authors and with real history. On the other hand the narrative world images connections to actual readers and to a world of interpretation which lies outside the text. Inherent to the fabric of the narrative world is the image of an implied reader. The text provides consistent pointers which encourage readers to build bridges between the world of the text and the world of the reader. In the Gospel of

Mark readers are encouraged to confront false religion and fickle followers not simply as literary constructs, but as present dangers. Readers are urged to find faith and discipleship beyond the walls of the text in their own world and in their own reality. Without such connections the text would prove unreadable and irrelevant. Readers are encouraged to imagine themselves in the world of the text and to transport the events of the text into their own world. The text thus presents itself as an island with a bridge. This bridge is a shadow image implied already in the narrative world. The reader creates the response to the text, but the text has already set the stage for the reader's response. The textual strategy is not an innocent image, but rather a demanding and insistent one. Through various techniques the text invites the reader to respond to the narrative, to construct this bridge, and to enter into the world of the text. By constructing this bridge the reader also invites the text to enter into the real world of the reader. When the text enters the world of the reader, it brings along its subtle power of polemic and persuasion.

The most important link between the narrative world constructed in the Gospel of Mark and the world of history and hermeneutics is the concept of kerygma (proclamation). The most certain 'historicity' implied in the Gospel of Mark is its kerygmatic nature. Implied in this narrative is a time and place in which the text operates as kerygma—as a central message and calling of faith. The Gospel of Mark bears witness to a kerygmatic identity and origin—it presents itself as a word from God which demands obedience from its hearers.[1] The text suggests other levels of historicity—the words and deeds of Jesus, the response of early followers, the times and places observed—but the primary historicity of the narrative is its intrinsic kerygmatic identity and demand. If the Gospel of Mark is kerygma, it is kerygma for some time, some place, some people. The kerygmatic nature of the Gospel of Mark imagines an intimate link to some objective history.

Hermeneutics is also rooted in the kerygmatic nature of the Gospel of Mark. The reader is free to avoid the narrative image presented by this text or to reject its claims, but the response of the reader does not alter the intrinsic orientation of the text. The Gospel of Mark presents itself as a word about God and from God—as a kerygma with claims

---

1. Mk 1.1 presents the narrative as 'the gospel of Jesus Christ'. Mk 1.14-15 centers the story on Jesus' proclamation of 'the gospel of God'. At the heart of this narrative is a central imperative: repent and believe in the gospel (Mk 1.15).

upon the reader. Thus, the most authentic hermeneutical moves are those which recognize the intrinsic kerygmatic possessiveness of this narrative. These claims may be accepted or rejected, but they must be recognized as inherent to the nature of this text.

For the Gospel of Mark this kerygmatic nature is grounded in an objective, faith-oriented, praxis-determined view of reality. This narrative constructs a view of the world that is more reactionary than reflective.[1] This courageous, decisive, action-oriented view of reality calls for a hermeneutic of similar tone. The Gospel of Mark resists the imposition of a subsequent, philosophical hermeneutic as the primary process of interpretation. The world-view of the Gospel of Mark suggests a faith-oriented, praxis-determined reading, both in its historical and in its hermeneutical images.[2]

Thus, history and hermeneutics may be linked to the narrative world of the Gospel of Mark through the concept of kerygma. The primary kerygmatic identity and demand of this narrative provides its most certain tone of historicity and its most productive hermeneutical key. While history and hermeneutics theoretically lie outside the parameters of the narrative world, the inner workings and the inner identity of this narrative image a bridge. This bridge joins the world of the narrative to the world of human events and to the world of human readers. Through this process the text is made readable. The narrative is at once tamed and unleashed. The text is tamed because it

---

1. The calling of the disciples in Mk 1.16-20 embodies this world-view. The calling is pragmatic and direct: 'Follow me, and I will make you to become fishers for humans'. The response is similar in tone: 'And immediately, leaving the nets, they followed him'.

2. In my opinion the hermeneutical suggestions of liberationist and of materialist readings hold some relevance for the world-view of the Gospel of Mark. For examples of liberationist hermeneutics, see L. Boff, *Jesus Christ Liberator: A Critical Christology for our Times* (Maryknoll, NY: Orbis Books, 1978); S.J. Croatto, *Exodus: A Hermeneutics of Freedom* (Maryknoll, NY: Orbis Books, 1981); G. Gutierrez, *A Theology of Liberation* (Maryknoll, NY: Orbis Books, 1973); J.L. Segundo, *The Liberation of Theology* (Maryknoll, NY: Orbis Books, 1976); J. Sobrino, *Christology at the Crossroads* (Maryknoll, NY: Orbis Books, 1980). For examples of materialist readings, see F. Belo, *A Materialist Reading of the Gospel of Mark* (Maryknoll, NY: Orbis Books, 1981); M. Clevenot, *Materialist Approaches to the Bible* (Maryknoll, NY: Orbis Books, 1985); L.J. Reynolds, 'Materialist Reading as a Hermeneutical Approach to Christian Proclamation' (unpublished ThM thesis; The Southern Baptist Theological Seminary, 1988).

becomes an object in the hands of readers; it thus becomes subject to interpretation, analysis, manipulation, reconstruction. At the same time the text is unleashed upon the reader and the reader's world. The reader is thus confronted by the focused power of the text, with all of its insistence and persuasion.[1]

Narrative Analysis and Passion Narrative

The primary goal of this investigation is a precise description of the narrative strategy which guides Mark 14–16. Particular attention will be given to the process of characterization. This analysis will employ grammatical categories to describe the content and the dynamics of the narrative portrait of Jesus in Mark 14–16. Initially the content and function of individual pericopes will be analyzed. This synchronic analysis will observe the operation of each pericope in both local and extended contexts. Particular focus will be given to the christological image which emerges. A comparative type of diachronic analysis will locate this narrative process alongside other possible uses of this material. Subsequently the investigation will focus the relationship of this christological portrait to the image of Jesus in the larger story of the Gospel of Mark. Various implications of this relationship will then be considered.

The history of research in the passion account suggests three options for understanding the Gospel of Mark. In one model the Gospel of Mark is a passion account to which other materials have been appended. A second model sees a narrative dialectic in which the passion story ultimately dominates. A third model suggests a unified narrative with a complex interaction of concerns. Each model carries decisive implications for the christological question as well as for the origin, nature and outlook of the Gospel of Mark. These questions have endured through various stages of critical research and remain open to inquiry.

Employing a formalistic analysis set within a *traditionsgeschichtliche* context, the analysis which follows will describe the dynamic narrative strategy which guides Mark 14–16. This investigation will

1. This linkage is established here in terms of the operation of narrative worlds and their relation to human history and interpretation. For a more philosophical, existential linkage of the Gospels to history and hermeneutics, see H. Weder, *Neutestamentliche Hermeneutik* (Zürich: Theologischer Verlag, 1986).

demonstrate that Mark 14–16 provides a multi-faceted portrait of Jesus which is constructed, clarified and amplified through its reciprocal relationship with the larger narrative.

The understanding that Mark 14–16 belongs inextricably to the larger world of this Gospel carries key consequences. The demonstration of the inherent unity of passion story and Gospel story demands renewed attention to the question of authorship and sources, to the nature and purpose of the Gospel of Mark, to the question of the Gospel genre, and, indeed, to the history of development of the Gospel traditions.

Chapter 2

MARK 14.1-42: THE PREPARATION AND BETRAYAL

The first section of the passion story extends from Mk 14.1-42 and contains four units (14.1-11; 14.12-26; 14.26-32a; 14.32-42). Synchronic analysis will be employed to describe the form and function of each of these units. Literary statements will be transposed into simple narrative sentences composed of agents and actions. These sentences will be organized as narrative motifs and their participation in individual stories will be observed. Subsequently the relationship to the larger contexts of the passion account and the Gospel of Mark will be focused. A comparative form of diachronic analysis will be used to set forth a larger field against which to highlight the operation of each pericope. This narrative analysis will give particular attention to the role of Mk 14.1-42 in the characterization of Jesus.

Mark 14.1-11: The Anointing Scene

Mk 14.1-11 opens the passion account with the story of the anointing of Jesus by an unnamed woman. This unit links the ministry of Jesus to his death and provides an interpretive preface to the events of the passion.

Synchronic Analysis
The motifs of Mk 14.1-11 may be plotted in the following manner:

>   *Introduction*
>   The leaders conspire   14.1-2
>   *Body*
>   The woman anoints   14.3
>   Some complain   14.4-5
>   Jesus responds   14.6-9
>   *Conclusion*
>   The leaders conspire   14.10-11

Narrative Morphology. This account is built around a simple frame. The introduction of the story employs a single motif to provide the setting for these events. The body of the unit narrates the primary action event through a single motif, then focuses contrasting responses to the deed of the woman. The extended response of Jesus provides the center of the account. The conclusion is provided by a single motif which validates the report of the introduction: the leaders are conspiring to put Jesus to death. The anointing story is thus constituted around three distinct narrative segments.

1. The inner scene (14.3-9) may be distinguished structurally and ideologically from the introduction (14.1-2) and the conclusion (14.10-11). The attempt in 14.1 to provide exact temporal location is unusual in the Gospel of Mark prior to the passion narrative.[1] Three different descriptions of the festival (τὸ πάσχα; τὰ ἄζυμα; τῇ ἑορτῇ) have stirred much debate.[2] Likely this series of references

---

1. The distinct use of temporal and geographical markers in the passion story has typically been seen as evidence of Mark's dependence upon a fixed passion account with precise time and place references. See, for example, K.L. Schmidt, *Der Rahmen der Geschichte Jesu: Literarkritische Untersuchungen zur ältesten Jesusüberlieferung* (Darmstadt: Wissenschaftliche Buchgesellschaft, 1964 [1919]), pp. 303-304; R. Pesch, *Das Markusevangelium* (HTKNT; Freiburg: Herder, 2nd edn, 1981), II, p. 17. In my opinion at least part of this phenomenon is explained by the type of tradition involved. Material such as the miracle stories and sayings could be framed and circulated in short, rather self-standing units and tended to lose time and location markers. In contrast the passion story required an extended narrative, a form in which time and place markers served more important functions and tended to be retained. Thus, patterns of retention/loss of time and place markers may reflect the intrinsic nature of the material as well as Markan redactional patterns.

2. See for instance Pesch, *Markusevangelium*, II, pp. 319-22, who argues that τὸ πάσχα refers in a general way to the entire festival. J. Jeremias ('πάσχα', *TDNT*, V, pp. 896-904) argues that in the New Testament τὸ πάσχα almost always refers to the seven-day feast of the Passover. He sees in Mk 14.1 the primary exception to this pattern. Thus, τὸ πάσχα refers explicitly to the Passover meal on 15 Nisan. J. Gnilka (*Das Evangelium nach Markus* [EKKNT; Zürich: Benziger Verlag, 1979], II, pp. 218-21) argues that Mark uses a Greek measure of time. Pesch (*Markusevangelium*, II, pp. 319-20) sees here a Jewish chronology. In spite of this, Gnilka and Pesch both locate the anointing on Wednesday. The Feast of Unleavened Bread (ἄζυμα) refers to an extended celebration from 15–21 Nisan, while the Passover (πάσχα) is celebrated in one Jewish day (from the evening which ends 14 Nisan to the evening which ends 15 Nisan). The phrase μετὰ δύο ἡμέρας places the anointing two days prior to the beginning of these feasts on 13

2. Mark 14.1-42: The Preparation and Betrayal

locates the anointing on 13 Nisan. Beyond serving as a temporal marker, 14.1 sets the story against the heightened religious piety and nationalistic fervor which accompanies these overlapping feasts. More significantly, Mk 14.1 shapes the ideological context through its introductory description of the death plot. The resistance of the priests occurs only in the environs of Jerusalem (11.18; 11.27; 14.1; 14.10; 14.43; 14.55; 14.60; 14.61; 14.63; 15.1; 15.11; 15.31), while the scribes oppose Jesus throughout his Galilean ministry (2.6; 3.22; 7.1; 7.5; 9.14, 16). Mk 14.1 joins these two lines of opposition into a death conspiracy in Jerusalem. The quest of the authorities is placed in the imperfect (ἐζήτουν), implying an iterative, continuing process. These opponents 'seek' (ζητέω) Jesus, an act which carries negative implications throughout the Gospel of Mark (1.37; 3.32; 8.11; 8.12; 11.18; 14.1; 14.11; 14.55; 16.6; συζητέω in 9.14, 16; 12.28). This negative seeking imagery is linked precisely to the death plot and to the volatility of the people here and in 11.18 and 12.12. Mk 14.1 exactly reproduces the imagery of 11.18: priests and scribes seek to kill Jesus but are hindered by the volatility of the people.[1] In this manner Mk 14.1-2 provides a focused context for the anointing story: amidst the season of religious piety and popular fervor, the religious leaders plot the death of Jesus.

2. Mk 14.10-11 also constitutes a distinct narrative segment. Here the priests are aided in their conspiracy by one of the Twelve, and their plot is sealed with a promise of money (14.11). This conspiracy is directly related to 14.1-2: the priests and the seeking motif are recalled, as is the need for discretion. In contrast, Mk 14.10-11 has no direct connections to the anointing scene in 14.3-9.[2]

Nisan, which begins on Tuesday evening and extends through Wednesday evening.

1. The reference to the people as the λαός in 14.2 is unusual, but λαός is likely a synonym for ὄχλος. In the Gospel of Mark ὄχλος is the standard form (some 38 times) and λαός is the exception (7.6; 14.2; with the textual tradition divided on 11.32). The argument of Gnilka, *Markus*, II, p. 220, that λαός, in distinction from ὄχλος, designates the crowd as the people of God, seems strained. In Mk 11.18 and 12.12 the crowd serves the same role as in 14.2, but is designated as the ὄχλος. The change in speakers should also be noted. In Mk 11.18 and 12.12 the narrator is speaking. The use of λαός in 14.2 represents the speech of the high priests and scribes. The use of λαός in 7.6 is drawn from the Old Testament.

2. Mt. 26.8 establishes this connection in a vague way by naming the disciples as the grumblers, as does a secondary textual tradition for Mk 14.4-5: W f^{13} D Θ 565 (it). Jn 12.4-5 inserts the information of Mk 14.10-11 directly into the anointing

Thus, Mk 14.1-2 and 14.10-11 constitute distinct narrative episodes within the anointing story. These segments are linked through similar images and create a separate environment over against the inner scene. This outer context conveys images of piety (religious authorities, Jewish feasts, membership in the Twelve), but it also bears the harsh reality of those who seek Jesus and the opportune time for his death.

3. Consequently the anointing scene in Mk 14.3-9 constitutes a narrative segment distinguishable from the outer context. Various elements demonstrate this contrast. (1) Mk 14.3 provides a new set of time and place markers for the internal story: Bethany, the house of Simon the leper, reclining. No direct connection is made between these markers and the outer setting (14.1). (2) The cast of characters has also shifted from the outer context (priests, scribes, Judas, the Twelve) to the inner story (Jesus, Simon?, a woman, some who grumble). (3) The hostility and betrayal of the outer frame is not explicit in this inner scene. (4) The report style of 14.1-2, 10-11 gives way in 14.3-9 to more direct narration dominated by sayings. Thus, Mk 14.3-9 stands apart from 14.1-2, 10-11.

In addition to its distance from the outer contexts, Mk 14.3-9 carries contrasting internal themes. The succint account of the anointing (14.3bc) is overshadowed by the extensive discussion about the meaning of this act (14.4-9). The woman does not take part in this conversation, and the participation of the grumblers is limited to their initial objection (14.4-5). The remainder of the story is occupied by sayings of Jesus which address four distinct concerns.[1] (1) The saying

---

scene and makes the connection explicit: Judas, the disciple who betrays Jesus, grumbles about this use of the ointment. This connection is not directly established in the Gospel of Mark. The information in 14.10-11 is more directly related to the arrest scene (14.43-52) and seems to be a preliminary report of Mk 14.43. If the omission of the elders in 14.43 by ℵ* A W 0112 $f^{1.13}$ (700). 1424 *al* is accepted, 14.1-2, 10-11 and 14.43 contain the same elements: priests and scribes, Judas, membership in the Twelve, the crowd. Quite possibly Mk 14.10-11 is shaped by 14.43, then joined to the anointing story. The likelihood that 14.10-11 is part of an editorial frame is strengthened by the use of εὐκαιρέω, which appears only here and in the editorial summary in Mk 6.31. In addition, the Twelve are mentioned in the passion story only in 14.10, 17, 20, 43. The editorial nature of 14.17 and 14.43 suggests that 14.10-11 is also an editorial report. The easy transition directly from 14.2 to 14.10 also suggests an editorial framing.

1. The association of four diverse sayings likely reflects editorial shaping. In particular the third and fourth sayings (14.8b-9) reflect a distinct interest in the death

2. Mark 14.1-42: The Preparation and Betrayal

in 14.6 designates the anointing not as a wasteful deed deserving reprimand, but as a good work (καλὸν ἔργον).[1] (2) The second saying (14.7-8a) addresses the validity of giving in behalf of the poor, but relativizes almsgiving in view of Jesus' presence. (3) The third saying (14.8b) introduces the burial theme and links it to the woman's deed. (4) The final saying (14.9) addresses the theme of the gospel and missionary proclamation.

The inner scene (14.3-9) creates a logical coherence between the first and second sayings. The qualitative distinction between religious acts finds radical application in the teachings of Jesus. The giving of all is valued above much giving (Mk 14.41-44); meeting human needs is greater than Sabbath restrictions (Mk 3.1-6; 3.23-28).[2] While singular, spontaneous works of mercy may be valued even above the ongoing care of the poor, a more important distinction is made here. The act of the woman has christological relevance. She has done extravagently what can be done only once: she has honored the departing messiah with an act of compassion. The antithetical form[3] emphasizes the urgency of the moment: 'but you do not always have me' (14.7c). Thus, the objections of the grumblers is answered in kind: giving to the poor is a good thing, but she has done the better deed.

---

of Jesus and its consequences; this represents a distinct line of thought over against the first two sayings. It is likely that the older form of the anointing story focused the reverent and extravagent compassion of the woman. This viewpoint is supported by R. Bultmann, *The History of the Synoptic Tradition* (trans. J. Marsh; Oxford: Basil Blackwell, 1963 [1921]), pp. 36-37; E. Lohse, *History of the Suffering and Death of Jesus Christ* (trans. M.O. Dietrich; Philadelphia: Fortress Press, 1967 [1964]), p. 18; and E. Schweizer, *The Good News according to Mark* (trans. D.H. Madvig; Richmond: John Knox Press, 1970), pp. 288-91.

1. 'Working a good work' (καλὸν ἔργον ἠργάσατο) is a Hebraism. The more typical expression of this motif is seen in Mk 3.41 (ἀγαθὸν ποιῆσαι) and in 14.7b (εὖ ποιῆσαι). For an extended discussion on the distinction of acts of love from almsgiving, see J. Jeremias, 'Die Salbungsgeschichte Mc 14, 3-9', *ZNW* 35 (1936), pp. 77-81. Jeremias argued that Jewish thought consistently valued works of love (גמילות חסדים) above almsgiving (צדקה). Among the more important works of love are preparation, burial and mourning for the dead. Jeremias saw a heightening of this distinction in the teachings of Jesus and in the life of the early church.

2. The process in Mk 3.1-6 parallels that of 14.1-11: the doing of good (3.4; 14.6) is set over against traditional religious duties (sabbath, alms). Both stories are followed by a death plot (3.6; 14.10-11).

3. πάντοτε γὰρ τοὺς πτωχοὺς ἔχετε...ἐμὲ δὲ οὐ πάντοτε ἔχετε.

The linkage of the anointing to Jesus' burial is not a logical connection, but rather a theological connection drawn from her deed. This interpretation does not grow logically out of the dialogue about her act, but is imposed upon the scene solely through the saying of Jesus. In this manner the death of Jesus provides the key to the poetics of this account.

In a similar manner the connection between the deed of the woman and the mission of the gospel is not logical but theological. Her deed, like the gospel message, announces the centrality of Jesus' death. In an ironic twist the woman who brought a memorial to honor Jesus is memorialized in the Gospel story.

The introduction to 14.9 (ἀμὴν δὲ λέγω ὑμῖν) places it among the decisive Amen-sayings (Mk 3.38; 6.11 [secondary insertion of Mt. 10.15]; 8.12; 9.1; 9.41; 10.15; 10.29; 11.23; 12.43; 13.30; 14.9; 14.18; 14.25; 14.30). Following the lead of Ernst Lohmeyer, Jeremias interpreted the worldwide proclamation of the gospel not as a missionary action, but as the final eschatological announcement. Thus, the woman will be remembered with mercy by God at the final hour.[1] While Jeremias builds upon the generally eschatological nature of the Amen-sayings in the Gospel of Mark, another important focus is developed through this form. In Mk 14.18, 14.25 and 14.30 eschatological concerns fall to the background and the Amen-saying focuses precisely upon the upcoming death of Jesus. Mk 14.9 also belongs to this use of the Amen-sayings. Thus, a decisive sayings formula is employed in 14.9 to focus the death of Jesus and its consequences. The Amen-formula also shows the eschatological impact of this event. The saying to the woman in Mk 14.9 repeats the theme of the Amen-saying in Mk 10.29-30: in the present the gospel demands a costly—sometimes extravagent—commitment, but it is ultimately rewarding.

Mk 14.9 also echoes the antithesis form (δὲ λέγω ὑμῖν). While the antithetical sayings typically contrast the teaching of Jesus and that of Jewish traditions (Mt. 5.22, 26, 28, 32, 34, 39, 44; Lk. 6.27), the Gospel of Mark uses the form to emphatically contradict routine interpretations and expectations (the expectation of Elijah in 9.13; the failure to watch in 13.37). In accordance with this tendency, Mk 14.9 emphatically contradicts the routine interpretation of the woman's deed as insensitive and wasteful.

---

1. J. Jeremias, 'Mc 14, 9', *ZNW* 44 (1952–53), pp. 103-107.

2. Mark 14.1-42: The Preparation and Betrayal

In this manner the composition of the inner scene provides a unique outlook. The sayings take precedence over the action, and the focus on the woman moves to the background of the story. The meaning of the event is transformed through various words of Jesus. With the introduction of the passion link in the third saying, the question about the poor also becomes background material. The use of the Amen-form brings the final saying to the foreground and addresses the ongoing situation of the Christian community.[1]

Thus, the inner scene contains a disparate collection of sayings which are joined through the passion focus. Almsgiving is affirmed, but the woman's gift is more urgent and important in view of Jesus' approaching absence. The anointing of Jesus points to his burial; the death of Jesus will form the center of the gospel story and the gospel mission. Through this process the elements of the inner story are unified and transformed by the hermeneutical impact of Jesus' death. As a result Mk 14.3-9 maintains a lively dialogue and a vivid contrast not only with 14.1-2, 10-11, but also with its own images.

4. Morphologically the anointing story is structured around three distinct narrative segments (14.1-2, 3-9, 10-11).[2] Mk 14.1-2, 10-11 are joined through common images and themes; this linkage forms an outer context which frames the contrasting images of the inner scene. Within Mk 14.3-9 diverse images are focused through sayings material and joined through the passion focus. Syntactical analysis will show that the interplay of these contrasting segments and images

---

1. Through these characteristics the inner scene echoes the form and function of the pronouncement stories. Various scholars have built upon this characteristic. M. Dibelius (*From Gospel to Tradition* [trans. B.L. Woolf; New York: Charles Scribners' Sons, 1966 (1919)], pp. 37-69) argues that the anointing story was not an original element in the passion story, but was first an independent paradigm. Bultmann (*History*, pp. 36-37) lists the anointing among the biographical apopthegms. V. Taylor (*The Formation of the Gospel Tradition* [London: MacMillan, 1953], pp. 74-75) accepts Bultmann's designation.

2. This structural contrast likely reflects the redactional process through which the story was developed and transmitted. While reconstruction of the redactional history is helpful, this analysis is more concerned with the effect of the editorial process upon the form and function of the text. Thus, morphological analysis will be used to describe the constitution of the text in formal terms. Issues of redactional history and intention will be considered primarily in relation to their effect upon the structure and interaction of the text.

creates a unique narrative significance which is greater than the sum of its constitutive parts.

Narrative Syntax. The syntactical interplay of these motifs creates a study in contrasts. At the center of this narrative process stands a vital line of characterization.

1. Mk 14.1-2 initiates this pattern of contrasts. This introduction provides the temporal and ideological setting for this account. Chronologically the story is set in the time of the Passover celebration and the festival of Unleavened Bread. This temporal marker also places the story within a decisive thought world: these events occur against the backdrop of the religious and cultic piety of the Jewish people. A second ideological marker is provided by the conspiracy of the religious leaders, who hope through deceit to seize Jesus and to kill him. A third ideological marker is provided by the presence of the crowds. The multitudes who attend the Jewish feasts with heightened messianic expectations offer a volatile, tumultuous backdrop for this unit. Against this temporal and ideological setting, Mk 14.1-11 initiates the story of Jesus' death.

2. The death conspiracy of the religious leaders (14.1-2) reappears in the conclusion of the story (14.10-11). A third conspirator is named as Judas Iscariot and labeled conspicuously as 'one of the Twelve' (14.10). Thus, the reported conspiracy has now reached into the inner circle of Jesus' followers. The co-operation of Judas actualizes the threats of 14.1-2. The chief priests gladly accept and reward Judas's offer. Taking up the concern of the religious leaders for the timing of the arrest (14.1-2), Judas now seeks the proper opportunity to betray Jesus (14.11b). The end of this account thus takes up and develops the conspiracy theme set forth in the opening lines. Through this intercalation the introduction and the conclusion now frame the anointing with images of deceit, conspiracy and death. In this manner the death conspiracy of the religious leaders provides the canvas against which this account paints a distinct image of Jesus.

3. The motifs and images in the body of the story create a stark contrast to the outer frame. While the characters in the introduction and conclusion are marked by religious standing (chief priests, scribes, one of the Twelve), the center of the story is inhabited by characters of low esteem. The religious leaders represent Jerusalem; the anointing occurs in Bethany. Chief priests occupy the temple—the

2. Mark 14.1-42: The Preparation and Betrayal

house of God—while Jesus occupies the house of a leper. Religious leaders perform the sacred, symbolic rites of Israel; chief among these is the approaching Passover meal. In contrast, a woman slips into Jesus' meal with Simon and performs a scandalous, seductive rite. The compassion of the woman inverts the deeds of Judas and the religious leaders and provides a sharp alternative to the hostility of the outer scene. Her act is extravagant, costing the equivalent of a year's wage.[1] Her deed is perhaps scandalous, bringing a woman into a men's feast. Her actions may be viewed as inflammatory, suggesting that Jesus is indeed the anointed one, the messiah of Israel.[2] Significantly, the story reports her deeds without comment or evaluation. Their scandal and their symbolic potential are not immediately addressed by the narrative. The woman is not named, and her reputation is not discussed. The evaluation of her actions is provided instead by the dialogue which results.

The center of the story and the height of the contrast is reached in Jesus' response to the woman and to her critics (14.6-9). Jesus sets a protective frame around the deeds of the woman: 'Leave her alone. Why do you bother her? She has worked a good work for me. . . She performed what she had' (14.6-8a). The symbolic value of the act is clarified through the interpretation of Jesus: her deeds are not a scandal to be rejected, but a welcomed gift of service. The extravagance of the gift and the link to Jesus' death set the anointing apart as an unrepeatable symbol. In Jesus' evaluation her incredible extravagance is justified by the urgency of his messianic work and the immediacy of his death. Jesus does not avoid the implications of her deed, but the messianic overtones of the act are carefully focused. The messianic anointing foreshadows not a revolution, but a crucifixion.

The deed of the woman receives its ultimate interpretation through the pronouncement which follows: 'Amen, I say to you, "Wherever

---

1. A denarius is equivalent to a day's wage in Mt. 20.2.
2. In the Old Testament anointing of the head is used for kings (2 Kgs 9.6; 1 Sam. 10.1), of prophets (1 Kgs 18.15-16) and in a general sense (Pss. 23.5; 133.2; 141.5). In contrast to Gnilka, *Markus*, II, pp. 223-24, I see here rather explicit messianic imagery. Etymologically the term messiah/christ (משיח, χριστός) designates the anointed of God. In addition, the anointing of the Spirit in Isa. 61 was applied to Jesus both directly (Lk. 4.16-20) and indirectly (Mk 1.9-13). In my opinion the act in Mk 14.3 already contains clear messianic overtones. The sayings in 14.6-9 tie this messianic imagery directly to the death of Jesus.

the gospel should be preached in the whole world, what she did shall be spoken of in memory of her"'(14.9). Thus, Jesus links her deed not only to his own messianic identity and destiny, but also to the future of the gospel itself.

4. The compassion of the inner scene (14.3-9) is framed against the hostility of the outer context (14.1-2, 10-11). These colliding worlds are connected by two narrative threads. The money motif plays a secondary role in both areas (14.5, 11). A more important connection is established around the motif of Jesus' passion. Both scenes portray people who accompany Jesus to his death. One group accompanies Jesus with hostility, conspiracy and betrayal; an unnamed woman accompanies Jesus with extravagant compassion and insight. In this manner the various elements and images of Mk 14.1-11 are gathered into a narrative piece marked by vivid contrast.

At the center of this narrative creation stands a distinct portrait of Jesus. Through its primary focus on the sayings material[1] Mk 14.1-11 gives sharp focus to the role of Jesus as teacher and as prophet. His pronouncements reveal the true meaning of present events and prophesy the shape of the future. Significantly, Jesus' words now center on his death. Thus, the mission of Jesus as teacher and prophet is joined with his passion destiny. Through this connection a decisive characterization of Jesus emerges from the narrative interactions of Mk 14.1-11.

The Passion Context. Beyond its internal structure and operations, Mk 14.1-11 plays an important role within the larger context of the passion narrative. The internal story is transformed through the passion saying in Mk. 14.8.[2] Because Jesus himself links the anointing to his burial, the account now provides a preview and commentary upon his death. The entire passion narrative is set against the backdrop of the religious piety of Israel. Jesus is shown as one rejected by religious structures and by one of his own followers (14.1-2, 10-11), but accepted by people like Simon and this unnamed woman. A story

---

1. Mk 14.1-11 fits no clear literary form, yet the interpretive focus falls precisely on the pronouncements of Jesus. Gnilka (*Markus*, II, pp. 222-23) notes the diverse attempts to categorize this text: rabbinical story, pronouncement, controversy, biographical scene, Bethany tradition.

2. Because Luke omits the burial saying (Lk. 7.36-40), his story deals with Jesus' ministry and has no relation to the passion story.

2. Mark 14.1-42: The Preparation and Betrayal

filled with elements typical of Jesus' ministry is centered upon his death. The failed attempt to anoint Jesus at the end of the passion story (16.1-8) is countered by the dramatic anointing which opens the passion narrative. Thus, Mk 14.1-11 transforms the anointing scene and employs it as a vital part of the larger story of Jesus' death.

The Gospel Context. Mk 14.1-11 plays a key role within the larger narrative context of the Gospel of Mark. Located at a vital juncture in the narrative, the anointing story recalls various themes and narrative elements from the ministry of Jesus, then links them to the death story.[1] These connections—some explicit and some more subtle and suggestive—establish a larger narrative pattern and effect.

1. The location of this story is important. Within the larger narrative the story serves two significant functions. First, Mk 14.1-11 provides a link between the ministry of Jesus and his passion. In the Gospel of Mark, Jesus' ministry is set in stages: his coming forth (1.1-15), his proclamation and ministry in Galilee (1.16-8.30), his journey to Jerusalem (8.31-10.52), and his ministry in and around Jerusalem (11.1-13.37). In some ways Mk 14.1-11 appears as the last act of Jesus' public ministry. At the same time the anointing story introduces the passion narrative. Because of this Mk 14.1-11 occupies the decisive juncture between Jesus' ministry and his passion.

The location of Mk 14.1-11 also makes it part of the frame for the passion narrative. Mk 16.1-8 concludes the passion account with the puzzling story of women who are unsuccessful in their attempt to anoint Jesus and of a message which they fail to proclaim. In contrast, Mk 14.1-11 prefaces the passion account with the story of a woman who successfully anoints Jesus and of a message proclaimed in all the world.

2. In addition to its important narrative location, the images of the anointing story suggest various connections to the wider narrative world. While many of these allusions are subtle and unfocused, they nonetheless establish an important narrative pattern. Mk 14.1-11 recalls various themes from Jesus' ministry and links them to the story of his death.

2.1. In the Gospel of Mark, Jesus' ministry is often met by blindness

1. I have given attention to the implications of this story for the purpose and meaning of the Gospel of Mark in 'Mark 14.1-9: A Gospel Within a Gospel', *Paradigms* 1/1 (1985), pp. 32-41.

and rejection. In particular the religious leaders pursue and harass Jesus (Mk 2.6-7, 16, 24; 3.2-6, 22; 7.1-5; 8.11; 10.2; 11.18, 27-28; 12.12, 13-17), and it is they who instigate his death (Mk 6.6; 14.1-2, 10-11, 53-56; 15.1, 11). The rejection prevalent through Jesus' public ministry emerges anew in the anointing story. Here Jesus is surrounded by hostile leaders (14.1-2), insensitive critics (14.4-5) and unfaithful followers (14.10-11).

2.2. Mk 14.1-11 also picks up the theme of Jesus' fellowship with common people,[1] then reflects this image upon the passion story. Here Jesus reclines in the house of Simon, who is designated as a leper.[2] Further, a woman slips into this scene.[3] Mk 14.1-11 thus confirms the wider portrait of Jesus as one who shares fellowship with common people.

2.3. Mk 14.1-11 also recalls the image of discipleship developed around the minor characters in the Gospel of Mark. Typically these minor characters are nameless and without background; they enter the story, fulfill their roles, then fade away. Significantly, the Gospel of Mark employs these minor characters as paradigms of obedience. Their obedience stands in sharp contrast to the rejection of the religious leaders, the abandonment of the crowds and the failure of the disciples. The Gospel of Mark provides an impressive line of minor characters—little people—who present models of true discipleship.[4] Mk 14.1-11 further develops this theme. Jesus characterizes the

---

1. In the Gospel of Mark, Jesus' ministry is characterized by his fellowship with lepers (1.40-42), tax collectors (2.14-17), unclean (5.25-34), sinners (2.15), possessed (1.39), sick (3.10; 5.1-20; 7.32; 8.22; 10.46-52) and common crowds (3.34-35; 7.14-16; 8.1-9; 10.1). In particular Jesus is known for his scandalous eating habits. He eats with tax collectors and sinners (2.14-17), he and his disciples refuse to fast (2.18-22), he defends the plucking of grain on the Sabbath (2.23-28), and he orders food for Jairus's daughter (5.43). Throughout his ministry Jesus' acceptance of outcasts and sinners is demonstrated by his sharing of table fellowship with them, even in violation of social and religious traditions.

2. While the disease may or may not be presently active, the stigma of leprosy raises medical and religious prohibitions (Lev. 13–14). Pesch (*Markusevangelium*, II, p. 331) rejects the possibility of an active disease or even that Jesus healed Simon earlier. In my opinion the designation of Simon as 'the leper' sustains a crucial narrative effect and characterizes Simon as an outcast.

3. The scandalous nature of her actions is supported by Schweizer, *Mark*, pp. 290-91.

4. Peter's mother-in-law arises from her sickness to 'serve' Jesus (1.31). A

woman's deed as true discipleship: 'working a good work' and 'doing what you have'. Her compassionate discipleship provides a christological sign focused on the death of the messiah, and it becomes a part of the gospel story.

2.4. Mk 14.1-11 reflects the eschatological urgency which surrounds the entire ministry of Jesus. Mk 1.1 marks the onset of a new age—'the beginning of the gospel of Jesus Christ'. Jesus announces the urgency of the present moment: 'the time has been made full and the Kingdom of God is drawn near. Repent and believe in the gospel' (Mk 1.14-15). In Jesus the messiah the time and the place of God's reign has come. Normal human activities are suspended in view of this urgency.[1] In light of the eschatological urgency present in Jesus, even some acts of religious piety are suspended.[2] Thus, the

---

leper demands that Jesus heal him, then goes out 'preaching' and 'announcing the word' (1.40-45). Tax collectors and sinners who eat with Jesus are said to 'follow' him (2.15-17). Legion, a healed demoniac, begins to 'preach' in Decapolis and to tell what Jesus has done for him (5.20), thus initiating the mission to the Gentiles. Jairus's faith is unwavering, even when his daughter dies (5.21-24, 35-43). The daughter of faith believes she will be healed if she touches the garment of Jesus. By this faith she is 'saved' and goes on her way in peace (5.25-34). A Syro-Phoenician woman demands of Jesus that he heal her daughter, and her request is granted (7.24-30). Those who witness the healing of a deaf and silent man go and 'preach' what they have seen (7.36). Bartimaeus insists that Jesus stop and give attention to his need. When Bartimaeus is healed, he throws aside his garment and 'follows' Jesus 'in the way' (10.46-52). An unnamed scribe who questions Jesus is 'not far from the Kingdom of God' (12.28-34). A widow who gives all she has gives the greatest of gifts (12.41-44). Some of the women who followed Jesus in Galilee witness the crucifixion and serve as deacons to Jesus (15.41). A Gentile centurion makes the true confession of Jesus' identity (15.39, 45). The followers of John the Baptist have shown that it is the place of disciples to bury their master (6.29), then Joseph of Arimathea fulfills his discipleship by burying Jesus (15.42-46). Simon Cyrene carries the cross of Jesus, and cross-bearing becomes a sign of discipleship (15.21). Women alone come to the tomb; they are the first to hear and the first sent to proclaim the resurrection message (16.1-8). In the Gospel of Mark these minor characters provide the true models for discipleship.

1. Fishermen are to abandon their nets to follow Jesus (Mk 1.16-20). Tax collectors leave their tax booths (Mk 2.14). Disciples are to lose their soul for Jesus and the gospel (8.35). Followers are to leave behind house and family and fields for the gospel (Mk 10.29). The rich are to go and sell all that they have and follow the messiah (Mk 10.21).

2. In Mk 2.18-20 fasting while the bridegroom is present is inappropriate. For the connection of Mk 14.7 to Mk 2.18-20, I am indebted to Duane A. Priebe ('The

Gospel of Mark shows in Jesus the dawning of a new age of messianic urgency and joy which suspends the routines of life. Mk 14.7-8 reflects this urgency and joy. For Jesus doing good for the needy is a crucial sign of righteousness—more important than even the Sabbath itself (Mk 3.1-6). Nonetheless the eschatological urgency of God's reign in Jesus justifies the costly, extravagant offering of this woman. She has done for Jesus what she could while she could. The duty to the poor remains forever, but she has seized upon an unrepeatable moment.

2.5. Mk 14.1-11 also reflects the careful christological pattern of the earlier narrative. In the Gospel of Mark the messianic secrecy motif limits the proclamation of Jesus as messiah or solely in terms of his miracles. In conjunction with this pattern of limitation the Gospel of Mark consistently interprets christological images and titles in light of Jesus' death.[1] Mk 14.1-11 continues this pattern of interpretation. The anointing in 14.3 recalls Old Testament images of the messiah as God's anointed one (Isa. 61). In the Gospel of Mark the context of this messianic anointing is crucial. Jesus is anointed as messiah in the midst of hostility and rejection, at the house of a leper, by an unnamed woman. Most significantly, Jesus is anointed not for enthronement, but for death. Thus, Mk 14.1-11 continues the central christological theme: Jesus is indeed the messiah, but the definitive signs of his messiahship are suffering and service, fellowship with sinners and death on the cross.

2.6. The final image recalled in the anointing story is the theme of the gospel. Although εὐαγγέλιον is used only seven times in the Gospel of Mark (1.1; 1.14; 1.15; 8.35; 10.29; 13.10; 14.9), it provides a central theme. The entire work is designated as the gospel of Jesus Christ (1.1); the central mission of Jesus is to preach the gospel of God (1.14-15); disciples are to surrender all in behalf of the gospel (8.35; 10.29). Most signicantly, disciples are to preach the gospel throughout the world (13.10). The anointing story recalls this theme through Jesus' prophecy of a time when the gospel will be preached

---

Woman Who Anoints Jesus: Mark 14:3-9' [unpublished paper presented to the Society of Biblical Literature, November, 1989]).

1. Schweizer, *Mark*, p. 180, summarizes this christological pattern: '...all the promises and expectations, including those implied by the title "Christ", are fulfilled in the suffering of the Son of Man and in man's acceptance of discipleship (8.27-38)'.

2. Mark 14.1-42: The Preparation and Betrayal

'in all the world' (14.9). This woman's story and her witness to the death of Jesus will become a part of that gospel and a part of its proclamation.

3. These varied patterns of interconnection provide a decisive narrative effect. Located at the juncture of Jesus' life and his passion, Mk 14.1-11 gathers important themes from Jesus' story into a dramatic christological portrait. This account initiates the story of Jesus' death by building upon the story of Jesus' public ministry. At the same time Mk 14.1-11 gathers important images from the life of Jesus and places them under the interpretive framework of his passion. In this manner the opening account of the passion narrative builds a crucial bridge between the story of Jesus' life and the story of his death.

Comparative Analysis

The Gospel of Mark locates the anointing story at the juncture of Jesus' ministry and his passion, then employs this account to bring the major themes of the Gospel under the influence of the passion theme. The story performs an important role within the passion account and within the larger setting of the Gospel of Mark. This story also appears in other forms and in other contexts. Diachronic analysis will investigate these alternate contexts and will set forth a comparative base—a phenomenological field—against which to highlight the narrative significance of Mk 14.1-11.[1]

Pre-Markan Contexts. Various scholars have attempted to reconstruct a pre-Markan account of the anointing story. An early and enduring theory sees an anointing story which existed independent of the passion account. While K.L. Schmidt presented a strong argument for the integrity of a pre-Markan passion narrative, he saw that the anointing scene interrupts the flow of the story. He concluded that this account was originally an independent, self-standing pericope.[2] Dibelius agreed that the anointing story was not original to the pre-

---

1. This analysis will not address the historical relationship between different accounts of this story. These various forms will be considered as co-texts—as alternate performances of a common story. In this methodology diachronic analysis provides a phenomenological description and comparison of these co-texts.
2. Schmidt, *Rahmen*, pp. 306-307.

Markan passion account.[1] Bultmann argued in a similar vein that the anointing in Mk 14.3-9 was a self-standing unit later added to the passion story. Bultmann suggested in addition that the passion emphasis of 14.8-9 was absent from this account.[2] Subsequent to this numerous scholars have embraced the idea that the anointing story first stood as an independent unit. Among these, many presuppose a stage at which the story carried no reference to the passion.

The existence of the anointing story as a self-standing unit without reference to the passion would present a sharp contrast to Mk 14.1-11. The hostility and rejection set forth in Mk 14.1, 10-11 would be missing, and no mention would be made of the religious leaders or of the religious feasts. The betrayal by one of the Twelve would also be absent. The only controversy present would be the grumbling and the rebuke of 'some' (14.4-5) over the waste of ointment. In addition, most who contend for such an account also argue for the absence of the passion focus of Mk 14.8b-9.[3]

An independent anointing story without reference to the passion would serve a distinct literary function. Such an account would understand the woman's deed as an extravagant act of reverence and honor. The anointing would also carry messianic implications, but these implications would remain undefined. Such a story might perceive Jesus primarily as political messiah or as divine miracle worker. Beyond this, various elements of the story become ambiguous. Without prior development the mention of the leper's house, a woman's service to Jesus and the preaching of the gospel throughout the world serve only as colorful details. This lack of definition and wider reference limits their impact to this singular context. Thus, this account would tell of the heroic deed of an unnamed woman toward a messiah whose mission remains unclear. The central focus of such a story would fall on Jesus' affirmation that she has 'worked a good work' (14.6).

1. Dibelius, *Tradition*, p. 181.
2. Bultmann, *History*, pp. 36-37, 263.
3. See, for example, Bultmann, *History*, pp. 36-37; Lohse, *Suffering and Death*, p. 18. Schweizer (*Mark*, pp. 288-91) suggests that the story originally focused the expressions of love in 14.7ac. Nonetheless Schweizer thinks that the passion link may be early.

2. Mark 14.1-42: The Preparation and Betrayal

A second possible context is suggested by those who see the anointing story as an integral part of a pre-Markan passion narrative.[1] The telling of such a story in the context of the passion account would be more akin to Mk 14.1-11, yet significant differences remain. In such a story the rejection by religious leaders and one of the Twelve might already impact the account. The deed of the woman would stand in sharp contrast to this rejection, and the link to the death of Jesus would be present. Nonetheless important elements of Mk 14.1-11 would be missing from this context. The hostility and rejection would lack the careful development provided by passages such as Mk 2.6-7, 16, 24; 3.2, 6, 22; 7.1-5; 8.11; 10.2; 11.18, 27-28; 12.13-14. Elements such as eating with outcasts, the priority of service, the role of women, the meaning and destiny of the gospel would lack the coherent definition and development provided by Mark 1–13. Operating solely with the framework of Mark 14–16, the anointing story would lose much of its referential and symbolic value.

The Gospel of Matthew. Mt. 26.1-16 places the anointing story in a context similar to that of Mk 14.1-11. Matthew's account follows the parable of judgment (Mt. 25.31-46). The introduction (Mt. 26.1-5) parallels Mk 14.1-2 and ties the story to the previous teaching and to the death of Jesus. Matthew's linkage of this account to the passion is explicit: the Son of Man will be handed over unto crucifixion (Mt. 26.2). Matthew notes that the conspiracy involves the chief priests and the elders, who meet in the courtyard of the chief priest Caiaphas. Thus, Matthew gives explicit detail to the hostility of the religious leaders and links this story beforehand to the crucifixion of Jesus.

The anointing scene is parallel to Mk 14.3-9: in Bethany at the house of Simon the leper, an unnamed woman anoints the head of Jesus. In contrast to the 'some' of Mk 14.4, Matthew tells that it is the disciples who grumbled at this use of the ointment (Mt. 26.8). Typical of his kindness to the disciples, Matthew omits the rebuke against them. The exact cost of the ointment is also omitted. A distinctive reference is made to the preaching of 'this' gospel (Mt. 26.13). Matthew's account of Jesus' reply is stylized, but it reflects no

---

1. See Pesch, *Markusevangelium*, II, pp. 328-29. D. Dormeyer (*Die Passion Jesu als Verhaltensmodell: Literarische und theologische Analyse der Traditions- und Redaktionsgeschichte der Markuspassion* [Münster: Aschendorff, 1974], p. 80) argues that 14.3 was part of the oldest passion account.

substantive differences. Mt. 26.14-16 also closes the story with the betrayal by Judas.

Thus, the anointing story in Mt. 26.1-16 differs little in form or function from the account in Mk 14.1-11. Matthew has softened the internal controversy and placed it upon the lips of the disciples. Externally, Matthew has made the connections to the hostility of the religious leaders and to the death of Jesus explicit. This story functions in much the same way as Mk 14.1-11: the public ministry of Jesus ends with a scene which gathers together various themes from his ministry and points to his death.

The Gospel of Luke. The anointing story is found in a sharply different context in Lk. 7.36-50. Luke places the story in the midst of Jesus' public ministry. Following a parabolic reference to Jesus as a friend of tax collectors and sinners (Lk. 7.34), Luke demonstrates Jesus' table fellowship with outcasts. This story also opens with the mention of a religious leader, but a strange twist appears. Here a Pharisee invites Jesus to eat at his home. The woman who approaches Jesus is unnamed, but not unknown; she has a sinful reputation on the streets of the city. With her vessel of ointment she approaches Jesus from behind. She covers his feet with her tears, wipes his feet with her hair, kisses his feet, then anoints his feet with ointment.

In Luke's account it is the Pharisee host who objects to this intrusion. His objection does not relate to money, but to the scandal of the event and to the identity of Jesus: a true prophet would know that she is a sinner. A dialogue follows between Jesus and the Pharisee, now named as Simon (Lk. 7.40). Significantly, the Pharisee addresses Jesus as 'Teacher' (Lk. 7.40). Jesus poses a parabolic riddle about forgiveness of debts (Lk. 7.41-42). Simon answers this riddle correctly: the one forgiven most will love most (Lk. 7.43). Jesus then contrasts the compassionate attention of the woman with the host's lack of hospitality (Lk. 7.44-47). In a final pronouncement Jesus proclaims forgiveness for this sinful woman. The pronouncement is first made to the Pharisee as a completion of the riddle. Jesus speaks to the woman for the first time in Lk. 7.48. His address is short and unadorned: 'Your sins are forgiven'. Controversy results and is articulated by those at the table: 'Who is this who even forgives sin?' (Lk. 7.49). Jesus sends the woman on her way with a final benediction: 'Your faith has saved you. Go in peace' (Lk. 7.50). Following this account Luke returns to

2. Mark 14.1-42: The Preparation and Betrayal 47

the ministry of Jesus and gives specific focus to the contribution of women (Lk. 8.1-3).

Thus, Lk. 7.36-50 narrates a sharply contrasting form and function for the anointing story. Various parallels link the account to Mk 14.1-11: eating as a guest, the presence of a religious leader, the mention of Simon, anointing by an unnamed woman, an alabaster jar, controversy over the act, the mention of denarii. At the same time Lk. 7.36-50 is unique. The story occurs early in Jesus' ministry, religious leaders do not threaten Jesus, the woman anoints Jesus' feet rather than his head, the objection raised centers on the identity of the woman and the identity of Jesus, the controversy is stirred by Jesus' proclamation of forgiveness, the objectors are unnamed. Missing from this account are the plotting of the religious leaders, the mention of leprosy, the connection to the death of Jesus, the linkage of the deed to the preaching of the gospel, and the betrayal by one of the Twelve.

Set within this contrasting narrative context, Luke's story produces a different portrait of Jesus. The messianic images of the anointing are avoided when the woman anoints the feet rather than the head. The story focuses now on the scandalous contact of Jesus with sin and with sinners. The Pharisee's embarassment and lack of hospitality provides a colorful backdrop for the sensuous compassion of this sinful woman. Luke's account delights in the narrative contrast between the religious leader and the sinful outcast. Here Luke posits a clear christological theme: Jesus is the teacher who eats and drinks with sinners and offers them forgiveness. Luke 15 develops the same theme from a theological perspective. Thus, Luke employs the anointing story to speak of Jesus' identity and mission among outcasts. To reinforce the internal images of this story, Luke frames the account (Lk. 7.34-35; 8.1-3) with Jesus' ministry among tax collectors and sinners and women.

The Gospel of John. Jn 12.1-8 presents another context for the anointing story. The Passover feast again provides the setting for this account (Jn 11.55). The people also play a role—they are curious about Jesus (Jn 11.56). Most significantly, the story is set against the attempt by the religious leaders (chief priests and Pharisees) to arrest Jesus (Jn 11.49-53, 57). The hostility of the religious leaders also follows the story (Jn 12.9-11). Against this setting Jn 12.1-8 tells the anointing story. Many similarities exist between Jn 12.1-8 and Mk 14.1-11: the Passover setting, Bethany, a meal, anointing by a woman, an objection, mention of the price and the poor, mention of burial, the betrayal by Judas, a pronouncement by Jesus. At the same time, sharp differences emerge. The event takes place six days before the Passover rather than two. The meal is at the house of a friend (Lazarus), and the woman is named (Mary). Mary anoints the feet, not the head. The objection is raised by Judas Iscariot, who is labeled a callous thief. The pronouncement of Jesus is simple and direct: 'Leave her. Let her keep it unto the day of my burial' (Jn 12.7). Missing from the account are the anointing of the head, the mention of her good work, and the preaching of the gospel in all the world.

While Jn 12.1-8 narrates precise details omitted in Mk 14.1-11, the form and function of the Johannine account are unique. Framed by the hostility of the religious leaders and the curiosity of the crowds, Jn 12.1-8 tells a story of private compassion and intimacy. Jesus stays at the house of friends (Jn 11.5). He is hosted by Lazarus, served by Martha, and anointed by Mary. In the midst of open hostility and in the shadow of the cross, Jesus is welcomed into a circle of friends. Nonetheless the hostility invades even the internal workings of the story. One of the disciples objects to this scene of compassion, and his objections in behalf of the poor are motivated by greed. Death also invades the inner scene: the anointing points to Jesus' burial (Jn 12.7). The host has been delivered from death by the guest, but the guest will die. The poor will remain, but Jesus must depart (Jn 12.8).

This unique account of the anointing enhances the portrait of Jesus. He is shown as one rejected by the world of religious leaders, yet loved by his own. Jesus' compassion for Lazarus, Martha and Mary (Jn 11.1-44) is returned in this scene. Followers who confess him as Lord, Christ, Son of God, Teacher (Jn 11.21, 27, 28, 32, 39) provide a place of safety and compassion. Still Jesus is taken from them through hostility and betrayal. Nonetheless, the one whom they bury (Jn 12.7) is himself the resurrection and the life (Jn 11.25-26). Thus, this account now embodies the Johannine focus on the mission and identity of Jesus.

Summary

The story of the anointing of Jesus was shown to operate in a variety of narrative contexts. Each context carried significant implications for the characterization of Jesus. The first possibility examined was that of an independent, pre-Markan story without reference to the death of

2. Mark 14.1-42: The Preparation and Betrayal 49

Jesus. Such a story would be missing any major controversy, and the deed of the woman would provide an example of extravagant reverence. This story would present an ambiguous messianic image open to various interpretations.

The second context examined placed the story in a pre-Markan passion narrative. This account would link the anointing to the hostility of the religious leaders and to the death of Jesus, but the details of the story would have no particular frame of reference outside the passion account.

Alternate performances of this story are found in the canonical Gospels. Matthew replicates the form and function of Mk 14.1-11, but influences the story by his own style and by at least one theological concern: he acquits the disciples of significant resistance to the ministry of Jesus. Luke narrates the anointing story in the midst of Jesus' ministry as an independent unit with no reference to the passion. The image of Jesus which emerges is typically Lukan: Jesus is the teacher who eats and drinks with tax collectors and sinners and women, then offers them God's acceptance and forgiveness. The Gospel of John gives explicit detail to various elements of the anointing story. The image of Jesus which emerges is thoroughly Johannine: Jesus is hated and rejected by the world, but he is loved by his own.

Thus, the anointing story was shown to exist in diverse contexts and to support a variety of images of Jesus. Seen over against these alternate contexts, Mk 14.1-11 creates a distinct narrative account and a unique characterization of Jesus. Morphological analysis showed that Mk 14.1-11 is constituted around five motifs distributed across three narrative segments. The syntactical interaction of these elements produces a decisive narrative effect. Mk 14.1-11 places the anointing story at the juncture of Jesus' public ministry and his passion. From this narrative perspective the anointing consummates the story of Jesus' life and initiates the story of his death. Likewise, Mk 14.1-11 links up with Mk 16.1-8 to form a narrative frame for the passion account. More significantly, Mk 14.1-11 insists that the passion narrative cannot stand alone as an independent account; instead, the passion story is deeply rooted in the story of Jesus' words and deeds. Conversely the words and deeds of Jesus are brought under the final interpretive frame of his death and resurrection. Through Mk 14.1-11 the life story and the death story of Jesus are welded together. The ultimate key to Jesus' mission and identity lies in his death; the story of Jesus' death radiates with referential and symbolic value gained from the events of his life.

At the center of these narrative transactions stands a distinct line of characterization. The authoritative teacher/prophet stands in view of his own death. Jesus is hated by religious leaders and betrayed by one near him. In contrast he is welcomed by the lowly, and he shares fellowship with these common people. Jesus is portrayed as God's anointed, but it is his death which provides the singular key to his messianic identity. The story of Jesus is narrated as a gospel story which will be proclaimed in all the world. Gathering and building upon major themes from Jesus' ministry, Mk 14.1-11 links the whole story of Jesus and the diverse images of Jesus to the scandal of the cross.

Mark 14.12-26: The Passover Meal

Mk 14.12-26 tells of Jesus' celebration of the Passover meal with his disciples. This story creates a dramatic local scene and provides important links to the larger story of Jesus.

Synchronic Analysis

The motifs of Mk 14.12-26 present the following structure:

Introduction
Disciples question	14.12
Jesus predicts	14.13-15
Disciples respond	14.16

Body
All come	14.17
Jesus prophesies	14.18
Disciples respond	14.19
Jesus prophesies	14.20-21
Jesus distributes	14.22a
Jesus interprets	14.22b
Jesus distributes	14.23a
Disciples drink	14.23b
Jesus interprets	14.24
Jesus prophesies	14.25

Conclusion
All depart	14.26

2. Mark 14.1-42: The Preparation and Betrayal

Narrative Morphology. Mk 14.12-26 employs fourteen motifs to present the Passover meal, with both action and description used to develop the significance of this scene. The introduction of the unit is rather complex, employing three extended motifs. The story opens with an unusual motif in which the disciples question Jesus. This inquiry sets the stage for the two motifs which follow—the reply of Jesus and the response of the disciples. Following this dense introduction the story shifts to the meal scene. The opening motif of the body accomplishes the transition to the table. In the remainder of the body sharp focus is given to the words and deeds of Jesus; only the question of the disciples (14.19) and the drinking of the cup (14.23b) break this concentration. In contrast to the complex introduction, a single motif concludes the unit and provides the transition to the following story.

1. Morphologically the Passover story is constituted around three distinct narrative segments (14.12-16; 14.17-21; 14.22-26).[1] The first segment (14.12-16), with its temporal markers (14.12a),[2] question (14.12b), answer (14.13-15) and fulfillment formula (14.16), is relatively self-contained.[3] Mk 14.12-16 is set off from the rest of the story by its reference to the followers of Jesus: here they are designated as disciples (μαθηταί), while 14.17-26 refers to them as the Twelve. Nonetheless Mk 14.12-16 presumes an attached meal scene. Thus, various scholars argue that Mk 14.12-16 has been intentionally structured to designate the following scene as a Passover

---

1. These segments almost certainly reflect an editorial linking of material. While various scholars attempt to reconstruct the stages and intentions which underlie this redaction, this analysis is concerned primarily with the narrative effect of this restructuring process.

2. The doubled time reference in 14.12 generates a host of difficulties. The first day of Unleavened Bread is 15 Nisan (the Passover), but the sacrifice of the Passover lamb (ἔθυον) is carried out on 14 Nisan. Bultmann (*History*, p. 264) calls the reference 'quite impossible in Jewish usage'. Pesch (*Markusevangelium*, II, p. 342) cites parallels in support of an eight-day feast of Unleavened Bread which begins on 14 Nisan. A simple solution would be provided by using a Greek time pattern which measured from morning (14 Nisan) to evening (15 Nisan) as one day which included both preparation and Passover; this, however, would place preparation and Passover in too close proximity.

3. Indeed, Bultmann (*History*, pp. 263-64) sees here a legendary variant of Mk 11.1-6 which has been framed as an introduction to the Passover meal. See also Schweizer, *Mark*, p. 294.

meal.¹ Significantly, two models for the structuring of Mk 14.12-16 have been suggested. A similar scene precedes the Jerusalem entry in Mk 11.1-6, and the parallels to 14.12-16 are extensive.² It is likely that Mk 11.1-6 and 14.12-16 are structured by the same hand.³ In addition, numerous parallels exist between Mk 14.12-16 and 1 Sam. 10.1-10.⁴ Mk 14.12-16 thus constitutes a separate narrative segment in distinction from the meal scene.

While Mk 14.12-16 invokes an extended concern with the preparation for Passover, its real focus centers around the instructions given by Jesus. The extensive cultic details required for Passover are not treated;⁵ attention is given instead to the details of Jesus' command. In addition, the segment climaxes with a fulfillment report in which the instructions of Jesus are vindicated (14.16). As a result the primary

1. Nothing in Mk 14.17-21 or 14.22-26 explicitly designates a Passover meal.

2.   Mk 14.12-16   Mk 11.1-6

  13. ... ἀποστέλλει δύο τῶν   1. ... ἀποστέλλει δύο τῶν
       μαθητῶν αὐτοῦ   μαθητῶν αὐτοῦ
       καὶ λέγει αὐτοῖς   2. καὶ λέγει αὐτοῖς
       ὑπάγετε εἰς τὴν πόλιν   ὑπάγετε εἰς τὴν κώμην
       καὶ ἀπαντήσει ὑμῖν   καὶ ... εὑρήσατε
  14. εἴπατε...   3. εἴπατε
       ὁ διδάσκαλος   ὁ κύριος
  16. καὶ ἐξῆλθον...   4. καὶ ἀπῆλθον
       καὶ εὗρον   καὶ εὗρον
       καθὼς εἶπεν αὐτοῖς   6. καθὼς εἶπεν ὁ Ἰησοῦς
       καί...   καί...

In addition, both scenes seem to reflect a Bethany tradition.

3. Gnilka (*Markus*, II, p. 232) argues that the redactor takes a single report from a fixed passion tradition and employs it in two forms. See also Taylor, *Mark*, p. 536. The extensive use of καί-parataxis (11 times) also supports the redactional nature of 14.12-16.

4. Among the similar images are the instructions about meeting persons bearing common objects, the prophetic imagery and the fulfillment report. Significantly, 1 Sam. 10.1-10 is prefaced by 1 Sam. 9.9, which explains the transition in terms from seer to prophet. Close connections between this passage and Mk 14 are rejected by Pesch (*Markusevangelium*, II, p. 341) but supported by Gnilka (*Markus*, II, p. 232). See as well the traditions in 1 Kgs 17.8-16 and in 2 Kgs 1.1-17.

5. Among these are preparation of the room, selection and slaughter of a sacrificial lamb, preparation of unleavened bread, preparation of the table and preparation of other meal elements. See Gnilka, *Markus*, II, p. 232; P. Billerbeck and H.L. Strack, *Kommentar zum Neuen Testament aus Talmud und Midrasch* (Munich: Beck, 1928), IV, pp. 41-76.

2. Mark 14.1-42: The Preparation and Betrayal

focus of this narrative segment is the prophetic foreknowledge employed by Jesus.¹ Various elements support this prophetic imagery.² In conjunction with this image Jesus implies that he will be recognized by a distinct title: the Teacher (ὁ διδάσκαλος in 14.14).³

Thus, Mk 14.12-16 generates an insistent image of Jesus as the teacher/prophet who instructs with power and insight. Beyond its role as an introduction to the Passover meal, 14.12-16 defines the ideological context: against the celebration of Passover and Unleavened Bread, Jesus is shown as the authoritative messenger of God.⁴

2. Mk 14.17-21 provides the second narrative segment in the Passover story. Both the isolation of this segment and its internal patterns are decisive.

2.1. Mk 14.17-21 distinguishes itself with a new set of time and place markers in 14.17-18 (an evening meal). The explanation of ἀνακειμένων (while reclining) with ἐσθιόντων (while eating) is unusual, particularly if 14.12-16 has prepared for the meal.⁵ In

---

1. In contrast Pesch (*Markusevangelium*, II, p. 343) sees the Passover preparation as primary and the prophetic imagery as secondary.

2. The extensive use of imperative (ὑπάγετε, ἀκολουθήσατε, εἴπατε, ἑτοιμάσατε) and future (ἀπαντήσει, δείξει) forms conveys the image of prophetic authority. In addition, the parallels to 1 Sam. 10.1-10, 1 Kgs 17.8-16 and 2 Kgs 1.1-17 all suggest prophetic images. More ambiguous prophetic images may be suggested by the seemingly familiar reference to 'my guest room' (τὸ καταλυμά μου). The open invitation to a guest room is found in the Elijah tradition (an upper room in 1 Kgs 17.15, 19-20, 23) and in the wandering proclaimer tradition (Mk 6.8-11; Mt. 10.1, 5-15; Lk. 9.1-6), and this imagery may belong to the teacher/prophet characterization.

3. The suggestion by Pesch (*Markusevangelium*, II, pp. 343-44)—that ὁ διδάσκαλος is employed as a code name (the rabbi) with no christological significance in order to avoid the death plot—is speculative. The use of ὁ διδάσκαλος is unexpected and unmotivated in this context, and it serves to confirm the prophetic Christology of 14.12-16.

4. Schweizer (*Mark*, p. 297) concludes in a similar manner that 'this passage serves two objectives: It puts the Lord's Supper into the place of the Jewish Passover and at the same time emphasizes that what happened on this day did not come upon Jesus as a catastrophe but was predicted by him, and that he chose to endure it'.

5. The use of κατάκειμαι can refer to reclining from either sickness (Mk 1.30; 2.4) or at table (Mk 2.15; 14.32). In contrast, the New Testament use of ἀνάκειμαι is only in reference to meals (for example, Mk 6.26; a secondary tradition uses it otherwise in Mk 5.40). Reclining at table requires one who serves, so ἀνάκειμαι is paired with διακονέω in Lk. 22.27 and Jn 12.2. F. Büchsel ('κεῖμαι', *TDNT*, III,

addition, the changed reference to the followers of Jesus—from disciples (14.12, 13, 14, 16) to the Twelve (14.17, 20)—sets this unit apart from the rest of the story.[1] Beyond this, nothing in the meal directly picks up the Passover theme announced in 14.12-16.[2] The repetition of 'while he (Jesus) was eating' in 14.22 also tends to separate 14.22-26 from the events in 14.17-21.[3] Thus, the table scene in Mk 14.17-21 forms a distinct narrative segment over against 14.12-16 and 14.22-26.[4]

2.2. The internal pattern of 14.17-21 creates a decisive effect. While 14.18 introduces a meal scene, only the τρύβλιον[5] in 14.20 relates to this theme. Indeed, the focus on the meal falls to the background, and three sayings of Jesus are placed in the foreground (14.18, 20, 21). Three themes dominate these sayings: betrayal, discipleship failure, the handing over of the Son of Man.

2.2.1. The first saying (14.18b) interrupts the meal with the prediction of betrayal. The betrayal motif is described as a παράδοσις—a handing over—and this prophecy echoes the predictions in 9.31 and 10.33. In contrast to 9.31 and 10.33 (where the Son of Man is handed

p. 655) says of Mk 14.18: 'Reclining at the passover was meant to signify that after the Exodus the Israelites were free men and not slaves. It was thus regarded as essential...'

1. This change is seen as evidence of a different tradition by J. Jeremias, *Die Abendmahlsworte Jesu* (Göttingen: Vandenhoeck & Ruprecht, 4th edn, 1953), p. 300; Schenke, *Studien*, p. 200; Schweizer, *Markus*, p. 294. Schenke, *Studien*, pp. 199-285, sees the whole unit, with the exception of the traditional saying in 14.21b, as Markan construction. Pesch (*Markusevangelium*, II, pp. 347-48) resists this interpretation.

2. Pesch (*Markusevangelium*, II, pp. 345-53) strains to see inherent signs of a Passover meal in elements such as the reclining and the specific mention of eating. His efforts are unconvincing. If the thesis of Pesch—that reclining distinguishes the Passover and feast meals from common meals, where participants sit at table—is followed, Jesus is never shown in a common meal scene in the New Testament!

3. The argument of Pesch (*Markusevangelium*, II, p. 348)—that καὶ ἐσθιόντων αὐτῶν in 14.22 is a marker separating the main meal from the Passover ritual—is unlikely.

4. Indeed, Mk 14.17-21 may reflect a separate tradition drawn from a common meal with the Twelve near the time of Jesus' death. The focus of this meal would be the astonishing betrayal by one of the Twelve and the suffering of Jesus which is at hand. The clear image which would emerge from such a story is that of the suffering prophet. For this type of proposal, see Bultmann, *History*, p. 264.

5. The term τρύβλιον may refer to various types of dinnerware.

2. Mark 14.1-42: The Preparation and Betrayal

over), 14.18 employs an active form and designates the actant ('one of you will hand me over').[1] While ἐξ ὑμῶν seems ambiguous, its antecedent is given in 14.17 as the Twelve. Thus, the first saying predicts not only that Jesus will be handed over; more importantly, he will be betrayed by one of the Twelve. This interruption of the meal scene is intensified by the use of the Amen-formula. In addition, the appositional description of the conspirator as 'one eating with me' sharpens the theme of betrayal by an associate. This phrase echoes the language of Ps. 41.10 and recalls the imagery of the suffering righteous.[2] The first saying thus frames the handing over theme with the nearness of the betrayer to Jesus. This imagery is strengthened through the Amen-formula and set forth against the meal scene as a stark prophecy: Jesus will be handed over by one who has shared his ministry and his fellowship.

2.2.2. The grieving question of the Twelve (14.19) is sandwiched between the first and second sayings. This succint report implies an extended query in which one after another (εἷς κατὰ εἷς) of the Twelve poses the question of guilt: 'It is not I, is it?'[3] This construction extends the focus on the Twelve as individuals rather than as a collective group.[4] Through this query the unthinkable prophecy of 14.18 is repeated twelvefold: Jesus will be handed over by one of his followers.

2.2.3. The focus on the betrayer is intensified through its repetition in the second saying (14.20). This saying provides an antiphonal response to 14.19: one after one the Twelve deny, but one of the

---

1. The use of the Son of Man title and the passive sense seems typical for this phrase and may be found in 9.31, 10.33, 14.21 and 14.41. This form focuses the destiny of the Son of Man. The change of the phrase in 14.18 shifts the focus to the betrayer of the Son of Man. In conjunction with this shift, the term becomes a title (ὁ παραδιδούς) in 14.42, 44. This same effect is achieved when the use of the title frames the reference in 14.43 to Judas as one of the Twelve.

2. See also the use of this phrase in 1QH 5.23-24.

3. Formulating the question with the use of μή expects a negative response.

4. The extensive use of εἷς (4 times) and ἐκεῖνος (2 times) in 14.17-21 demonstrates this individual focus. To what extent the actions of Judas are paradigmatic for a larger group is a question of narrative effect and association. Likely, this focus on individual responsibility is primarily a dramatic emphasis of the closeness of the betrayer and only secondarily a theological motif of individual versus corporate responsibility. D. Dormeyer (*Verhaltensmodell*, p. 100) and Pesch (*Markusevangelium*, II, p. 353) see here a theological motif of individual responsibility.

Twelve will betray. In content Mk 14.20 simply repeats the images of the first saying. The verbless phrasing of this second saying creates an asyndeton which repeats the theme with stark emphasis: the betrayer is one of the Twelve at the table.

The intercalation produced from these elements creates a dramatic narrative effect and focuses the betrayal of Jesus by one of his followers. This imagery is posed in 14.18 by the transformation of the phrase in order to focus the role of the betrayer and by the use of the Amen-formula. Repetition and broken grammar are used to dramatize this theme in 14.20. Sandwiched between these two sayings, the twelvefold query of 14.19 provides an extended echo of the theme. Through this complex narrative arrangement the central premise is presented with somber intensity: the Son of Man is betrayed by one of his followers.

2.2.4. The third saying (14.21) repeats the central theme, but it also provides further development. The standard formulation of the παράδοσις prophecy stands at the center of the saying (ὁ υἱὸς τοῦ ἀνθρώπου παραδίδοται as in 9.31; 10.33; 14.41). Building around this standard form, 14.21 explicates crucial aspects of this prophecy. (1) The one handed over is identified as the Son of Man (in contrast to 'me' in 14.19, 20). (2) His going up[1] fulfills the Scriptures.[2] (3) The betrayal of the Son of Man is a crime for which the betrayer stands condemned. This third logion unites vital aspects of Jesus' ministry: a didactic/prophetic saying employs eschatological images[3] to focus the departure of Jesus as fulfillment of the Old Testament.

2.3. Thus, Mk 14.17-21 employs three sayings and a query to focus the παράδοσις theme. The handing over of Jesus is posited, but

---

1. Here ὑπάγω is apparently a euphemism for the arrest of Jesus. In normal usage departure or dismissal is implied (Mk 5.34; 14.13). The Fourth Gospel develops this term into a full theological metaphor for the return of Jesus to the Father. In no other use is death an explicit element of this term. As recently as Mk 14.13 the term means a journey into Jerusalem (which is always 'up'), and this seems to be the image applied to the arrest of Jesus in 14.21. The use of ὑπάγει as a death metaphor, as in Pesch, *Markusevangelium*, II, p. 351, seems to come from outside this scene.

2. The Gospel of Mark assumes, but does not explain, that the death of the Son of Man is rooted in Old Testament texts. This same assumption is found in 9.12. Mk 1.1-3 may root the entire story of Jesus (including his death) in the Isaianic message of the Suffering Servant.

3. The eschatological use of the Son of Man title is seen in Mk 13.26, 32; 14.62. In addition, 14.21c may imply eschatological judgment.

2. Mark 14.1-42: The Preparation and Betrayal

primary focus is given to the details and implications of this process. In this manner the internal operations of 14.17-21 focus a stark christological portrait. This process and its images are only vaguely connected to the meal setting (14.17) and even less connected to the Passover setting (14.12, 16). This internal focus and the distinction from surrounding material show that Mk 14.17-21 is constituted as a distinct segment within the larger story of the Passover meal.[1]

3. Mk 14.22-26 constitutes a third segment within the Passover story. The imposition of a third temporal/place marker (while eating) sets this unit apart from the discussion of betrayal in 14.17-21.[2] In addition, the lack of explicit Passover elements or references creates distance between this scene and the preparations in 14.12-16. While connections exist between all three units of the Passover story,[3] 14.22-26 presents a separate narrative segment.

The scene in 14.22-26 is structured around the meal elements but focused around the sayings material. Apart from these interpretive logia the meal elements lose their significance.[4] The first saying (14.22c) identifies the bread with the body of Jesus, but offers no further explanation. The second saying (14.24) similarly interprets the cup as the blood of Jesus. Having established these connections, the remainder of the second saying fills out the imagery: the death of Jesus establishes a new covenant, and this covenant is for 'the many'.[5] In Jewish imagery the blood is a concrete symbol for life; thus, the pouring out of blood means death. As in Exod. 24.8, the giving of life

---

1. Schenke (*Studien*, p. 203) confirms this analysis: 'Mk 14, 17-21 presents, literary critically, a narrative piece which may be separated from the context'.

2. As a result 14.22 begins with three participles (eating, taking, blessing). The information in 14.22 provides the proper opening to a meal scene, as Mk 6.41 and 8.6 show.

3. For example, neither Jesus nor the disciples is named in 14.22-26 ('he' and 'they' are used throughout), assuming prior designation of their roles.

4. Pesch (*Markusevangelium*, II, pp. 354-64) goes to great lengths to demonstrate parallels with the Passover ritual.

5. Pesch (*Markusevangelium*, II, p. 358) sees 'the many' primarily as a reference to Israel. Gnilka (*Markus*, II, p. 246) correctly sees a wider primary reference which encompasses all people. The death of God's servant for the many, including the Gentiles, has its model in Isa. 53. In Isaiah as in the Lord's Supper traditions the death of the servant is linked to God's forgiveness of sin. This *pro nobis* imagery has already been employed as a prophetic Son of Man saying about the passion in Mk 10.45.

is associated with the establishment of a covenant. Significantly, the Exodus covenant is confirmed by eating and drinking in eschatological glory (Exod. 24.9-11). Employing these images, the logion in Mk 14.24 links the death of Jesus to the framing of a covenant. While sacrificial images may be present, the focus of this saying is primarily covenantal, with the traditional concept of the covenant widened by attaching it to the death of Jesus and to the need of the many. The emphasis that 'all' (πάντες) participate prepares for the contrasting failure of 'all' in 14.27, 50.[1]

The final saying (14.25) culminates the covenant theme and links it to the Kingdom. A vow of abstinence is set in which Jesus refrains from wine until a future celebration.[2] This new wine will be taken in the Kingdom.[3] In this manner the death of Jesus and his future are linked to the initial theme of his preaching: the Kingdom of God (1.14-15). Thus, the final saying unites three important images of Jesus—prophetic teaching, eschatology, passion—and places them in the Amen-form at the end of the meal scene.

The conclusion in 14.26 has transformed the hymn—which could reflect a Passover element—into a dismissal scene. The departure to the Mount of Olives rather than to Bethany is significant for the accounts which follow.[4]

4. This analysis shows that Mk 14.12-26 is constituted morphologically around three distinct narrative segments. The meal theme—which is explicitly a Passover meal only in 14.12-16—guides the structure of each segment, yet the primary focus in each unit is given

---

1. Schweizer (*Mark*, p. 303) finds historical cause for the emphasis that all drank of the wine. He argues that this phrase 'is probably aimed against any tendencies toward asceticism or frugality which would eliminate the wine from the celebration of the Lord's Supper'. The narrative effect operates in a quite different direction. Through syntactical connections the denials (14.31) and failure (14.27, 50) of 'all' become doubly tragic, for 'all' had shared his cup (14.23).

2. No explicit reference is made to the role of the disciples in this celebration. This omission is covered by Mt. 26.29, which makes explicit the participation of the disciples in the future celebration.

3. Significantly, Jesus' preaching of the Kingdom is characterized as new wine (Mk 2.22) which requires new skins. Linguistically the use of καινός (2.22; 14.25) and the reference to 'that day' (2.20; 14.25) may also connect 2.18-22 and 14.22-26.

4. I have argued for strong theological symbolism attached to the Mount of Olives in 'Which Mountain is "This Mountain"?: A Critical Note on Mark 11.22-25', *Paradigms* 2/1 (1986), pp. 33-38.

2. Mark 14.1-42: The Preparation and Betrayal

to the words of Jesus.[1] It is through these sayings that crucial didactic, prophetic, eschatological and passion images are framed around the meal theme. Syntactical analysis will show the powerful narrative effect generated through these morphological patterns.

Narrative Syntax. The syntactical interaction of these motifs creates a dramatic story and a unique focus on the identity of Jesus. Central to this process is the characterization of Jesus as the prophet of God.

1. The opening motif (14.2) provides the temporal setting, introduces the actants and imposes the Passover theme on all three segments of the story. Consequently this meal focus guides the plotting of the entire account. In the second motif (14.13-15) Jesus sends the disciples to prepare this meal with a prediction that they will be met by a ready host and a prepared room. In the narrow sense Mk 14.16 provides an answer to the disciples' question (14.12) and sets the stage for the meal; in the wider sense this motif shows the sudden and certain fulfillment of Jesus' prediction. The introduction thus serves an unusual function in this story. In addition to providing the primary setting, the actants and the major plot elements for this account, Mk 14.12-16 initiates the central narrative pattern. The disciples share an intimate season with Jesus, guided by his words of instruction and prediction. They do as Jesus commands, and they see his words fulfilled before their eyes. The introduction thus creates the paradigm of prophecy and fulfillment which will shape the plot of this story and its portrait of Jesus.

2. The body of the story is guided by intense focus on the words of Jesus. The prophecy of betrayal is set forth in a stark Amen-saying (14.18), then repeated in more intense and specific terms: the Son of Man will be handed over by one of the Twelve at the table (14.20-21). These prophetic words are followed by prophetic deeds. The traditional breaking of bread is accompanied by a new interpretation: the bread now represents the broken body of Jesus (14.22). A second distribution and interpretation follows. Jesus shares the cup associated with the old covenant, but links its meaning to a new covenant formed through his death (14.24). Thus, typical meal elements have been designated as Passover elements and provide the occasion for Jesus to instruct and to interpret. The Old Testament images of Exodus and

---

1. As in 14.1-11, various formal similarities may be seen between 14.12-26 and the pronouncement stories.

covenant are now employed as symbols which define the mission and identity of Jesus. Jesus' instruction and interpretation provide at the same time a prediction: his death lies close at hand and will provide the foundation of a new deliverance and a new covenant. The supper scene closes with a final prophecy which moves beyond the scope of Jesus' life and death to the future Kingdom (14.25). Thus, the body of the story is framed around a meal scene designated as the Passover, but it is focused upon the instruction and prophecy of Jesus.

3. Through these narrative processes, Mk 14.12-26 creates a unique christological portrait. Intense focus is given to the image of Jesus as teacher and prophet, particularly through his words. These sayings provide both instruction and prediction. Jesus, the Teacher (14.14), directs the preparation of the Passover, and the disciples see the immediate fulfillment of his prediction (14.12-16). The meal itself intensifies the focus on Jesus as teacher/prophet. Jesus knows of both his betrayal and his betrayer, and he is able to warn the disciples of this event. Jesus teaches a new meaning for the traditions of the Passover, linking them directly to his death. Jesus' death is for his followers (14.24). Jesus also gives instruction and prophecy about the ultimate outcome of these events (14.25). Thus, the meal story in Mk 14.12-26 identifies Jesus as the teacher and prophet whose passion insures the coming of the Kingdom.

4. Mk 14.12-26 also confirms the validity of Jesus' prophecy. The narrative creates a growing pattern of authenticity and reliability around the words of Jesus through the use of narrative prolepses— references to events which have not yet occurred in the narrative.[1] Through this technique a paradigm of prophecy/fulfillment is established. (1) Jesus speaks beforehand of the water bearer and of the readiness of the room and the host (14.13-15), then disciples and readers see the immediate fulfillment of this prediction. (2) Jesus predicts that one of the Twelve will betray him (14.18, 20), and the reader knows that the betrayal by Judas is already underway (Mk 14.1-2, 10-11). These predictions provide internal prolepses which are quickly fulfilled within the text. For the narrative these examples are programmatic. Set at the beginning of the passion story, this

---

1. On the narrative role of prolepses, see G. Genette, *Narrative Discourse: An Essay in Method* (trans. J.E. Lewin; Ithaca, NY: Cornell University Press, 1980). On the role of prolepses in biblical texts, see R.A. Culpepper, *Anatomy of the Fourth Gospel* (Philadelphia: Fortress Press, 1983), pp. 54-70.

model carries a strong primacy effect; it insists that all of Jesus' instructions and predictions are reliable. Thus, the story leaves no doubt that the suffering symbolized by the bread and wine will soon occur. External prolepses—predictions made but not fulfilled within the narrative—are also to be taken as reliable. Seen through the lens of this prophetic paradigm, the future of the Kingdom (14.25) is certain.

5. Thus, Mk 14.12-26 designates the meal scene as a Passover tradition and uses it to generate a vital narrative portrait. Through his sayings the meal scene focuses the identity of Jesus as the true teacher and prophet of God. In the words and in the death of this prophet the coming of the Kingdom is insured.

The Passion Context. The unique images of Mk 14.12-26 interact in vital ways with the larger passion context. In particular, the focus on the prophetic words of Jesus is expanded. The prophecy of Judas's betrayal (14.18, 20) is fulfilled within the passion story (14.1-2, 10-11; 14.43-46), and the theme of abandonment is expanded to include Peter and all of the disciples (14.27; 14.29-31; 14.37-42; 14.50-52; 14.54, 66-72; 16.8?). This expansion also has a linguistic base: all (πάντες) share Jesus' fellowship (14.23), all deny his prophecy (14.31), all forsake him (14.27, 50). Thus, the theme of discipleship failure focused in the Passover story provides an internal prolepse which is expanded and fulfilled within the context of the passion account.

In addition, the passion account expands the focus on the future of the Kingdom. The saying in Mk 14.25 is an external prolepse—it can be fulfilled only outside the framework of the narrative. A similar prediction is set forth at the trial of Jesus as a warning of judgment (14.62). Beyond this, the future is addressed in the words of the messenger at the tomb (16.7). Thus, the prophecy of the Kingdom set forth in the Passover scene is expanded and clarified within the context of the passion narrative.

Most significantly, the passion account actualizes the Passover prediction of Jesus' death. Through Passover imagery Mk 14.12-26 defines a new covenant of redemption around the approaching death of Jesus. This pattern employs the Passover scene to present the meaning of Jesus' death prior to and in the absence of the passion event. Mk 14.12-26 thus provides beforehand the interpretive framework for understanding the subsequent death of Jesus. In the narrative world of the Gospel of Mark the eucharistic interpretation is not allowed to stand apart from the narration of the passion (as it does in 1 Cor. 11.23-26), and the passion event is not allowed to stand apart from this interpretation.

Thus, the framing and interaction of Mk 14.12-26 against the passion narrative provides a determinative interpretive context. Because the passion story provides the fulfillment of events narrated (but not fulfilled) within Mk 14.12-26, the reliability of the narrative is heightened. The paradigm of prophecy/fulfillment established in the Passover scene is extended through the passion context.

The Gospel Context. Mk 14.12-26 carves out a decisive image of Jesus: he is the true teacher and prophet whose death brings the new covenant of the Kingdom. This model of prophetic certainty is extended and intensified within the context of the passion story. This view of Jesus also plays an important role within the larger narrative context of the Gospel of Mark. The images of the Passover meal suggest various connections with the larger story. These suggestive formal links[1] are part of a larger narrative world, its patterns and its effects.

1. The prophetic Christology is taken up and developed through various formal connections. In Mark 1–13 Jesus issues several prophetic announcements (Mk 8.31; 9.1; 9.31; 10.32-34; 13.1-37), but none of these predictions is fulfilled prior to the passion story. Thus, Mark 1–13 affirms the prophetic identity of Jesus but offers no demonstration.[2] Over against this pattern, the passion focus on the fulfillment of prophecy is crucial. The paradigm of prophecy/ fulfillment established in the Passover story and strengthened through the passion account provides a sure standard by which to evaluate the earlier words of Jesus. In numerous ways Mk 14.12-26 and the

---

1. Within this analysis the question of whether an author or source intends these connections is secondary. From a formal perspective potential connections are created by the act of framing a narrative world. This analysis is concerned primarily to show the narrative effect of these interactions. While some of these connections are explicit and demonstrable, others are more suggested and implicit in nature. A variety of potential narrative patterns will be analyzed in terms of their narrative interaction with and effect upon local images of Mk 14.12-26.

2. Mk 11.1-6 provides a possible exception to this pattern.

2. Mark 14.1-42: The Preparation and Betrayal

passion context validate the prophetic images set forth in Mark 1–13.

1.1. The key cycle of prediction in Mk 8.31, 9.31 and 10.32-34 is confirmed. Jesus offers three announcements of his death in Jerusalem (8.31; 9.31; 10.32-34); this prophecy is fulfilled in Mark 14–16. These predictions also speak of the hostility and abuse Jesus will suffer; the passion account fulfills this prophecy. In addition, these three predictions speak of the resurrection; this prophecy is validated in Mk 16.1-8. Within the context of Mark 1–13 these three predictions are external prolepses which remain unfulfilled. The passion story changes these predictions into internal prolepses whose fulfillment is experienced by disciples and readers alike. Through this strategy the paradigm of prophecy/fulfillment initiated in 14.12-26 is extended into the public ministry of Jesus and the reliability of Jesus' words is affirmed.

1.2. The prophetic certainty generated by Mk 14.12-26 exerts its influence upon other prediction units. Various prophecies in Mark 1–13 remain unfulfilled, even in the passion account.[1] Nonetheless the Gospel of Mark provides a clear standard of interpretation by which unfulfilled prophecies are to be read. Beginning in Mk 14.1 Jesus is shown as the true prophet whose words and death insure the coming Kingdom. Some predictions of Jesus are fulfilled immediately (14.12-16; 14.18, 20). Other fulfillments follow (14.50-52). Ultimately Jesus' threefold prophecy of his suffering, death and resurrection is realized in detail. Through this pattern a paradigm of prophecy/fulfillment is established in the Passover scene and extended through the passion context. Consequently this local narrative image insists that all of Jesus' words will be fulfilled. The process of prophetic fulfillment which begins within the Passover scene will end with the coming of the Son of Man and the celebration in the Kingdom. Thus, Mk 14.12-26 exerts a crucial hermeneutic for the reading of Mark 1–13.

---

1. Some will see the Kingdom of God before their death (9.1). The temple complex will be destroyed (13.2). False messiahs will come (13.6). Wars, earthquakes and famines will precede the end-time (13.8). Believers will be brought to trial (13.9). The gospel will be preached unto all the nations (13.10). Persecution shall divide family members (13.13). Some shall endure and be saved (13.13). The desecrating sacrilege will appear (13.14). Unparalleled suffering will occur (13.19-20). False christs and false prophets will work wonders (13.22). The heavenly bodies shall dissipate (13.24-25). The Son of Man shall come in the clouds with much power and glory (13.26). The elect shall be gathered from all the earth (13.27). None of these predictions are fulfilled within the Gospel of Mark.

2. In addition to this development of prophetic Christology, Mk 14.12-26 suggests formal narrative links with other stories. The Gospel of Mark narrates two feeding miracles in the midst of Jesus' public ministry. The feeding of the five thousand in Mk 6.32-46 is a thoroughly Jewish story which gives sharp focus to the role of Jesus as teacher and shepherd of the people (6.34). This account draws extensively upon the imagery of the Old Testament[1] and transports the theological milieu of the Exodus into the feeding story. Mk 6.32-46 thus tells of the calling and nurturing of a shepherdless people of God. In addition, Mk 6.32-46 leaves itself open to a variety of eucharistic interpretations.[2] Beyond this, the feeding story suggests images of the eschatological messianic banquet.[3]

While Mk 6.32-46 narrates a thoroughly Jewish feeding story, these basic themes are repeated in a Gentile context in the feeding of the four thousand (Mk 8.1-10).[4] Through this mirroring technique the

---

1. The shepherd imagery of Mk 6.34 is drawn from the Old Testament (Num. 27.17 and elsewhere). The mention of green grass in Mk 6.39 draws upon the shepherd imagery of Ps. 23. Twelve baskets (6.42) may be symbolic of twelve tribes of Israel. Like Israel of old the people receive bread in the wilderness.

2. L. Schenke (*Die Wundererzählungen des Markusevangelium* [SBB; Stuttgart: Katholisches Bibelwerk, 1974], pp. 231-34) posits a stage in which the present eucharistic experience of the second generation of Christians dominated the understanding and the application of this story. See also Schweizer, *Mark*, p. 138; Taylor, *Mark*, pp. 321-22, 324, 356-57; J. Schreiber (*Theologie des Vertrauens: Eine redaktionsgeschichtliche Untersuchung des Markusevangeliums* [Hamburg: Furche Verlag, 1967], p. 169).

3. Examples of the expectation of a messianic banquet may be seen in Isa. 25.6; 55.1?; 65.13; *1 En.* 62.14; *2 Bar.* 29.8; *Pirke Abot* 3.20. This expectation appears in the synoptic tradition in Mt. 8.11-12, 22.1-14 and 25.1-13. Taylor (*Mark*, p. 324) supports this view of Mk 6.32-46: 'it is a foreshadowing of Messianic Feast, and thus, of the perfecting of the Kingdom'. A. Schweitzer (*The Quest of the Historical Jesus: A Critical Study of its Progress from Reimarus to Wrede* [London: A. & C. Black, 1948 (1906)], pp. 374-79) sees both the feeding in Mk 6 and the Lord's Supper as eschatological sacraments: 'With the morsel of bread which He gives His disciples to distribute to the people He consecrates them as partakers in the coming Messianic feast, and gives them the guarantee that they, who had shared His table in the time of His obscurity, would also share it in the time of His glory'. E. Schweizer (*Mark*, pp. 139-40) does not see clear images of an eschatological banquet.

4. For further development of this relationship, see E.K. Broadhead, *Teaching with Authority: Miracles and Christology in the Gospel of Mark* (Sheffield: JSOT Press, 1992), pp. 117-23.

feeding in Mk 8.1-10 takes over the ideological significance of Mk 6.32-46: Jesus, the teacher and shepherd, is calling out a new people of God. In similar fashion, this story also carries eucharistic and eschatological overtones.

Read in isolation both of these feeding stories might permit an overly enthusiastic christological understanding: through the eucharist Christ may be experienced anew as the miracle-working deliverer and as the coming Lord. Various scholars point to historical situations in which such a Christology was drawn from the feeding miracles.[1]

Over against these enthusiastic possibilities the meal scene in Mk 14.12-26 provides an important interpretive lens through which to view the feeding miracles. Like the feeding stories the Passover meal draws upon extensive Old Testament imagery and employs eucharistic and eschatological overtones. The image of Jesus as teacher is focused in both traditions (6.34; 14.14). The reader is thus encouraged to understand the feeding miracles in light of the Passover account. The narrative linkage of these three meal scenes provides a powerful line of characterization. Any enthusiastic or eschatological christological images supported by the feeding miracles must be read in light of the death of Jesus. Those who would follow Jesus and share his experiences must tread the way of the cross.

3. In a similar manner, the interaction of Mk 14.12-26 within the wider narrative provides an important standard by which to understand the Son of Man title. Various images of the Son of Man are open to enthusiastic interpretation: the Son of Man has authority to forgive sins upon the earth (Mk 2.10), he will come with great power and glory (Mk 13.26), he will be seated at the right hand of power (Mk

---

1. See Schenke, *Wundererzählungen*, pp. 231-34; V.K. Robbins, 'Last Meal: Preparation, Betrayal, Absence', in *The Passion in Mark* (ed. W. Kelber; Philadelphia: Fortress Press, 1976), pp. 21-40. Robbins says that 'Mk knows Christians who recount miracles of Jesus in the setting of ceremonial eating and focus upon breaking bread as the act through which the powers of the risen Lord are manifested in their midst'. In the view of Schweitzer (*Quest*, p. 379) this link of eschatology and sacrament provided the key to the growth of Christianity in a Hellenistic world: 'If Christianity as the religion of historically revealed mysteries was able to lay hold upon Hellenism and overcome it, the reason of this was that it was already in its purely eschatological beginnings a religion of sacraments, a religion of eschatological sacraments, since Jesus had recognised a Divine institution in the baptism of John, and had Himself performed a sacramental action in the distribution of food at the Lake of Gennesareth and at the Last Supper'.

14.62). Numerous scholars argue that Mark's use of the Son of Man title presents a redactional correction of false or insufficient Christologies.[1] In conjunction with this potential for misunderstanding, Mk 14.12-26 provides a careful interpretation of this christological title. In an ironic reversal, this Son of Man who will come with power and glory (13.26) is now handed over to sinners, to suffering and to death (14.21). Ultimately the Passover scene views the Son of Man as the one whose death establishes the new covenant and ushers in the Kingdom.

4. Finally, Mk 14.12-26 participates in the larger narrative description of the Kingdom of God. Within Mark 1–13 the concept of the Kingdom remains open to various interpretations. Emphasis is given alternately to its nearness (1.15), its development (4.26-29; 4.30-32) and its sudden inbreak (9.1). Mk 14.12-26 joins all of these images of the Kingdom to a central christological theme. The eschatological celebration in the Kingdom has a stark precedent in the Passover meal which foreshadows Jesus' death. The reign of the Son of Man in the Kingdom of God is preceded by the betrayal and death of the Son of Man in Jerusalem. Consequently the various images of the Kingdom set forth in Mark 1–13 are given a new, ironic interpretation through the passion focus of Mk 14.12-26.

5. Thus, Mk 14.12-26 takes part in the shaping of a larger narrative world. These patterns of intratextual exchange generate a unique christological portrait. Jesus is the true teacher and prophet of God, the shepherd and leader of the new community. Jesus is the Son of Man who will die for the new covenant and the coming Kingdom.

Comparative Analysis

The Gospel of Mark employs the Passover story to characterize Jesus as teacher, prophet, Son of Man. This local image plays an influential role in the context of the passion narrative and in the larger setting of the Gospel of Mark. The story in Mk 14.12-26 also appears in other

---

1. N. Perrin ('Towards an Interpretation of the Gospel of Mark', in *Christology and a Modern Pilgrimage: A Discussion with Norman Perrin* [ed. H.D. Betz; Missoula, MT: Scholars Press, rev. edn, 1974]) saw the Son of Man title as a corrective of θεῖος ἀνήρ Christology. He is supported in this position by various scholars. W. Kelber (*The Kingdom in Mark: A New Place and a New Time*; Philadelphia: Fortress Press, 1978]) argues that Mark corrects a false apocalyptic understanding of the Son of Man title.

2. Mark 14.1-42: The Preparation and Betrayal

narrative contexts and creates other effects. Diachronic analysis will use these alternate performances to set forth a comparative base against which to highlight the narrative significance of Mk 14.12-26.[1]

Pre-Markan Contexts. Many interpreters have tried to recover a pre-Markan version of the Passover scene. One line of reconstruction argues that the Passover story first existed as an independent unit. Dibelius suggested that the story circulated as an independent Last Supper tradition which served cultic needs. This ancient, self-contained account provided the basis for the writing of both Mark and Paul. Dibelius argued that this tradition was not a Passover celebration and that it contained no inherent soteriological interpretation.[2] Bultmann argued that Mk 14.22-25 reflects an ancient, independent cult legend from Hellenistic circles and held no reference to the Passover.[3] Taylor argued that the meal scene is likely an isolated unit of tradition derived from a primitive Christian liturgy. In contrast to Bultmann, he argued for Palestinian origins.[4] Taylor also suggested that the Last Supper meal was not a Passover meal.[5] Gnilka argues similarly for an independent story which is older than the passion account; he too believes that this meal was not the Passover.[6] Various other scholars support a similar reconstruction.[7]

---

1. This analysis does not primarily address the historical relationship between different accounts of this story. These various forms will be considered as co-texts—as alternate performances of a common story. In this methodology diachronic analysis provides a phenomenological description and comparison of these co-texts.
2. Dibelius, *Tradition*, pp. 205-11.
3. Bultmann, *History*, pp. 266, 277.
4. V. Taylor, *The Gospel according to Mark* (London: MacMillan, 1953), pp. 542-43.
5. Taylor, *Mark*, pp. 664-67.
6. J. Gnilka, *Das Evangelium nach Markus* (EKKNT; Zürich: Benziger Verlag), II, pp. 240-43.
7. See, for example, Dormeyer, *Die Passion*, pp. 100-110; Lohse, *Suffering and Death*, p. 36; E. Haenchen, *Der Weg Jesus: Eine Erklärung des Markus-Evangeliums und der kanonischen Parallelen* (Berlin: Töpelmann, 1966), pp. 478-83; P.J. Achtemeier, *Invitation to Mark* (Garden City, NY: Image Books, 1978), pp. 198-200; Schweizer, *Mark*, pp. 300-305; W. Schenk, *Der Passionsbericht nach Markus: Untersuchungen zur Überlieferungsgeschichte der Passionstraditionen* (Gütersloh: Gerd Mohn, 1974), pp. 189-93; L. Schenke, *Studien zur Passionsgeschichte des Markus: Tradition und Redaktion in Markus 14, 1-42* (Würzburg: Echter Verlag, 1971), pp. 319-28.

Thus, an important line of scholarship sees behind Mk 14.12-26 an independent Lord's Supper tradition which makes no mention of the Passover. Such a tradition would serve a unique function and would create a different portrait of Jesus. Important elements would likely be missing from this account: the betrayal motif, the connection to the feast of Unleavened Bread, the Passover imagery, the focus on Jesus as teacher and prophet. In this form the story would serve an important function in the cultic and liturgical practices of the early church. This use of the story would highlight the symbolic and sacramental role of the bread and wine, and the soteriological significance of the death of Jesus would be central. Such a story would also carry a distinct Christology. The death of Jesus becomes a sacrifice; believers are to share in this event through participation and identification. Participation in this eucharist provides an eschatological experience. Such an independent Last Supper tradition would operate in sharp distinction from the story in Mk 14.12-26.

A second reconstruction locates the Passover meal as part of an independent, pre-Markan passion narrative.[1] Within such a literary context the story would possibly retain its Passover setting, the betrayal story, the image of Jesus as prophet, the focus on Jesus' death, and the eschatological view of the Kingdom. Important elements would be missing from this context. The development of the prophetic image of Jesus would be limited, since no literary link would be established to the prophecies in Mark 1–13. This story would provide no commentary on the feeding miracles and their Christology. The complex irony of the Son of Man title would be weakened. The christological importance of Jesus' death would be developed, but its impact would be localized. The operation of this story solely within a passion context would dissolve the unique connection between the passion Christology and the wider portrait of Jesus' mission.

The Gospel of Matthew. Mt. 26.17-30 takes over the Passover story and weaves it into a different literary ethos. The basic outline of the account is unchanged: the disciples prepare for the meal, the bread and wine are linked to Jesus' death, the eschatological focus remains, a

1. See, for example, Pesch, *Markusevangelium*, II, pp. 354-64; T.A. Mohr, *Markus- und Johannespassion: Redaktions- und traditionsgeschichtliche Untersuchung der Markinischen und Johanneischen Passionstradition* (ATANT; Zürich: Theologischer Verlag, 1982), p. 205.

2. Mark 14.1-42: The Preparation and Betrayal

hymn closes the unit. At the same time significant differences emerge. The prophetic element is missing from the preparation for the meal (Mt. 26.17-20). Instead, Jesus issues a command which the disciples obey. As elsewhere the Gospel of Matthew creates a more positive image of the disciples. While Mt. 26.20 acknowledges the presence of the Twelve, Mt. 26.23 removes the stark focus on the betrayer as one of the Twelve. The disciples then address Jesus respectfully as 'Lord' (Mt. 26.22). The addition of Mt. 26.25 to the story puts the blame squarely on the shoulders of Judas. The contrast in the wording of the question distinguishes Judas from the rest of the disciples: Judas addresses Jesus as rabbi, but they address him as Lord. Thus, Mt. 26.17-25 blunts the sharp image of discipleship betrayal and blames Judas alone for this crime. This elaboration and redirecting of the betrayal theme also softens the focus on Jesus and his words.

Beyond this, Mt. 26.28 makes explicit the soteriological meaning of the cup. Jesus' death for the many provides the means of forgiveness. The eschatological reference is also redirected. The circumlocution 'Kingdom of my Father' (Mt. 26.29) breaks the explicit linguistic link to the Kingdom of God. This version of the story makes no reference to the Son of Man. The ending of the account is identical to Mk 14.26.

Thus, Mt. 26.17-30 employs the Passover story in a different literary context. While the basic form and setting of the story are unchanged, this account has differing concerns. Typical of Matthew's Gospel, the scandal which surrounds the disciples is softened. This concern is developed at the expense of the sharp focus on Jesus as the true teacher and prophet. An explicit soteriology is focused around Jesus' death, and a Matthaean image of the Kingdom emerges.

This alternate literary context impacts the christological focus of the story. Jesus is less prophetic, less controversial and less enigmatic in this account. Jesus is the savior whose death offers forgiveness and foreshadows the coming Kingdom; the disciples are faithful, respectful followers who will carry forward this work.

The Gospel of Luke. This story appears with a different outlook in Lk. 22.7-39. The preparation of the banquet preserves the predictive elements (Lk. 22.7-16), and the story names Peter and John as those sent (Lk. 22.8). The significance of the meal scene is made explicit: Jesus is about to die, and the meal will foreshadow the coming fullness of the Kingdom of God (Lk. 22.15-16). The giving of the bread is marked by a second eschatological reference to the Kingdom (Lk. 22.17-18). The sharing of bread is designated as a memorial tribute to Jesus (Lk. 22.19). A second cup is given, pointing to the new covenant through the shedding of blood (Lk. 22.20). Significantly, the prophecy of betrayal of the Son of Man follows the meal scene. The mention of the Twelve and the focus on Judas are absent.

Thus, the meal scene in Lk. 22.7-23 centers on the saving significance of the death of Jesus and the future fulfillment of the Kingdom. This scene is presented as a memorial tribute gathered around the death of Jesus. While employing the basic elements seen in Mk 14.12-26, some change in focus is evident.

In addition, Lk. 22.24-38 provides a new setting for the story. In this account the death of Jesus is related to the demands of discipleship. The argument over who is greatest is to be replaced by service which imitates Jesus (Lk. 22.24-27). Faithfulness in following Jesus will be rewarded (Lk. 22.28-30). Peter's failure and renewal is predicted, as is his leadership of the disciples (Lk. 22.31-34). The difficulties that will fall upon the disciples in conjunction with the death of Jesus are foretold (Lk. 22.35-38). This focus on the destiny of the disciples gives particular attention to the future. The disciples will be assigned a kingdom (Lk. 22.29); there they will eat and drink with Jesus, and they will sit on thrones of judgment over the twelve tribes of Israel (Lk. 22.30). In the immediate future Peter will fall away, then return as leader of the disciples (Lk. 22.31-34). Lk. 22.24-38 thus interprets the meaning of Jesus' death precisely for the future of those who follow him.

This unique form and setting of the story has an effect on its christological portrait. While Jesus is prophet and teacher, the Son of Man who is betrayed unto death, the founder of the Kingdom covenant, Lk. 22.7-39 gives its central focus to the impact of these events upon those who follow Jesus. The death of Jesus provides a new covenant between Jesus and his disciples. One betrays him, but the others are faithful. Peter, who abandons Jesus, will become their leader. The disciples will serve and suffer, but they will also rule with Jesus in the fullness of the Kingdom. In this manner the christological focus of the meal scene gives way to distinct ecclesiological concerns.

The Gospel of John. The meal scene serves a radically different function in Jn 13.1-31. Various elements of this story parallel the Passover

2. Mark 14.1-42: The Preparation and Betrayal

meal of Mk 14.12-26.[1] At the same time Jn 13.1-31 offers a unique form and setting for the meal. Important elements and themes are missing. While the story occurs at Passover season, it is not a Passover meal. No mention is made of a cup or bread, and the new covenant imagery is absent. These concerns are replaced by various Johannine themes. Jesus is the teacher and Lord who is about to depart. His last meal is marked by his pastoral concern for his followers. Jesus' love for his own is demonstrated in his washing of their feet. Judas betrays Jesus and departs into the night. The Son of Man will be glorified, and God will be glorified.

This reshaping of the meal story has significant impact upon the Christology of this account. The image of Jesus which emerges is thoroughly Johannine. Jesus, the faithful teacher and prophet and Lord, loves his own until the end. The Father has given all things into his hands. Jesus comes from God and will return to God. Jesus has loved and served his own, and they are to follow his example. All of this will be to the glory of God.

The Lord's Supper Tradition. The meal story appears in yet another form in 1 Cor. 11.23-26. Here the account is an independent tradition without mention of the Passover. The story has become a tradition which can be received ($\pi\alpha\rho\acute{\epsilon}\lambda\alpha\beta o\nu$) and handed on ($\pi\alpha\rho\acute{\epsilon}\delta\omega\kappa\alpha$). The night of betrayal is mentioned (1 Cor. 11.23). The bread and the cup are central to this tradition, and their soteriological significance is explicit. The death of Jesus establishes a new covenant in his blood. In particular the meal is understood as a memorial (1 Cor. 11.24-25) which is to be repeated as a proclamation of the Lord's death. This celebration holds in view the coming of the Lord (1 Cor. 11.26), and this tradition carries precise ethical implications for the community of faith (1 Cor. 11.17-22, 27-33).

Thus, 1 Corinthians offers a distinct form and use of this account. Focusing on the death of Jesus, the meal serves the liturgical and confessional needs of the church. This tradition carries a distinct christological understanding. Jesus is Lord (11.20; twice in 11.24; 11.26;

---

1. The story is set in the Passover season and speaks of the departure of Jesus (Jn 13.1). A meal scene provides the setting and plot of the account. The betrayal by Judas is central. A symbolic act provides a christological focus. Jesus is pictured and named as teacher (Jn 13.14). The disciples question their own faithfulness (Jn 13.22-25). The Son of Man is mentioned (Jn 13.31).

twice in 11.27; 11.32), the savior whose death and blood establish a new covenant. Jesus is the crucified messiah (11.26), the judge (11.32) and the coming Lord of the church (11.26). This Lord's Supper tradition is taken up in various forms in subsequent literature (*Gos. Eb.* 7; *Did.* 9.1-5; Justin, *Apology* 1.66.3).

Summary

The meal scene which preceded Jesus' death was shown to operate in a variety of narrative contexts, each of which provides a distinct understanding of the mission and identity of Jesus. One alternative reconstructed an independent pre-Markan tradition which made no reference to the Passover. This account gives unique focus to the image of Jesus as the savior and the coming Lord and plays an important role in the liturgical and confessional life of the church. The tradition recalled by Paul in 1 Corinthians 11 and developed in subsequent literature seems to demonstrate this form of the story.

A second alternative places the story within the framework of an independent, pre-Markan passion account. Within this limited context the story picks up various christological images. Jesus is betrayed by his own disciples, and the death of Jesus provides the key to his mission and identity. The Old Testament images of the Passover are fulfilled in the passion of Jesus. The Son of Man who is betrayed unto death will drink this wine anew in the Kingdom.

This account is placed into wider narrative contexts by each of the Evangelists, and these accounts each generate a unique image of Jesus. Mt. 26.17-20 presents Jesus as the savior whose death brings forgiveness of sins and foreshadows the coming of the Kingdom. His work will be carried forward by faithful, reverent disciples. Lk. 22.7-39 tells of Jesus as prophet, as teacher, as the Son of Man betrayed unto death, as the giver of the new covenant, but particular attention is given to the destiny of the disciples. Jesus will bring his followers into the new covenant. They will be restored to faith, and they will serve him. Ultimately the disciples will eat and rule with Jesus in the Kingdom of God. This story emphasizes Johannine Christology in Jn 13.1-31. Jesus has come from God, and he will return to God. Jesus is the teacher and Lord who cares for his own sheep. In and through the community of his followers, Jesus will glorify God.

Set over against these various literary contexts, the Passover meal in Mk 14.12-26 offers a unique christological portrait. Constructed from

2. Mark 14.1-42: The Preparation and Betrayal

three distinct segments, the narrative syntax places at the center of this story the image of Jesus as the teacher and prophet who dies for the people. At the same time Mk 14.12-26 interacts with various christological images from the wider narrative. Jesus is the one betrayed through hostility and deception. He is the host who calls forth a new people of God. He is the one who renews the Passover and establishes a new covenant. Jesus is the teacher who instructs his followers in the way of faith. He is the true prophet who leads the way into the future. Jesus is the suffering Son of Man who will come with power and glory. He is the proclaimer whose message culminates in his death. Through a variety of narrative transactions Mk 14.12-26 brings these christological images under the sharp focus of Jesus' death. In this manner the Passover story helps to gather the entire narrative and its various images into a coherent portrait.

Mark 14.26-32a: The Prophecy of Betrayal

Mk 14.26-32a predicts the abandonment of Jesus by his followers. This prophecy plays a decisive role in the plot of the passion story and provides an important element in the characterization of Jesus.

Synchronic Analysis
The motifs of Mk 14.26-32a may be plotted in the following manner:

Introduction	
All come	14.26
Body	
Jesus prophesies	14.27-28
Peter responds	14.29
Jesus prophesies	14.30
Peter responds	14.31a
All respond	14.31b
Conclusion	
All depart	14.32a

Narrative Morphology. Mk 14.26-32a employs seven motifs to predict the abandonment of Jesus. Verse 26 serves as a bridge by taking part in both the Passover scene and the prophecy scene. The story is introduced and concluded by simple motifs which transport actants to and from the scene. An antiphonal dialogue between Jesus and the disciples occupies the center of the story. Apart from the movement at the beginning and end, this story is devoid of action. Mk 14.26-32a presents instead a heated debate between Jesus and his disciples.

1. Morphologically this story is constructed around a single narrative segment with two distinct foci. The scene is played out between the departure from the meal (14.26) and the arrival in Gethsemane (14.32a). No particular time markers are present, and no time or place transitions occur within the scene. Thus, the framing of Mk 14.26-32a creates a single stable episode.

Within this episode two distinct foci are developed through a point–counterpoint dialogue. Four sayings of Jesus (14.27a, 27b, 28, 29) are countered by responses from Peter and others (14.29, 31bc, 31d). Future constructions dominate the sayings of Jesus (σκανδαλισήσεσθε, πατάξω διασκορπισθήσονται, μετὰ τὸ ἐγερθῆναι με, προάξω, ἀπαρνήσῃ), while the speech of the disciples is strewn with negatives (ἀλλ' οὐκ ἐγώ, οὐ μὴ δε απαρνήσομαι). Through this construction all concern for setting and action is displaced by a central focus on the dispute between Jesus and his followers.

2. The most extensive line of this dialogue focuses the σκανδαλίζομαι (to be scandalized) theme.[1] This theme is set forth by Jesus in

---

1. The Gospel of Mark uses σκανδαλίζω eight times (4.17; 6.3; 9.42, 43, 45, 47; 14.27, 29). It occurs in 4.17 in the midst of the sower parable. Some who gladly receive the word are rootless and temporary, so they are immediately σκανδαλίζονται by trouble and persecution on account of the word. This parable is played out in Mk 6.3, where the people of Jesus' home town hear him but are ἐσκανδαλίζοντο in him. The σκανδαλίζομαι theme is developed fully through the sayings in Mk 9.42-48. In 9.42 the term is presented as a threat to the faith of the little ones, and the judgment against one who scandalizes is worse than death. In Mk 9.43, 45, 47 such a scandal leads to eternal damnation and should be removed, even at the cost of a hand, a foot or an eye. Against this background Mk 14.27, 29 presents a stark prophetic warning—all of the disciples will be scandalized. Thus, the use of σκανδαλίζω provides a dramatic warning about the loss of faith. G. Stählin ('σκάνδαλον', *TDNT*, VII, pp. 339-58) roots the use of σκάνδαλον and σκανδαλίζω in the thought and speech of the Old Testament and Judaism, with little relation to Greek thought. Stählin concludes that 'In the NT as in the OT what is at issue in σκάνδαλον is the relation to God... The σκάνδαλον is an obstacle in coming to faith and a cause of going astray in it. As in the OT it is the cause of both transgression and destruction... for a fall in faith is the fall in the absolute sense'. Stählin insists that 'the force of the verb σκανδαλίζω is even stronger than that of the noun σκάνδαλον in the NT. Whereas σκάνδαλον is only an "occasion of falling" which might lead to a fall or not, σκανδαλίζω is the "cause of a fall" and σκανδαλίζομαι the actual "taking place of the fall"' (p. 345). Pesch (*Markusevangelium*, II, p. 379)

2. Mark 14.1-42: The Preparation and Betrayal

terse form in the initial saying: all will be scandalized (14.27a).[1] This theme is echoed in the curt response of Peter in 14.29.[2] Thus, the σκανδαλίζομαι theme is established in 14.27a, 29 by a sharp and pregnant dialogue between Jesus and Peter.

This initial presentation is developed through two subsequent cycles (14.30-31a; 14.31b) which intensify and extend the theme. In 14.30 Jesus echoes and intensifies the charge of 14.27a in various ways: (1) The second saying is directed specifically to Peter; (2) the charge is placed in the form of an Amen-saying; (3) the immediacy of the danger is emphasized through three time references;[3] (4) the predicate is changed from a scandal (σκανδαλίζομαι) to a denial (ἀπαρνέομαι), and the tense has changed from the passive to the active; (5) the denial will not occur once, but three times. The repetition of Peter's rejoinder (14.31) undergoes a corresponding intensification: (1) he speaks more intensely (ἐκπερισσῶς ἐλάλει); (2) he makes a death vow; (3) he uses the emphatic οὐ μή (in no way).

A third cycle (14.31b) takes up this intensified form of the theme and extends it in various ways. (1) The intensity of Peter's rebuke is maintained by the use of ὡσαύτως (likewise). (2) The rejoinder is extended to include the entire group. (3) The use of πάντες creates an ironic echo of 14.23; all who shared the cup with Jesus now dispute his word. (4) The use of the imperfect form (ἔλεγον) implies an ongoing dispute.

Thus, the σκανδαλίζομαι theme is given precise focus through the

opposes this understanding of the term for Mk 14.27.

1. The use of πάντες (all) recalls the participation of all in the cup (14.23) and points ahead to the denial and failure by all (14.31, 50).

2. The use of the first class conditional (εἰ plus the indicative) accepts the condition, with Peter declaring himself the one exception. The stark rejoinder of Peter (ἀλλ' οὐκ ἐγώ) forms an echoing contrast to the grieving query of the Twelve in 14.19 (μήτι ἐγώ). The use of μή by the Twelve is a question expecting a negative response; Peter's insistent οὐ μή is a stark declaration of his power and faithfulness.

3. The three time references produce increasing specificity. The use of σήμερον is a Markan *hapax legomenon* and provides a general time reference. The phrase ταύτῃ τῇ νυκτί employs a Jewish chronology which places the events of the early morning watch on the same calendar day as the prediction on the prior evening—thus the denial will occur in the first half of the calendar day. The use of ἢ δὶς ἀλέκτορα φωνῆσαι likely designates sunrise (the ban against roosters in Jerusalem seems generally ignored). Consequently the denial will occur on this date in the hours before sunrise.

words of Jesus, then heightened through three cycles of development. Within this thematic line the primary focus is given to the destiny of the disciples and only consequently to the impact upon Jesus. This theme dominates the flow of Mk 14.26-32a and controls its level of intensity.

3. Within the narrative development of the σκανδαλίζομαι theme, a separate theme is focused around the destiny of the shepherd (τὸν ποιμένα) in 14.27b-28. This distinct theme articulates a different set of metaphors and employs a contrasting pattern of development. The shepherd/sheep imagery echoes the prophetic word in Zech. 13.7, and this allusion is made explicit through the citation formula (ὅτι γέγραπται).[1] While the σκανδαλίζομαι theme was developed through repetition, intensification and extension, this second focus is developed through analogy. In 14.28 the imagery of the smitten shepherd and the scattered sheep is applied directly—without clarification[2]—to Jesus (με has its antecedent in 14.27). This second theme gives primary attention to the destiny of Jesus, with consequent concern for the destiny of the followers.[3]

4. While Mk 14.27a, 29-31 and Mk 14.27b-28 focus different themes,[4] they share various narrative connections. Both themes are

---

1. In a similar way Mk 1.2-3 invokes the Isaianic world through the use of γέγραπται. Gnilka (*Markus*, II, p. 252) argues that the shepherd is already a messianic image in Zechariah. Significantly, the shepherd prophecy in Zech. 13.7 is followed by a prophecy of the trial and restoration of a small remnant (Zech. 13.8-9). In a similar manner Mk. 14.28 may imply some manner of restoration in Galilee. Willi Marxsen focused the role of this prophecy in his programmatic redactional analysis of the Gospel of Mark. For Marxsen (*Mark*) the saying in 14.28 is wholly redactional and points not to a restoration, but to the approaching parousia in Galilee.

2. The shepherd imagery is thus used as a metaphor rather than a simile.

3. *Contra* Schweizer (*Mark*, p. 306), who sees the main emphasis in 14.27b-28 on the failure of the disciples and Jesus' going before them.

4. The distinction in focus, tone, intensity and development between 14.27a, 29-31 and 14.27b-28 most likely reflects editorial insertion of the shepherd theme. The objection of Peter (14.29) does not address the shepherd theme, but picks up the σκανδαλίζομαι theme directly from 14.27a. Thus, Mk 14.27a, 29-31 may be read as a self-standing unit in which the σκανδαλίζομαι theme is intensified and extended through cycles. Mk 14.27b, 29-31 is seen as an editorial insertion by numerous scholars. See, for example, Gnilka, *Markus*, II, p. 252; Schweizer, *Mark*, pp. 306-308; Schenk, *Passionsbericht*, pp. 223-28. Schenk discusses the formal distinction of 14.27b-28, but also presents extensive philological arguments for seeing this material as Markan redaction. The absence of 14.28 from the Fayyum

2. Mark 14.1-42: The Preparation and Betrayal

concerned for the interlaced destiny of Jesus and his followers. Both employ strands of prophetic imagery.[1] Both concerns are structured around sayings and dialogue. Mk 14.27b-28 presumes the prior identification of Jesus and the disciples (με and ὑμᾶς in 14.28). Morphologically Mk 14.26-32a connects two distinct foci into one stable episode. Syntactical analysis will show how the interplay of these elements generates a coherent narrative unit with a decisive image of Jesus.

Narrative Syntax. The syntactical interaction of these motifs generates a vital narrative effect. This process provides plot movement and articulates an important image of Jesus.

1. The opening motif picks up the concluding movement of the Passover meal and uses it to initiate the plot of this account. The fellowship and meal Christology symbolized by the hymn of departure provide a stark and ironic contrast to 14.27-31. In particular, the covenantal theme which concludes in the hymn provides an ironic backdrop for the prophecy of a broken fellowship. This motif also provides geographical setting: the Mount of Olives. Within the story no symbolic images are developed around this setting. Thus, Mk 14.26 provides a simple, functional introduction to the story, but creates a stark backdrop for the prophecy of betrayal. This story closes as it began—with a simple transitional motif which moves the disciples to another setting and another story (14.32a).

2. Sandwiched between these transitional motifs is a stark scene of prophecy. The functional introduction and conclusion create an isolated vignette. The lack of precision about time or place and the absence of action events focuses this isolated scene precisely upon the dialogical exchange.

Various techniques highlight the authority of Jesus' words—prediction, Old Testament citation, Amen-formulation, repetition, specification. The growing intensity of Jesus' predictions is countered by a corresponding intensification in the disciples' rejoinder. Through these techniques the σκανδαλίζομαι theme provides the predominant narrative focus and tone. This theme focuses primarily on the destiny

---

fragment does not validate this claim, since the fragment abbreviates this story in other ways as well.

1. This imagery is both retrospective (citation of the Old Testament) as well as prospective (announcement of future events).

of the disciples, and only consequently on the destiny of Jesus. The σκανδαλίζομαι theme ends abruptly (14.31-32a) and offers no hope of redemption.

3. Imbedded within this predominant narrative line is an important christological focus (14.27b-28). The internal syntax of this shepherd theme is vital. The citation from Zechariah gathers the mantle of Old Testament prophecy around the image of Jesus. In addition, the subjectless form presents this prophecy not simply as information but as a direct word from God. The predictive element in the saying heightens this prophetic aura.

The prophetic Christology established through the citation (14.27b) is applied directly to the saying in 14.28. In line with this prophetic authority the resurrection of Jesus is articulated with unconditioned certainty. This predictive element in 14.28 is specified by time (post-resurrection) and place (Galilee).

The internal syntax of 14.27b-28 thus creates a stark prophetic Christology in the midst of the betrayal focus. This prophetic image is rooted retrospectively in the mighty works of God in the Old Testament and prospectively in the future of the Risen One. Numerous elements of characterization are gathered into this prophetic Christology. Didactic images are present in Jesus' unique interpretation of the Old Testament. Prophetic overtones may be heard in the use of Old Testament scenes and in the prediction of future events. Eschatological images are present in the promise of deliverance. The passion theme emerges in the focus on striking down. Messianic overtones are reflected in the shepherd imagery. Thus, the internal syntax of Mk 14.27b-28 provides a carefully nuanced characterization of Jesus as the prophet of God.

4. The role of 14.27b-28 in the external syntax reshapes the entire episode. In the midst of the total and unrelieved failure stands a prophetic image of Jesus. Through the shepherd motif the failure of the Twelve is linked to the larger failure of Israel (Zech. 13.7). At the same time the hope of a new flock (Zech. 13.8-9; Mk 14.28) is offered to the disciples. Through this syntactical arrangement the flow of the σκανδαλίζομαι theme is met by the counterflow of the shepherd theme. The focus on discipleship failure is met by a stark prophetic Christology. The unrelieved failure of the disciples is met by the promise of the Risen One. The debacle in Jerusalem is countered by the promise of Galilee. The closed prophecy of denial and the broken

2. *Mark 14.1-42: The Preparation and Betrayal* 79

fellowship are countered by an open prophecy of renewal and an open-ended symbol of hope—Galilee.[1]

5. Thus, the syntactical pattern of Mk 14.26-32a creates a vital narrative effect. Set against the covenantal promise of 14.24, the σκανδαλίζομαι theme provides a dramatic prophecy focused on the failure of the disciples. This failure will be intense (even Peter), widespread (all) and sudden (this night). This failure will be a loss of faith which denies the basic bond of discipleship. Jesus has foretold these events, but all of the disciples rebuke his prophecy.

At the center of this episode is a vital line of characterization. Jesus is surrounded by disciples who dispute his words and turn a deaf ear to his message. Through his teaching Jesus is again shown as the true prophet of God. His pronouncements provide the fulfillment of the Old Testament and foretell the events of the future. Significantly, Jesus' instruction and prophecy centers on his death. He is the shepherd who is struck down through rejection and betrayal. In another place and another time this shepherd will go before his people again.

---

1. The narrative ambiguity of Galilee echoes through the subsequent traditions and through the history of research. Matthew tied Galilee to the appearance traditions (Mt. 28.8-20). Because of his concern for the Jerusalem appearances, Luke omitted this prophecy and reduced Galilee to a memory (Lk. 24.6). The Fourth Gospel maintained Jerusalem appearances (Jn 20.11-29), but tied Galilee to one strand of appearance traditions (Jn 21.1-23). Following a fantastic resurrection narrative set in Jerusalem, the *Gospel of Peter* seems to prepare for a Galilean appearance, but the text breaks off at this point (*Gos. Pet.* 15.59-60).

The history of research is equally divided on the role of Galilee. Traditionally Mk 14.28 and 16.7 have been read in line with the larger appearance traditions—so Pesch, *Markusevangelium*, II, pp. 381-82; Taylor, *Mark*, p. 549. Lohmeyer (*Markus*, pp. 311-12) and Marxsen (*Mark*, pp. 75-95) saw in the Galilee motif a distinct Markan concern with the imminent parousia. This line has been developed by N. Perrin, W. Kelber and others. A few scholars see in the Galilee focus neither parousia nor appearance, but a renewed call to a Gentile mission in the place where discipleship began. See, for example, G.H. Boobyer, 'Galilee and Galileans in St Mark's Gospel', *BJRL* 35 (1953), pp. 334-48; C.F. Evans, 'I will go before you into Galilee', *JTS* 5 (1954), pp. 3-18. D. Crossan ('Empty Tomb and Absent Lord', in Kelber [ed.], *The Passion in Mark*, pp. 148-49) sees here a distinct symbol which embodies past, present and future in the Markan community.

From the standpoint of formalistic narrative analysis Galilee presents a symbol with a past (calling and ministry in Galilee) and a future (I will go before you into Galilee). Nonetheless, the basic sense of the term remains unfocused. Consequently Galilee remains an open-ended symbol in the Gospel of Mark.

The Passion Context. This portrait of Jesus interacts in various ways with the larger passion story, creating a mutual pattern of reinterpretation. The predicted appearance in Galilee (14.28) is paired with the appearance promise (16.7). The prophecy of abandonment repeats and intensifies the betrayal theme from the anointing and the Passover stories (Mk 14.1, 10-11, 18, 20-21, 42). This imagery will be expanded around the death of Jesus (Mk 14.44-45, 50-52, 66-72; 16.8). The predicted failure by all (πάντες) is realized in 14.50. The particular focus on Peter (14.29-31) is expanded in the scene of denial (14.66-72). In a similar way the focus on Jesus as teacher and prophet takes part in a larger narrative scheme. As throughout the passion (Mk 14.8, 21, 23-24), the prophecy in 14.26-32a points to Jesus' death. Thus, the precise focus in Mk 14.26-32a on Jesus as the rejected teacher/prophet who dies for the people helps to generate and to reinforce the extended portrait of Mark 14–16.

Conversely, the passion context has an effect on the internal operations of Mk 14.26-32a. Within this story the predictions of Jesus remain unfulfilled. The wider passion context changes these predictions into internal prolepses whose fulfillment is experienced by the reader (with the exception of the προάξω theme). This narrative transaction confirms and strengthens the image of Jesus as the true prophet of God.

The Gospel Context. The image of Jesus created in Mk 14.26-32a intersects the larger narrative world at vital points. This interaction sponsors reciprocal lines of interpretation and solidifies the text as an irreducible whole. Various narrative connections—some explicit and some suggestive—join Mk 14.26-32a to the larger world of the narrative.[1]

1. The σκανδαλίζομαι theme intensifies a concern central to Mark 1–13. These disciples have been chosen and called by Jesus (1.16-20; 3.13-19), and they have been given the mysteries of the Kingdom (4.11). Nonetheless the Gospel of Mark characterizes the disciples through growing obstinance and blindness (4.13, 40-41; 5.30-32; 6.35-37, 49-52; 8.4, 27-30, 31-33; 9.6, 9-10, 11-13, 14-28, 30-32, 33-

---

1. These connections are based on formal patterns of narrative morphology and syntax. The question of whether an author intends these connections is a separate issue. These links are offered here as narrative connections which impact the local and the extended significance of the narrative.

2. Mark 14.1-42: The Preparation and Betrayal

37, 38-41; 10.23-27, 32, 35-45). This lack of courage and understanding intensifies around the message of Jesus' death (8.31-33; 9.31-32; 10.32-45). Consequently Mark 1–13 develops a growing focus on discipleship failure. Mk 14.26-32a picks up this theme and gives it precise definition in terms of Jesus' death. As the passion predictions implied, the threat to Jesus intensifies the failure of the disciples. In Mk 14.26-32a the theme of discipleship failure is crystallized in the prophetic words of Jesus.

2. Mk 14.26-32a also interacts with important christological themes from Mark 1–13. Chief among these is the portrait of Jesus as prophet/teacher. While the Gospel of Mark seldom narrates the content of Jesus' teaching, the image of Jesus as teacher is central. The story of Jesus (1.1) opens against a prophetic backdrop (1.2-3). The entire narrative centers in Jesus' teaching/preaching of the Kingdom of God (1.14-15). The initial characterization of Jesus tells of one who teaches with amazing authority (1.22). This authority is demonstrated not only through his words, but especially through his deeds (1.23-39). Within the Gospel of Mark the miracle stories give distinct focus to the power of Jesus the teacher.[1] One response to the teaching of Jesus is hostility and rejection (Mk 2.6-7, 16, 24; 3.2-6, 22; 7.1-5; 8.11; 10.2; 11.18, 27-28; 12.12, 13-17). Ultimately the Gospel of Mark links this hostility over Jesus' teaching to the plotting of his death (Mk 3.6; 11.18; 12.12; 14.1-2, 61-64; 15.1, 11). Mark 1–13 thus gathers disparate narrative elements and patterns to generate a distinct Christology: Jesus teaches with amazing authority, and this teaching leads to his death. Mk 14.26-32a repeats and intensifies this characterization in the proximity of the cross. Jesus is the teacher and prophet who instructs his followers. His teaching fulfills the Old Testament and points the way to the future. Even here among his disciples, the words of Jesus are met by rejection. Most important, his final instructions center on his death and on the days ahead.

3. Various other narrative connections are suggested by the form and function of Mk 14.26-32a. These connections confirm the reciprocal lines of interpretation which transect the Gospel of Mark.

3.1. Significantly, the prophecy in Mk 14.26-32a is given from the Mount of Olives. Within the local context of the passion narrative this

---

1. I have shown that the image of Jesus as one who teaches with authority is central to the miracle traditions in the Gospel of Mark. See Broadhead, *Teaching with Authority*.

setting carries no particular symbolism. When read within the larger narrative context this setting is vital. Within the Gospel of Mark the Mount of Olives serves as the antithesis of the Temple Mount.[1] Consequently the Mount of Olives provides a crucial narrative antisymbol to all that is represented by Jerusalem and its temple.[2] This symbol also has positive implications. From the Mount of Olives, while sitting opposite the temple, Jesus instructs his followers about the future (Mk 13.3-37). Thus, the Mount of Olives provides a decisive narrative antithesis to the Jerusalem traditions and a vital symbol for the future of the Christian community. Mk 14.26-32a takes up this symbol and links it to the death of Jesus. From the Mount of Olives (14.26), Jesus gives two crucial prophesies: (1) he will be struck down and his followers scattered, and (2) he will be raised up and will go before his community into Galilee. Mk 14.26-32a takes up this unusual narrative symbol to articulate the importance of Jesus' death and resurrection.

3.2. The focus on the resurrection (14.28) draws upon a wider development. The resurrection focus belongs to each of the passion prophecies in the midst of Jesus' ministry (8.31; 9.31; 10.32-34). This line of prophecy is fulfilled through the empty tomb (16.7). Thus, the prophecy in 14.28 also takes part in this wider narrative tradition.

3.3. In a similar way the Galilee theme (14.28) operates against a wider context. The Jerusalem experience (11.1–16.8) provides an interlude in a larger story written against a Galilean backdrop. Jesus emerges from Galilee (1.9) and carries his message of power throughout the synagogues of Galilee (1.39). The end of this narrative is built upon a renewal of the story in Galilee (16.7). Mk 14.28 sustains this concern and is impacted by this larger narrative strategy.

3.4. The shepherd imagery plays an extended role in the Gospel of Mark. The feeding story in Mk 6.35-44 is built upon the image of Jesus as shepherd (6.34), and the people are characterized as a flock in need of a leader. Significantly, this shepherd/flock imagery is built upon an Old Testament citation (Num. 27.17) and focuses the role of Jesus as teacher. Mk 14.26-32a echoes both the pattern and the

---

1. Broadhead, 'Which Mountain is "This Mountain"?', pp. 33-38.
2. The Mount of Olives stands 'opposite' the city and the temple (Mk 13.3). In his last days Jesus ventures into both city and temple, but he returns to his place on the Mount of Olives (Mk 11.1; 13.1-3; 14.26). Thus, the narrative directs the movement of Jesus away from Jerusalem and the temple and toward the Mount of Olives.

imagery of Mk 6.34, but makes one important extension: the image of Jesus as shepherd and teacher is now linked precisely to his death.

3.5. A closer reading of Mk 14.26-32a suggests a subtle formal connection between Peter's objections and the sower parable (Mk 4.3-20). Peter's insistence that he alone will remain faithful—even in the face of death—reflects an assertive commitment which will not endure the trials of even this one day. The concrete image of Peter in 14.29-31 is captured in the metaphorical language of the sower parable. Peter is among those who hear the word and receive it with joy, but their faith is shallow and temporary (4.16). Their enthusiasm will fail in the face of trial and persecution (4.17). This suggestive linkage is built upon two linguistic connections. Like the disciples, the enthusiastic hearers are scandalized by trials (σκανδαλίζονται in 4.17; σκανδαλισθήσεσθε in 14.27a). In particular, the obstinacy of Peter (ὁ Πέτρος) is most like that of the rocky soil (τὰ πετρώδη). Significantly, both passages are rooted in the instruction of Jesus and address the coming test of faith.

4. Morphologically Mk 14.26-32a constitutes a single episode with two distinct foci. The syntactical interweaving of these elements produces intense light on the failure of the disciples. This theme is met by the counterflow of the prophetic shepherd tradition, creating a lively scene. This episode corresponds in significant ways with the passion context and is linked to the larger narrative through a variety of formal patterns. Through these narrative forms and patterns a crucial image of Jesus emerges: he is the rejected teacher and prophet, the smitten shepherd of God who will go before the new community.

Comparative Analysis

Mk 14.26-32a portrays Jesus as the rejected prophet, the smitten shepherd, the future hope. This local image maintains a reciprocal relationship with the wider narrative world of the Gospel of Mark. The prediction of abandonment also appears in other narrative contexts and creates differing images of Jesus.[1] These alternate forms of this material will be used to highlight the distinct narrative performance of Mk 14.26-32a.

---

1. This analysis will not address the historical relationship between different accounts of this story. These various forms will be considered as co-texts—as alternate performances of a common story. In this methodology diachronic analysis provides a phenomenological description and comparison of these co-texts.

Pre-Markan Contexts. The material in Mk 14.26-32a may have circulated as one or more independent sayings. As words of the Lord or as fulfillment of the Old Testament, such material would carry self-authentication. Its primary significance would derive not from any literary context or theological coherence, but from its inherent claim to be authoritative teaching of Jesus. A number of scholars reconstruct a stage in which the material in Mk 14.26-32a circulated in such a form. Eduard Schweizer suggests that the saying in Mk 14.28 was handed down at first as a saying of the risen Christ, as in Mk 16.7. He also argues that the quotation from Zech. 13.7 circulated independently in the church. Schweizer further argues that the saying to all the disciples and the words to Peter circulated as separate traditions of what Jesus said.[1] Marxsen argued that Mk 14.28 was an individual saying inserted into the story by Mark.[2] Lohmeyer argued that 14.27, 29 were dominical sayings.[3]

Various scholars thus point to a stage in which this material existed as one or more independent logia. This form of the material would provide a different christological focus. As self-standing sayings of the Lord, these traditions would take on the power and outlook of orality.[4] In such form this material would provide a self-authenticated, living voice. This pattern tends toward an enthusiastic Christology in which the immediate presence of the risen Lord is experienced by the believer. This use of the material in Mk 14.26-32a would likely offer an enthusiastic image: Jesus is the living Lord who may be experienced anew in his words.

A second line of reconstruction views Mk 14.26-32a as an integral part of a pre-Markan passion story. Dibelius argued that the account in 14.26-31 'constitutes an essential part of the Passion-story'.[5] Gnilka agrees with Marxsen that 14.28 shows a Markan concern with Galilee, but he specifies further that Mk 14.27a, 29-31 is pre-Markan and

1. Schweizer, *Mark*, pp. 305-308.
2. Marxsen, *Mark*, pp. 75-76.
3. Lohmeyer, *Markus*, pp. 310-13.
4. See W. Kelber, *The Oral and the Written Gospel: The Hermeneutics of Speaking and Writing in the Synoptic Tradition, Mark, Paul, and Q* (Philadelphia: Fortress Press, 1983).
5. Dibelius, *Tradition*, p. 115; see also pp. 183, 215.

2. Mark 14.1-42: The Preparation and Betrayal

belongs to the larger passion tradition.[1] Pesch argues that all of 14.26-31 is an integral part of the fixed, pre-Markan passion tradition.[2]

Within this narrative setting the story takes on the influence of narrativity and a clear focus on the death of Jesus. In contrast to oral tendencies this account would relate the story of Jesus as a past event. Further, this pattern would limit superficial enthusiasm by linking the sayings of Jesus directly to the cross. This form of the story would develop important themes: abandonment by the disciples, Jesus as teacher and prophet, the resurrection appearance. In this context the interaction with Mark 1-13 would be missing. Consequently the referential value of these themes would be limited to the passion context.

The Gospel of Matthew. The prediction of abandonment also appears in Mt. 26.30-36a. While this version of the story makes stylistic changes, the substance of the account is identical to Mk 14.26-32a. In addition, this story also operates within the context of the passion account. Thus, Mt. 26.30-36a operates locally with the same basic form and function as Mk 14.26-32a. Missing from this context are the various narrative links established between Mark 1-13 and the prediction of abandonment. The failure of the disciples is softened in the Gospel of Matthew, since these are the leaders of the new community. The focus on the teaching of Jesus roots in his words (Mt. 5-7) more than in his deeds. In these ways Mt. 26.30-36a draws upon a different referential world and participates in a distinctly Matthaean portrait of Jesus and his followers.

The Gospel of Luke. In the Gospel of Luke the departure to the Mount of Olives (Lk. 22.39) is followed immediately by the Gethsemane scene (22.40-46). The prediction of betrayal is omitted at this point because Luke has placed a similar scene at the Passover table (22.31-34). This unique dialogue is used to reflect similar themes. Peter will fall away but be restored (22.31-32). Peter rejects this possibility, vowing faithfulness unto death (22.33). Peter's denial will be sure and quick—before the first cockcrow (22.34). Central to this account is the restoration of Peter and his future role as leader of the disciples (22.32). The failure of Peter is due to Satan (22.31), and his

1. Gnilka, *Markus*, II, p. 252.
2. Pesch, *Markusevangelium*, II, pp. 377-85.

86 *Prophet, Son, Messiah*

restoration is insured by Jesus (22.32). Consequently Lk. 22.31-34 describes the fall and rise of Peter in tragic, yet heroic terms.

In Luke the continuity of the Christian community is insured by Jesus, but the focus of this future falls on the ministry of the disciples. This use of the material empties its christological impact. Jesus remains a prophetic and caring leader, but the focus on the death and resurrection of Jesus has been redirected.

The Gospel of John. The Gospel of John has scattered the elements of this story across several scenes. At the same time the various themes of this story have been incorporated into the wider Johannine portrait of Jesus. In Jn 18.1 Jesus crosses the Kidron valley and enters an unnamed garden. The arrest scene follows (18.2-11). As with the Gospel of Luke, the prediction of betrayal is missing from this account. Jn 16.32 vaguely reflects the Zechariah citation with its shepherd imagery, but the Johannine focus on the Father dominates the saying. An account of Peter's resistance is found in Jn 13.36-38. Peter insists that he will go with Jesus now, even unto death (13.37). Jesus affirms that Peter will follow him unto death, but later (13.38). For the present Peter will deny Jesus before the next cockcrow (13.38). The restoration, ministry and death of Peter are addressed again in Jn 21.15-19. Following the resurrection Jesus questions the love of Peter and sends him to minister to the Christian flock. Particular concerns of the Johannine community are addressed in this final discussion (21.20-23).

Thus, the Gospel of John has addressed similar issues by scattering this material across several units. At the same time the focus of the material now serves specific Johannine interests. Questions about the life and leadership of the Christian community are addressed by this use of the material. Most significantly, the christological image has been shaped into a thoroughly Johannine portrait. Jesus is the good shepherd who departs to the Father. He loves his own and makes provision for their future. Peter and the Beloved Disciple will lead the community into that future.

Fayyum Manuscript. A fragmentary manuscript from the third century contains an excerpt from an unknown gospel. One part of this manuscript contains the prediction of abandonment. Significantly, this text links the sayings in Mk 14.27, 29, 30 by omitting the Galilee pre-

2. Mark 14.1-42: The Preparation and Betrayal 87

diction in Mk 14.28. Because of the fragmentary nature of this manuscript, the wider narrative context is missing.

Summary

The prediction of Jesus' abandonment, death and resurrection was shown to operate in differing literary contexts and to construct varying images of Jesus. At one stage the material may have operated as independent sayings. In this form the words of Jesus fulfill the Old Testament and prophesy about future events. This form of the material is open to an enthusiastic Christology in which the power and presence of the Lord are experienced anew.

A second reconstruction placed this material within the framework of a pre-Markan passion story. Within this context the enthusiasm of the oral tradition is now linked to the passion Christology. This account operates within the referential world of the passion story to show Jesus as prophet and teacher, crucified messiah, risen Lord, shepherd of the new community.

This material has been taken over by the Evangelists. While the local form and function of the story are unchanged in the Gospel of Matthew, the material now interacts with a different referential world and partakes in a distinct portrait of Jesus. In the Gospel of Luke this material helps to focus the role of the disciples in the future community. While Jesus insures the life of his community through the disciples, the material has lost its sharp christological focus. The Gospel of John uses this material at various places to address particular concerns. Most significantly, the christological force of this material has been aligned with the predominant elements of Johannine Christology.

When seen over against these alternate contexts and performances, the form and function of Mk 14.26-32a is singular. Set as an interim scene between the Passover meal and the Gethsemane scene, the story provides a crucial commentary on prior and subsequent events. Important themes from the earlier narrative are reinforced: the disciples fail Jesus at his point of need, Jesus' teaching and prophecy fulfills the Old Testament, the Mount of Olives symbolizes a new direction for the followers of Jesus. Beyond this, the story prepares for the scenes ahead: Jesus will die and his followers will be scattered, Jesus will be raised, he will go before his community into Galilee. Most importantly, Mk 14.26-32a provides a sharp focus on the mission and identity of Jesus: he is the true teacher and prophet, the smitten shepherd of God's people, the Risen One.

Mark 14.32-42: Gethsemane

Mk 14.32-42 creates a dramatic scene of prayer and abandonment at the close of Jesus' ministry. This story plays an important role within the passion account and provides a focused commentary on earlier images of Jesus.

Synchronic Analysis

The motifs of Mk 14.32-42 provide a balanced structure:

Introduction	
All come	14.32a
Body	
Jesus commands	14.32b
Jesus grieves	14.33
Jesus commands	14.34
Jesus prays	14.35-36
Jesus questions	14.37
Jesus commands	14.38
Jesus prays	14.39
Jesus questions	14.40
Jesus commands	14.41
Conclusion	
Jesus commands	14.42

Narrative Morphology. Simple motifs introduce and conclude the Gethsemane scene. These motifs use transition (coming in 14.32a; command to depart in 14.42) to frame the central story. In the body of this unit Jesus is the subject of each motif. Thus, the motifs of 14.32-42 focus the image of Jesus in the midst of his followers.

1. Morphologically this account is built around three distinct cycles of instruction, prayer, return. These overlapping cycles (14.33-38, 38-40, 41) employ two patterns of reduction. (1) The larger group of disciples (14.32) is reduced to three (14.33), then to Jesus alone (14.35, 39). (2) The pattern of instruction, prayer, return is reduced from a full report (14.32b-38) to summary reports (14.39-40, 41). The reduction in participants serves as a focusing device which intensifies through isolation of characters. The second pattern of

2. Mark 14.1-42: The Preparation and Betrayal

reduction provides narrative emphasis through cyclical repetition. Thus, Mk 14.32-42 is constituted around a primary sequence (instruction, prayer, return) which has been developed through techniques of isolation and repetition.

2. This morphological pattern supports two thematic lines. The first ideological line continues the theme of discipleship failure from 14.26-32a.[1] This theme operates in the two outer settings (disciples, the Three). The role of the larger group of disciples is unfocused— they are commanded only to sit (14.32)—but they share, through association, the guilt of failure. More meaningful commands are given to the Three—remain and watch (14.34), watch and pray (14.35)— and their failure is focused more precisely—sleeping (14.37), weakness of the flesh (14.38), heavy eyes (14.40), inability to speak (14.40). Ultimately Jesus accepts their sleep as their response to his trials and his commands (14.41). Thus, the external layers of the story realize the predicted downfall of Jesus' followers. This fall is defined as a failure to watch and pray, it is focused around the image of sleep and it climaxes in the act of betrayal (14.41).

The second ideological stream is seated in the inner setting, where Jesus prays alone (14.35-36, 39). This second stream provides a christological focus set against a theological backdrop. The explicit articulation of the prayer theme invokes the presence of God both indirectly (14.35) and directly (14.36). These two descriptions provide intensification and sharpen the theological focus. In particular, 14.36 makes four direct appeals to God (αββα, πατήρ, σοι, συ). Within this theological gestalt a sharp christological portrait is framed. The reverence of Jesus is displayed in his submission (ἔπιπτεν ἐπὶ τῆς γῆς) and in his confession (πάντα δυνατά σοι). The prayer of Jesus climaxes with a cry of obedience (οὐ τί ἐγὼ θέλω ἀλλὰ τί σύ).[2] Thus, the inner scene portrays Jesus as the faithful and

---

1. In contrast to H.G. Kuhn ('Jesus in Gethsemane', *EvT* 12 [1952–53], pp. 260-85) I find 'paranetic' an inadequate description of this material. This line of thought employs paranetic material, but it belongs to a much larger focus on discipleship failure. The passage articulates condemnation as much as paranesis. On the other hand, W. Kelber ('Mark 14.32-42: Gethsemane', *ZNW* 63 [1972], pp. 166-87) has pressed the role of discipleship failure far beyond its local function as backdrop and contrast for the christological focus.

2. The absence of the final predicate creates an aposiopesis which serves a mimetic purpose—the stark, broken grammar embodies the pathos of the scene.

obedient Son who prays in the hour of agony to the Father.

In this manner the story moves by stages between an external setting (disciples), an intermediate setting (Jesus and the Three) and an inner setting (Jesus alone before God). Jesus' movement between these settings sustains a cyclical pattern which creates narrative focus, intensity and duration. Two vital streams of thought flow through this structure. The outer scenes are anthropological, focusing the failure of the disciples; the inner scene provides a sanctuary of prayer and focuses key christological concerns. These two streams merge in a final sequence of sayings (14.41-42).[1]

3. This complex morphological pattern likely reflects the compositional process behind this account. Mk 14.32-42 appears to contain a foundational tradition which has been joined to a wider stream of editorial activity.[2]

A.T. Robertson (*A Grammar of the Greek New Testament in the Light of Historical Research* [Nashville: Broadman Press, 1914], p. 1203) defines aposiopesis as 'a conscious suppression of part of a sentence under the influence of a strong emotion like anger, fear, pity'.

1.   Much debate has circulated around whether Mk 14.32-42 is characterized by a sequence of doublets (disciples/Three; commands in 14.32, 34; indirect/direct prayer in 14.35, 36; general/specific conclusion in 14.41) or by the use of trilogies (three disciples; three cycles of prayer). In my analogy two streams of thought flow through the story—one anthropological and one christological. The anthropological stream of failure and warning employs two patterns of reduction and is built around a tripartite schema.

2.   A long history of research has produced three conflicting categories of analysis. (1) Bultmann (*History*, pp. 267-68) argued for an independent legend at the ground layer. The account in 14.32-42 is seen as a secondary development of this tradition. This line of analysis has been followed by Linnemann (*Studien*, pp. 27-32) and Schenke (*Studien*, pp. 461-56; *Der gekreuzigte Christus*, pp. 126-29). In a similar vein Schweizer (*Mark*, pp. 309-11) argues that a single shorter version of this story has been expanded through sayings material and allusions to the Old Testament. (2) Kuhn ('Gethsemane', pp. 260-85) sees two strong lines of tradition merged into one account. In Kuhn's reconstruction one tradition is christological (14.32, 35, 40-42) and one is paranetic (14.33-34, 36-38). Schenk (*Passionsbericht*, pp. 193-206) attempts to anchor Kuhn's analysis to a tradition characterized by its use of a grammatical form—historical presents. Schenk's argument that tense changes to the historical present signal a distinctive source or tradition is difficult to support in view of the common use of such changes in various types of literature. (3) The Gethsemane scene was understood as a unified, indissoluble whole by Lohmeyer (*Markus*, p. 313). Pesch (*Markusevangelium*, II, p. 386) supports this analysis. Both argue that Mark has taken over the story intact from his sources. The

2. Mark 14.1-42: The Preparation and Betrayal

3.1. One sequence of material appears to be foundational in nature. The location of the scene seems early and unmotivated. The ambiguous χωρίον is clarified by Γεθσημανί, yet no further specification is given. No redactional influence surfaces in the reference to Gethsemane.[1] While the Gospel of Mark makes extensive use of geographical symbolism,[2] Gethsemane appears only in this scene.[3] Because the Gethsemane location reflects no redactional or aetiological interests, it is likely a foundational element of this account.

In addition to this location, the tradition of Jesus' lament/prayer is foundational. The αββα address in 14.36 reflects a strong liturgical tradition tied to sonship (Rom 8.15; Gal 4.6) as well as the Lord's Prayer tradition (Mt. 6.9; Lk. 11.2). In contrast, the fatherhood of God is not a major theme in the Gospel of Mark (11.25; 13.32).[4] In addition, the confession that 'all things are possible' echoes a foundational Christian tradition found in various forms and contexts (Mk

---

position of Kelber ('Gethsemane', pp. 166-87) appears at first reading to expand upon Bultmann's thesis of a ground tradition with secondary expansions. Pesch (*Markusevangelium*, II, p. 386) incorrectly lists Kelber in this tradition. A close reading shows that Kelber affirms the basic unity of Mk 14.32-42. In sharp contrast to Lohmeyer and Pesch, Kelber argues that Mark did not inherit a unified story, but created one. His design was to generate a polemic against his own opponents through his focus on the absolute fall of Peter and the disciples. Kelber ('Gethsemane', p. 176) concludes, 'Mark is not merely the redactor, but to a high degree the creator and composer of the Gethsemane story'.

This overview of the history of research in Mk 14.32-42 demonstrates the inherent liabilities and the lack of consensus which characterize reconstruction, particularly in this passage. Moving beyond this impasse, this analysis gives primary attention to the narrative effect of joining such contrasting images within a text.

1. The Gospel of Mark typically clarifies Aramaic terms (3.17; 5.41; 7.11; 7.34; 14.36; 15.22; 15.34), yet the etymology of Γεθσημανί remains uncertain. See Kelber, 'Gethsemane', p. 174.

2. Among these are the seashore, the wilderness, the house, the mountain, Galilee. This use of geography was seen by Lohmeyer and has received renewed attention in recent studies. See, for example, W. Kelber, *Mark's Story of Jesus* (Philadelphia: Fortress Press, 1979); Broadhead, 'Which Mountain is "This Mountain"?'.

3. Only Mk 14.26 ties Gethsemane to the Mount of Olives. This narrative link, which is external to this pericope, provides the basis for traditional designations of the Gethsemane site, while the description as a garden was provided by Jn 18.1.

4. The Gospel of Luke has 12 references to God as father, the Gospel of Matthew has 42, and the Gospel of John has 68.

11.22-26; Mt. 17.20; Lk. 17.6; 1 Cor. 13.2). Beyond this the symbolic use of ποτήριον (cup) reflects a metaphor used widely in early Christianity.¹ The linkage of the cup to Jesus' death in Jn 18.11 demonstrates its existence outside the synoptic tradition. In a similar way the metaphorical use of ὥρα (the hour) in 14.35 as a decisive moment of judgment or death is found in numerous settings and traditions.² The linkage of the hour to the Father/Son relationship in Jn 17.1 confirms the wide circulation of this imagery. Thus, various elements suggest that the direct prayer of Mk 14.36 belongs to a foundational Gethsemane tradition. Mk 14.35 provides an indirect reflection of this tradition.

The lament in Mk 14.34 is based on allusion to various Old Testament psalms³ and may be foundational. The addition of ἕως θανάτου (to the point of death) likely represents an extension of the scriptural allusion, though it may be based on Jon. 4.9 LXX or 1 Kgs 19.4. The appearance of the lament in a similar form in Jn 12.27 demonstrates the wider circulation of this tradition.

Thus, the account in Mk 14.32-42 seems to be framed around a foundational Gethsemane tradition of Jesus' lament/prayer. This tradition (14.34a, 35-36) provided a singular focus on the experience of Jesus and was likely introduced by the Gethsemane setting and the command to wait (14.32).

3.2. In contrast to the constitution of Mk 14.32, 34a, 35-36 upon widespread traditions, the discipleship theme reflects various literary patterns distinctly characteristic of the Gospel of Mark. (1) The use of καί plus ἔρχομαι to narrate the movements of Jesus and his disciples is a frequent introductory phrase in the Gospel of Mark (5.38; 8.22; 10.46; 11.15; 11.27).⁴ (2) The separation of the Three for decisive events in Jesus' ministry is a typical pattern found in Mk

1. The ποτήριον is employed in a variety of Lord's Supper traditions (Mk 14.23; Mt. 26.27; Lk. 22.17, 20 [twice]; 1 Cor. 10.16, 21), as a symbol of social ministry (Mk 9.11; Mt. 10.42) and as a death metaphor (Mk 10.38, 39; 14.36; Mt. 20.22, 23; Lk. 22.42; Jn 18.11).

2. See, for example, Mt. 24.36-50, Lk. 12.40 (Son of Man!) and the extensive Johannine development of ὥρα. Numerous parallels exist within the New Testament and in other literature.

3. See, for example, Pss. 42.5, 6, 11; 43.5.

4. C.H. Turner, 'Marcan Usage: Notes, Critical and Exegetical, on the Second Gospel', *JTS* 29 (1925), pp. 225-26; J.C. Hawkins, *Horae Synopticae: Contributions to the Study of the Synoptic Problem* (Oxford: Clarendon Press, 1899), p. 12.

5.21-31, 35-43 and 9.2-8.[1] This separation is marked by the use of παραλαμβάνει (5.40; 9.2; 14.33). (3) The extended use of καί-parataxis (16 times) is a typical construction in the Gospel of Mark. (4) The use of the historical present (15 times) is also characteristic. (5) The use of ἄρχομαι plus a present infinitive in 14.33 reflects typical style.[2] (6) The use of θαμβεῖν and ἐκθαμβεῖσθαι is unique to the Gospel of Mark.[3] (7) The καὶ πάλιν linkage is typical.[4] (8) The use of an imperfect periphrastic (ἦσαν plus the participle in 14.40) belongs to the wider editorial patterns. (9) The abrupt use of the γάρ clause (14.40) is characteristic.[5] (10) The obsession with trilogies belongs distinctly to the editorial pattern of the Gospel of Mark.[6]

These various literary patterns suggest that the discipleship theme (14.33, 34b, 37-41ab) shares the same editorial pattern as the larger text of the Gospel of Mark. This material is likely shaped as a narrative explication of the predictions in Mk 14.19, 27, 30.

Various narrative images are developed within this discipleship material. (1) The culpability of the disciples is made clear by more specific commands to abide, watch, pray (14.34, 38). (2) The sorrow of Jesus becomes life-threatening (ἕως θανάτου in 14.34). (3) Peter's name reverts to Simon (14.37). (4) A paranetic concern is developed (14.38). (5) The imagery of blindness is suggested, as is the image of muteness (14.40). (6) An eschatological focus is developed (14.41). (7) This failure is linked to the betrayal (14.41, 42). (8) The Christology of the suffering Son of Man is focused (14.41).

4. Thus, Mk 14.32-42 is constituted around two clear lines of thought. A foundational christological concern is present in the

1. This pattern was seen as Markan as early as 1901 by W. Wrede, *The Messianic Secret* (trans. J.C.G. Greig; Cambridge: James Clark, 1971 [1901]), pp. 352-53.

2. Turner, 'Marcan Usage', *JTS* 28 (1927), pp. 352-53.

3. E. Schweizer, 'Die theologische Leistung des Markus', *EvT* 24 (1964), p. 340.

4. Turner, 'Marcan Usage', *JTS* 29 (1928), pp. 283, 286, 287.

5. C.H. Bird, 'Some γάρ Clauses in St Mark's Gospel', *JTS* NS 4 (1953), pp. 121-87.

6. See Kelber, 'Gethsemane', p. 171 n. 25. Gnilka (*Markus*, II, p. 257) sees trilogies as a canon of folk literature, while Pesch (*Markusevangelium*, II, pp. 15-20, 387) sees the use of trilogies as evidence of an extensive pre-Markan passion narrative.

Gethsemane tradition of Jesus' lament/prayer (14.32, 34a, 35-36). The discipleship tradition reflects the larger editorial style of the Gospel of Mark and focuses the repeated failure of the closest followers of Jesus. The embedding of the christological theme within the larger discipleship focus and the joining of the two themes in a concluding sayings sequence produces a singular narrative line.[1] This complex morphological scheme provides the basis for lively patterns of syntactical interchange.

Narrative Syntax. The narrative significance of Mk 14.32-42 is greater than the sum of its components. The morphological elements which constitute Mk 14.32-42 are shaped by important interrelationships. These patterns of internal syntax generate a vital narrative statement.

1. The anthropological focus on discipleship failure (14.33, 34b, 37-41ab) serves as the host for various other concerns and transactions. The narrative images built upon this theme help to shape the larger account.

1.1. The first of these syntactical transactions may be seen in the development of sufficient grounds for the charge against the disciples. The initial command—simply to sit (14.32)—provides sparse grounds for condemning the followers. Only in the focused charge to the Three (remain and watch, 14.34) and to Peter (watch and pray, 14.38) can such a charge be supported.

1.2. In a similar manner the sleeping of the disciples is developed into a charge of failure. The initial command (14.32) does not condemn or even forbid sleep. Only when the narrative identifies sleep as a refusal to watch and to pray does it become a failure. The sleep of the disciples is defined further as a door to temptation and as an indication of weakness (14.38). Ultimately sleep impairs the vision

---

1. This compositional analysis distinguishes itself from Bultmann's thesis in that neither tradition is seen as a secondary expansion of the other. In contrast to Kuhn and Schenk the streams of tradition are not seen as indicative of the entire passion story, but are localized in effect.

In distinction from a rather contradictory history of research, this analysis is concerned primarily for the syntactical effect of this process upon the local story and for the role of this scene within the larger narrative. Thus, the union of anthropological and christological lines in 14.32-42 is valued not primarily as a signal of traditional sources or authorial intention, but as a catalyst in the production of narrative significance.

2. Mark 14.1-42: The Preparation and Betrayal

of the disciples and leaves them mute (14.40). A typical biological response is thus transformed through the syntax of this account into a deadly failure.

1.3. Through the addition of ἕως θανάτου (to the point of death) the sorrow and agony of Jesus becomes life-threatening. Only in this form can the prayer/lament be tied explicitly to the passion Christology. In addition, the fatal aura of Jesus' grief intensifies the failure of the disciples.

1.4. The definition of Jesus' agony as life-threatening and the consequent intensification of the disciples' failure occasions the didactic focus of 14.34, 38. The command to watch and pray is thus transformed beyond its initial biological focus and its original audience of disciples; watchfulness and prayer now address spiritual needs inherent in human nature.

1.5. The failure of the disciples is applied precisely to Peter. This transition is accomplished through Jesus' question in 14.37. Peter alone is queried, and he is addressed by his old name (Simon). Consequently the syntax of this story defines sleeping as a deadly failure and makes Peter the chief culprit (14.37).

1.6. Thus, the internal syntax of 14.32-42 employs the discipleship focus to sponsor a scene of increasing danger and failure. The sleep of the disciples is defined as a moral flaw indicative of human existence and as a spiritual danger. The failure of the disciples is defined as a complete fall and an absolute abandonment of identity.

2. The imbedding of the christological theme (14.32, 34a, 35-36) into this account realigns the story in major ways. (1) Jesus is portrayed as the faithful Son who watches with prayer and obedience. (2) This messianic presence transforms the call to watch and pray (14.38) from a general paranesis to an urgent necessity in view of the hour. (3) In a similar manner the presence of the messianic hour transforms the temptation (14.38) from a general warning to a stark, immediate danger of absolute failure. (4) The impending sense of eschatological urgency sponsored by the 'watch and pray' command (14.38; 13.35, 37) becomes distinctly christological and is precisely linked to the suffering and death of Jesus. (5) The eschatological emphasis of the 'hour' (14.41) is linked directly to the 'hour' of Jesus' suffering (14.35). Thus, the imbedding of the christological theme within the larger story of discipleship failure provides a stark syntactical realignment. Ambiguous images of failure are transformed

into fatal flaws. General warnings become christological and eschatological imperatives. The critical urgency of this hour is linked directly to the suffering of Jesus, the obedient Son.

3. The union of the anthropological theme and the christological theme completes the realignment of this scene. These two streams are joined in the final sequence of sayings (14.41c-42). The failure of the disciples is given renewed intensity through the reintroduction of the betrayal theme (παραδίδοται) and the designation of one of the followers as ὁ παραδιδούς. At the same time the christological theme reaches its summit in 14.41. The Son who accepts the cup in obedience is now designated as the suffering Son of Man (14.41). The concluding eschatological reference to the 'hour' (ὥρα in 14.35, 37, 41) draws upon both streams of thought. The hour of Jesus' agony and death (14.35) and the single hour of Peter's failure (14.37) become ultimate, eschatological moments.[1] The paranetic command to watch and pray becomes an eschatological imperative. This syntactical maneuver establishes a crucial hermeneutic: the eschatological destiny of the Son of Man is to be found in the present suffering of Jesus and the eschatological danger is to be found in the present weakness of his followers.[2] The two streams which flow through Mk 14.32-42 converge in one stark, terse saying: 'It is done. The hour has come' (ἦλθεν ἡ ὥρα).[3] The failure of the disciples is ensured, and the destiny of the Son is decided.

---

1. The language of 14.41c-42 reflects the opening of Jesus' ministry in 1.14-15, where the time (καιρός) is fulfilled and the Kingdom, like the betrayer, has drawn near (ἤγγικεν in 1.15; 14.42).

2. Various scholars support this connection. Gnilka (*Markus*, II, p. 261) sees this impact: 'With verse 35 the suffering struggle of Jesus is christologically focused and is designated as apocalyptic'. Schenke (*Studien*, p. 558) says that 'Mark 14.32-42 makes it clear that what Christians expect to see in the Parousia can be seen precisely in the suffering'. Schweitzer (*Quest*, p. 390) argued for the thoroughly eschatological nature of this passage as well as the entire passion event.

3. The use of ἀπέχει is enigmatic. Typically ἀπέχω means to be at a distance. This distance is spatial in Mt. 14.24, Lk. 7.6, 15.20 and 24.13, but spiritual in Mk 7.6. The term means to keep one's distance or to abstain from in Mt. 15.8, 1 Thess. 4.3, 5.22, 1 Tim. 4.3 and 1 Pet. 2.11. The term has a documented commercial use—to receive payment in full and to give a receipt—in the papyri and the ostraca. The use of ἀπέχω to designate the full development or compensation of a process is found in the New Testament. The ultimate payment for evil is addressed through this term in the Sermon on the Mount (Mt. 6.2, 5, 16) and in the Sermon on the Plain (Lk.

2. Mark 14.1-42: The Preparation and Betrayal

4. At the center of these syntactical exchanges stands an important christological process. The focus on Jesus in 14.32, 34a, 35-36 provides a counterflow which contrasts the abject failure of the disciples. More significantly, the christological focus placed at the center of this account creates a sphere of influence around which various images circulate.

4.1. The lament/prayer scene invokes prophetic images. The withdrawal for prayer belongs to the characterization of a prophet.[1] The language of lament carries a prophetic echo.[2] In addition, the focus on the Son of Man and the 'hour' (14.41) echoes prophetic expectations similar to those found in Daniel.[3] Beyond this the internal language of this account suggests prophetic authority.[4] The intimate dialogue with God also belongs to the characterization of a prophet.[5] Most significantly, Jesus' awareness of the presence and the import of the 'hour' reflects prophetic understanding.

6.24). The term may also refer to complete payment for good in Phil. 4.8 and Phlm. 15, where the term is used of Onesimus. H. Hanse ('ἔχω', *TDNT*, II, p. 828) notes the difficulty of ἀπέχει in Mk 14.41: 'For this there are no parallels and we have to decide as best we can'. Some choices are less preferable than others. The Western gloss of ἀπέχει τὸ τέλος reflects Luke's reworking of the difficulty (Lk. 22.37) and proves of little help. Also of little help is the Vulgate translation (*sufficit*) meaning 'for what suffices?' W. Bauer, W. Arndt and F. Gingrich (*A Greek–English Lexicon of the New Testament and other Early Christian Literature* [eds. F. Gingrich and F. Danker; Chicago: University of Chicago Press, rev. edn, 1979], pp. 84-85) noted the common use of οὐδὲν ἀπέχει to mean 'nothing hinders' and suggested that ἀπέχει refers to the hindrance provided by the drowsiness of the disciples. Likewise, the suggestion of Hanse—'it is not in place'—offers little substance. Gnilka (*Markus*, II, p. 263) ties the term to a temporal line. In my opinion the commercial use of the term lies in the background of Mk 14.41. The most likely reading is that the arrival of the 'hour' brings the full completion of the two lines of thought. The failure of the disciples has reached its apex in the betrayal of Jesus. At the same time the obedience of the Son to suffering and death has come full term.

1. Abraham withdraws from his companions to pray in Gen. 22.5. Moses withdraws from the people to speak with God (Exod. 19.3, 25). A similar image of withdrawal and suffering may be found in Jeremiah's lament (Jer. 15.15-18).

2. This imagery is formalized in the Lamentations of Jeremiah.

3. See, for example, Dan. 7.13; 11.40, 45 in the LXX.

4. The speech of Jesus employs seven imperative forms (καθίσατε, μείνατε, γρηγορεῖτε [twice], προσεύχεσθε, καθεύδετε, ἀναπαύεσθε) and one cohortative (ἄγωμεν).

5. See, for example, Exod. 33.11-23; 1 Kgs 19.9-10, 14; Jon. 4.1-11.

4.2. The lament/prayer scene also focuses the image of Jesus as Son of God. The address to God (αββα, πατήρ) establishes this image, and the prayer supplies its content. Jesus is portrayed as the faithful and obedient Son, then this imagery is cast against the failure and betrayal of his followers.

4.3. The Son of Man Christology is invoked by the saying in 14.41. Closely attached to this image is the theme of betrayal and the coming of the 'hour'.

4.4. These various christological images circulate around a stark passion Christology. The lament inserts the suffering theme at the heart of the pericope, and the addition of ἕως θανάτου[1] makes the passion focus explicit. In addition, metaphors such as the cup and the hour support the passion emphasis. This central passion focus extends its images into the discipleship story and provides the hermeneutical key to other christological images. The prophet suffers alone in view of his death. The obedience of the Son of God leads to his passion. The Son of Man is handed over to die.

5. Thus, the syntax of Mk 14.32-42 generates a vital narrative episode. An extended anthropological focus demonstrates and warns of human weakness, then connects this failure precisely to Jesus' suffering. A contrasting christological stream links the death of Jesus directly to his obedience to God. These contrasting streams and the images which they support converge in a stark portrait. The passion of Jesus marks the arrival of the ultimate hour. Surrounded by human weakness and divine power, the Son is abandoned to obedience.

The Passion Context. This solemn christological image is connected in important ways to various other elements of the passion story. Within the context of the passion account the abandonment in 14.32-42 fulfills the earlier prediction of Jesus (14.26-32a).[2] This immediate, precise fulfillment confirms the image of Jesus as true prophet. Beyond this Mk 14.32-42 extends the earlier portrayal of Jesus as one who suffers

---

1. The extension of the lament through 'until death' may be drawn from Jon. 4.9 or from 1 Kgs 19.4.

2. Specific details from 14.26-32a are taken up in 14.32-42: (1) the abandonment occurs 'this night' (14.30); (2) Peter is the most resistant (14.29) and the most culpable (14.39); (3) all of the disciples resist Jesus and all fail (14.27, 31; 14.32b); (4) the Old Testament imagery is employed in both scenes (14.27b; 14.34); (5) the failure is threefold (14.30; 14.41).

2. Mark 14.1-42: The Preparation and Betrayal

and dies (14.21, 27). The image of Jesus as the Son of Man who is betrayed (14.41) also develops an earlier focus (14.21). The mention of the cup (14.36) recalls the cup of Jesus' suffering and death (14.23-24). The death of Jesus, implied in various scenes (14.1-2, 10-11, 18-20, 21, 22-25, 27-28), is now made explicit (14.34). Thus, various concerns of the passion story are crystallized in the christological images of the Gethsemane scene. Conversely the prophetic tone generated by Mk 14.32-42 is deepened by its interaction with the passion context in which it operates.

The Gospel Context. The images of the Gethsemane story gain their sharpest focus in the wider context of the gospel narrative. Various formal connections—some explicit and some suggestive—link this account with the wider text and generate a reciprocal field of interpretation.[1] These patterns of interconnection are decisive for the shaping of narrative significance and provide important clues to the identity of the Gospel of Mark.

1. The theme of discipleship failure set forth in 14.32-42 now operates against the backdrop of Mark 1–13. Within this framework the disciples' failure to watch becomes part of a consistent and extended pattern. Various narrative locations confirm that their spirit is willing, but their discipleship is incomplete.[2] In particular their insight and courage fails around the issue of Jesus' death (8.31-32; 9.31-32; 10.32-45). This important and carefully developed theme is given stark demonstration in Jesus' last hour: the disciples sleep when they should watch and pray, their eyes are heavy, and they do not know how to answer Jesus. The failure of the disciples in Mk 14.32-42 thus gives summary focus to an extended narrative image.

2. In addition, this story unites all of the prophecies of betrayal. The various images and predictions of abandonment (3.6; 8.31; 9.31; 10.32-34; 14.18, 20; 14.27, 28, 30) are brought together in a final prophetic word: 'Behold, the Son of Man is betrayed into the hands of

---

1. These implicit and explicit formal narrative connections may or may not reflect authorial intent and the use of related sources. These varying degrees of intratextual exchange are argued here on formalistic grounds and prove central to the process of signification.
2. The disciples fail to understand the parables (4.13; 9.32), they are fearful and lose faith (4.40-41; 9.6; 10.32), they ask inappropriate questions (5.31; 6.36; 8.4; 9.10, 34; 10.24, 35-37), they argue with Jesus (8.32), they are impotent (9.18).

sinners' (14.41). Set in the shadow of the cross, this prophecy rings with certainty and finality.

3. In conjunction with this discipleship theme, the Gethsemane story interacts with various christological images from Mark 1–13. (1) The image of Jesus as the obedient Son of God is set forth at the beginning of the Gospel in the baptism scene (1.11), and the following verses show Jesus in the wilderness, confronting temptation (1.12-13). This opening scene sets the stage and the pattern for the public ministry of Jesus. Mk 14.32-42 closes the life of Jesus with a similar scene. In Gethsemane Jesus addresses God as Father and offers obedience to the will of God (14.36). At the end of his ministry Jesus prays to God in a lonely place. Thus, Mk 14.32-42 joins with Mk 1.9-13 to provide a distinct interpretive frame. Throughout his ministry Jesus is the reverent, obedient Son of God. (2) The Son of Man Christology, while open to images of present power (2.10) and future glory (13.26-27), is focused around the suffering and death of Jesus (8.31; 9.12; 9.31; 14.21). Mk 14.41 confirms this use of the Son of Man title in relation to his suffering. (3) In addition, the Gethsemane story confirms and extends the passion Christology posited at various places in Mark 1–13. Most significantly, the threefold prediction of passion and suffering (8.31; 9.31; 10.32-34) is recapitulated in three scenes of abandonment in the face of death (Mk 14.32-42).[1]

4. A sequence of formal connections is established between the Gethsemane account and the disciples' request in 10.35-40. (1) The sons of Zebedee are central to both accounts (10.35; 14.33). (2) The imagery of the cup represents the destiny of Jesus in both stories (ποτήριον in 10.38, 39; 14.36). (3) The disciples who boast that 'we are able' (δυνάμεθα in 10.39) are 'not able' (οὐκ ἴσχυσας) in 14.37. (4) Those who do not know what they are asking (10.38) do not know what to answer (14.40). (5) Both stories are set against the context of the passion (10.33-34; 14.34-36, 41-42). Through this connection the arrogant request of 10.35-40 foreshadows the dangers and the demands of discipleship—a prophecy realized in 14.32-42.

5. The naming of Peter takes on new significance in connection with the wider narrative. Jesus calls Simon in Mk 1.16, then visits his house in 1.29. In the appointment scene of 3.13-19 Jesus calls aside (προσκαλεῖται, ἀπῆλθον in 3.13) his followers, and Simon is the

---

1. Kelber ('Gethsemane', pp. 181-87) sees the tripartite use of passion prediction and discipleship failure as the key for understanding Markan theology.

2. Mark 14.1-42: The Preparation and Betrayal

first of the Twelve to be appointed. With his appointment Simon's name is changed to Peter. The etymology of the new name reflects a rock-like character, and the changing of the name reflects—as in the Old Testament—a new identity and vocation.[1] Seen against this backdrop, the calling aside (παραλαμβάνει in 14.33) and the renaming (14.37) become crucial signs. The reversion to the name Simon in 14.37 suggests a narrative reversal of Peter's appointment and a narrative abandonment of his identity and vocation.[2]

6. The Gospel of Mark creates a reciprocal interpretive relationship between the Gethsemane scene and the transfiguration story (Mk 9.2-10). (1) Both stories use παραλαμβάνω to designate the calling apart of disciples (9.2; 14.33). (2) A mountain setting is used in both scenes (9.2; 14.26; implicit in 14.32-42). (3) Peter, James and John are chosen to accompany Jesus through a decisive experience (9.2; 14.33). (4) A change in demeanor is narrated (9.2; 14.33). (5) Peter is singled out as a representative (9.5; 14.37). (6) The number three is significant (three tents in 9.5; three cycles in 14.41). (7) Stark γάρ phrases are used to indicate the tone of the stories (9.6 [twice]; 14.40). (8) The disciples do not know what to answer Jesus (9.6; 14.40). (9) Jesus is designated as the Son of God (9.7; 14.36). (10) The Son of Man title is used in association with Jesus' death (9.9, 12; 14.41). (11) Both scenes are framed by the impotence of the disciples (οὐκ ἴσχυσαν in 9.18; οὐκ ἴσχυσας in 14.37). This extensive line of connections unveils a decisive hermeneutic: every vision of the Son of God and the Son of Man must be filtered through the experience of his suffering and death.

7. Most significantly, the Gethsemane scene provides a hermeneutic for reading Mark 13. Various interconnections are established between the stark Gethsemane scene and the apocalyptic imagery of Mark 13. (1) The inner circle of three is central to both scenes (13.3; 14.33). (2) The theme of betrayal (παραδίδωμαι) is important (13.9,

---

1. Examples are found in Abraham, Sarah and Jacob. The same imagery is implicitly applied by Luke to Paul.
2. This change has already been prefigured in Mk 8.33, where Jesus addresses Peter as Satan. While the narrator continues to use the Peter title, Jesus never again uses his name in the story. The message to 'Peter' in Mk 16.7 may signal a narrative reversal of this fall. Obviously this switching of names may represent layers of tradition and a corresponding historical background to this process. Whatever the historical background of this transaction, its formal narrative significance remains decisive.

11, 12; 14.41, 42). (3) The concept of the 'hour' (ὥρα) is employed (13.11, 32; 14.35, 41). (4) Endurance (ὑπομέων, μένω) is the sign of true discipleship (13.13; 14.34). (5) Death (θάνατος) is important in both accounts (13.12; 14.34). (6) In both scenes disciples are commanded to pray (13.18; 14.38). (7) Both stories employ the image of sleep (13.36; 14.37, 40, 41). (8) The image of the Son of Man stands at the center of both scenes (13.26; 14.41). (9) The command to watch provides the primary exhortation in both units (βλέπω in 13.5, 9, 33; γρηγορέω in 13.34, 35, 37; 14.34, 37, 38).

7.1. These narrative links suggest that Mark 13 should be read in view of Mk 14.32-42. Having established this linkage through the Gethsemane scene, the passion account establishes further links to Mark 13.[1] These extensive links encourage the reader to understand Mark 13 and Mk 14.32-42 in a dialogical relationship. Through this relationship the apocalyptic imagery of Mark 13 is joined to the Gethsemane scene. This connection realigns the christological focus of Mark 13 in important ways. The prophet who speaks of apocalyptic wonder now stands in the shadow of the cross. The Son of Man who will come in the clouds of heaven with power and great glory is now betrayed into the hands of sinners. The decisive 'hour' is the hour of the cross. Thus, the Gethsemane scene dramatically impacts the interpretation of Mark 13.

7.2. This impact is most evident in relation to the image of prophecy in the Gospel of Mark. Of all the predictions in this narrative, those in Mark 13 are most problematic. Apocalyptic images of cosmic destruction stretch the imagination of skeptics and believers (13.24-25). Even signs and wonders can be misleading (13.22), false prophecy abounds (13.22) and false christs will lead many astray (13.22). Even the less spectacular prophecies prove troublesome.

---

1. The symbolism of the Mount of Olives (13.1, 2, 3) and the mountain (13.14) may be taken up in the setting of Mk 14.26. The mention of the cockcrow and the division of the day into watches (13.35) is repeated in the story of Peter's denial (14.30, 68, 72). The abandonment of the garment (13.16) is realized in Mk 14.51-52. The image of betrayal by one's family (13.12) is reflected in the betrayal by one of the Twelve (14.10, 20, 43). The promise of trials and abuse before religious and political authorities (13.9-11) is realized in the passion context (14.53-65; 15.1-20). The prophecy of the preaching of the gospel to all nations (13.10) is repeated in relation to Jesus' death (14.9). Outside of the passion context the image of the fig tree (13.28) is developed in Mk 11.12-14, 20-25.

2. Mark 14.1-42: The Preparation and Betrayal

Some are ambiguous and obscure (13.14). The literal fulfillment of some predictions seems difficult (13.2). Read in isolation, the predictions of Mark 13 have difficulty establishing the reliability of Jesus' prophecy.

Significantly, the linkage of Mark 13 to the Gethsemane account provides stark narrative confirmation for the reliability of Jesus' prophecies. Through this connection Mark 13 partakes in a world which confirms the reliability of Jesus' prophecy. The trustworthiness of Jesus the prophet was established early in the passion story (14.12-26), then developed through various scenes. This extensive pattern of prophecy/fulfillment generates a sense of confidence around the words of Jesus, and Mk 14.32-42 partakes in this growing image of reliability. Jesus is shown again as the prophet who knows his own destiny as well as that of his followers. Because of extensive connections between Gethsemane and Mark 13 the reader is encouraged to see Mark 13 in the same light—as reliable prophecy.

In addition, the Gethsemane story suggests that fulfillment of the prophecies of Mark 13 is already underway. The hour (Mk 13.11, 32; 14.35, 41) is now at hand. Betrayal and death are near (Mk 13.9, 11, 12; 14.34, 41, 42). The time for endurance (13.13; 14.34) and prayer (13.18; 14.38) has come. The danger of sleep is present (13.36; 14.37, 40, 41). The command to watch (13.5, 9, 33, 34, 35, 37; 14.34, 37, 38) is already valid. The prophecies concerning the Son of Man (13.26; 14.41) are being fulfilled.

7.3. Through these interconnections the Gethsemane scene helps to draw the apocalyptic images of Mark 13 into the mainstream of the narrative strategy. The apocalyptic Christology of Mark 13 is tied decisively to the present suffering of Jesus. In particular, the portrait of Jesus as the futuristic prophet and the coming Son of Man is linked to the passion Christology. Jesus is the Son of Man who is handed over to sinners, the prophet who moves consciously toward his own death.

7.4. Conversely Mark 13 impacts the reading of the Gethsemane story and the passion account. Gethsemane ends in failure and betrayal, but the wider narrative suggests an alternate ending. The reader now knows the future of the Son of Man who dies in humiliation; he will come again with power and glory. The reader knows that the prophet abandoned by his own holds the keys to the future. The present danger of sleep and the command to watch play a central role in this future. Disciples must watch and endure, for Jesus has shown them all things beforehand (13.23). Like the passion (14.36) the consummation lies in the hands of God (13.32). In this manner the local events of 14.32-42 are cast against the cosmic images of Mark 13.

8. Thus, the Gethsemane story participates in a crucial pattern of intratextual exchange. The extensive imagery of discipleship failure is now played out in the shadow of the cross. The prophecies of betrayal are gathered into a sharp focus in the last hours of Jesus. The image of Jesus as the faithful, obedient Son of God frames his entire ministry. The developing passion Christology is crystallized. The futuristic images of Mark 9 and Mark 13 are set forth as reliable prophecy whose fulfillment has begun. Expectations of the resurrection (9.2-13) and the parousia (13.1-37) are joined to the passion hermeneutic. Images of Jesus as prophet, Son of God, Son of Man are linked to his death. Prayer and watchfulness are demanded, for the hour is near.

Comparative Analysis
The Gospel of Mark employs the Gethsemane story to generate a solemn christological focus. This image interacts with various elements from the earlier narrative and points ahead to the death of Jesus. This account also appears in other narrative contexts. Phenomenological description and comparison of these co-texts provides a field against which to highlight the narrative operations of Mk 14.32-42.[1]

Pre-Markan Contexts. Various attempts have been made to reconstruct the form and use of the Gethsemane story prior to its inclusion in the Gospel of Mark. Bultmann argued that Mk 14.32-41 is an individual story not intended for its present context in the Gospel of Mark.[2] For Bultmann the story acts as a faith or cult legend.[3] Bultmann saw this account as a late construction not belonging to the passion context. A few others have supported the theory of a self-standing Gethsemane tradition.[4] Such a story would lose the solemn focus provided by the passion context. The images of betrayal, suffering and the threat of

1. In this study diachronic analysis is used primarily to establish a performance field rather than a history of the tradition.
2. Bultmann, *History*, pp. 267-68.
3. Bultmann, *History*, p. 306.
4. W. Grundmann, *Das Evangelium nach Markus* (Berlin: Evangelische Verlagsanstalt, 1959), pp. 396-403.

death would become ambiguous. Likewise, the failure of the disciples would be less significant, and the exhortation to watch and pray would become a general maxim. Apart from the passion context the christological portrait of such a story would be quite different: Jesus would be shown as a heroic figure who must endure the frailties of those about him.

A more likely reconstruction places the Gethsemane story as one element of a fixed pre-Markan passion account. Dibelius suggested that the Gethsemane scene is based on the Old Testament and is a part of the earliest passion tradition.[1] Schenke argues that the Gethsemane story was connected already to other passion traditions.[2] Lohmeyer saw here a unified story which Mark has taken over largely unchanged into his narrative.[3] Pesch emphasizes that this account was already a part of the fixed, pre-Markan passion tradition.[4] In this form the story would have important connections to the rest of the passion account. The emphasis on Jesus as the suffering prophet and Son of Man would be developed in conjunction with other parts of the passion. The developing theme of betrayal would be addressed. The failure of the disciples in the passion account would be continued. Images of Jesus as teacher and leader would be focused. Missing from this presentation would be the various links to Mark 1–13. The Son of God image would lose its resonance with Mk 1.9-13. The passion Christology would have a limited field of reference. Most important, the cross-references to Mark 9 and 13 would be missing. Such a presentation of the Gethsemane story would place it at the center of the passion account, but its effect would be localized.

A third reconstruction sees here the blending of two lines of tradition. According to this theory two separate accounts of the events at Gethsemane have now been woven into a single story. One line of tradition (14.32, 35, 40-42) is strongly christological. This material focuses the consciousness of Jesus that the hour of the Son of Man has come and that his handing over to sinners will fulfill the will of God. A second line of tradition (14.33-34, 36-38) is paranetic in its tendencies.[5] Standing in isolation these traditions would provide a

1. Dibelius, *Tradition*, pp. 211-13.
2. Schenke, *Passionsgeschichte*, pp. 461-560.
3. Lohmeyer, *Markus*, p. 313.
4. Pesch, *Markusevangelium*, II, pp. 385-86.
5. H.G. Kuhn, 'Jesus in Gethsemene', *EvT* 12 (1952–53), pp. 260-85;

singular christological or paranetic focus. It is likely that no reference to or interaction with other traditions would be provided.

Werner Kelber argues that Mark is responsible for almost all of the Gethsemane story.[1] Kelber sees only the location in Gethsemane and the prayer of 14.35-36 as pre-Markan. Beyond these elements the focus on the failure of Peter and the disciples is a Markan theme addressed to opponents at work in his own day. Kelber sees this form of the story addressed against the false Christology of a group Kelber labels the 'Peter-Christians'.

The Gospel of Matthew. The Gethsemane account also appears in Mt. 26.36-46. The language of the story bears a Matthaean style, but the content is essentially unchanged. The harsh word that the disciples 'did not know what to answer him' (Mk 14, 40) is omitted. Beyond this the story replicates the form and the context of Mk 14.32-42. The Matthaean context of the story creates a new connection for the prayer of Jesus. His prayers in Gethsemane (Mt. 26.39, 42) echo the Lord's Prayer given in the Sermon on the Mount (Mt. 6.9-13). Both prayer scenes address God as Father (Πάτερ in 6.9; τοῦ πατρός μου in 26.29, 42, both with some textual variations). Mt. 26.39 asks for the will of God in a way that indirectly recalls Mt. 6.10: 'not as I will, but as you [will]'). The request in Mt. 26.42 is a precise echo of Mt. 6.10: 'Let your will be done' (γενηθήτω τὸ θέλημά σου in both verses). Mt. 26.44 notes a third instance of this request. The will of God is to be the desire of the disciple (Mt. 6.10) and is the only door to the Kingdom (Mt. 7.21). This prayer occupies the center of Jesus' desires, but the disciples miss this concern.

The Gospel of Luke. Lk. 22.39-46 presents the Gethsemane account in abbreviated form. The description of Jesus' emotions is omitted and replaced by a single command to pray (Lk. 22.40). The three scenes of prayer are reduced to a single account. Likewise Jesus discovers the disciples sleeping only one time (Lk. 22.45). Strangely this account

---

Schenk, *Passionsbericht*, pp. 193-206. See Gnilka, *Markus*, II, p. 256, for a summary of this position. In contrast, Schweizer (*Mark*, pp. 309-311) argues for the expansion of a single, shorter version of this story through the addition of sayings material and Old Testament images.

1. Kelber, 'Gethsemane'. Kelber supports this view through analysis of linguistic and thematic factors in the Gethsemane story.

explains that the disciples sleep from sorrow (Lk. 22.45). Luke also has here an indirect echo of the Lord's Prayer (Lk. 11.2; 22.42). The story ends with a solemn exhortation: 'rise and pray that you may not enter into temptation' (Lk. 22.46). In various manuscripts a description of Jesus' agony has been added (Lk. 22.43-44).[1]

This version of the Gethsemane scene creates a different focus on Jesus. The concern for abandonment and betrayal is missing. Likewise the focus on Jesus as prophet and as the Son of Man is absent. No mention is made of the 'hour'. Only the prayer in Lk. 22.42 and the description in Lk. 22.43-44 relate the story to the death of Jesus. The solemn christological focus of Mk 14.32-42 has been redirected, and the issue of prayer provides the focus of this account. Prayer is contrasted to sleep and provides a way through the temptation (Lk. 22.46). The story suggests that the scene of Jesus at prayer is customary (Lk. 22.39). Jesus also encourages his followers to pray (Lk. 22.40, 46). This exhortation to 'pray that you may not enter into temptation' (Lk. 22.40, 46) frames the story and provides its central message. Thus, Lk. 22.39-46 blends the image of Jesus as one who prays into an exhortation for disciples to pray.

The Gospel of John. Images of the Gethsemane story may be found in Jn 12.27. Here the soul of Jesus is troubled, and mention is made of the Father. The concept of the 'hour' is central to this account, and Jesus embraces the hour and death as a part of his destiny. This saying has been placed within a pre-passion discourse which concludes Jesus' public ministry. The 'hour' provides the primary Johannine image for Jesus' destiny (Jn 2.4, 7.30; 8.20; 12.23, 27; 13.1; 17.1). This 'hour' is a moment of glory by which both the Son of Man (12.23) and the Father (12.27-28) will be glorified. It is a departure to the Father (13.1) which will glorify both Father and Son (17.1). While Jn 12.27 employs images of Gethsemane, its Christology is thoroughly Johannine. Images of betrayal, abandonment and death are exchanged for a departure to glory. Typical of the Fourth Gospel, elements such as the 'hour' have multiple levels of meaning. Thus, this material has been set in a different context and now bears a distinct Johannine Christology.

---

1. Luke 22.43-44 is added in ℵ*.2 D L Θ Ψ 0171 f^1 𝔐 lat sy$^{c.p.h}$ bo^{pt}.

Polycarp. Some of the sayings material from Mk 14.32-42 is found in Polycarp's *To the Philippians* (7.1-2). This series of paranetic exhortations draws upon various New Testament texts, particularly 1 John. This exhortation includes the call to watch unto prayer as a way to avoid temptation. In addition, a saying of the Lord is cited: 'The spirit is willing, but the flesh is weak'. Thus, this material has now been drawn into an epistolary context and used to warn against false doctrine, false teaching and unethical practices. While the passage mentions the coming of Christ in the flesh, the cross and the resurrection, the major concern of the passage is heresy, not Christology.

Summary
The material from the Gethsemane story was shown to operate in a variety of narrative contexts. These alternate literary settings and performances have a sharp impact on the christological focus of this material. Various pre-Markan uses of the material were suggested. In one reconstruction the material operated in two distinct streams—one christological and one paranetic. Another reconstruction described the unit as a self-standing story which presented a heroic image of Jesus as one who endures the frailties of his followers. A third reconstruction placed the Gethsemane story in a fixed, pre-Markan passion account. This story would show Jesus as the suffering prophet and the Son of Man betrayed into the hands of sinners. Nonetheless its narrative impact would remain localized within the context of the passion story. A fourth reconstruction sees the Gethsemane story as a tool in Mark's polemic against heretical Christology and discipleship in his own time.

The Gospel of Matthew replicates the use of the material in Mk 14.32-42, but it also creates an echo of the Lord's Prayer. The Gospel of Luke employs this echo and uses the account to call the disciples to watchfulness and to prayer. The Gospel of John uses selective elements of the Gethsemane material to develop the Johannine concept of the 'hour'. In Polycarp the material is used to counter heresy and to encourage faithfulness. This comparative type of diachronic analysis shows the narrative potential of the Gethsemane material; this story is capable of performance in a wide range of narrative contexts and is able to generate sharply differing images of Jesus.

Over against this broad and varied history the narrative effect of Mk 14.32-42 is distinctive. Operating within the local frame of the passion and within the wider world of the gospel narrative, Mk 14.32-

2. Mark 14.1-42: The Preparation and Betrayal

42 draws upon a host of literary images, connections and allusions. Images of discipleship failure are gathered from the wider narrative and played out in the context of Jesus' approaching death. The prophecies of betrayal are now realized in the internal and external experience of Jesus. From the beginning of his story to its end Jesus is the Son of God who pleases the Father. Jesus is shown to be the Son of Man handed over to sinners, the prophet who suffers and dies. Clear lines of interpretation are drawn between this image of Jesus and the wider narrative. Mark 13 becomes reliable prophecy already underway. Enthusiastic images of the Risen One, the apocalyptic prophet, the coming Son of Man are gathered into the story of the passion. A final word of exhortation is given by the teacher: watch and pray. For Jesus and for disciples the hour is near.

Conclusion

The four stories in Mk 14.1-42 play a vital role in the account of Jesus' death. The passion story is initiated and embodied by a private anointing scene. The Passover meal joins images from the Old Testament to the death of Jesus. The prediction of betrayal points to the events ahead. The scene in Gethsemane sets the stage for the arrest and trial of Jesus. In various ways these accounts generate the plot line of the passion story and create a vivid image of Jesus.

Plotting

Mk 14.1-42 provides two major plot functions: prediction and symbol. Each of these stories speaks of future events which will be pivotal in the gospel story. The anointing scene (Mk 14.1-11) tells that Jesus will be killed and buried and that the gospel will be preached throughout the world. In addition, this story foreshadows the betrayal and arrest. The Passover scene (14.12-26) points to the betrayal of Jesus, to his suffering and death and to the coming of the Kingdom. Mk 14.26-32a predicts the abandonment by the Twelve, the resurrection and the experience in Galilee. The Gethsemane scene speaks of the imminent arrest and death. Thus, each of these stories operates within the plot line as narrative prophecy.

At the same time these accounts create various narrative symbols. An anointing provides a symbol for the death of the messiah. Bread and wine symbolize the giving of Jesus' life. The shepherd imagery from the Old Testament provides a symbol for the passion. In Mk 14.32-42 the destiny of Jesus is a cup to be taken and an hour which has come. Thus, the four stories in Mk 14.1-42 make an important contribution to the plotting of the passion story. The Gospel of Mark employs these stories as narrative prophecies which predict and embody the death of Jesus.

Characterization
Beyond their contribution to the plotting of the passion narrative, these stories play a key role in the characterization of Jesus. Central to each account is the image of Jesus as one who dies for the cause of God. In addition to this primary focus various other images of Jesus emerge. Mk 14.1-42 shows Jesus as the true prophet of God whose words are reliable and sure. Jesus is the teacher and shepherd who continues to lead the flock of God. He is hated by religious leaders, betrayed and abandoned by those near him, but welcomed and loved by outcasts and sinners. Jesus is the founder of the new covenant, the Son of Man who will bring the Kingdom. Jesus is the innocent sufferer, the obedient Son, the fulfillment of the Scriptures. Mk 14.1-42 thus employs a host of vivid images to sketch the portrait of Jesus. Significantly, each of these character sketches is carved out against the backdrop of a second line of characterization—the failure, abandonment, and betrayal of the disciples.

The patterns of characterization generated in Mk 14.1-42 interact in important ways with the larger story of Jesus' ministry. Standing at a decisive juncture in his journey, the anointing story (Mk 14.1-11) gathers various images from the ministry of Jesus and links them to his death. This initial pattern is taken up in the scenes that follow. In particular, Mk 14.1-42 takes up the image of Jesus as one who teaches with authority, then links it to the portrait of Jesus as the faithful prophet of God who dies in behalf of the people. In a similar process other images are taken over and joined to the passion Christology. The shepherd who feeds the flock of God (Mk 6.32-46; 8.1-10) is smitten. The Risen One (9.2-13) must suffer and die. The Son of Man (Mk 13.26) will be betrayed, the messiah will be put to death, the Son of God will die. Through a strong pattern of intratextual exchange the opening stories of the passion account take up and develop images from the life and ministry of Jesus. Thus, the narrative of Jesus' death is deeply rooted in the story of his life.

2. Mark 14.1-42: The Preparation and Betrayal

Identity

Four initial stories in the passion account were analyzed in terms of morphological composition, syntactical interaction and narrative effect. Dramatic syntactical relationships and extended patterns of interconnection were demonstrated in each account. Distinct lines of plotting and characterization were sponsored by these processes. Most significantly, a profound christological pattern emerges from this interplay of formal narrative elements and processes.

Through this formalistic analysis the fundamental pattern and identity of the Gospel of Mark begins to emerge. In light of these narrative strategies the description of Martin Kähler—passion narratives with extensive introductions—is called into question. Numerous elements in Mk 14.1-42 show that the passion story is rooted in and realigned by the story of Jesus' ministry. Formalistic analysis implies that material outside of the passion narrative provides not simply an introduction to the passion story, but its very foundation and framework.

Formalistic analysis also suggests the view of Theodore Weeden—the Gospel of Mark engenders an open christological conflict in favor of passion Christology—provides an inadequate model. Mk 14.1-42 was shown to root formally and ideologically in the wider pattern of Jesus' words and deeds. Numerous themes from the earliest days of Jesus' ministry are taken over without correction. In addition, various themes from the passion narrative are themselves critically realigned through the power and wonder of Jesus' ministry.

The dynamic patterns of syntactical interaction and the extensive connections focused by formalistic analysis demonstrate the need for a more complex, interconnected model for the Gospel of Mark and its christological portrait. The patterns which were demonstrated in Mk 14.1-42 must be tested against the remainder of the passion story.

Chapter 3

MARK 14.43–15.15: THE ARREST AND TRIAL

The second major section of the passion narrative extends from Mk 14.43–15.15 and contains four accounts (14.43-53a; 14.53-65; 14.66-72; 15.1-15). This unit narrates the betrayal and arrest, the denial, and the trial scenes. Synchronic analysis will focus the internal form and function of each account. Particular attention will be given to the plotting of these stories within the passion narrative and within the wider Gospel context. Comparative analysis will be used to set forth a larger performance field against which these stories operate. Special attention will be given to the characterization of Jesus which emerges from this process.

Mark 14.43-53a: Betrayal, Arrest, Abandonment

Mk 14.43-53a narrates the betrayal by Judas, the arrest by religious authorities and the abandonment by the disciples. This brief account climaxes the movement of Mk 14.1-42 toward the betrayal and arrest of Jesus. At the same time this unit sets in motion the events which lead to the crucifixion.

Synchronic Analysis

The motifs of Mk 14.43-53a present the following framework:

    Introduction
        Judas comes   14.43a
        The crowd comes   14.43b
        The narrator informs   14.44

    Body
        Judas betrays   14.45
        The crowd seizes   14.46
        One strikes   14.47

3. *Mark 14.43–15.15: The Arrest and Trial*

Jesus questions	14.48
Jesus instructs	14.49
All flee	14.50
The youth flees	14.51-52
Conclusion	
Jesus departs	14.53a

Narrative Morphology. The story of Jesus' arrest employs eleven motifs. The account opens with a complex introduction built around three motifs. Uniquely the movement which opens the scene centers around Judas and the crowd. Jesus is stationary, and his location is taken over from the prior scene.[1] A second unique element is introduced in the voice of the narrator. This seldom-used motif informs the reader of the prior agreement between Judas and the crowd and clarifies the kiss of betrayal. The introduction thus gathers the various actants around Jesus and sets the stage for the scene of betrayal and arrest.

The body of the story carries the central plot action. A brief sequence of events (betrayal, seizure, striking) leads to the central focus on the words of Jesus. Following Jesus' words comes a second sequence of events (fleeing).

The conclusion of the story is also distinct. While Jesus' departure is common as a concluding motif, this use is ironic: Jesus is arrested and taken away for trial.

Morphologically Mk 14.43-53a is constituted around two action sequences (14.43-47; 14.50-53a) and a series of pronouncements (14.48-49). Two distinct christological streams flow through this structure, and a crucial image of Jesus is generated.[2]

1. The first action sequence is framed in 14.43-47. The opening motif assumes the presence of Jesus and the disciples, then invokes the presence of Judas, the mob and the religious leaders.[3] The narrator's

---

1. E. Schweizer (*The Good News according to Mark* [trans. D.H. Madvig; Atlanta: John Knox, 1970], p. 316) suggests a location other than Gethsemane. While this may be historically plausible, the formal arrangement of this story assumes the previous location and time frame.

2. While this segmentation likely reflects the redactional history of 14.43-53a, primary concern is given here to the narrative effect of this morphological arrangement.

3. The naming of the three religious groups—chief priests, scribes, elders—is a precise echo of the prophecy in 8.31 and the questioners of 11.27. The chief priests

comment in 14.44 completes the preparation for the scene. The staccato sequence of action which follows provides the basic plot structure for the story. Various elements from the scene become poignant symbols—the Twelve, a kiss,[1] the rabbi title,[2] the sword. This curt sequence initiates a thought stream of violent betrayal, seizure, abandonment, and it provides the foundational frame for this account.[3]

2. The concluding action sequence in 14.50-53a completes the plotting of this account. The departure from the scene is accomplished through two sharply contrasting images. (1) The flight of the followers is shown through two separate motifs. Mk 14.50 narrates the abandonment by all in brief and stark terms. This abandonment is significant for its breadth (all) and for its intensity (fleeing). Mk 14.51-52 duplicates this abandonment with increased precision and intensity—a solitary follower flees naked into the night.[4] Both flight

and the scribes are found in 14.1. The three parties are named at the beginning of both trial scenes (14.53; 15.1).

1. On the use of καταφιλέω, see G. Stählin, 'καταφιλέω', *TDNT*, IX, pp. 140-41, and W. Bauer, W. Arndt, F. Gingrich, *A Greek–English Lexicon of the New Testament and Other Early Christian Literature* (trans. and rev. W.F. Arndt and F.W. Gingrich; Chicago: University of Chicago Press, 1957, 1979), p. 420. The use of καταφιλέω to signify a kiss of greeting or farewell is widespread. Of particular interest is the kiss of betrayal in the Old Testament. A kiss may characterize deception (Gen. 27.26-27), political seduction (2 Sam. 15.5), temptation (Prov. 7.13), flattery (Sir. 29.5), an enemy desiring safety (Prov. 27.6) or murder (2 Sam. 20.9). Joab's betrayal of Amasa combines the kiss and the sword (2 Sam. 20.9-10). Extensive parallels to the kiss of betrayal are found outside of the Bible in Hellenism, India, Persia and Egypt.

2. The rabbi title is used by Peter in untranslated form in Mk 9.5 and 11.21. Bartimaeus addresses Jesus as ραββουνί in 10.51. The term is translated as 'teacher' and employed as a title in Mk 4.38; 5.35; 9.17, 38; 10.17, 20, 35; 12.14, 19, 32; 13.1; 14.14. The translated form is used equally by disciples, by common people and by opponents. Thus, the use on Jesus' lips seems to be neutral.

3. Mk 14.43-46 has been widely seen as a unified complex. See, for example, E. Lohmeyer, *Das Evangelium nach Markus* (Göttingen: Vandenhoeck & Ruprecht, 1953), p. 321; Schweizer, *Mark*, p. 173. Typically, R. Pesch (*Das Markusevangelium* [HTKNT; Freiburg: Herder, 2nd edn, 1980], II, pp. 397-404) sees the entire scene as a unified account. The striking and healing in 14.47 are enigmatic and undeveloped and may be subsequent to 14.43-46, yet a coherent narrative flow is maintained throughout 14.43-47.

4. The enigmatic flight of the youth has been explained in various ways.

3. *Mark 14.43–15.15: The Arrest and Trial*

motifs echo with apocalyptic overtones.[1] (2) In stark contrast to the flight of the followers the departure of Jesus is a forced procession to judgment and death (14.53a).

Thus, two sequences of action (14.43-47; 14.50-53a) are employed to frame a violent scene of betrayal, seizure and abandonment. A logical coherence connects these two sequences and provides the foundational structure of the scene.

This sustained plot sequence reflects no evidence of an independent existence. Various elements demonstrate the symbiotic connection between 14.43-47 and 14.50-53a and the surrounding context. (1) The identity of Jesus is assumed throughout. (2) The presence of the

---

(1) Numerous scholars, finding no motivation for this account, conclude that Mk 14.51-52 presents a historical recollection from an unnamed follower. Among those who hold this view are B. Weiss, *Das Markusevangelium* (Berlin: Hertz, 1872), pp. 408-409; E. Gould, *The Gospel according to St Mark* (New York: Charles Scribner's Sons, 1896), p. 276; A.E.J. Rawlinson, *St Mark* (London: Methuen, 1925), pp. 215-16; H. Branscomb, *The Gospel of Mark* (London: Hodder & Stoughton, 1937), pp. 270-71; Lohmeyer, *Markus*, pp. 323-24; V. Taylor, *The Gospel according to St Mark* (London: MacMillan, 1959), pp. 561-62; M.-J. Lagrange, *Evangile selon Saint Marc* (Paris: Gabalda, 1974), pp. 396-97; C.E.B. Cranfield, *The Gospel according to St Mark* (Cambridge: Cambridge University Press, 1959), pp. 438-39; P. Carrington, *According to Mark* (Cambridge: Cambridge University Press, 1960), p. 321; E. Haenchen, *Der Weg Jesu* (Berlin: de Gruyter, 1968), p. 502; Schweizer, *Mark*, pp. 316-17. (2) Some take this view further, suggesting that the scene is an autobiographical note by Mark—so Rawlinson, *Mark*, pp. 215-16; Lagrange, *Marc*, pp. 396-97. (3) Others argue that this story—like much of the passion narrative—is built upon Old Testament allusions. Amos 2.16 and Gen. 39.12 are seen as possible sources for this construction. This argument is supported by C.G. Montefiore, *The Synoptic Gospels* (London: MacMillan, 1927), I, pp. 349-50; F.C. Grant, *Interpreter's Bible* (New York: Abingdon Press, 1951), VII, p. 886. (4) R. Scroggs and K. Groff ('Baptism in Mark: Dying and Rising with Christ', *JBL* 92 [1973], pp. 531-48) connect this passage to Mk 16.5 and interpret it in terms of a Christian baptism ritual.

In contrast to the various historical settings reconstructed in these hypotheses, the narrative effect of Mk 14.51-52 is sharp and profound. Mk 14.50 sets forth the flight theme in absolute finality: all fled. While a more stark expression of the flight theme seems impossible, Mk 14.51-52 serves precisely this function. Here the flight theme is intensified through repetition, isolation and embarassment. Further, the final flight of the solitary youth provides a proper and ironic parallel to the departure of Jesus: one flees for safety while the other is led away to die.

1. For the apocalyptic use of flight see Mk 13.14-20; Rev. 6.15-17; *1 En.* 62.10. See also Amos 2.16.

disciples is assumed, but not explicit. (3) No time or place markers are provided. (4) The departure to the high priest (14.53) assumes the arrest scene. Thus, the plotted sequence in 14.43-47 and 14.50-53a displays intrinsic connections to the surrounding environment.[1]

3. A second ideological stream emerges from the pronouncement sequence in 14.48-49. This sequence contains no actions and provides no extension of the plot line. In contrast to the plot function of 14.43-47 and 14.50-53a this pronouncement sequence functions in the realm of characterization.

3.1. Three sayings traditions are united in this segment. The first saying (14.48b) describes the scene of arrest. Repeating the imagery of 14.43, Jesus describes the crowd as a deadly mob with swords and staves.[2] Conversely Jesus is seen by the crowd as a ληστής—as a thief and rebel.[3] Through this bifocal imagery the arrest of Jesus is described as a violent seizure. This description operates against the backdrop of various images from the Old Testament.[4]

3.2. The second saying invokes a separate and quite disparate imagery—the teaching of Jesus in the temple. His teaching by day (καθ' ἡμέραν)[5] insists that the message of Jesus is an open

---

1. The connections between the arrest and the larger passion context are affirmed by R. Bultmann, *The History of the Synoptic Tradition* (trans. J. Marsh; Oxford: Basil Blackwell, 1963 [1921]), p. 279; Taylor, *Mark*, pp. 557-58; J. Gnilka, *Das Evangelium nach Markus* (EKKNT; Zürich: Benziger Verlag, 1979), II, pp. 266-68; Schweizer, *Mark*, pp. 315-19; Pesch, *Markusevangelium*, II, pp. 397-404.

2. Like the μάχαιρα, the ξύλον is an instrument of death. Eusebius, 2, 23, 18, notes that James the Just was struck with a ξύλον. The term is also used of the gallows, and consequently of death on a cross. This use is found in the Old Testament in Gen. 40.19, Deut. 21.23, Josh. 10.26 and Est. 5.14. The New Testament application to the cross largely reflects this Old Testament use. See, for example, Gal. 3.13 (Deut. 21.23); Acts 13.29 (see Josh. 10.27); Acts 5.30; 10.39; 1 Pet. 2.24. This connection between ξύλον and crucifixion seems too remote to impact the arrest scene.

3. The term can mean either a robber or a revolutionary. Josephus, *War* 2.254, connects the term to σικάριος, and the connection is made to Barabbas in Jn 18.40. For wider discussion of the term, see M. Hengel, *The Zealots: Investigations into the Jewish Freedom Movement in the Period from Herod I until 70 AD* (trans. D. Smith; Edinburgh: T. & T. Clark, 1989 [1961]), pp. 24-46, 337-41.

4. See in the LXX Hos. 7.1; Obad. 1.5; Ezek. 22.9ab.

5. The Gospel of Mark narrates only a limited period of temple teaching; thus, the translation 'daily' presents difficulty. More plausible—and more consistent with

3. Mark 14.43–15.15: The Arrest and Trial

demonstration, not a secret revolution.[1] Only the conclusion of the logion with καὶ οὐκ ἐκρατήσατε με (14.49b) links the temple teaching to the arrest scene.

3.3. The third saying provides an elliptical fulfillment formula (14.49c). This broken phrase is enigmatic. What event fulfills the scripture is unclear, and which text is fulfilled is uncertain. Thus, the third logion accents the fact of fulfillment with little attention to its details.[2]

3.4. In this manner Mk 14.48-49 joins three disparate sayings into a focused image. The violent seizure of Jesus by night contrasts his teaching in the temple by day. This pronouncement sequence adds nothing to the plot structure but proves crucial for the characterization of Jesus.

3.5. The pronouncement sequence in 14.48-49 exhibits no intrinsic relation to the two action sequences. The pronouncements are introduced as Jesus' answer (ἀποκριθείς in 14.48), but no question has been posed. The identity of Jesus, which is assumed in 14.43-47 and 14.50-52, is restated in 14.48. The response of Jesus does not address

---

the local emphasis of Mk 14.43-53a—is a translation of 'by day' (so Schweizer, *Mark*, p. 318). In this manner the brief period of Jesus' public temple instruction provides a contrast to the secretive nature of the arrest. Particular emphasis would emerge from the contrast of activity by day and by night.

1. Images of Mal. 3.1 may be echoed here. The narrative antecedent for this saying is found in Mk 12.27-40. The narrative effect of this logion is to contrast the violent and secretive arrest by night with the open teaching of Jesus in the daytime.

2. Within the pronouncement sequence the fulfillment formula relates only vaguely to the arrest. The connection to various Old Testament passages remains general (see perhaps Pss. 37.14; 71.11; Jer. 26.8; 37.13-15). In my opinion the fulfillment formula has become ambiguous only through its subsequent use in the arrest scene. In its present form the reader struggles to find the fulfillment in the preceding events of the arrest. More likely the fulfillment formula first related to the fleeing of the followers. This pattern is already present in Mk 14.27-28, where the predicted abandonment fulfills Zech. 13.7. Likely the fleeing of Mk 14.50-52 invites the reference to Mk 14.27-28 and occasions the fulfillment formula. This formula is prospective in function, introducing Mk 14.50-52 as the fulfillment of Mk 14.27 and Zech. 13.7. One line of the textual tradition ([N] W [Θ f^{13} 565 *al* aur c l vg] sy$^{(s)}$) supports this focus by emphasizing that it was disciples who fled and by connecting their flight directly to the fulfillment formula with τότε. Thus, the third saying likely related first to the flight of the disciples in fulfillment of Mk 14.27 and Zech. 13.7. The embedding of the pronouncement sequence in the arrest scene creates a retrospective focus on the arrest and renders the fulfillment formula ambiguous.

the betrayal by Judas, the striking of the servant or the presence of the authorities. Similarly the abandonment by his followers (14.50-52) is not presupposed in the sayings. The pronouncements in 14.48-49 thus sustain a distinct narrative stream of thought and imagery.[1]

4. Thus, Mk 14.43-53a is constituted around a two-part action sequence (14.43-47, 50-53a) which seems foundational. This sequence sustains a distinct narrative stream focused on the violent betrayal, seizure and abandonment of Jesus. A second, somewhat intrusive stream emerges from the pronouncement sequence of 14.48-49. Three unconnected logia are focused around the arrest of Jesus and function in the service of characterization. Syntactical analysis will show how the interplay of these morpological components generates an important scene and a vital narrative image of Jesus.

Narrative Syntax. The syntactical interaction of these elements generates a dynamic narrative effect. This narrative pattern advances the plotting of the passion story and sustains a vital prophetic Christology. This syntactical process operates upon Mk 14.43-53a in a variety of ways.

1. A process of representation is at work in this passage. The introduction of Judas as 'one of the Twelve' (14.3) casts his actions over against the larger group of apostles. The crowd is sent from the chief priests, scribes, elders, and it acts in behalf of the religious leaders (14.43).[2] The option of violent resistance is represented by a solitary bystander (14.47). The abandonment by the followers is embodied in the naked flight of the youth (14.51-52). Thus, various actants function in the story as representatives of larger groups and embody different responses to Jesus.

2. The action sequence (14.43-47, 50-53a) which sustains the frame and plot of this account produces a prophetic focus. (1) The story

---

1. Likely this sayings collection has a point of origin in distinction from the plot frame of 14.43-47, 50-53a. The separate origin of the sayings sequence is supported in various forms by E. Linnemann, *Studien zur Passionsgeschichte* (Göttingen: Vandenhoeck & Ruprecht, 1970), pp. 41-69. The three distinct emphases of the logia—arrest, teaching, fulfillment of Scripture—suggest the sayings circulated independent of each other. Likely the arrest scene in 14.43-47, 50-53a provides the first occasion for the merger of these disparate sayings into a pronouncement sequence.

2. Schweizer, *Mark*, p. 318, notes that the reproach of Jesus is more properly addressed to the absent leaders than to those who carry out their orders.

3. Mark 14.43–15.15: The Arrest and Trial

opens in the midst of Jesus' instructions ('while speaking'). The arrest scene is thus framed around the image of Jesus as teacher. (2) The coming of Judas in 14.43 provides immediate fulfillment of the prediction in 14.42. This fulfillment is confirmed through the identification of Judas as ὁ παραδιδούς (14.42, 44; see also 14.18, 21). (3) The exact listing of the religious authorities takes up the prophecy of 8.31. (4) The address of Jesus as rabbi recalls his activity as teacher and prophet. (5) The flight of Jesus' followers fulfills the prophecy of 14.27 and the words of Zech. 13.7. (6) The naked flight of the youth echoes the prophecy of Amos 2.16. (7) The departure of Jesus in 14.53a fulfills the ὑπάγω prophecy of 14.21. (8) The abandonment of the prophet reflects an Old Testament pattern.[1] The action sequence of Mk 14.43-47, 50-53a thus provides plotted fulfillment of various prophetic images, allusions, predictions. Consequently the action sequence characterizes Jesus as the end of a long line of prophets who suffer violence at the hands of the people.[2]

3. The sayings sequence (14.48-49) focuses the prophetic Christology from a different perspective. (1) The numbering of Jesus among the thieves echoes an Old Testament image (Isa. 53.12). (2) The teaching ministry of Jesus is recalled. Significantly, the emphasis on the temple correlates to the hostility of the religious authorities. This saying may also invoke the images of Mal. 3.1. In particular, the model of Jeremiah may be invoked: following his temple sermon (Jer. 7.1-15) the prophet is arrested (Jer. 26.8-9). (3) The fulfillment formula ties Jesus' words explicitly to the prophetic image. The arrest of Jesus is narrated as a part of this prophetic line, as Jesus had predicted in Mk 14.21. The proverb of Mk 6.4 may also be echoed in this scene: a prophet is not without honor except among his own people. Thus, the sayings collection of Mk 14.48-49 invokes a host of scattered allusions and images to focus the role of Jesus as the rejected prophet of God.

4. This complex morphological frame and the accompanying syntactical interplay produce a vital, pre-trial judgment upon the identity and the destiny of Jesus. Three disparate sayings collaborate

---

1. See, for example, Exod. 16.2-3; Num. 12.1-8; 1 Kgs 19.10, 14; Jer. 26.8.
2. This prophetic image fulfills the parable of Mk 12.1-12. On the violent destiny of the prophets, see O.H. Steck, *Israel und das gewaltsame Geschick der Propheten: Untersuchungen zur Überlieferung des deuteronomistischen Geschichtsbildes im Alten Testament, Spätjudentums und Urchristentum* (Neukirchen–Vluyn: Neukirchener Verlag, 1967).

in a pronouncement sequence which focuses Jesus' prophetic identity. This sayings collection is embedded within a plotted sequence of betrayal, seizure, abandonment. This action sequence provides the plotted fulfillment of Jesus' prophetic identity. Thus, Mk 14.43-53a is formed by two narrative streams which circulate and merge into a vital narrative Christology: Jesus is the rejected prophet of God.

The Passion Context. This vivid scene in Mk 14.43-53a interacts in important ways with other parts of the passion story. Various elements predicted and foreshadowed in earlier scenes come to pass in this account. The hostile ambitions of the religious leaders (14.1-2, 11) are realized here (14.43, 46, 53a). The predicted betrayal by one of the Twelve (14.10, 20) comes to pass (14.43). The quest for an opportune time (14.10) is realized (14.44). The predicted failure of the disciples (14.27, 29, 31) occurs in this story (14.50-52). Thus, various plot expectations set forth in Mk 14.1-42 are realized in the scene of betrayal, arrest and abandonment.

In addition, Mk 14.43-53a sets in motion the events which lead to Jesus' death. The scene of betrayal, arrest and abandonment puts in place the plot elements necessary for the trial and crucifixion which follow (14.53–15.37). Mk 14.43-53a thus provides an important link in the larger plot line of the passion story.

Most significantly, Mk 14.43-53a interacts with the larger passion focus on Jesus as the rejected teacher and prophet. Various prophecies of Jesus are fulfilled in this story: he is betrayed by one of the Twelve (14.20, 43) and abandoned by all (14.27, 50-52). The prophecies of the Old Testament are fulfilled in his words (14.21, 27, 49). Mk 14.43-53a thus interacts with the passion context to create a number of internal prolepses—predictions which are realized within the narrative. This close linkage of prophecy and fulfillment takes up and enhances a central christological image: Jesus is the true teacher, the reliable prophet of God.

Mk 14.43-53a also picks up the careful linkage of this prophetic image to the passion Christology. Through the images of betrayal, abandoment and death which pervade this scene the passion Christology is brought into this account and linked closely to the image of Jesus as teacher and prophet. The rabbi is handed over by one of his disciples; the teacher is rejected by religious leaders and abandoned by his followers. The fulfillment of his words leads to his

3. *Mark 14.43–15.15: The Arrest and Trial*

death. Thus, Mk 14.43-53a interacts with the larger passion story to amplify the portrait of Jesus as the true teacher and prophet of God, rejected and abandoned by the people.

The Gospel Context. The images of Mk 14.43-53a prove even more significant within the larger Gospel context. Various degrees of linkage are established between this scene and earlier stories. These connections provide reciprocal lines of interpretation between the story of Jesus' life and the story of his death.

1. Numerous narrative images developed in the wider narrative are taken up in the scene of betrayal, arrest and abandonment. The consistent but fruitless plotting of the religious authorities (Mk 3.6; 11.27-28; 12.12-13; 14.1-2, 10-11) is successful at last. The continuing theme of discipleship failure (4.13, 40-41; 5.30-32; 6.35-37, 49-52; 8.4, 27-30, 31-33; 9.6, 9-10, 11-13, 14-28, 30-32, 33-37, 38-41; 10.23-27, 32, 35-45; 14.10-11, 27-31, 32-42, 45, 50-52) reaches its zenith when all abandon Jesus. The image of Jesus as prophet is authenticated in the fulfillment of his words. The extensive focus on Jesus' fulfillment of Scripture (1.2-3; 4.12; 7.6-7; 8.18; 9.11-13; 11.9-10, 17; 12.10-11, 36; 14.27, 34) reaches a high point in Mk 14.49. The threefold prophecy of Jesus' passion (8.31; 9.31; 10.32-34) begins to unfold. The extensive focus on passion Christology becomes a concrete event. Thus, Mk 14.43-53a interacts with general themes and images developed in the wider Gospel narrative.

2. Beyond this, specific passages from Jesus' ministry shed new light on Mk 14.43-53a. This pattern of interconnection sustains the interpretive link between Jesus' life and his death.

2.1. Various images link the betrayal and arrest to the temple scene in Mk 11.15-19. (1) Both stories occur in the area of Jerusalem. (2) The Twelve are important in both accounts (11.11; 14.43). (3) Both stories employ night and darkness as metaphors (11.11, 19; 14.17). (4) The teaching of Jesus in the temple is central to both accounts (11.15-18; 14.49). (5) This teaching fulfills the Old Testament (11.17; 14.49). (6) Religious leaders play a hostile role in both stories (11.18; 14.43). (7) The crowd is present in both scenes (11.18; 14.43). (8) Both stories employ the image of a thief (λῃστής in 11.17; 14.48).

These extensive narrative links encourage the reader to interpret the temple scene and the betrayal scene in relationship to one another. This relationship clarifies various elements in Mk 14.43-53a. Jesus is arrested because he has stirred the anger of the religious authorities. The teaching of Jesus is the cause of this anger. In particular, the implications of his message infuriate the religious authorities. Jesus' teaching in the temple offers an alternative to the traditional authority of the religious leaders (11.28). Jesus implies that in his words he takes up the mantle of the Old Testament prophets and fulfills the Scriptures. At the same time the words of Jesus offer critique and condemnation of the religious authorities. Like the corrupt leaders of old (Jer. 7.11) they have made the house of God into a den of thieves. It is this authoritative, prophetic teaching of Jesus which amazes the crowds and inspires the anger of the religious authorities (11.18).

Thus, the scene in Mk 14.43-53a is clarified by the images of Mark 11. The one who implies that the temple is in the hands of thieves (11.17) is handed over as a thief in the night (14.48). His teaching and his prophecy imply an identity and a mission which threatens the traditions and power of the religious structures of Israel. The religious authorities understand this threat and act quickly to end it. Readers of the Gospel are encouraged to see what the religious authorities see. The christological claim which emerges is precise: in his words and in his deeds, Jesus has claimed to be the true prophet of God sent to the people of Israel.

At the same time Mk 14.43-53a completes the images of the temple scene. Prophetic Christology in 11.15-19 has its culmination in the passion Christology. Jesus' prophetic words and deeds provide the charge for his death (14.58; 15.29). Thus, the narrative linkage of these two accounts provides a vital understanding of Jesus' destiny: he will die as the rejected prophet.

2.2. This decisive link between the teaching/prophecy of Jesus and his death is reinforced by Mk 12.1-12. Numerous images link this parable to the arrest scene. (1) The image of Jesus the teacher is central to both stories (12.1; 14.43, 45, 49). (2) Clear symbols of Israel are employed in both scenes—the vineyard (12.1) and the temple (14.49). (3) The hostility of the religious leaders lies behind both stories (12.12; 14.43). (4) Both accounts make reference to the Old Testament or its images. (5) The rejection of God's messenger stands at the center of both scenes.

As a consequence the parable in Mk 12.1-12 reinforces the arrest scene. Jesus is the final prophet sent with the message of God. The keepers of the vineyard and the temple have rejected that message, and

3. *Mark 14.43–15.15: The Arrest and Trial*

they will kill the messenger. This rejected prophet is the Beloved Son (12.6). Those who put him to death will face the judgment of God (12.9).

In this way Mk 11.15-19 and 12.1-12 provide depth and texture for the images of the betrayal scene. The death of Jesus is tied precisely to his prophetic activity and the hostility which it produces. The linkage of these three scenes defines and reinforces this christological image in a way that no one of the stories could do alone. The Gospel of Mark thus entwines these accounts in a crucial narrative relationship to generate a distinct image of Jesus: he is the prophet of God rejected and killed by his own people.

2.3. This linkage of Jesus' activity as teacher/prophet to his death is reinforced in other passages. The extended activity in Mk 11.27–12.44 joins the teaching ministry of Jesus to his death. This teaching activity occurs in Jerusalem in the temple (11.27) and is directed to the chief priests, scribes and elders (11.27; 14.43). The first question concerns the authority behind Jesus' prophetic words and deeds (11.28). Subsequently the question of authority is addressed to various religous groups—chief priests, scribes, elders (11.27), Pharisees and Herodians (12.13), Sadducees (12.18), scribes (12.28). In this manner Mk 11.27–12.44 gives unusual focus to the content of Jesus' teaching and precisely defines his audience: Jesus sets forth the authority of his teaching before the religious leaders of Israel. At the end of this dialogue the religious authorities are silent (12.34). Mk 12.35-37 provides a definitive summary to this activity. Jesus teaches in the temple (12.35), and his words fulfill the Old Testament (12.36). Beyond this, his teaching implies a decisive claim: the messiah is not only David's son, but also David's Lord. Those who listen to the Holy Spirit should know this (11.36). The messiah is Lord over David's line, over David's tradition, over David's temple.

2.4. Thus, the larger narrative system develops carefully and consistently the link between the prophetic teaching of Jesus and his death. This image provides the key to the arrest scene of Mk 14.43-53a. Through this process the hostility of the religious leaders and the grounds for Jesus' arrest are made clear, and the question of mission and identity is focused with inescapable clarity. Jesus teaches and acts with authority (1.22) as one sent from God. He has taken upon himself the image and the task of God's final messenger. He will die as the rejected prophet of God.

3. Against this larger interpretive context the images of Mk 14.43-53a become haunting and ironic. When Judas identifies Jesus as 'Rabbi' and betrays him, the irony is overwhelming. Jesus is indeed the true teacher and prophet from God, and he will die for the people. Jesus is arrested as a thief in darkness; in reality he is the messenger of God teaching by day in the temple and fulfilling the words of the Old Testament. The one rejected and killed 'in truth teaches the way of God' (12.14). Thus, the concise images of Mk 14.43-53a are completed through the commentary of Mk 11.15-19, 12.1-12 and 12.13-14. This interconnected sequence sustains a narrative effect which far exceeds the isolated effect of 14.43-53a. Operating within the larger world of the narrative the simple arrest scene moves outward into images of increasing complexity and intensity. A stark portrait of Jesus emerges: he is the messiah, the Beloved Son of God. Jesus is the final prophet from God, rejected and killed by his people.

Comparative Analysis
The betrayal scene appears in various other narrative settings. These alternate accounts provide a comparative literary base against which to view the operation of Mk 14.43-53a.[1]

Pre-Markan Contexts. Various scholars attempt to reconstruct the form and function of the arrest scene prior to its use in the Gospel of Mark. The existence of this story as an independent unit is doubtful. Nonetheless some have argued for such a stage.[2] As an independent account the betrayal scene would have little frame of reference, and its function would be limited.

A more likely reconstruction sees the betrayal story as an integral part of the earliest passion tradition.[3] Within this context the betrayal

---

1. As noted in Chapter 1, diachronic analysis will be used to provide a phenomenological description rather than historical reconstruction.
2. Linnemann (*Studien zur Passionsgeschichte*, pp. 41-69) concludes that the story has joined three independent pieces of tradition. (1) A collection of biographical apophthegms has been used in Mk 14.43, 48, 49b. (2) A narrative of the betrayal by Judas can be seen in Mk 14.44-46. (3) Fragments from a narrative which explains the role of the disciples in the passion appear in Mk 14.47, 50-52.
3. See Bultmann, *History*, p. 279; Taylor, *Mark*, pp. 557-58; Gnilka, *Markus*, II, pp. 266-68; Schweizer, *Mark*, pp. 315-19; Pesch, *Markusevangelium*, II, pp. 397-404.

scene would provide direct fulfillment of the predictions in Mk 14.27-31. As he predicted, Jesus is arrested and his disciples flee. At the same time this unit initiates the trial and crucifixion scenes. While this account would serve a vital role in the story of Jesus' death, its referential value would be limited to the framework of the passion tradition.

The Gospel of Matthew. The form and function of the betrayal story in Mt. 26.47-57a is similar to that of Mk 14.43-53a. Matthew also places the account between the Gethsemane scene and the first trial of Jesus. Matthew omits the scribes from the list of religious authorities and omits Judas's request to lead Jesus away without harm (Mk 14.44). A response from Jesus is added in Mt. 26.50: 'Friend, why are you here?' A distinct sayings tradition is inserted in Mt. 26.52-54. Following the violence against the servant of the high priest, Jesus commands that the sword be put away. Two further sayings explain this command. The first explanation is an ethical standard: one who lives by the sword will die by it (Mt. 26.52). The second saying provides a theological interpretation of the arrest: God is able to stop this process, but this event is predestined as the fulfillment of Scripture (Mt. 26.53-54). Thus, a sequence of sayings traditions now reinterpret the focus of this scene. Following this a saying about Jesus as the temple teacher arrested as a thief is employed (Mk 14.48-49 = Mt. 26.55-56a). Mt. 26.56b reduces the flight of the disciples to a single statement and omits the account of the naked flight.

Thus, Mt. 26.47-57a takes over the basic form and function of the betrayal scene in the Gospel of Mark. Typical Matthaean changes in style and focus may be seen. A decisive new focus emerges through the added sayings traditions. A stark critique of violence is issued by Jesus (Mt. 26.52). Further, the arrest and its consequences are seen as events which God allows in fulfillment of the Old Testament. Thus, the scene now operates in a different narrative context and carries a distinct shape and function.

The Gospel of Luke. Lk. 22.47-54a employs the betrayal scene in a differing form. The explanation about the crowd and the arrangement of the signal is missing. The focus falls instead on the actions of Judas. Jesus responds to Judas with a question: 'Judas, would you betray the Son of Man with a kiss?' (Lk. 22.48). The insertion of dialogue continues when one asks permission to use the sword (Lk. 22.49). Lk. 22.50 explains that it was the right ear that was severed. The reply of Jesus is added in Lk. 22.51: 'No more of this'. A description of the crowd is provided in Lk. 22.52; among them are chief priests, temple officers and elders. The temple activity of Jesus is described, but the mention of teaching is absent (Lk. 22.52b-53). The focus on the fulfillment of Scripture is missing; it is replaced by a different logion which employs two distinct metaphors. Jesus' arrest marks the coming of their hour and the rising power of darkness (Lk. 22.53b).

While Lk. 22.47-54a places the betrayal scene in a similar context between Gethsemane and the first trial, this account of the story is unique. Direct mention of Jesus' teaching activity is omitted. In its place the extended use of logia focuses the teaching role of Jesus. Various details have been added to the story, and several elements and images have been clarified or emphasized. The story now operates in essentially the same manner as Mk 14.43-53a, but with a Lukan focus.

The Gospel of John. Jn 18.2-12 employs the betrayal scene to advance a different image of Jesus. Judas comes with soldiers and officers from the chief priests and the Pharisees (Jn 18.3). Jesus is in charge throughout this scene. He knows beforehand all that is to occur (Jn 18.4). He questions the crowd (Jn 18.4, 7), and they draw back at his words (Jn 18.6). Ultimately Jesus issues a command to the crowd: 'If you seek me, let these ones go' (Jn 18.8). At the center of the story are two christological signals: Jesus answers twice with the theologically rooted ἐγώ εἰμι (Jn 18.5, 8). Jesus' commands fulfill the word about losing none of his followers (Jn 18.9). Extensive detail is added to the incident with the sword: Peter bears the sword and Malchus receives the blow (Jn 18.10). No concern for the healing of the servant is mentioned. The command to put up the sword relates instead to the destiny of Jesus: he is to drink this cup because it is from the Father (Jn 18.11). The arrest of Jesus is reduced to a single verse (Jn 18.12).

Thus, the Gospel of John has taken the betrayal and arrest and wrapped it in the images of Johannine thought. Jesus is the one sent from the Father who is obedient in all matters. Jesus understands all things, and he is in control of his destiny to the end. The crowds are under the command and control of Jesus. They are able to take him only because he has chosen this way. Even as Jesus goes he makes

3. Mark 14.43–15.15: The Arrest and Trial

provision for his own. Jn 18.2-12 thus employs the arrest scene to highlight the Johannine portrait of Jesus as he draws near to his death.

The saying on teaching in the temple has been woven into the trial scene in Jn 18.20. Here Jesus bears witness to the Jewish authorities that his ministry was done openly in their synagogues and in the temple. This logion now becomes a part of a Johannine witness to the light which Jesus brings to the world.

Summary

The story of Jesus' arrest and betrayal was shown to operate in various narrative settings. As an independent unit this story would convey biographical images and details of Jesus and his followers. As part of a pre-Markan passion account the story would fulfill the earlier predictions of Jesus and would set in motion the events of his death. The Gospel of Matthew takes over the basic form and function of this account, but reshapes it in various ways. In similar fashion the Gospel of Luke sets the narrative within a Lukan framework. More significantly, the Gospel of John employs the story to create a sharp christological focus. The central action of the story is reduced to a single verse, but various images and metaphors are highlighted. As a result a distinctly Johannine image of Jesus emerges.

Over against these comparative settings and performances, the arrest story in Mk 14.43-53a is unique. Various elements of the plot line are advanced in this account. Most significantly, this story sets in motion the events which lead to Jesus' death. Beyond this plot function the story provides a crucial characterization of Jesus. Central to this image is the portrait of Jesus as teacher and prophet. Two contrasting lines of interpretation emerge around this prophetic Christology. The narrative argues carefully that Jesus is the true prophet sent from God: his predictions come to pass; his teaching in the temple provides an open witness; his words fulfill the Old Testament. Another line of interpretation sees Jesus as a false prophet who is worthy of death; thus, religious authorities come by night to seize him. Through these lines Mk 14.43-53a creates a sharp portrait: Jesus is the rejected teacher and prophet.

The local image focused in Mk 14.43-53a interacts in important ways with other elements of the passion story. Various predictions from the passion story are fulfilled in this account, and the image of Jesus as prophet is heightened. In particular, the link between prophetic Christology and passion Christology is strengthened. The passion context declares that the prophet of God will be rejected and he will die.

Most significantly, the image of Jesus focused in Mk 14.43-53a participates in a vital dialogue with the larger Gospel context. This dialogue produces extensive intratextual connections and sustains vital lines of reciprocal interpretation. The wider tradition of Jesus' prophetic words and deeds is linked directly to his death. His teaching ministry is shown as the catalyst for the anger of the religious authorities. His words draw upon the Old Testament and provide a sharp critique of the religious leaders of Israel. The story of Jesus' death is linked in a vital way to the events of his life. Drawing upon the full depth of his ministry, Mk 14.43-53a provides—on the eve of the passion—a profound study in characterization. Jesus is the true, authentic prophet of God. Consequently he will suffer and die at the hands of his own people.

Mark 14.53-65: The First Trial

Mk 14.53-65 narrates the first trial scene. This account culminates the earlier movements of the passion story and provides the foundation for the crucifixion of Jesus.

Synchronic Analysis

The motifs of Mk 14.53-65 may be plotted in the following manner:

Introduction
- Jesus comes — 14.53a
- Leaders come — 14.53b
- Peter comes — 14.54

Body
- Leaders seek — 14.55
- Witnesses testify — 14.56
- Witnesses testify — 14.57-59
- Chief priest questions — 14.60
- Jesus is silent (passive) — 14.61a
- Chief priest questions — 14.61b
- Jesus answers — 14.62
- Chief priest judges — 14.63-64a
- All judge — 14.64b
- Some torture — 14.65

Conclusion
—

3. *Mark 14.43–15.15: The Arrest and Trial*

Narrative Morphology. The introduction of the unit is relatively extensive. The movement of Jesus by force opens the scene and links the story to the arrest. Further movement brings the religious leaders together. A final transition brings Peter into the story. The introduction of Peter is distinct, for he plays no role in the trial scene. Instead, this strategy sets the stage for the following scene in which Peter denies Jesus. This maneuver links the two accounts in a reciprocal relationship. Thus, the introduction in Mk 14.53-54 brings the major actors onto the stage and joins Peter's denial to the trial of Jesus.

The body of the story narrates the trial scene. Central to this account are the false witnesses, the questioning and judgment by the chief priest, the responses by Jesus, the pronouncement of judgment and the scene of torture.

The typical conclusion is missing, with no movement or transition made to the following scene. Instead, the mention of Peter in the introduction is recalled and developed into a related scene. This unusual form creates an interpretive link between the trial of Jesus and the denial by Peter.

Morphologically Mk 14.53-65 is built around a singular line of plotted action (14.53-59, 63-65) and a concentrated dialogue sequence (14.60-62). This formal arrangement sustains the structure and outlook of this scene.

1. The extended line of action (14.53-59, 63-65) is built around a simple plot frame. This basic structure has been filled out and extended through various elements.

1.1. The basic content of this scene is provided in a few strokes. (1) Jesus is led to the high priest (14.53a). (2) The Sanhedrin seeks testimony to support a death sentence (14.55a).[1] (3) The verdict is given (14.64). (4) Jesus is abused (14.65d).

1.2. This basic account has been filled out through various details and images. The gathering of the Sanhedrin (14.53b), the failure to find a charge (14.55b-56), the temple charge (14.57-59),[2] the high

---

1. On the power of the Sanhedrin to pronounce a death sentence, see the discussion by Gnilka, *Markus*, II, pp. 284-86; P. Winter, 'The Trial of Jesus and the Competence of the Sanhedrin', *NTS* 10 (1963–64), pp. 494-99. See also E. Dabrowski, 'The Trial of Jesus in Recent Research', *SE* 1 (1968), pp. 21-27.

2. On the history of the temple charge, see Schweizer, *Mark*, pp. 329-30; Gnilka, *Markus*, II, p. 276. Gnilka sees here an apocalyptic theme introduced into

priest's outburst (14.63), and the details of the abuse (14.65abc) extend the basic story into a detailed and nuanced account.

1.3. Most significantly, the narrator's intrusion in 14.54 creates a distinct narrative focus.[1] This comment invokes a new cast of characters (Peter and the servants, ὑπηρέται) and a new setting (the fire [literally φῶς, the light] outside in the courtyard). The intrusive comment in 14.54 breaks the flow of the story to generate a new ideological line, yet this new impetus remains undeveloped at this point. Neither the broken flight, the distance from Jesus nor the fellowship with the ὑπηρέται who abuse Jesus (14.65) is given clear narrative significance in this context.

1.4. The result is a strong narrative line marked by condemnation and abuse. The narrative roots this oppression precisely in the theological zeal of Israel's leaders (14.53, 55, 60). The resulting charge—blasphemy—echoes this orientation, as do the rending of the garment and the death penalty (14.63-64). This imagery is enforced linguistically throught the multiple use of κατά: ἐξήτουν κατά (14.55); κατ' αὐτοῦ (14.56, 57); καταλύσω (14.58); κατέκριναν (14.64). Consequently the language and imagery of the action line produces a clear portrait: Jesus is condemned and abused at the hands of religious authorities.

2. A dialogical cluster (14.60-62) is woven into this action sequence. This conversation makes a vital contribution to the configuration of the scene.

Formally the sayings material is built around two question/answer cycles.[2] The first cycle (14.60-61a) focuses the high priest as Jesus' interlocutor. The initial query is general and ambiguous, and it evokes no response from Jesus.[3] In contrast the second cycle (14.61b-62) is

the passion story prior to Mark's redaction. See also Pesch, *Markusevangelium*, II, pp. 433-35.

1. Almost all interpeters see 14.54 as Markan framing of the trial of Jesus with Peter's denial (14.54, 66-72). Significantly, the Gospel of John employs a similar intercalation (Jn 18.15-27). On the role of intercalations in the plotting of the Gospel of Mark, see G.A. Wright, 'Markan Intercalations: A Study in the Plot of a Gospel' (unpublished PhD dissertation, The Southern Baptist Theological Seminary, 1985).

2. This doublet is also present in 15.2-4, suggesting a related pattern of framing for 14.53-56 and 15.1-15.

3. The silence theme is predominant in Mk 15.1-15. In contrast, 14.62 reverses this theme with a dramatic confession by Jesus. It is possible that consistent silence represents the authentic response of Jesus, but the silence may also be a secondary

3. Mark 14.43–15.15: The Arrest and Trial

specific and evokes a dramatic response. The focus of the query shifts from the question of Jesus' deeds to the question of his identity. The blunt inquiry by the high priest is met by two stark pronouncements. The ἐγώ εἰμι answer provides a radical affirmation of the titles used by the high priest. This claim is extended in a Son of Man saying based on Dan. 7.13 and Ps. 110.1. While the first question/answer cycle serves a preparatory role, the verbal cluster climaxes in the stark pronouncements of 14.62.

3. This verbal sequence (14.60-62) cannot be separated from the context of the trial. The presence of the high priest and the focus of his first query presume the search for condemning testimony. In a similar manner the response of the priests in 14.63 presumes a confession in the order of 14.62. Thus, the basic line of this account resists further reduction.

4. Only the intrusive comment in 14.54 is separable. The situation of Peter plays no role in this scene. Two tenuous linguistic connections tie Peter's situation loosely to this account. (1) The central role of the chief priest (14.53, 55, 60, 61, 63) is echoed in the location of 14.54 in the courtyard of the high priest. (2) Peter sits together and warms himself with the ὑπηρέται. Subsequently Jesus is abused by the ὑπηρέται (14.65). While this insertion creates a different focus, no distinct segment or episode is developed at this point.

5. Thus, Mk 14.53-65 constitutes a single episode with two distinct foci. A basic frame (14.53a, 55a, 64, 65d) is developed into an extensive sequence of plotted action (14.53-59, 63-65). This action sequence focuses the condemnation of Jesus at the hands of religious authorities. Woven into this sequence and serving as its summit is a dialogical sequence (14.60-62) which focuses the identity of Jesus. At the level of the narrative the two lines are interwoven into a singular, non-reducible episode. The intrusive focus on Peter has been joined to this scene to prepare for the following sequence in 14.66-72.

6. This morphological configuration has been explained in diverse ways. This account is described as a secondary construction by various scholars.[1] A second theory argues that two independent accounts have

---

influence from the Old Testament—see, for example, Isa. 53.7. The significant but contrasting role of the silence in the two trials suggests a related pattern of framing for these two scenes.

1. The theory of a secondary construction has three basic forms. (1) For some

been joined in 14.53-65.[1] A third line of research argues for a basic account which has been filled out through *traditionsgeschichtliche* development.[2]

scholars Mark is responsible for this account. Among those who support this view are P. Winter, 'Mark 14, 53b.55-64 ein Gebilde des Evangelisten', *ZNW* 53 (1962), pp. 260-63; S. Schulz, *Die Stunde der Botschaft: Einführung in die Theologie der vier Evangelisten* (Hamburg: Furche Verlag, 1967), pp. 131-34; J. Donahue, 'Temple, Trial, and Royal Christology (Mark 14.53-65)', in W. Kelber (ed.), *The Passion in Mark: Studies in Mark 14–16* (Philadelphia: Fortress Press, 1976), pp. 61-79. Noting the historical problems involved, Donahue concludes that 'the Mkan narrative of Jesus before the Sanhedrin must be bypassed as a primary source for historical reconstruction' (p. 62). Donahue finds the purpose of Mark's construction in another direction: 'Mk has constructed the trial narrative in such a way that it embodies major theological concerns of his Gospel. The trial itself is considered an entree to Mk's theology' (p. 62).

(2) Other scholars argue that an earlier narrative layer shapes the construction of this account. This position is articulated by F. Hahn, *The Titles of Jesus in Christology: Their History in Early Christianity* (London: Lutterworth Press, 1969 [1963]), p. 173.

(3) Others believe that particular elements have been expanded into a secondary account. Dibelius (*Tradition*, pp. 182-83, 192-93) argued that this account grew out of the temple charge in 14.58 and that the addition of the confession in 14.62 brought this scene into the passion story. Others argue that the report in 15.1 has been expanded into a full account in 14.53-65. Among these are Bultmann (*History*, pp. 269-70) and A. Klostermann (*Das Markus-Evangelium nach seinem Quellenwert für die evangelische Geschichte* [Göttingen, 1867], p. 155).

1. Linnemann, *Studien*, pp. 109-35, finds one pericope (14.57, 58, 61b, 60b, 61a) modeled on Mk 15.1-15 and focused on the image of Jesus' silent suffering. A second pericope (14.55, 56, 60a, 61c, 62, 63, 64) focuses the messianic claim. In a similar process, Schenk (*Passionsbericht*, pp. 229-43) separates a layer marked by historical presents (14.53b, 55, 56, 61b, 62a, 63, 64; 15.1b) and an apocalyptic-gnostic stream (14.53a, 57, 58, 60, 61a, 65b; 15.1b). In my opinion such detailed reconstruction is excessive and oversteps the limits both of the historical sources and the methodological approach.

2. Among these are Gnilka, *Markus*, pp. 274-95; G. Schneider, 'Jesus vor dem Sanhedrium', *BL* 11 (1970), pp. 1-15; *idem*, 'Gab es eine vorsynoptische Szene "Jesus vor dem Sanhedrium"?', *NovT* 12 (1970), pp. 22-39; *idem*, *Die Passion Jesu nach den drei älteren Evangelien* (Munich: Kösel, 1973), pp. 55-64, argues for a pre-Markan tradition which parallels Luke's trial scene. Schenke (*Der gekreuzigte Christus*, pp. 26-46) argues that Mk 14.53a, 55-56, 60-61, 63-65 formed an original scene to which Mark added 14.53b, 57-59, 62. Dormeyer (*Verhaltensmodell*, pp. 149-50, 157-74, 288-90) sees remains of a primitive martyr story (14.55) at the base of this scene. This core has been expanded by a

3. Mark 14.43–15.15: The Arrest and Trial

While diverse elements participate in this account and suggest separate lines of origin, these elements have been woven together in a manner that resists reduction. With the exception of 14.54, the removal of single elements tends to destroy the coherence of this scene. Mk 14.62 provides a clear example. While this confession appears to represent a distinct, separable interest,[1] the removal of 14.62 in its entirety dissolves the story.[2] Mk 14.62 already presumes the question of 14.61, and the response of 14.63-64 is senseless apart from some dramatic confession on Jesus' part. Thus, the text bears two contrasting traits: it appears to be a collaboration of separate incidents and elements, yet these elements are joined in a compositional line which resists partition. Thus, evolutionary or artificial patterns of composition prove difficult to demonstrate.

At the same time the scene in Mk 14.53-65 presents a host of historical problems.[3] In addition, the trial scene reflects extensive

---

christological redaction (14.56, 61b, 62a, 63, 64, 65b) and by a final redaction which poses Jesus as a model for conduct (14.53b, 57-61a, 62ab, 65ac). In my opinion Mk 14.55 provides an insufficient core to demonstrate the influence of an Acts of the Martyrs genre.

1. N. Perrin ('Mark 14.62: The End Product of a Christian Pesher Tradition?', in *A Modern Pilgrimage in New Testament Christology* [Philadelphia: Fortress Press, 1974], pp. 10-22) argues that Mk 14.62 is an independent product formed from two streams of pesher tradition. In a similar manner Schweizer (*Mark*, pp. 329-30) implies a distinct path for the temple charge of 14.58. Dibelius (*Tradition*, pp. 182-83) argued for a separable role for the temple charge. Various other elements have been viewed as separable.

2. Perrin maintains the continuity by retaining the ἐγώ εἰμι answer as an original part of the story.

3. See E. Lohse, 'συνέδριον', *TDNT*, VII, pp. 867-68; J. Blinzler, *The Trial of Jesus* (trans. I. McHugh and F. McHugh; Westminster, MD: Newman, 1959), pp. 149-63; Donahue, 'Temple, Trial, and Royal Christology', pp. 61-62.

Numerous discrepancies exist between this account and rabbinic trial regulations. (1) The night trial (Mk 14.53; 15.1) violates the command that capital trials be held by day (*m. Sanh.* 4.1). (2) Legal procedures were banned on sabbaths and feast days (*m. Sanh.* 4.1; Mk 14.1, 12). (3) The death sentence was not to be pronounced on the same day as the trial (*m. Sanh.* 4.1; Mk 14.64). (4) The blasphemy charge concerned pronouncement of the divine name (*m. Sanh.* 7.5; Mk 14.62). (5) Trials were usually held in official chambers rather than the high priest's residence (*m. Sanh.* 11.2; Mk 14.56-59). (6) The manner of Jesus' death is Roman in both the charge (claim to kingship) and the mode of execution (crucifixion).

These discrepancies have been countered from two directions. (1) Historicity has interest in and correlation to Old Testament images.[1] Beyond this, various scholars find here an account guided more by (Markan) theological concerns than by historical interests.[2] Consequently historical, theological and compositional factors combine to suggest that Mk 14.53-65 has been intentionally constructed to form a coherent theological complex echoing Old Testament themes.

One possible model for the composition of the trial in Mk 14.53-65 is a basic report pattern which underlies the construction of both trial scenes. (1) The gathering of the Sanhedrin to Pilate (15.1) takes up the quest for a death sentence (3.6; 11.18; 12.12; 14.1-2). This simple report avoids the discrepancies between the religious trial and the rabbinic prescriptions and insures the possibility of a death sentence. (2) The dual line of questioning (so 14.60-61) by Pilate focuses precisely on a political charge—sedition—and is supported by the accusations of the priests (15.2-3). (3) The silence of Jesus (14.61a; 15.5) prevents self-incrimination. (4) The affirmation of Jesus' innocence (14.55b, 59; 15.14) signifies the charges are unjust. (5) The abuse of Jesus is noted (14.65; 15.15b), as is the death verdict (14.64b; 15.15b).

Elements from this basic pattern have been taken up into a detailed account (14.53-65) which clarifies the role of the religious authorities in the death of Jesus.[3] More significantly, this trial occasions the most

been argued by designating the religious trial as an illegal prelude to a legal politial trial—see, for example, W. Lane, *The Gospel according to Mark* (NICNT; Grand Rapids: Eerdmans, 1974), pp. 528-30. (2) Others contend that the pre-70 Sanhedrin was dominated by Saducees and the rabbinic prescriptions are latter—so Blinzler, *Trial*; Lohse, 'συνέδριον'.

1. R. Pesch (*Der Prozess Jesu geht weiter* [Freiburg: Herder Verlag, 1988], pp. 65-66) notes the correlation between the trial of Jesus and Pss. 22, 27, 31, 34, 35, 37, 38, 39, 40, 41, 42, 43, 54, 55, 69, 71, 86, 88, 109, 118, as well as Isa. 50 and 53. In particular the two lines of witnesses (Num. 35.30; Deut. 19.15), the silence and the abuse echo Old Testament images. See also A. Suhl, *Die Funktion der alttestamentlichen Zitate und Anspielungen im Markusevangelium* (Gütersloh: Gerd Mohn, 1965).

2. See, for example, Donahue, 'Temple, Trial, and Royal Christology', pp. 61-79.

3. The framing of the religious trial under the influence of a foundational report would clarify some of the difficult elements in 14.53-65. (1) The possibility of the death penalty is never questioned, but stoning is never suggested. (2) The temple charge suggests political sedition, as would the basic account. (3) The insistence that the testimony is unreliable parallels the judgment of Pilate. (4) It becomes necessary

3. *Mark 14.43–15.15: The Arrest and Trial*

decisive christological confession in the Gospel of Mark (14.62).[1]

This compositional pattern reflects a basic knowledge of Jesus' appearance before the religious authorities and their quest for his death as well as an awareness of a foundational report which sketches the pattern of Jesus' trial. While this composition may reflect the work of a single author—the Evangelist Mark—such a composition more likely emerges from the ongoing reflection of a community. The strong connections to the foundational report, the thorough immersion in Old Testament images, and the coherence of the story line all suggest an extended period of reflection and a wider compositional community.

Narrative Syntax. This unique narrative configuration provides the base for a decisive syntactical strategy. As a result Mk 14.53-65 provides an important account for the passion story and generates a vital characterization of Jesus.

1. The trial scene creates a high drama in which the religion of Israel judges one of its own. The gravity of the trial is shown when the chief priest speaks for the nation in questioning and in judgment. Various witnesses are called, but their testimony is shown to be false and without power to condemn. The temple charge is mentioned, but it is defused. Instead, the story gives central focus to the dialogue between Jesus and the chief priest. Jesus will be judged not on the testimony of others, but upon his own witness. The judgment is meted out in three stages: the condemnation of the chief priest, the death sentence by the entire group, and the torture by the others. The central charge is blasphemy—making a false claim in relation to God.

2. The drama of this trial scene draws upon various Old Testament images. The concept of Israel judging one of its own has a lengthy heritage (Exod. 18.13-27; Deut. 1.12-18; 16.18-20). The blasphemy charge and the corresponding death sentence is rooted in the Torah: 'One who blasphemes the name of the Lord shall be put to death'

---

to note the silence of Jesus (since it is in the foundational report), even though this silence is reversed. (5) Jesus is abused and mocked prior to his trial before Pilate. These various elements and the questionable standing of the first trial may be explained by a common frame which underlies both trial narratives.

1. On the retrospective and prospective role played by 14.62 within the Gospel of Mark, see N. Perrin, 'The High Priest's Question and Jesus' Answer (Mark 14.61-62)', in Kelber (ed.), *The Passion in Mark*, pp. 80-95.

(Lev. 24.16). The image of prophetic confrontation has a rich history (1 Kgs 18.17-40; Jer. 27–28). While the prophetic conflict is sometimes between prophets of Yahweh and prophets of Baal (1 Kgs 18.17-40; Jer. 2.8-9), the conflict is typically between two groups who claim to represent the God of Israel. The guidelines for identification and punishment of false prophecy are gathered from the Old Testament (1 Kgs 13.11-32; 22.13-38; Jer. 5.12-13, 30-31; 6.13-14; 8.10-11; 14.13-16; 23.9-40; 27.8-22; 28.1-17; Hos. 4.4-6; Mic. 2.6-11; 3.5-8; 3.11). The death sentence against a false prophet comes from the Torah (Deut. 13.1-5; 18.15-22). The rending of the garments as a sign of horror is found in 2 Kgs 18.37 and 19.1. Thus, the scene of conflict and judgment between Jesus and the chief priest reflects the heritage of Israel. Central to this scene is the question of who is the authentic bearer of the word of Yahweh.

3. The most crucial product of this account is its christological portrait. The syntax of the story gives a singular focus to the characterization of Jesus. The plot line contains no surprises. The discrediting of the witnesses and the defusing of the temple charge remove these secondary elements. The witness of Jesus and the judgment of the religious leaders now carries the entire weight of the drama. Consequently the identity of Jesus provides the central focus.

3.1. The prophetic image developed in earlier stories comes to full expression in this scene. Standing before the religious leadership of Israel, Jesus is clearly portrayed as one who claims to speak for God. The trial focuses on the truth of this assertion. Various elements confirm the prophetic claim. Witnesses say he predicted the fall of the temple (Mk 14.58). Jesus predicts the future coming of the Son of Man (14.62). The words of Jesus provide fulfillment of the Old Testament (Dan. 7.13; Ps. 110.1). Lest the reader miss the imagery, those who torture Jesus mock him as one who claims the gift of prophecy (14.65). Thus, the presence of the prophetic claim is explicit. At the same time the story makes clear the rejection of this claim by the religious authorities. Consequently the image of Jesus as prophet stands at the center of the trial scene. Jesus, through his own words and deeds, has claimed to speak for Yahweh. This claim is rejected by the religious leaders of Israel, and Jesus is condemned to death as a false prophet who blasphemes the name of God.

3.2. The trial scene asserts various other christological images. The chief priest articulates the concern which is primary: 'Are you the

Christ?' (14.61). Thus, the trial is ultimately about the mission and identity which Jesus claims in the name of God. The answer of Jesus is explicit: 'I am' (14.62). The use of ἐγώ εἰμι relates this claim precisely to the power, the name and the identity of Yahweh (Exod. 3.5-6, 13-14; Mk 6.50). Within the Jewish context of this scene the ἐγώ εἰμι answer rings with unqualified clarity: 'By God I am the messiah'.

3.3. The question of the chief priest makes explicit a second christological concern: 'Are you the Son of God?' (the son of the Blessed One in 14.61). Jesus answers with the ἐγώ εἰμι. Jesus' claim is thus made explicit before the leaders of Israel: he is the messiah, the Son of God.

3.4. The answer of Jesus extends the christological description. Jesus is also the Son of Man who will come with power and judgment (14.62). Because he knows this future and proclaims it to the leaders of Israel, Jesus is also the prophet of God who fulfills the Scriptures.

3.5. The religious leaders do not miss these claims and their implications. If the claims of Jesus are correct, then his prophetic rebuke of Israel's leadership is also true. If the chief priest is the true leader of Israel and bears the truth of God, then Jesus is a false prophet worthy of death. The verdict is quick, decisive and unanimous: Jesus has claimed the voice and the name of Yahweh, and they judge him worthy of death (14.63-64). He is condemned, sentenced and tortured as a false prophet.

4. Like each of the preceding pericopes Mk 14.53-65 reaches its zenith in a pronouncement by Jesus. The syntax at work in this scene dissolves the testimony of the witnesses and the temple charge, then focuses precisely on the question of Jesus' identity. The question posed in 14.61 is answered emphatically by the pronouncements of 14.62. As a result this episode makes testimony and confession the structural and ideological key to this scene. This stark confession of Jesus amidst the scene of condemnation provides the catalyst for the death charge, initiates the passion sequence and provides the decisive christological confession in the Gospel of Mark.

The Passion Context. The sharp drama and the explicit Christology of the trial scene interacts in important ways with the larger passion story. These interconnections provide new levels of narrative substance and depth.

1. The prophetic image developed in the anointing, Passover, prediction, Gethsemane and arrest scenes reaches it climax in Mk 14.53-65. Various predictions come into view. The prophecy of burial (14.8) becomes more likely. The broken body and shed blood of the Passover scene move toward realization. The images of the smitten shepherd and the scattered sheep are confirmed. The nearness of the hour and the handing over of the Son of Man are realized (14.41). The treatment of Jesus as a thief (14.48) comes to pass. Thus, the prophetic image of Jesus is confirmed in the trial scene. Beyond this the prophetic focus is shown to be the primary element in the passion story: Jesus is condemned and abused as a false prophet. Thus, the trial scene completes the linkage of prophecy and passion in the portrait of Jesus.

Conversely the careful development of the prophecy image in the earlier stories provides a crucial backdrop for the trial scene. Jesus' claim to bear the words of Yahweh and the implications of this claim provide the basis for the trial scene. The dynamics of the trial flow around the conflicting evaluations of this claim. If Jesus is a true prophet, the religious leaders are false; if the religious leaders speak for God, Jesus is a false prophet worthy of death. Nothing in the trial scene guides the reader in the evaluation of these conflicting claims. How then is the reader to arbitrate these two conflicting voices about the work of God? Mk 14.1-52 provides the proper context from which the reader is to pass judgment on the identity of Jesus. The prophetic image has been presented and authenticated through these earlier scenes. The words of Jesus are fulfilled immediately in the Passover preparation. The predicted betrayal by one of the Twelve and abandonment by all his followers has come true. The prophetic insight about his death in the anointing and Passover scenes demonstrates Jesus' authenticity. The crucial role played by his words of instruction and interpretation point to his identity. His life and death fulfill the Scriptures. Thus, the trial of Jesus as one who claims to speak for Yahweh is set against a carefully plotted sequence in which Jesus speaks and acts as the faithful prophet of God.

2. In a similar fashion the focus on Jesus' identity as the messiah (14.62) picks up the images of Mk 14.1-11. In this anointing scene the messianic images are clear, but implicit. In the trial scene these messianic images are taken up and give explicit confirmation in the words of Jesus (14.62). Here, as in the anointing scene, the messianic

3. *Mark 14.43–15.15: The Arrest and Trial*

identity of Jesus is linked directly to his death.

3. The image of Jesus as the Beloved Son of God is also taken up and heightened. In particular, this concern builds upon the image of Jesus as the faithful Son in the Gethsemane story. In both scenes the identity of Jesus as the Son of God is linked explicitly to his destiny of suffering and death.

4. The Son of Man title also plays an important role in the wider passion context. The Son of Man imagery was linked to the passion Christology in the Passover scene (14.21). This linkage was confirmed by the Gethsemane story (14.41). In the midst of the trial scene Jesus takes up the Son of Man imagery (14.62). Because this saying is followed by the death sentence (14.63-64), the trial scene confirms the linkage of Son of Man expectations to the death of Jesus.

The Son of Man imagery in 14.62 may also address a crucial narrative gap. At the end of the passion story comes the promise of an appearance in Galilee (ὄψεσθε in 16.7). While 16.7 takes up the wording and promise of 14.28, a connection to 14.62 may be justified.[1] While the ὄψεσθε experience of 16.7 is largely undefined, the ὄψεσθε prediction of 14.62 is specific and dramatic: the Son of Man will be seen at the seat of power and coming with the clouds of heaven. Thus, Mk 14.62 may provide substance for the promise of 16.7.

5. As a result of these interconnections Mk 14.1-52 provides decisive evidence which guides the reader through the conflicting claims of the trial scene. The words and deeds of Jesus have demonstrated his identity. From the perspective of the reader the witness of Jesus before the chief priest is true: he is the messiah, the Beloved Son, the Son of Man, the prophet of God.

The Gospel Context. The trial scene in Mk 14.53-65 is played out in crucial ways against the images of the larger Gospel narrative. This pattern of interconnection creates vital lines of reciprocal interpretation and establishes the unity of the narrative.[2]

1. The trial scene fulfills various plot concerns from the wider story. The thematic development of the hostility of the religious

---

1. This connection is developed by Perrin, 'The High Priest's Question and Jesus' Answer'.

2. Despite his rigid historicistic approach Pesch (*Markusevangelium*, II, p. 443) acknowledges the decisive impact of the wider narrative world: 'In the framework of the Gospel of Mark new light from the wider context falls upon our scene'.

leaders and their death plot against Jesus (Mk 3.6; 11.18, 27-28; 12.12-13; 14.1-2, 10-11) reaches its zenith in the trial scene. The absence of the disciples confirms the larger theme of abandonment. More definitively, the three passion predictions (8.31; 9.31; 10.32-34) are being fulfilled with precision. Thus, the trial scene acts as an extension of the drama of Jesus' life and ministry.

2. Most significantly, the trial scene plays a culminative role in the larger christological strategy. Mk 14.62 does what the rest of the Gospel of Mark has refused to do—it places explicit christological claims on the lips of Jesus. In the previous developments of the narrative the messianic identity of Jesus is veiled in secrecy. While a part of this motif is a traditional element in miracle stories,[1] a significant portion of this secrecy is a literary device which explains the failure to recognize Jesus as messiah during his ministry.[2] The Gospel of Mark makes extensive use of this motif (Mk 1.24-25, 34, 44; 3.11-12; 4.11-12; 7.36; 8.26, 30; 9.9). While demons and even disciples sometimes articulate christological claims (Mk 1.24; 3.11-12; 8.27-38), Jesus distances himself from these attempts to make public his identity. Thus, the Gospel of Mark accepts traditional christological affirmations with great hesitancy.

The logion in Mk 14.62 provides a dramatic reversal of this literary pattern. Here the messianic secrecy is broken open in the presence of religious leaders and witnesses. The hesitant acceptance of christological images is replaced by the definitive ἐγώ εἰμι on the lips of Jesus. In one brief stroke the trial scene makes explicit the identity of Jesus: he is messiah, Son of God, Son of Man, teacher and prophet of God. Thus, the narrative establishes a crucial relationship between the ministry of Jesus and the trial scene: all of the implied Christology of the Gospel of Mark is made explicit here through the testimony of Jesus.

3. The reverse is also true: the christological images confirmed by Jesus in Mk 14.62 are filled out by the larger Gospel context. Various images and titles demonstrate this reciprocal influence.

3.1. The prophetic image in the trial scene is given substance and depth by the careful portrait of Jesus as one who teaches with

1. See U. Luz, 'Das Geheimnismotiv und die markinische Christologie', *ZNW* 56 (1965), pp. 361-64.
2. W. Wrede, *The Messianic Secret* (trans. J.C.G. Greig; Cambridge: James Clark, 1971 [1901]).

3. Mark 14.43–15.15: The Arrest and Trial

authority (1.22). From the beginning the teaching activity of Jesus is linked not only to his power, but also to his death (3.6; 11.18; 12.12). Thus, the condemned prophet is the one who taught with power and wisdom throughout Galilee.

3.2. The confession that Jesus is Son of God is made explicit in Mk 14.62, but the content of this title is provided by the earlier story. The opening lines of the narrative assert this identity for Jesus (1.1). The divine voice confirms this destiny at his baptism (1.11). Demons acknowledge Jesus' sonship (1.24; 3.11; 5.7). The divine voice authenticates this relationship at the transfiguration (9.7). Parabolic images drawn from the Old Testament focus this identity (12.1-12). The Gethsemane scene confirms Jesus' faithfulness to the Father. Significantly, Mk 9.7, 12.1-12 and 14.32-42 each link the Son of God imagery to the death of Jesus. Apart from these connections Mk 14.62 provides a confession open to various interpretations.[1] Set within the larger context of the Gospel narrative, the assertion now provides a carefully hewn image: Jesus is the faithful, beloved Son who will give his life in obedience to the Father.

3.3. In a similar manner the Son of Man title receives its definition through the larger Gospel context. Standing alone this title implies dramatic apocalyptic images (Mk 13). While not negating the stark power of this title, the Gospel of Mark sets this imagery within a larger framework. The Son of Man is one who serves and gives his life (10.45). He will suffer much and be treated with contempt (9.12). The Son of Man will suffer and die (8.31; 9.31; 10.32-34). The Son of Man is handed over to sinners (14.21, 41). Through this linkage the dramatic images of Mark 13 are drawn into the passion Christology. The Son of Man title now provides an ironic union of power and suffering. This ironic characterization emerges only through the reciprocal lines of interpretation which traverse the narrative.

3.4. The confession that Jesus is the Christ receives its ultimate definition from the larger narrative world. The trial scene explicitly links Jesus' messianic identity and his passion destiny. The Gospel narrative fills out this christological confession. Jesus the messiah (1.1) teaches and preaches and heals in the power of God. His ministry

---

1. See, for example, the extensive attempts in modern scholarship to link the Son of God title to some form of θεῖος ἀνήρ Christology. In narrative terms the wilderness testimony (1.12-13) and Peter's response to the transfiguration (9.5-6) demonstrate the possibility of misuse and misunderstanding of Jesus' identity.

is marked by wonder, wisdom and authority. At the same time none of his miracles and none of his words sufficiently reveal his identity. His mission is a mystery cloaked in secrecy. Only in the context of suffering, service and the cross is the identity of Jesus fully seen. Through these reciprocal connections the confession in Mk 14.62 completes the preface in Mk 1.1: Jesus is indeed the Christ, the Son of God, but the definitive sign of his messiahship is suffering, service and death.

4. Thus, the trial of Jesus locates the clearest christological confession within the context of Jesus' death. In one brief and dramatic phrase set upon the lips of Jesus the whole of his identity is unveiled: he is the Christ, the Son of God, the Son of Man, the true teacher and prophet of God. Drawing upon various elements of Jesus' life story to fill out the content of these images, Mk 14.53-65 proclaims the true identity of Jesus in the shadow of the cross.

5. More than any other episode the trial scene in Mk 14.53-65 demonstrates the vital lines of connection which stream across the Gospel of Mark. Mk 14.62 provides an explicit christological clarity missing from the remainder of this Gospel. Significantly, the most direct christological description is uttered by Jesus himself as a confession that invokes the name of Yahweh. At the same time the dramatic confession of 14.62 is largely void of depth and content. As a result the explicit images of 14.62 remain open to various interpretations and misunderstandings. Only in connection with the wider world of the Gospel of Mark do the titles of 14.62 gain depth and precision.[1]

Consequently the most decisive moment of the gospel story engages the whole world of the narrative to declare the destiny and identity of Jesus. The morphological configuration and syntactical processes

---

1. Perrin ('The High Priest's Question and Jesus' Answer') gave particular attention to the relation of 14.62 to the narrative world of the Gospel of Mark. Perrin argued that Mk 14.61-62 '*functions* both retrospectively and prospectively in Mk. Retrospectively, it is the climax of the christological concerns of the Evangelist, and it marks the formal disclosure of the Messianic Secret. Prospectively, it prepares the way for the christological climax of the centurion's confession; it interprets the crucifixion/resurrection of Jesus as the enthronement/ascension of Jesus as the Christ and Son of Man; and it anticipates the parousia. These verses take on a new significance as they are examined from the literary-critical standpoint of their function in the Gospel' (p. 95).

3. *Mark 14.43–15.15: The Arrest and Trial*

operative in this account further demonstrate the inherent nature of the Gospel of Mark as an intricate and ironic narrative whole.

Comparative Analysis

The trial of Jesus before the religious leaders is also used in other narrative settings. These alternate performances and the images which they produce provide a comparative base for analysis of the trial scene.[1]

Pre-Markan Contexts. The story of Jesus' trial before the religious authorities presents a historical and a literary puzzle. Various attempts at reconstructing the history of this tradition demonstrate its complexity, and no consensus has been reached on the development of this passage.[2] Many scholars see here a secondary joining of different traditions. Following the lead of Bultmann, reconstructions of this process have been offered by Linnemann and by Schenk.[3] Others have argued that the trial scene existed prior to the passion story as an independent layer of ground tradition.[4] Pesch insists that the account is integral to the extensive, fixed pre-Markan passion tradition.[5] As an independent tradition the story might be valued because of its report of the details of Jesus' trial and because of its strong witness to the identity of Jesus as the messiah. As a part of an extended tradition this story would partake in a larger passion report and in its larger witness to the identity of Jesus.

The Gospel of Matthew. The trial before the religious authorities is told in Mt. 26.57-68. This story occupies the same context between the arrest and the denial by Peter. Internally the story is almost identical to Mk 14.53-65. Matthew has only one chief priest and identifies him

---

1. On the use of diachronic analysis as phenomenological description and comparision of co-texts see Chapter 1.
2. For summaries of the research on this passage, see Schenke, *Der gekreuzigte Christus*, pp. 23-26; Linnemann, *Passionsgeschichte*, pp. 109-13; Pesch, *Markusevangelium*, II, p. 428.
3. Bultmann, *History*, pp. 269-71, 284, 305; Linnemann, *Passionsgeschichte*, pp. 109-35; Schenk, *Passionsbericht*, pp. 239-43.
4. Dormeyer, *Verhaltensmodell*, pp. 149-50, 157-74; Schenke, *Der gekreuzigte Christus*, pp. 23-46; Gnilka, *Markus*, II, p. 277.
5. Pesch, *Markusevangelium*, II, pp. 424-46.

as Caiaphas (Mt. 26.57). Matthew reports the presence of false witnesses, then tells of two witnesses who level the temple charge against Jesus (Mt. 26.60-62). The chief priest asks about the identity, questioning Jesus here in the name of God (Mt. 26.63). In an unusual move Mt. 26.63 replaces the circumlocution 'the Blessed One' with the name for God. The answer of Jesus in Mt. 26.64 is distinct: 'You have said'. The Son of Man saying is taken over (Mt. 26.64), and the response of the religious leaders is similar. The abuse by the others is reported in a similar manner, with the exception that Jesus is addressed as the Christ (Mt. 26.68). Thus, Mt. 26.57-68 reports the trial scene with few significant changes.

The Gospel of Luke. The trial scene is also narrated in Lk. 22.54-71. Following the transition to the trial scene Luke tells the story of Peter's denial (Lk. 22.55-63). This denial is followed by the torture scene (Lk. 22.63-65). The trial itself is placed on the following day (Lk. 22.66). Significantly, Luke makes specific mention of the Sanhedrin. The line of false witnesses is omitted, as is the silence of Jesus. The central question has been split into two parts. The question about Jesus as messiah appears in Lk. 22.61, and the question about the Son of God follows in Lk. 22.70. Jesus responds to the first question with a rebuke: they will not listen if he speaks, nor will they speak if he questions them (Lk. 22.68). The second question is answered with an indirect use of ἐγώ εἰμι: 'you are saying that I am' (Lk. 22.70). In some sense this ironic answer turns the table and places the religious authorities on trial. Inserted between these two questions is the saying about the Son of Man (Lk. 22.69). This series is followed by the verdict, but the charge of blasphemy is omitted (Lk. 22.71). Thus, Lk. 22.54-71 relates the basic elements of the trial scene, but sharply alters their style and order of presentation.

The Gospel of John. Jn 18.13-24 tells a similar account within the Johannine framework. Jesus is led to Annas, the father-in-law of Caiaphas (Jn 18.13). Caiaphas's ironic comment about the death of one for the nation is recalled (Jn 18.14). Here Jesus is accompanied by Peter and by the 'other disciple' (Jn 18.15-16). Peter is brought to the trial scene through the privileged role of the other disciple. Following this introduction comes the opening scene of Peter's denial (Jn 18.17-18). The interrogation by the high priest is unique. The question of

3. Mark 14.43–15.15: The Arrest and Trial

the high priest does not center on the identity of Jesus, but on the disciples and on the teaching of Jesus (Jn 18.19). This question allows an extended answer on the activity of Jesus (Jn 18.20-21). At the center of this response is the open witness of Jesus to the Jewish people. The torture is replaced by a slap from an officer (Jn 18.22). The reponse of Jesus affirms his role as a true witness (Jn 18.23). Following this account Jesus is sent to Caiaphas, but no report is given of this scene.

The Gospel of John thus narrates the first trial scene in a different context and creates a distinct focus. The image of Jesus which emerges differs from the portrait in the Synoptic Gospels, yet it reflects consistent Johannine concerns. The 'other disciple' plays a central, faithful role in the story. Jesus provides the true and faithful witness to the work of God. The light of this revelation has been made available to the Jewish people, but they have rejected it (Jn 1.9-11).

Others. Isolated elements from the trial scene are found in various other literary contexts. The temple charge has become a logion in the *Gospel of Thomas* (71), and the abuse scene is reported in the *Gospel of Peter* (3.9).

Summary

The trial scene was shown to operate in several narrative contexts. Prior to the Gospel of Mark this scene may have served as an apologetic report or as an element of a passion tradition. The use of the story in the Gospel of Matthew and in the Gospel of Luke differs little from Mk 14.53-65. In contrast various elements of the trial scene have been used in Jn 18.13-24 to develop the Johannine form of the gospel story and to advance the Johannine portrait of Jesus.

In comparison with these various performances the trial scene in Mk 14.53-65 is distinctive. This scene plays a primary role in the story of Jesus' death and generates a decisive focus on the identity of Jesus. Ultimately the question of Jesus' identity is played out in the presence of the leaders of Israel. Secondary elements are pushed aside, and the conflict between Jesus and the religious authorities takes priority. The central issue in this confrontation is the question of who speaks with authority for Yahweh. The question of the chief priest cuts through to the decisive issue of Jesus' identity. The response of Jesus is clear and unqualified. The verdict is swift and harsh.

146 *Prophet, Son, Messiah*

The image of Jesus which emerges is crucial: he is the Christ, the Son of God, the Son of Man, the prophet and teacher from God. These images shatter the secrecy motif and give explicit definition to the mission and identity of Jesus. At the same time the full content of these christological images is provided by the story of Jesus' ministry. Thus, the trial scene in Mk 14.53-65 sustains a vital relationship with the larger story of Jesus. Before the religious authorities and in the shadow of the cross the identity and the destiny of Jesus is made plain. From the beginning of his life (1.1) to its end (14.62), the one condemned to death by the leaders of Israel is messiah and Son of God.

Mark 14.66-72: The Trial of Peter

Following close upon the trial of Jesus comes the scene of Peter's denial. This account picks up various images from Mk 14.53-65 and forms an addendum to the trial scene. At the same time Peter's denial concludes a number of themes developed in the wider narrative.

Synchronic Analysis
The motifs of Mk 14.66-72 may be plotted in the following manner:

    Introduction
    —

    Body
Servant comes	14.66
Servant identifies	14.67
Peter denies	14.68a
Peter departs	14.68b
Cock crows	14.68c
Servant identifies	14.69
Peter denies	14.70a
Bystanders identify	14.70b
Peter denies	14.71
Cock crows	14.72a
Peter remembers	14.72b

    Conclusion
Peter departs	14.72c

Narrrative Morphology. The typical introduction in which the actors are transported to the scene is missing from this account. Because of this Mk 14.54 provides the setting for the denial scene. This technique

3. *Mark 14.43–15.15: The Arrest and Trial* 147

creates an intimate link between the trial of Jesus and the denial by Peter. The denial story is shaped around the central dialogue between Peter and his accusers. This dialogue is structured by the repeated claims of the witnesses and the repeated denial of their claims by Peter. The scene builds upon three cycles of identification and denial (14.67-68, 69-70a, 70b-72a). The cockcrow marks the end of the first and the third cycle (14.68c, 72a). The three cycles are drawn into a unity by the motif of remembrance (14.72b). The implied movement at the end of the story (14.72c) provides a typical conclusion.[1]

Morphologically Mk 14.66-72 is built around a basic report of Peter's denial.[2] This foundational report has been developed in creative ways and joined through various connections to other material.

1. The basic report of Peter's presence is narrated in 14.54, 66-68b. The genitive absolute construction in 14.66a recalls the setting of

---

1. The meaning of ἐπιβαλών is not certain. The term generally means to throw over or to seize. This use is found in the New Testament in passages such as 1 Cor. 7.35; Mk 14.46; Mt. 26.50; Acts 4.3; 5.18. The intransitive may mean to cast oneself onto something. This use is found in Mk 14.37. For the use of ἐπιβάλλω in the New Testament period, see F. Hauck, 'ἐπιβάλλω', *TDNT* I, pp. 528-29. For discussion of possible translations and meanings of Mk 14.72, see Bauer, Arndt and Gingrich, *Lexicon*, pp. 289-90; Taylor, *Mark*, pp. 576-77. Luke and Matthew likely found this phrase difficult, since both transform it. The Fourth Gospel avoids the problem entirely. The violent image of Mk 4.37 may apply here in the sense that Peter is seized or stricken by grief. The use of ἐπιβάλλω in 14.72 forms an ironic contrast to 14.46. The seizure of Jesus leads to trial and death; Peter is seized with grief but remains free.

2. Various scholars argue that this report of the leading apostle's failure is included primarily because of its historical foundations. Representatives of this position are Taylor (*Mark*, pp. 571-72); A. Loisy, who argued: 'If there is an actual reminiscence from Peter anywhere in the Second Gospel it is most certainly in the story of the denial in the form in which it is found in Mark', cited in Taylor, *Mark*, p. 572. In a similar vein Pesch (*Markusevangelium*, II, p. 448) argues that 'everything speaks for the idea that the factuality of the denial of Jesus by Peter in the courtyard of the high priest's palace in the night of the arrest of Jesus as historical information was the first and final ground for the development of our narrative unity in the framework of the pre-Markan passion story'.

In contrast another line of scholarship argues that a traditional report of Peter's presence at the trial has been used by Mark to generate or to further an anti-Petrine polemic. Among those supporting this position are J. Schreiber, 'Die Christologie des Markusevangeliums', *ZTK* 58 (1961), pp. 154-83; K. Dewey, 'Peter's Curse and Cursed Peter (Mark 14.53-54, 66-72)', in Kelber (ed.), *The Passion in Mark*, pp. 96-114.

14.54 and was employed at the time when 14.53, 55-65 was placed inside this story. The concluding phrase in 14.68c (καὶ ἀλέκτωρ ἐφώνησεν) is based on debatable textual grounds[1] and serves to tie this scene to the prediction in 14.30. Thus the foundational report likely circulated around four elements. (1) Peter's presence at the scene of the trial is noted (14.54, 67).[2] (2) The recognition of Peter as an associate of Jesus is reported (14.66b-67). (3) Peter's denial of this claim is asserted (14.68a).[3] (4) Peter's departure is implied (14.68b). Significantly, this basic account serves as an incidental report scene and provides no harsh condemnation of Peter.[4]

2. The inner dynamic of the foundational report has been developed through a variety of narrative techniques. This development transforms the elements of the basic report into an explosive scene of denial.

2.1. The denial report has been framed around a temporal device—the cockcrow. This time marker is attached to 14.68 as a comment.

---

1. The phrase is omitted in a strong line of manuscripts: ℵ B LW Ψ* 892 pc c sy^s sa^{mss} bo. The 25th edition of Nestle-Aland omitted this phrase, though the 26th edition accepts the inclusion of καὶ ἀλέκτωρ ἐφώνησεν by A C D Θ Ψ^c 067 $f^{1.13}$ (1424) 𝔐 lat sy$^{p.h}$ (sa^{mss} bo^{ms}); Eus. If the phrase is seen as original its omission from significant texts might be explained as an attempt to harmonize Mk 14.68 with Matthew and Luke, who do not contain this phrase. On the other hand attempts to correlate Mk 14.68 with the prophecy in 14.30 would explain the secondary insertion of this phrase. Consistent with the evidence which does not place 14.68c in the foundational report, the designation of 14.72 as the second cockcrow (ἐκ δευτέρου) is omitted in p) ℵ C*^{vid} L pc c.

2. The insistence that Peter was 'with the Nazarene' (μετὰ τοῦ Ναζαρηνοῦ) echoes the language of Mk 3.14 and 5.18, and it provides a clear metaphor for discipleship.

3. A startled and frightened response is suggested by the language of Peter's reply. The grammatical use of synonyms with the οὔτε...οὔτε construction is technically incorrect. For various explanations of this phrasing, see Taylor, *Mark*, pp. 573-74. Taylor likewise saw a correlation between the form and function of this statement: 'It may well be that to press such distinctions, or to object that the verbs are synonymous, is equally out of place in considering an unpremeditated reply from a speaker who is taken aback' (p. 573).

4. Peter does not directly deny Jesus, but pretends ignorance of the girl's claims. Dewey ('Peter's Curse', p. 108) confirms this view of the basic story: 'Whereas in the tradition Peter's confrontation with the maid is a private one, Mk amplifies it to public proportion; in the former Peter is evasive, in the latter he is pushed to an outright cursing of Jesus. A weak Peter is transformed into a hostile Peter, an opponent.'

3. Mark 14.43–15.15: The Arrest and Trial

The cockcrow in 14.72 is correlated to 14.68 by its designation as the second (ἐκ δευτέρον) cockcrow. The denial by Peter is thus framed by these two temporal markers. This device provides the background sense of a ticking timepiece, it may emphasize the concentrated framework of Peter's denial[1] and it may provide a sense of finality to the night of arrest and betrayal. The cockcrow thus provides, within the local narrative context, a temporal frame for the scene of denial.

2.2. The basic report of Peter's denial has been extended and intensified by a pattern of threefold repetition. Through this technique the report has been narrated in stages. This staging technique creates a retarding pattern and a growing intensity which climaxes in the third denial.[2]

3. Beyond these internal developments the composition of 14.54-55, 66-72 sustains important external connections. These morphological links have a decisive impact on the form and function of this account.

3.1. The twofold cockcrow (14.68, 72) serves internally as a temporal frame for the story. At the same time this literary device provides an external link to the prophecy of 14.30. This temporal and prophetic link creates a vital interpretive connection between 14.30 and Peter's denial.

3.2. Remembering (ἀνεμνήσθη) serves as a literary device which connects the story explicitly to the prophecy of 14.30. Through this technique Mk 14.54, 66-72 becomes an explicit scene of prophetic fulfillment.

3.3. The threefold staging of this scene provides an internal pattern of retardation, intensification and culmination. Externally this device provides exact fulfillment of Jesus' prediction—you will deny me three times—and confirms the link to 14.30.[3]

3.4. The denial scene has been separated into two parts (14.54;

---

1. Pesch (*Markusevangelium*, II, p. 449) argues that the time between the first and second cockcrow is about one hour. This focus is supported within the narrative by the temporal notice of the passing of a 'little time' (μετὰ μικρόν in 14.70).

2. A similar pattern is found elsewhere in the Gospel of Mark. See, for example, the Gethsemane story in 14.32-42.

3. Scholars are divided over the source of this threefold pattern. Some see here a traditional pattern typical of folk literature. Among these are Gnilka, *Markus*, II, p. 290; Pesch, *Markusevangelium*, II, pp. 447-53. Others argue the threefold pattern is distinctly Markan. Among these are Dewey, 'Peter's Curse'; Dormeyer, *Verhaltensmodell*, pp. 150-55; Schenk, *Passionsbericht*, pp. 215-23. Regardless of its origin or intent, the narrative effect of this pattern is decisive.

14.66-72) and used as a frame for the trial scene (14.53, 55-65). This intercalation creates a textual frame and sustains a decisive narrative relationship between these two accounts.[1]

4. This complex morphological pattern likely reflects the compositional process behind this account. A basic account reported the presence of Peter and his attempt to avoid arrest. Through a process of circulation and reshaping this report has become a dramatic scene of indictment. Through reflection upon the wider story of Jesus—such as Gethsemane and the trial—vital connections have been established to the image of Jesus as the rejected prophet.

This process echoes both intentionality and competence in the development of this scene. The structured intentionality of this text makes an evolutionary pattern of accretion unlikely. Conversely the nuanced depth of competence and reflection behind this text points beyond the work of a single author and a straightforward redaction. It is more likely that the artful arrangement of this text echoes the work of a wider theological circle and an extended period of use, reflection and reshaping. The morphology of this scene suggests that this community practiced a hermeneutic of reflective discipleship in which such stories were linked to the factual reports about Jesus, to prophetic Scriptures and sayings, and to present demands of discipleship.

5. While scholars generally find here no clear genre lines,[2] important connections exist between 14.66-72 and the pronouncement stories. Typically pronouncement scenes are based on enigmatic events which are clarified through a culminating pronouncement. This final saying not only clarifies the scene but also provides a distinct characterization of Jesus.[3] Mk 14.66-72 echoes this compositional pattern. The denial scene is ultimately gathered under the prophetic

---

1. Scholars are almost unanimous in the evaluation that the framing technique represents a Markan redactional pattern. In my opinion more attention should be given to the possibility that intercalation represents a wider pattern of traditional storytelling. See, for example, the Homeric story of Odysseus's scar discussed in E. Auerbach, *Mimesis: The Representation of Reality in Western Literature* (trans. W. Trask; Princeton, NJ: Princeton University Press, 1953 [1946]), pp. 3-23. A similar flashback is employed to tell of the death of the Baptist in Mk 6.7-31. The Johannine use of intercalation in this scene (Jn 18.15-18, 25-27) may speak against the origin of this technique with Markan redaction.

2. Gnilka (*Markus*, II, p. 291) declares that 'By genre standards it can hardly be designated'.

3. See, for example, Mk 2.23-28.

3. *Mark 14.43–15.15: The Arrest and Trial*

word of 14.72. Significantly, Mk 14.72 provides not a pronouncement, but a recollection of a past saying. Through a process of remembering (ἀνεμνήσθη) the prophetic word of 14.30 is placed as the culmination of this scene. This transaction clarifies the scene of denial and characterizes Jesus as the true and faithful prophet of God.[1]

6. Consequently the story of Peter's denial presents a unique and informative morphology. An elemental report noted the presence of Peter and his resistance to attempts to identify him with Jesus. Internally this report has been structured around a temporal frame (cockcrow) and given dramatic effect through a threefold staging. External connections have been established with the prophetic saying of 14.30 and with the first trial scene (14.53-65). Syntactical analysis will show how the interplay of these compositional elements creates a dynamic narrative effect and a vital christological portrait.

Narrative Syntax. The syntactical arrangement operates upon these compositional elements to create a scene of drama with vital interpretive weight. Various syntactical patterns contribute to the narrative effect of this scene.

1. A simple report scene has been transformed into a complex drama of indictment. This is accomplished by blending two syntactical strategies—repetition and detailing. The threefold staging of Peter's resistance enlarges the significance of his denial. In addition, the details of resistance become more dramatic and more indicting by stages. In the first stage (14.67-68) Peter claims lack of understanding about the question of the girl—'I do not know or understand what you are saying'—then leaves the courtyard. The second staging (14.69-70a) simply repeats the drama of denial, but the generic aorist (ἠρνήσατο) of the first denial has become an iterative imperfect (ἠρνεῖτο) in the second denial. Through this technique the denial by Peter is presented as an extended process. In addition, the second denial expands the audience to include the bystanders (τοῖς παρεστῶσιν). The third staging (14.70b-72a) provides the height of the drama. The circle of witnesses against Peter has grown from one (the girl) to a group (the bystanders in 14.70b). The charge is now

---

1. Likely the transfer from a pattern of citation of Scripture and logia to a process of recollection reflects the hermeneutical situation of the later Christian community. The words of Jesus are applied to their own context through a process of remembrance and reflection.

supported by additional evidence: you are a Galilean (14.70c).[1] Most significantly, the response of Peter takes its starkest form: he begins to curse and swear, and he makes a direct denial of Jesus (14.71). In similar fashion the cockcrow is presented in dramatic style—it occurs immediately (εὐθύς) after the denial, and this is the second cockcrow (14.72a). The threefold staging and the development of the details combine to provide a strategy of intensification which climaxes in the third denial. Through this syntactical pattern Peter's simple resistance has been transformed into a dramatic scene of profane denial and rejection of his discipleship.[2]

2. This dramatic denial has been tied precisely to the prophecy of Mk 14.30. The numbering of the cockcrow (14.68c, 72a) and the designation of the three denials provide precise agreement with the details of 14.30. At the plot level this connection provides exact fulfillment of an earlier scene. Beyond this the connection to 14.30 advances the prophetic characterization of Jesus. Thus, the basic report of Peter's resistance has been syntactically shaped into a prophetic element central to plotting and characterization.

3. This complex staging of the denial and its nuanced images of

---

1. Zealotic implications may be present in the use of the Galilean designation. M. Hengel (*The Zealots: Investigations into the Jewish Freedom Movement in the Period from Herod I until 70 AD* [trans. D. Smith; Edinburgh: T. & T. Clark, 1989 (1961)], pp. 56-59) argues for a zealotic group who were called Galileans. In Hengel's view these were the followers of Judas of Galilee, who led the revolt around the time of Jesus' birth. On the role of Judas of Galilee, see Hengel, *The Zealots*, pp. 76-145.

2. It is very likely that this narrative pattern correlates to the historical situation of the early community of faith. Jesus had promised that they would stand as witnesses (martyrs) before Sanhedrins, synagogues, governors and kings (Mk 13.9). These followers have been called to endurance (13.13). Within the history of early Christianity this trial of faith centered around one's confession/denial of Jesus. Later parallels seem to confirm this situation, though these sources may be themselves shaped by Christian interests. Justin, *Apol.* 1.31.6 reports that Barkochba freed Christians from the most difficult penalties if they would deny and slander Jesus Christ. Pliny reported a similar view of Trajan. From the context of the second century CE Pliny (*Ep.* 10.96.3) described the inquiry against Christians: 'I will ask you if you are Christians, and when you confess, I will ask you a second and third time under the threat of punishment'. For further discussion of this see Gnilka, *Markus*, II, p. 293; H. Merkel, 'Peter's Curse', in E. Bammel (ed.), *The Trial of Jesus: Cambridge Studies in Honour of C.F.D. Moule* (London: SCM Press, 1970), pp. 66-71.

3. Mark 14.43–15.15: The Arrest and Trial

prophecy have been interwoven into the story of Jesus' trial (14.53, 55-65). The undeveloped report about Peter (14.54) serves notice of the connection to Jesus' trial. The absence of a conclusion in the first trial guides the reader to understand the denial scene in close relation to the trial scene. The opening lines in 14.66 draw upon the setting in 14.54, creating an intercalation. Thus, the syntactical operations of this account create a reciprocal relationship with the trial scene of Jesus.

Beyond this narrative linkage the form of the denial story grows out of the trial scene. Witnesses initiate the charge and play a vital role in both accounts (14.56, 57-59, 60; 14.66-67, 69, 70). The crucial issue in both stories is the question of identity (14.61; 14.67, 69, 70). In both scenes the response of the accused provides the central focus (14.62; 14.68, 70, 71). Symbolic elements (tearing the garment in 14.63; the cockcrow in 14.68, 72) follow the testimony of the accused.

Through these techniques of narrative linkage and parallel construction Mk 14.53-65 and 14.66-72 are presented as co-temporal mirror images. In the inner scene Jesus is on trial. Outside of the judgment hall Peter is also on trial. The contrast between the two trial scenes is ironic. In the trial of Jesus witnesses testify falsely against him. In the trial of Peter the witnesses speak the truth. The center of Jesus' trial comes in his certain witness to his own identity. The center of Peter's trial is his threefold denial of his identity as a follower of Jesus. The irony is inescapable. Over against false testimony Jesus bears witness to his true identity; over against true witnesses Peter lies about his identity. The ultimate irony emerges in the conclusion of these trial scenes. The lying Peter goes out free and without harm. Jesus, who speaks the truth, is bound and tortured.

This intertwining of the trial of Jesus with the trial of Peter enlarges the images of each scene. This expansion is most evident in the characterizations which emerge from these units. Over against the faithfulness of Jesus the threefold denial by Peter becomes a paradigm of cowardice and abandonment. Over against the scene of Peter's denial the portrait of Jesus as the faithful, courageous witness from God is cast in large images across the narrative.

4. The narrative effect of these syntactical patterns is extensive. Through this schema historical elements and reports from the story of Jesus have been gathered into complex accounts with theological

focus. The story of Peter's denial has been linked into an extended plot line and a larger drama. A decisive critique has been addressed against the followers of Jesus. As elsewhere Peter serves as the focus of the word to the disciples.[1] A crucial christological image is supported. Seen over against the dramatic denial by Peter, the confession of Jesus confirms his faithfulness as prophet, Son, messiah.

The Passion Context. The story in Mk 14.66-72 interacts in significant ways with the larger passion account. These connections establish this scene within the passion context.

1. Several lines of connection are established to earlier events in the passion story. (1) The denial scene draws its setting from Mk 14.54 and participates in the first trial narrative. (2) Peter's threefold denial takes up the theme of abandonment from Mk 14.50-52. Subsequently the denial scene provides the ultimate expansion and completion of the disciples' failure. (3) In addition, the prophecy of Mk 14.26-31 is fulfilled. As predicted, all of the disciples have abandoned Jesus (14.50-52). In both scenes the final spotlight falls on Peter. The sharp rejection of this prophecy by Peter (14.29, 31) is matched by his threefold denial of Jesus (14.68, 70, 71). The prediction of Jesus in Mk 14.30 is fulfilled precisely in Mk 14.66-72. Lest the reader miss this connection, the remembrance by Peter confirms this completion of the prophecy. (4) The staging of Peter's denial in three scenes mirrors the faithfulness of Jesus and the failure of the disciples in the three prayer scenes in Gethsemane (14.32-42).

2. The denial scene also plays an important role in the further plotting of the passion story. In particular, this story helps to describe and position the major actants in the death of Jesus. The role of the religious leaders was established in the trial scene: they reject Jesus and plot his death. The role of the political leaders will be established in the second trial of Jesus (15.1-20): they provide the instruments of death. The role of the disciples is established in the denial scene: Jesus is betrayed, denied and abandoned by his own.

3. Thus, the denial scene in Mk 14.66-72 is vital for the narration of the passion story. Through this account the theme of betrayal and abandonment by the disciples is completed. The images of this failure are then sharpened and enlarged by the contrast with the trial of Jesus.

---

1. See, for example, Mk 8.32-33; 9.5-6; 11.21; 14.29-31; 14.37-38.

3. Mark 14.43–15.15: The Arrest and Trial

At the same time the denial scene sharpens the christological image. Jesus is the true prophet, for his words have come to pass. He is the true witness from God who goes to his death in obedience and faithfulness.

The Gospel Context. The denial scene also plays an important role in the wider narrative context. Various lines of connection link the denial to the larger story world.

1. This story provides the completion of a theme developed carefully through the narrative—the failure of the followers of Jesus (Mk 4.13, 40-41; 5.30-32; 6.35-37, 49-52; 8.4, 27-30, 31-33; 9.6, 9-10, 11-13, 14-28, 30-32, 33-37, 38-41; 10.23-27, 32, 35-45; 14.10-11, 27-31, 32-42, 45, 50-52). This failure is consummated in Peter's denial. Throughout the narrative Peter serves as the focal point for the activity of the disciples. He is among the first called (1.16-20). He is first to confess that Jesus is the Christ (8.29). He articulates the demands of discipleship: 'Behold, we have left all and we have followed you' (10.28). Peter is present at two of the most intimate moments of Jesus' ministry: the scene of transfiguration (9.2-10) and the Gethsemane scene (14.32-42). He points out the fate of the fig tree (11.21). Peter protests most at the prophecy of Jesus' death (8.32). He protests most at the prediction of abandonment (14.29, 31). Peter is singled out in the resurrection promise (16.7). In various ways Peter serves in the Gospel of Mark as a representative for the followers of Jesus (14.31b). He is the lightning rod for the characterization of Jesus' followers. In some sense Peter is the ideal, the best hope for the disciples. Thus, his failure in Mk 14.66-72 completes the characterization of the disciples. Jesus has been betrayed (14.45), abandoned (14.50) and denied (14.66-72) by his followers. Even Peter has failed; especially Peter has failed. Mk 14.66-72 takes up the image of the disciples' cowardice, misunderstanding and abandonment and brings this central theme to completion.

2. A vital connection is established between Peter's failure and the prophecies of Mark 13. The testing of Peter is foreshadowed in the warning to believers (13.9, 13). Peter's denial recalls the instructions about faithful testimony (13.9, 11; see 8.38). Peter's failure recalls the command to watch (13.9, 33, 37). These loose narrative connections are accompanied by a linguistic connection—the use of the cockcrow as a temporal device in both scenes (13.36; 14.68, 72).

3. A loose narrative connection is likewise established with the story of the fig tree (11.12-14, 20-26). (1) Formally both stories participate in an intercalation. (2) In both accounts the middle element focuses the death plot by religious authorities (11.18; 14.63-64). (3) A curse is central to both scenes (11.14; 14.71). (4) Peter stands out in both accounts (11.21; 14.66). (5) Both stories circulate around remembrance of a prophetic saying (11.21; 14.72). Thus, the stories of the fig tree (11.12-14, 20-26) and of Peter's denial (14.66-72) overlap in form and function.

4. The artful use of the threefold pattern establishes connections throughout the narrative. The Gospel of Mark presents a narrative world in which triplets abound.[1] Some sequences are obvious: in Gethsemane Jesus prays and finds the disciples sleeping three times (14.32-42); Pilate asks three series of questions to the crowd (15.1-15); the crucifixion occurs in three stages of three hours each (15.21-39). Other uses of the threefold pattern occur at intervals. Foremost among these are the three passion predictions (8.31; 9.31; 10.32-34). Significantly, each of these predictions is built around a triadic internal pattern: prediction, rejection by the disciples, instruction. The call and commission of the disciples is given in three scenes (1.16-20; 3.13-19; 6.7-13, 30). Three dramatic episodes employ the boat setting (4.35-41; 6.45-52; 8.14-21).[2] The bread conflict is threefold (6.35-44; 8.1-10; 8.14-21). Three temple scenes precede the passion story (the first in 11.11; the second in 11.15-19; the third starts in 11.27 and ends in 13.1-2). Characters are also grouped in threes: Peter, James,

---

1. On the redactional use of triads, see F. Neirynck, *Duality in Mark: Contributions to the Study of the Markan Redaction* (ETL 31; Leuven: Leuven University Press, 1972), pp. 110-11. On the narrative role of triads, see D. Rhoads and D. Michie, *Mark as Story: An Introduction to the Narrative of a Gospel* (Philadelphia: Fortress Press, 1982), pp. 154-55. On the use of the threefold pattern in the Gospel of Mark, see D.E. Nineham, *The Gospel of St. Mark* (Baltimore: Penguin Books, 1963), p. 392; T.A. Burkill, *Mysterious Revelation* (Ithaca, NY: Cornell University Press, 1963), pp. 232, 243-44; Dormeyer, *Verhaltensmodell*, pp. 130-31, 153, 199, 213-14. For Pesch (*Markusevangelium*, II, pp. 15-16) this threefold pattern provides the key to the structure of the passion narrative. An overview of research on triads in the Gospel of Mark may be found in N. Petersen, 'The Composition of Mark 4.1–8.26', *HTR* 73 (1980), pp. 192-93 n. 23.

2. For discussion of the boat pattern, see R. Tannehill, 'The Disciples in Mark: The Function of a Narrative Role', *JR* 57 (1977), pp. 398-400; Petersen, 'The Composition of Mark 4.1–8.26', pp. 194-217.

3. Mark 14.43–15.15: The Arrest and Trial

John; elders, priests, scribes; three women at the tomb.

An important series of threefold structures focuses the failure of the disciples. The three boat scenes (4.35-41; 6.45-52; 8.14-21) stage the conflict between Jesus and his followers. The three bread scenes (6.35-44; 8.1-10; 8.14-21) demonstrate their failure to understand. The rejection which follows each passion prediction (8.32; 9.32; 10.35-37) confirms this obstinence. The Gethsemane scene (14.32-42) embodies this failure through the imagery of sleep. The threefold denial by Peter participates in this extended narrative chain; indeed, Peter's denial provides the climactic expression of this theme. The local and extended effect of this pattern is significant.[1] Thus, the dramatic curse of Peter in 14.66-72 is an intrinsic part of a larger narrative stream.

5. Consequently the denial scene in Mk 14.66-72 participates in an intricate series of relationships with the larger story. These lines create a pattern of interconnection and reciprocity which reshapes the significance of this scene and underscores the larger unity of the narrative.

Comparative Analysis

The denial scene appears in other literary settings. These different contexts and forms may sustain different narrative functions. In addition, these alternate uses of this story provide a comparative field for analysis.[2]

Pre-Markan Contexts. Various reconstructions of the denial scene have been attempted. Bultmann argued that the denial originated as an independent unit which he described as 'legendary and literary'.[3] This unit was not part of the earliest passion account, since it was linked

---

1. Concerning the narrative impact of this threefold pattern, Rhoads and Michie (*Mark as Story*, p. 55) contend that 'a threefold series is no mere repetition of similar events, but involves a progressive development. Each incident uncovers more about the characters or the conflicts, and the third episode fully reveals the dynamic of that entire series... The series thus creates suspense for the reader, who comes to anticipate a buildup to a dramatic climax. The reader is thereby prepared to view the three episodes of a series in relation to each other. That is, when the series unfolds, the reader then looks back from the perspective of the third scene and understands more clearly the issues involved in the first and second scenes.'

2. On the use of diachronic analysis as phenomenological description and comparison of co-texts, see Chapter 1.

3. Bultmann, *History*, p. 269.

well to the preceding material, but not to what follows.[1] Dibelius argued that the account of Peter's denial is not a soteriological presentation of the passion and was not an element of the oldest passion story.[2] The story is told instead from the interest of the church in Peter as the recipient of the first resurrection appearance.[3] In the independent form suggested by Bultmann and Dibelius the denial scene would have no real christological interests. Many have suggested that the account was preserved because of its historical value.[4] Others, following Dibelius, see here a theological interest in the role of Peter. In each case the story would serve a functional, if somewhat embarassing, role in the reports of the early church.

A second line of reconstruction sees the denial scene as an integral part of the pre-Markan passion story. Consistent with his reconstruction of the passion tradition, Rudolf Pesch champions the argument that Mk 14.66-72 was a vital part of the earliest passion narrative.[5] In this form the denial scene would interact with various elements of the passion tradition. Its interaction with the trial of Jesus would be evident and would play an important role. In this context the denial scene would also fulfill the prediction in Mk 14.27-31. Thus, this form of the story would provide a solid element in the wider passion story. The sharp contrast to the christological images of the trial scene would be present. Within this context the theme of discipleship failure would be limited, and the story would tend to become largely anecdotal.

The Gospel of Matthew. Mt. 26.69-75 takes over the denial scene with few significant changes. A number of verses reflect modification in style and clarification of difficult elements. The description of the servant girl has been compressed, and Jesus is described as a Galilean (Mt. 26.69). A different servant girl provides the second identification of Peter (Mt. 26.71). The second denial is accompanied by an oath (Mt. 26.72). Mt. 26.73 explains that Peter's speech identifies him as a Galilean. The confusing count of the cockcrow has been reduced to

1. Bultmann, *History*, pp. 269, 278.
2. Dibelius, *Tradition*, pp. 214-16.
3. Dibelius, *Tradition*, pp. 214-16.
4. See, for example, the argument of Taylor, *Mark*, pp. 571-72: 'The desire to warn the primitive community of the perils of apostasy and to present vividly an authentic tradition accounts adequately for the narrative' (p. 572).
5. Pesch, *Markusevangelium* II, pp. 446-47.

one instance, both in the prediction and in the fulfillment (Mt. 26.35, 74-75). Mt. 26.75 notes that the weeping of Peter was bitter. Thus, Mt. 26.69-75 takes over the basic form and function of the denial story. Matthew has typically altered the language and simplified the elements of this account. Beyond this the scene differs little from Mk 14.66-72.

The Gospel of Luke. Lk. 22.54-62 provides a continuous account of the denial prior to the trial scene. Thus, the sandwiching technique of Mk 14.53-72 has been abandoned. Beyond this Luke adds colorful elements to the account. Peter's oaths are omitted, but his responses are vivid. Peter's reply to the first identification is sharp: 'I do not know him, woman' (Lk. 22.57). A different person identifies Peter (Lk. 22.58) and receives a similar response: 'Man, I am not' (Lk. 22.58). The third denial is also colorful: 'Man, I do not know what you are saying' (Lk. 22.60). The second response of Peter provides a play on the confession of Jesus. Jesus' answer to the high priest builds on the 'I am' (ἐγώ εἰμι) construction (Lk. 22.70). The answer of Peter employs a contrasting phrase: 'I am not' (οὐκ εἰμί in Lk. 22.58). Like Matthew, Luke avoids the counting of the cockcrow (Lk. 22.60). Lk. 22.61 intensifies the drama by telling that Jesus turns and looks at Peter at the moment of his denial. This device, rather than an intercalation, links the denial to the trial scene. As in Matthew, Peter weeps bitterly.

Thus, Lk. 22.54-62 provides a distinct version of the denial scene. The sandwiching technique has been broken, and significant alterations are presented in the dialogue material. At the same time the Lukan version of the denial serves a similar function and creates a parallel image to Mk 14.66-72.

The Gospel of John. The Johannine version of the denial scene (Jn 18.15-18, 25-27) employs the sandwiching technique, but in a manner distinct from Mk 14.53-72.[1] Peter is identified here as Simon Peter,

---

1. Dewey ('Peter's Curse', pp. 104-105) finds here evidence of direct dependence of the Fourth Gospel upon the Gospel of Mark. She argues that four elements of Markan redaction have been adapted by John: (1) the intercalation pattern; (2) the use of θερμαινόμενος; (3) framing the trial of Jesus with Peter's warming himself; (4) a stage in which Peter has no discourse. Dewey concludes, 'These observations also argue against the existence of multiple versions of the denial story in the tradition

and he is accompanied by the 'other disciple' (Jn 18.15). The maiden in this account controls access to the door (Jn 18.17). The first scene of questioning and denial occurs prior to the narration of the trial of Jesus (Jn 18.17). This opening scene ends with the note that Peter was 'standing and warming himself' with the servants and officers (Jn 18.18). Following the trial scene (Jn 18.19-24) the narrative repeats the 'standing and warming himself' comment (Jn 18.25). Those around the fire instigate the second identification and denial (Jn 18.25). The language of the first two denials is identical: 'I am not' (Jn 18.17, 25). The third identification is by a relative of the man Peter injured (Jn 18.11, 26). The third denial is followed by the cockcrow, but no remembrance or interpretation accompanies this symbol (Jn 13.38; 18.27).

Thus, the Gospel of John has employed a distinct form of intercalation to intertwine the trial of Jesus and the denial by Peter. The contrast between Peter's denial and the faithful witness of Jesus confirms the Johannine image of Jesus as one who speaks the truth from God. Typically, the role of the 'other disciple' is significant. Various new details emerge in the Johannine version of the denial. Beyond this, the Johannine form of the story is largely anecdotal.

Summary

Comparative analysis revealed a number of possible narrative contexts for the scene of Peter's denial.[1] One reconstruction of the pre-Markan

and support the more probable view that later versions of the story are a combination of a knowledge of pre-Markan tradition, of Mk (in the case of Jn, a knowledge of the Synoptics), plus the creativity of later redactors: Mt, Lk, and Jn' (p. 105). Dewey does not miss the implications of this pattern for the question of composition history: 'These correspondences suggest that theories of Gospel sources and dependence must allow for greater flexibility. Inter-Gospel contacts appear much more fluid, and it is at least possible that Jn knew the Synoptics and perhaps even post-Synoptic traditions. We might opt for more recent views of oral and folk traditions and for greater creativity and selectivity on the part of the Evangelists rather than for strict and rigid limitations of dependence' (p. 105, n. 28). In my opinion more attention should be given to the possibility that the use of intercalation represents a wider pattern of tradition and transmission rather than a uniquely Markan pattern. Nonetheless, the specific and extensive similarities between the denial scene in Mk 14.66-72 and Jn 18.15-18, 25-27 suggest common knowledge of some form of this story.

1. This comparative analysis also supports the theory that a basic report under-

context suggests that the story operated as an independent anecdote about Peter. Such a story would speak to the historical or theological interest of the church in the role of Peter. A second reconstruction placed the story in a fixed pre-Markan passion tradition. Within this context the denial completes the prophecy in Mk 14.27-31 and provides a sharp contrast to the trial scene. Matthew and Luke have shaped the story in various ways, but both retain the basic function of the denial scene. The Gospel of John narrates a distinct version of the denial but accomplishes similar results.

When seen against the field of these various alternatives, Mk 14.66-72 operates uniquely within the context of the Gospel of Mark. Peter's resistance is narrated as a story of dramatic failure and denial. The intercalation of the trial scene into the denial story creates a pattern of mutual interpretation. The prophecy of Jesus is fulfilled through Peter's denial and emphasized by the crowing rooster. The theme of discipleship failure is played out in its fullness. This image of failure is enlarged by the faithful testimony of Jesus. At the same time the failure of Peter dramatizes the portrait of Jesus: he is the faithful and courageous witness, the Son of God who is about to die.

Mark 15.1-15: The Trial before Pilate

Mk 15.1-15 presents the second stage of Jesus' trial. This scene plays a vital role in the plotting of the death story and in the characterization of Jesus.

---

lies Mk 14.66-72. The four elements of the basic report are present in all four Gospels (with Peter's departure implied in John). In contrast, Matthew, Luke and John treat elements not in the basic report with more flexibility. All three replace the awkward counting of the cockcrow with a simple report. Luke finds the intercalation of the trial scene unnecessary and ties the two scenes through Jesus' looking at Peter. John finds the connection to the prophecy of betrayal unnecessary.

Synchronic Analysis

The motifs of Mk 15.1-15 may be plotted as follows:

Introduction
All come 15.1

Body
Pilate questions	15.2a
Jesus answers	15.2b
Chief priests condemn	15.3
Pilate questions	15.4
Jesus is silent (passive)	15.5a
Pilate is amazed (passive)	15.5b
Narrator informs	15.6-7
Crowd demands	15.8
Pilate questions	15.9
Narrator informs	15.10
Chief priests incite	15.11
Pilate questions	15.12
Crowd demands	15.13
Pilate questions	15.14a
Crowd demands	15.14b

Conclusion
| Barabbas departs | 15.15a |
| Jesus departs | 15.15b |

Narrative Morphology. Transition to and from this scene provides the typical introduction and conclusion. This framing makes the scene a closed unit, though it has close connections to what precedes and follows. The intervention of the narrator creates an unusual set of motifs and provides information vital to the advance of the narrative. The body of the story employs an extended question-and-answer sequence.

Morphologically the second trial scene is structured around a basic report which has been developed through a variety of techniques. This development creates extensive ties to the surrounding context.

1. A foundational report provides the basic pattern of the second trial scene.[1] (1) The gathering of the religious authorities is reported

---

1. In my opinion the careful development of the trial scene provides a general sketch of the foundational report but permits no detailed separation of tradition and redaction. Nonetheless, Hahn (*Titles*, p. 173) defines 15.1, 3-5, 15b as the 'still discernable older report'. Dormeyer (*Verhaltensmodell*, pp. 174-86) seeks further

(15.1). (2) The political charge is established in a hearing before Pilate.[1] (3) The story recalls the silence of Jesus in the face of his accusers (15.5). (4) The innocence of Jesus is asserted (15.10, 14). (5) The death sentence is focused (15.15). (6) The abuse of Jesus is reported (15.15).

2. This foundational report stands in continuity with the basic pattern behind the first trial scene (14.53-65).[2] Various elements suggest that the two trial scenes reflect a common foundational report. (1) The naming of the three religious groups and their condemnation of Jesus is cited in both scenes (14.53; 15.1).[3] (2) Both trials highlight the role of the chief priests (14.60; 15.3, 11). (3) A twofold line of questioning is addressed to Jesus (14.60-61; 15.2, 4). (4) A third line of questioning is addressed to the assembled group (14.63-64; 15.9-14). (5) The silence of Jesus is highlighted (14.60; 15.5). (6) The innocence of Jesus is affirmed (14.55-59; 15.10, 14). (7) The interest in the death sentence underlies both accounts (14.55, 64; 15.13, 14).[4] (8) The abuse of Jesus is focused (14.65d; 15.15).

precision and sees an older report in 15.1b, 3, 5, 6, 11, 7, 15.

1. Gnilka (*Markus*, II, p. 298) notes that only a non-Jew (Pilate) employs the King of the Jews title for Jesus and concludes that 'in this perspective this expectation carries a primarily political character'. Pesch (*Markusevangelium*, II, p. 457) incorrectly identifies the political charge with the religious charge of 14.61: 'The question... of Pilate repeats in a Gentile formulation... the question of the high priest in 14.61'. Schweizer (*Mark*, p. 336) reaches a similar conclusion.

2. Pesch (*Markusevangelium*, II, p. 454) notes agreement between the following verses: 14.60a/15.2a; 14.60b/15.4a; 14.61a/15.4b; 14.61b/15.4a; 14.61c/15.2b; 14.62a/15.2c. Pesch explains this correspondence through the tendencies of the narrator and the legal nature of the material.

3. Strickly speaking the designation of the priests, elders and scribes alongside the Sanhedrin (15.1) is tautological. Mk 15.1 exhibits obvious parallels to 14.53. Taylor (*Mark*, p. 578) argued that 15.1 provides the original reference to the actions of the priests and likely stood at the beginning of the trial process.

4. It is ironic that the Sanhedrin, which perhaps cannot execute, pronounces a death sentence, while Pilate, who can execute, pronounces no formal sentence. This foundational element has been clarified from two perspectives: the impetus behind the execution is found in the religious authorities (3.6; 11.18; 12.12; 14.1), but only Pilate holds the power of execution. Thus the execution of Jesus is ultimately a political event, as the means of death (crucifixion) demonstrates. Gnilka (*Markus*, II, p. 303) incorrectly blends the two scenes: 'The Sanhedrin pronounced the death sentence; Pilate was only the enforcer'. In my opinion the death sentence, while it serves the aims of the religious authorities, is primarily political in nature.

3. This foundational report has been developed into a full narrative segment through various techniques. (1) The nature of the political charge has been detailed. Pilate poses the question of sedition (claim to kingship), which presents a capital crime. The ambiguous response of Jesus (σὺ λέγεις) to the political charge is also noted.[1] (2) Pilate's response to Jesus' silence is described (θαυμάζειν in 15.5).[2] (3) The Barabbas incident is reported and linked to the fate of Jesus (15.6-14).[3]

4. The second trial scene has been constructed in a manner that resists reduction into traditional and redactional layers. The foundational report and its development have been woven together into an inseparable narrative constellation. Numerous elements demonstrate this interconnection. (1) The religious threat has been joined with the political charge. This union is supported by the use of πάλιν (15.4), which assumes the political question (15.2) and links it to the religious charges (15.3). (2) The report of Jesus' silence assumes his prior response (15.2). This connection is supported by the note that Jesus no longer (οὐκέτι) answers Pilate. (3) The role of the crowd in the death sentence (15.6-14) is assumed in the report of Pilate's decision (15.15). (4) The situation of Barabbas (15.6-14) is assumed in the report of his release (15.15). Thus, the traits of the narrative resist attempts to reduce this scene to a traditional stratum and secondary developments. Through various lines of assumption and interconnection the elements

---

1. The question of whether σὺ λέγεις means yes or no is debated. For discussion of possible nuances, see Gnilka, *Markus*, II, p. 300, especially n. 21.

2. Gnilka (*Markus*, II, p. 300) correctly notes that Pilate's amazement is more than a psychological description. A similar response in Mk 5.20 notes the power of God at work in an unexpected way.

3. Numerous scholars see the Barabbas incident as a break in the story. See, for example, Lohmeyer, *Markus*; R. Schnackenburg, *The Gospel according to St Mark* (trans. W. Kruppe; New York: Crossroad, 1981). Gnilka (*Markus*, II, p. 305) reaches the opposite conclusion: 'the trial of Jesus and that of Barabbas are, in narrative terms, tightly woven together'. The issue of the Passover amnesty proves difficult. Evidence for an ongoing custom of Passover amnesty is absent. Some have suggested that the amnesty of 15.6-14 was a one-time event, though 15.6 suggests otherwise. Schweizer (*Mark*, pp. 335-36) concludes that 'It is both possible and probable that this represented a single case of clemency which was reported here to form a contrast to the condemnation of Jesus...' For detailed discussion of the issues involved, see Gnilka, *Markus*, II, pp. 300-301, 305-309; Pesch, *Markusevangelium*, II, pp. 461-62.

3. *Mark 14.43–15.15: The Arrest and Trial*

of Mk 15.1-15 have been framed into a coherent narrative scene.

5. This morphological arrangement likely reflects the distinct compositional history and interests underlying this scene. Several textual patterns suggest the process of composition.

5.1. Mk 15.1-15 exhibits a conscious parallel to the first trial scene. This relationship suggests a foundational report common to both scenes as well as a conscious dovetailing of elements from the two stories. For example, the explicit role of the religious authorities in general and the chief priest(s) in particular which was developed in 14.53-65 operates as a summary focus in 15.1, 3, 11. A second example is provided by Jesus' silence. Both scenes maintain the silence of Jesus alongside a verbal response. The silence of Jesus in 14.60-61 is secondary to his decisive reply in 14.62. Conversely Mk 15.2-5 subordinates an ambiguous reply (15.2) to the decisive silence of Jesus (15.5).[1] Thus, Mk 15.1-15 has been constructed with a conscious interconnection to 14.53-65.

5.2. The development of the foundational report exhibits a concern for the positioning of social groups. Various groups are presented, and their role in Jesus' death is clarified. (1) Religious authorities— particularly the chief priests—provide the motivation for Jesus' death. (2) Secular authority declares Jesus innocent, but nonetheless provides the means of execution. (3) The crowd operates under the sway of the authorities and demands the death of Jesus. (4) The followers of Jesus are conspiciously absent. Thus, the second trial scene is composed with an interest in the polemics and apologetics of social location and identification.

5.3. The second trial scene is structured around a distinct christological interest. The narrative takes particular care to affirm the innocence of Jesus, to demonstrate his suffering in silence, and to note his abuse.

---

1. Schweizer (*Mark*, pp. 336-37) argues that the church had little interest in the details of Jesus' trial before Pilate. The one exception to this pattern is the interest in Jesus' silence. Schweizer argues that 'The silence of Jesus... was the only feature which continued to impress the church, because it revealed Jesus' will to suffer'. In my opinion the silence of Jesus reveals nothing of a psychological or volitional character. While internal aspects of Jesus' silence remain beyond our grasp, the external function is clear: Jesus is here sketched in prophetic images from the Old Testament.

5.4. This compositional strategy most likely echoes the extended reflection and activity of an editorial community. The creative development of the foundational report and the nuanced interconnection with the first trial suggest a lengthy process of composition and circulation. In addition, the concern for identification and positioning of various groups reflects interests and values more communal than personal. The shape of the second trial scene most likely emerges from extended reflection, circulation and composition within a community of believers.

Narrative Syntax. Morphological analysis demonstrated the complex compositional patterns present in the second trial scene. Syntactical analysis will show how the components of Mk 15.1-15 have been staged in a manner that creates various narrative dynamics.

1. The question-and-answer format generates a sequence of syntactical connections. This format sustains a dialogical trial scene similar to the trial of Jesus in Mk 14.53-65 and the trial of Peter in Mk 14.66-72.

2. The story of Jesus' destiny is framed around the Barabbas report, creating a type of intercalation. As in other intercalations in the Gospel of Mark, the middle element provides commentary on the outer elements.[1] This intercalation is dominated by irony. Barabbas, who is guilty of murder (15.7), goes free while Jesus, who is innocent (15.10, 14), is taken away to die.[2] This irony is extended by the sense of Barabbas's name. The freed criminal is called βαραββᾶς—literally, 'son of the father'—but Jesus, the true and innocent Son, is sentenced to die.[3] This intertwining of Jesus' destiny with that of Barabbas provides a dramatic and ironic depth for the trial of Jesus.

3. A linguistic frame is created around the παράδοσις theme. At

---

1. See, for example, the interpretive role of the death of the Baptist for the sending of the disciples in Mk 6.7-30.

2. Pesch (*Markusevangelium*, II, pp. 462-63, 467) argues—incorrectly in my view—that Barabbas may be innocent and that this scene does not yet contrast the innocence of Jesus with the murderous rebellion of Barabbas.

3. Unlike other instances (Mk 10.46), no translation of the name is provided. While such explicit irony may appear at first reading to be contrived, such nomenclature is not unusual. For discussion of the use of βαραββᾶς as a name see Pesch, *Markusevangelium*, II, p. 462, especially n. 8; Gnilka, *Markus*, II, p. 301. Thus, the ironic sense of the name does not impact the question of its historicity or non-historicity.

3. *Mark 14.43–15.15: The Arrest and Trial*

the beginning of this scene (15.1) Jesus is handed over to Pilate. At the end of the scene (15.15) Pilate hands Jesus over to abuse and death. Thus, the entire trial is framed as the παράδοσις of Jesus.

4. Decisive use is made of threefold patterns in the second trial. The scene is structured around three separate lines of questioning (15.2; 15.4-5; 15.8-14). This syntactical strategy impacts the scene in dramatic ways.

4.1. The threefold staging of the trial employs a familiar narrative technique. This pattern encourages the reader to connect this story with the first trial, with Peter's trial and with various other scenes (Gethsemane, transfiguration, passion predictions).

4.2. The threefold staging creates a process of delay and intensification. This technique of retardation and increasing drama reflects a wider narrative pattern with an important impact.[1]

4.3. As with other scenes, the threefold pattern reaches its summit in the third stage. Mk 15.1-15 accomplishes this climax through two techniques. (1) Because this story embraces an established pattern, the third line of questioning may be presumed as the structural climax of the scene. (2) This structural climax is enhanced by the internal pattern of the story. The first line of questioning ends with an ambiguous reply (15.2). The second line of questioning fades away into the silence of Jesus (15.5). Thus, the brief exchange between Pilate and Jesus offers little substance. The charge of the religious leaders is not confirmed, the King of the Jews title is not accepted and the response of Pilate is not judgment but amazement. Thus, the internal strategy of this story reduces the impact of the opening questions and locates the culminative focus in the third line of questioning.

Significantly, the third line of questioning (15.8-14) centers on the dialogue between Pilate and the people. In this way the story throws its central verdict upon the crowd and the religious leaders who guide them. The silence of Jesus creates a narrative realignment which requires that Pilate and the crowd answer for their actions. In some sense it is not Jesus but Pilate and the people who are on trial.

4.4. This climactic third line of questioning is developed through further use of triads. The third sequence of questions is itself built around three sets of questions to the crowd. (1) In 15.9 Pilate asks if they desire Jesus' release. (2) In 15.12 Pilate asks what he should do

---

1. See especially the discussion on Mk 14.66-72.

with the King of the Jews. (3) The third question brings to a climax the exchange between Pilate and the crowd. Thus, the third line of questioning reaches its summit in Pilate's third question to the people. This doubly climactic moment provides the ultimate verdict on Jesus: he is innocent.

5. Following upon the climactic verdict of innocence, the sentence to abuse and death (15.15) provides a study in ironic reversal. The effect of this syntactical maneuver is powerful. The handing over to crucifixion in 15.15 is built upon the threefold demand of the crowd (15.13, 14).[1] The reality of the death sentence is established through a single verb—σταυρόω. This pronouncement reverberates with concentric waves of horror and grief: Jesus will die, he will be executed as a criminal, he will be tortured and crucified.

6. The syntactical strategy of this story creates a sharp focus on the role of different participants. This scene guides the reader to understand various contributions to the death of Jesus. Religious authorities initiate and motivate the death of Jesus. Secular authorities provide the process of condemnation and the means of death. The crowds act as a persuasive mob which chants for Jesus' crucifixion.[2] The disciples are absent. Thus, the strategy of this story helps the reader to evaluate various groups of actants.

7. The syntax of this story also makes significant contributions in the area of plot functions. While the death threat has been present since 3.6, this scene makes Jesus' death a real possibility. In addition, the trial scene demonstrates the process of condemnation and clarifies the role of various participants. Significantly, Mk 15.1-15 transforms the death theme into an execution,[3] and more significantly, into a crucifixion.[4]

8. The syntactical strategy at work in Mk 15.1-15 provides a

1. The use of πάλιν in 15.13 creates an unnarrated first cry. While the logical effect is questionable, the narrative effect is clear: the cry of the crowd is an iterative, growing demand which climaxes in the third appeal for crucifixion (15.14).

2. The ironic reversal of the cry of the crowd in Mk 11.9-10 ('hosanna') and in 15.13-14 ('crucify') is inescapable.

3. While the death theme is prevalent, death as legal execution is, at best, only implicit prior to 14.53.

4. Incredibly Mk 15.13 provides the first mention of crucifixion. The cross is used as a metaphor for discipleship in 8.34. While the impact of cross terminology is limited prior to the second trial, τὸν ἐσταυρωμένον becomes a decisive christological title in 16.6.

3. Mark 14.43–15.15: The Arrest and Trial

climactic focus on the identity of Jesus. Amidst the frantic verbiage of religious leaders, secular authorities and a frenzied crowd, the narrative sketches a decisive image of Jesus. This Christology is based on the details of the trial scene and framed in the imagery of the Old Testament. In his hour of need Jesus is abandoned by his followers: 'My friends and companions stand aloof from my plague, and my kinsmen stand afar off' (Ps. 38.11). His condemnation by religious authorities recalls 'those who seek my life lay their snares, those who seek my hurt speak of ruin, and meditate treachery all the day long' (Ps. 38.12). He is silent before his accuser 'like a speechless man who does not open his mouth' (Ps. 38.13). His accuser is amazed, recalling the Scriptures: 'So shall he startle many nations; kings shall shut their mouths because of him' (Isa. 52.15). He is abused in the place of another as one 'wounded for our transgressions, he was bruised for our iniquities; upon him was the chastisement that made us whole, and with his stripes we are healed' (Isa. 53.5-6).[1] He is sentenced, and 'by oppression and judgment he was taken away' (Isa. 53.8). He is condemned to be 'cut off out of the land of the living' (Isa. 53.8).

These connections support two decisive lines of Christology. (1) The life and death of Jesus is prophetic, both in its content and in its manner. He is the fulfillment of the Scriptures and is himself God's ultimate prophet. (2) The prophetic mission of Jesus reaches its summit in his martyrdom. He embodies the Old Testament images of suffering innocence and completes the destiny of the Suffering Servant.

---

1. In my opinion Mk 15.1-15 does not use Barabbas to focus the death of Jesus in behalf of others, but to sharpen and contrast the innocence of Jesus. Attempts to see the release of Barabbas in relation to Mk 10.45 or to subsequent theories of vicarious atonement import a theology not focused in this passage. See, for example, the argument of Schweizer, *Mark*, p. 338, who says that 'the idea of vicarious suffering is suggested by placing side by side Barabbas who was set free and Jesus who was handed over to be crucified'. This connection is also attempted by Gnilka, *Markus*, II, p. 303. In my opinion the death of Jesus is linked to Isa. 53.4-6 and is connected more directly to the chanting mob and the absent disciples than to the solitary figure of Barabbas. Thus, the death of Jesus is an 'offering in relation to the many', as Mk 10.45 predicts. The early Christian focus on Jesus' death 'for us' emphasizes not the replacement of the individual, but rather the fulfillment of the Old Testament: 'Christ died in behalf of our sins according to the scriptures' (1 Cor. 15.3). Thus, the primary reference in Mk 15.1-15 is not the Barabbas connection but the Old Testament—most likely the Servant imagery of Isa. 53—and the needs of the many.

The trial before Pilate unveils the ultimate destiny of Jesus. The attempt to label Jesus as 'King of the Jews' (15.2, 9, 12) is not accepted by Jesus or by the crowd. The story focuses instead upon a different image. The innocence of Jesus is established through the judgment of a secular authority and through allusion to sacred texts. His silence in the face of abuse and judgment confirms his identity as the suffering prophet of God. The portrait of Jesus stands forth in stark clarity: he is the one of whom the prophet spoke:

> He was oppressed, and he was afflicted, yet he opened not his mouth; like a lamb that is led to slaughter, and like a sheep that before its shearers is silent, so he opened not his mouth. By oppression and judgment he was taken away; and as for his generation, who considered that he was cut off out of the land of the living, stricken for the transgression of my people? And they made his grave with the wicked and with a rich man in his death, although he had done no violence, and there was no deceit in his mouth (Isa. 53.7-9).

The Passion Context. Important narrative connections have been established between the second trial scene and the larger account of the passion. These links creates lines of reciprocal interpretation.

1. The weaving of the second trial scene into the passion story creates a coherent plot line. Because of this a logical sequence of events clarifies the process of execution. The seeming incongruence between an impotent Sanhedrin and the reality of Jesus' death is clarified by the legal process in Mk 15.1-15. While the religious authorities provide the motivation for the death of Jesus, the death plot is completed when Pilate provides the instrument of judgment and execution. Thus, Mk 15.1-15 provides a bridge which allows the hostility of the religious authorities to come to full expression in the crucifixion scene (15.20b-37).

In addition, the plot function of various groups is clarified. The role of the religious leaders was established in the first trial scene (14.53-65). The role of Jesus' followers was demonstrated in the trial of Peter (14.66-72). The trial before Pilate now confirms the role of the religious authorities and demonstrates the role played by political authority and popular demands in the death of Jesus. Thus, Mk 15.1-15 completes the cast of those who lead Jesus to his death.

2. Explicit connections are established between Mk 15.1-15, the trial of Peter (14.66-72) and the first trial scene (14.53-65). The death of Jesus is narrated within a complex constellation of envy (15.10),

cowardice (14.71), violence (14.65; 15.15), conspiracy (14.55), lying (14.56), mob incitement (15.11), expediency (15.15) and miscarriage of justice (15.14-15). These intricate lines of interaction place the death of Jesus within a host of influences and interests and resist the construction of a simplistic, anti-Jewish polemic by the reader.[1]

3. At the same time the trial before Pilate completes the image of Jesus as the prophet of God. The prophetic Christology becomes explicit only in connection with the passion narrative. The earlier scenes of the passion story establish Jesus as a prophet through his predictions and instructions. This prophetic Christology is linked to the approaching death of Jesus through various techniques. Mk 15.1-15 completes this image by showing the innocent suffering of Jesus as the Suffering Servant. While Jesus is characterized earlier through his words, this scene focuses his identity through his silence. Thus, both sides of the prophetic destiny are confirmed in the person of Jesus: he is the authentic prophet who speaks for God, yet suffers in silence before his accusers. Drawing upon various Old Testament images, this scene collaborates with the larger passion story to generate a complex, yet vivid characterization of Jesus as God's prophet.

The Gospel Context. Lines of reciprocity are drawn across the breadth of this narrative. These connections take various forms and generate a pattern of mutual interpretation.

1. A number of linguistic connections join the second trial to the larger narrative world. The condemnation of Jesus (κατηγορέω) by religious authorities is not limited to the passion context, but is developed throughout Jesus' ministry. This theme is established linguistically near the beginning of Jesus' ministry (3.2) and comes to completion in the second trial scene (15.3, 4). In a similar manner the death plot is initiated and completed in an assembly (συμβούλιον in 3.6; 15.1). Similarly the amazement which accompanies the ministry of Jesus is established early (5.20; 6.6) and is completed in the trial scene (15.44).

A widespread linguistic connection is established around the act of crying out (κράζω). In the Gospel of Mark κράζω is used solely to present differing responses to Jesus. Demons cry out at his presence

---

1. In my opinion assertions such as that of Schweizer (*Mark*, p. 337) that 'it is upon the authorities alone that Mark places the blame' overlook the complex constellation of interests and influences which surrounds the death of Jesus in the Gospel of Mark.

and command (1.26; 3.11; 5.5, 7; 9.26). Those in need cry out for aid (9.24; 10.47, 48). The centurion cries out in confession (15.39). Within this linguistic constellation the role of the crowd becomes significant. They embody two opposing responses to Jesus. In 11.9 they cry out with hosannas in affirmation of Jesus. In the second trial the crowd cries out for the crucifixion of Jesus (15.13, 14). Thus, the response of the crowd in Mk 15.1-15 provides one element in a larger narrative strategy.

Most significantly, a linguistic pattern is established around the theme of the handing over (παραδίδωμαι). The Gospel of Mark employs παραδίδωμαι some twenty times, eighteen of which participate in a singular theme.[1] In the Gospel of Mark παραδίδωμαι presents a martyrological theme. This imagery is established around the destiny of the Baptist. His handing over to imprisonment and death (1.14) initiates the coming forth of Jesus. This imagery is then applied extensively to the ministry of Jesus. The narrative foreshadows the handing over as early as 3.19, then uses the term three times as a prophecy on the lips of Jesus (9.31; twice in 10.33). This theme is developed fully within the context of the passion story. The plotting and prediction of Jesus' παράδοσις (14.10, 11, 18, 21, 41, 42, 44) comes to fulfillment in the second trial scene, which is framed by the παράδοσις theme (15.1, 10, 15). Significantly, Jesus predicts that the παράδοσις destiny shared by the Baptist and by the Christ will also be shared by the disciples (13.9, 11, 12). Thus the handing over of Jesus in the second trial scene is an inseparable element in an extensive narrative pattern.

2. In addition to these linguistic interconnections, various plot elements participate in intricate and widespread literary connections. The various plot expectations for arrest and trial by secular authorities (3.6; 9.31; 10.33; 14.41, 48) are fulfilled in the trial before Pilate. The crowd which prevented the death of Jesus (11.18; 12.12; 14.2) now calls for his crucifixion (15.13, 14). Religious and political authorities collaborate in the death plot (Pharisees and Herodians in 3.6; chief priests, elders, scribes, Sanhedrin, Pilate in 15.1). Thus, Mk 15.1-15 gathers various elements from the larger narrative and completes them in the scene of Jesus' condemnation before Pilate.

3. The portrait of Jesus is enlarged dramatically by the interaction

1. Exceptions are found in 4.29, which refers to the yielding of fruit and in 7.13, which uses the term to speak of human traditions and customs.

3. Mark 14.43–15.15: The Arrest and Trial

of Mk 15.1-15 with the Gospel context. The narrative introduces Jesus as 'one who teaches with authority' (1.22). Jesus' powerful words and wondrous deeds demonstrate the authority of his preaching/teaching. The narrative then establishes a close link between the teaching of Jesus and the hostility which leads to his death (3.6; 11.18; 12.12, 13). Thus, the wider narrative portrays Jesus from the beginning as the wondrous proclaimer whose teaching leads to his death.[1] The trial scene in Mk 15.1-15 completes this complex image. Building upon the portrait of Jesus as powerful teacher from the larger narrative and upon the sharp focus on Jesus as the authentic prophet in the passion account, Mk 15.1-15 shows Jesus as the righteous prophet who silently bears judgment and condemnation. The scene closes with the beginning of the death march. In this manner the link between the prophetic teaching activity of Jesus and his passion is completed. The story of Jesus' life is linked to the story of his death. A vital and complex image of Jesus is cast across the scene of his death: he is the wondrous teacher, the righteous prophet who suffers and dies at the hands of sinners.

Comparative Analysis
The trial before Pilate is told in other narrative contexts. These alternate performances create a comparative field against which to highlight the form and function of Mk 15.1-15.[2]

Pre-Markan Contexts. Attempts to establish a pre-Markan form and use of this story prove inconclusive. A host of scholars argue for a historical basis for the account,[3] and this would explain its preservation. The story about Barabbas is seen by many as a secondary addition to this account.[4] If the account existed as an independent unit, almost all theological connections with the larger story would be missing. As an independent unit this story would fill out the historical report of Jesus' trial before Pilate by showing Jesus in images from the Old Testament.

---

1. See E.K. Broadhead, *Teaching with Authority: Miracles and Christology in the Gospel of Mark* (Sheffield: JSOT Press, 1992).
2. See Chapter 1 on the comparative role of diachronic analysis in narrative criticism.
3. See, for example, Bultmann, *History*, p. 279; Gnilka, *Markus*, II, p. 296; Taylor, *Mark*, p. 577.
4. Bultmann, *History*, p. 272; Dormeyer, *Verhaltensmodell*, pp. 179-86.

Others have argued more successfully that the trial before Pilate was an integral part of the earliest passion tradition.[1] In this form the story would play a crucial role in the plotting of the death story. The historical aura of this event would be preserved. The motivation and the implementation of the death sentence would be explained through this account. The image of Jesus as the suffering righteous one would remain intact.

The Gospel of Matthew. Mt. 27.1-26 makes stylistic changes and expands the trial before Pilate. Matthew refers to Pilate consistently as the 'governor' (Mt. 27.11, 15, 21). The trial is put on hold while the fate of Judas is reported (Mt. 27.3-10). Jesus' brief answer and silence before Pilate are maintained. The silence of Jesus is emphasized with the comment that he answered 'not one word' (Mt. 27.14). In the report about Barabbas the description of his crimes is omitted. In the Gospel of Matthew the Christ title is employed by Pilate to replace the 'King of the Jews' title (Mt. 27.17, 22). The image of Jesus as the righteous, innocent one is expanded by the dream of Pilate's wife (Mt. 27.19). The guilt of the people is enlarged by the addition of Pilate's handwashing (Mt. 27.24-25). This guilt is accepted by the people when they cry, 'His blood (be) upon us and upon our children' (Mt. 27.25).

Thus, Mt. 27.1-26 presents a distinct form of the trial scene. This account makes explict the image of Jesus as the suffering righteous one. The report that Jesus is King of the Jews is replaced by the Christ title. Particular focus is given to the guilt of the leaders and of the Jewish people in the death of Jesus. This expanded and dramatized account of the trial before Pilate serves the same basic function as Mk 15.1-15.

The Gospel of Luke. Lk. 23.1-25 alters and expands this scene in various ways. Here the charges against Jesus are made clear: he is guilty of insurrection (Lk. 23.2, 5). Pilate repeatedly declares Jesus innocent and resists his death (Lk. 23.4, 14, 15, 20, 22). Lk. 23.6-12 tells of a third trial before Herod. Here Jesus is silent, and no verdict is given. Herod's conclusion is reported instead by Pilate (Lk. 23.15). At the end of the trial before Herod, Jesus is mocked but not beaten.

---

1. See, for example, Gnilka, *Markus*, II, p. 298; Pesch, *Markusevangelium*, II, pp. 454-68.

3. *Mark 14.43–15.15: The Arrest and Trial*

This form of the story tends to remove the burden of guilt from Pilate and place it squarely on the people.

Thus, Lk. 23.1-25 narrates the political trial of Jesus in a distinct form and emphasizes differing elements. Specific charges of insurrection motivate the trial. Pilate does not employ titles for Jesus, but repeatedly declares him innocent. Herod confirms this opinion. Jesus is handed over at the insistence not of the political authorities, but of the Jewish people.

The Gospel of John. Jn 18.28–19.17 presents a sharply different image of the political trial. The religious authorities lead Jesus before Pilate, but they will not enter the praetorium (Jn 18.28). In an ironic presentation the religious leaders plot murder but avoid ritual defilement. Pilate comes out to the people, and a lengthy debate over the validity of the trial ensues (Jn 18.29-32). The purpose for the trial is explained at two levels: it fulfills the wishes of the leaders for a death sentence, and it fulfills the prophecy of Jesus concerning the means of his death (Jn 18.31-32).

Returning to the inner scene, Pilate asks Jesus the question that appears in Mk 15.2: 'Are you the king of the Jews?' (Jn 18.33). In contrast to other versions of the trial the answer of Jesus is extensive (Jn 18.34-37). Following an opening rejoinder to Pilate (Jn 18.34), Jesus responds to the question of kingship. This lengthy discourse before Pilate provides a clear christological statement: Jesus indeed has a kingdom, but his kingdom is a heavenly one (Jn 18.36). The mission of Jesus is defined in his third response: he has come into the world to bear witness to the truth (Jn 18.37-38). Thus, the identity of Jesus is made explicit in his witness before Pilate. Following this testimony Pilate goes out to the Jewish people and declares Jesus innocent (Jn 18.38). The offer of release is then made by Pilate (Jn 18.39). The crowd requests instead the release of Barabbas, who is a thief (Jn 18.40). Following the abuse by the soldiers (Jn 19.1-3), Pilate presents Jesus before the people with his verdict: 'I find no crime in him' (Jn 19.4). The Johannine account makes the role of the religious leaders clear: it is they who cry out, against Pilate's wishes, for the death of Jesus (Jn 19.6, 7). Their charge is clarified in Jn 18.7: Jesus has claimed to be the Son of God.

Another round of questioning follows inside the praetorium. Here the silence of Jesus is implied (Jn 19.10), but Jesus responds with a rejection of Pilate's authority. The charges become political in Jn 19.12: Jesus has claimed to be a king over against Caesar. The King of the Jews title is central in the remainder of the story. From the judgment seat Pilate presents Jesus at a sacred season to the Jewish people as their king (Jn 18.13-14). The repeated cries for crucifixion end in a decisive exchange between Pilate and the chief priests: 'Shall I crucify your king?' 'We have no king but Caesar' (Jn 19.15). At the end of this scene Pilate hands Jesus over to his death (Jn 19.16).

Thus, the Gospel of John has taken the frame of the trial before Pilate and narrated an extensive account. The characterization of Pilate is developed, and he declares the innocence of Jesus in a variety of ways. The responses of Jesus are explicit and lengthy. He rejects the authority of Pilate, and he is unswayed by the events before him. At the same time Jesus bears clear witness to his identity and his mission: he has come to bear witness to the truth, and he will reign over a kingdom not of this world. In addition, Jn 18.28–19.17 places the blame for the death of Jesus on the Jewish people in general and on their leaders in particular. At the end of the story the chief priest pronounces the verdict upon himself and his people: they have abandoned the Father and crucified the Son.

Other. The *Acts of Pilate* (3.2; 4.4-5; 9.4-5) also narrates the political trial of Jesus. This narrative draws heavily upon the Johannine tradition and provides a sympathetic view of Pilate.

Summary

The scene of Jesus' trial before Pilate appears in various narrative contexts and creates diverse images. The Gospel of Matthew expands and dramatizes the story, but uses it in a fashion similar to the Gospel of Mark. The Gospel of Luke uses the account to emphasize the charge of insurrection, the innocence of Jesus in the eyes of Pilate and Herod, and the guilt of the Jewish people in the death of Jesus. The Gospel of John generates from this scene a series of debates which place the blame for the death of Jesus on the Jewish people and their failed leadership. A clear Johannine image of Jesus emerges: he is God's witness to the truth who rules over an eternal kingdom.

This comparative analysis of the trial before Pilate helps to focus the images of Mk 15.1-15. Various elements from the wider narrative are gathered into this account. The expectations for trial and

3. Mark 14.43–15.15: The Arrest and Trial

condemnation are fulfilled. The roles of the religious leaders, the political authorities and the people are demonstrated. The motivation and the means of the death scene are clarified. The plot line is carried forward to the point of the crucifixion. Over against these images of conspiracy, violence and murder, a sharp portrait of Jesus emerges. In the face of violence and condemnation, Jesus is the righteous servant and prophet of God who suffers at the hands of his own people.

Conclusion

The four stories of Mk 14.43–15.15 play a vital role in the account of Jesus' death. Formal analysis of these narrative units demonstrates their vital contribution to issues of plotting, characterization and narrative identity.

Plotting

These scenes provide significant advances in the plot line of the passion story. Building upon the prophetic Christology and the narrative symbolism generated in Mk 14.1-42, these stories plot the journey of Jesus to the cross. In doing so various images generated in Mk 14.1-42 are realized in the scenes of Mk 14.43–15.15, providing a prophetic paradigm. The predictions of betrayal, arrest and abandonment are fulfilled. The hostility of the religious authorities unfolds in the first trial scene. The failure of the disciples is completed in Peter's denial. The death sentence is passed in the trial before Pilate. Thus, various narrative expectations from the first section of the passion story come to objective reality in Mk 14.43–15.15. Through this process a narrative bridge is constructed between the predictions and symbols of Jesus' death (14.1-42) and the cross event (15.16–16.8). Through the scenes of Mk 14.43–15.15 the motivation and the means of Jesus' death are put in place. Because of this the scene of Jesus' death is preceded by a series of interpretive images and by a logical sequence of causation.

Characterization

Beyond this contribution to the plotting of the passion story, the four scenes in Mk 14.43–15.15 play a vital role in the characterization of Jesus. Complex lines of identification traverse these scenes.

1. The arrest scene (Mk 14.43-53a) develops the image of Jesus as the true teacher and prophet sent from God. Through various

narrative techniques the arrest story draws upon the temple scene (11.15-19) and upon the parable of the vineyard (12.1-12, 13-14). The proclamation of Jesus is shown to be the catalyst which stirs the anger of the religious authorities and motivates his arrest. Consequently the arrest scene provides a crucial link between prophetic images of Jesus and the passion Christology. Moving outward from the simple lines of the arrest story, a complex portrait comes into focus: Jesus is the ultimate teacher and prophet, sent from God but rejected by his own people.

2. The first trial scene extends the image of Jesus as prophet through his own testimony. With explicit reference to the name of God, Jesus acknowledges his identity as messiah, Son of God, Son of Man, true prophet. The religious authorities pose a different view of Jesus: he is a false prophet worthy of death. These conflicting claims are mediated through the prior images of the passion story: Jesus is the authentic prophet and his claims are reliable.

This focused portrait of Jesus plays a central role in the larger christological strategy. The secrecy, mystery and misunderstanding which surround Jesus are broken through his own witness. In the shadow of the cross the identity of Jesus is unveiled. Here the Christology implicit in Jesus' life is made explicit in the story of his death. Conversely the content of this christological confession is filled out and given substance by the images of the larger narrative. In this manner the images of Jesus' life flow into and are completed by the story of his death.

3. While the scene of Peter's denial (14.66-72) is void of christological images, it too makes a contribution to the portrait of Jesus. In the character of Peter the failure of Jesus' followers is focused and consummated. Through narrative linkage and parallel construction this scene is joined to the trial of Jesus. This technique enlarges the stark portrait of cowardice and failure. At the same time the denial provides a backdrop for the characterization of Jesus. In sharp contrast to the denial scene, Jesus stands forth as the faithful, courageous witness to the work of God.

4. The trial before Pilate (15.1-15) completes a complex sequence of characterization. This story wraps Jesus in the cloak of the Old Testament servant who suffers in silence. Various elements and titles are suppressed in order to focus the suffering of God's prophet. This picture complements the larger christological portrait. Earlier images

3. Mark 14.43–15.15: The Arrest and Trial

of Jesus as the wondrous teacher and as the authentic prophet of God are completed in this trial scene. Jesus is shown to be the righteous prophet who bears judgment and condemnation in silence.

5. Thus, Mk 14.43–15.15 draws upon various elements from the life of Jesus to present a decisive christological portrait. Significantly, this characterization is sketched in the shadow of the cross and announced through the testimony of Jesus. The mystery of Jesus' identity is revealed with sharp clarity: he is the messiah, the Son of God, the Son of Man, the ultimate messenger of God who dies at the hands of sinners. Hostile religious leaders, cowardly disciples, abusive authorities contrast the character of Jesus. Through strong and complex lines of intratextual connection this prophetic passion Christology is deeply rooted in the story of Jesus' life. The decisive revelation unfolds precisely against the sentence of death. The light which falls across the identity of Jesus marks the dawning of his final day.

Identity

The four scenes in Mk 14.43–15.15 were focused in terms of morphological construction, syntactical dynamics and narrative effect. Internal syntactical relationships and external connections were demonstrated in each of these scenes. Key attention was given to the patterns of plotting and characterization sustained by this process. Particular focus was given to the christological portrait generated by this interplay of narrative elements and strategies.

The narrative characteristics demonstrated through this formalistic analysis provide important clues to the identity of the Gospel of Mark. A symbiotic relationship was shown to operate between Jesus' passion and his ministry. Various elements of the passion story refer back to Jesus' ministry for definition, perspective, clarity, direction, confirmation. Explicit christological titles are filled out through reference to Jesus' words and deeds. The implied Christology of Jesus' ministry undergirds the passion Christology. These vital lines of interconnection suggest that Martin Kähler's identification of the Gospel of Mark as a passion narrative with an extended introduction is insufficient and stereotypical.

In view of this formalistic analysis the description by Theodore Weeden—that the Gospel of Mark embodies an ongoing christological polemic and employs the passion story as corrective Christology—also proves insufficient. The arrest of Jesus is linked precisely to the power of his words and deeds. The decisive christological confession of Mk 14.62 incorporates the very titles and images which dominate Jesus' ministry. Thus, the passion story and the life story are shown to circulate in reciprocal patterns of realignment.

The syntactical patterns and the extensive interconnections focused by formalistic analysis demonstrate the interlaced coherence exhibited by the Gospel of Mark in its language, structure and outlook. These narrative patterns suggest a complex intentionality which undergirds the composition of this Gospel. Present compositional models do not adequately explain this complex intentionality. Compositional theories based on evolutionary accretion of traditions through various life settings do not explain the intentionality and coherence present in the narrative language, structure and thought. While reference to a final editor or evangelist may account for the intentionality of this narrative, a singular redaction does not explain the complex internal and external staging of these stories and their nuanced connection to the Old Testament.

Thus, the narrative patterns demonstrated in Mk 14.43–15.15 confirm the inadequacy of traditional descriptions of the Gospel of Mark and the failure of current theories of composition to account for the organization and operation of this Gospel. At the same time the narrative characteristics focused through formalistic analysis provide the groundstock for a fundamental re-evaluation of the basic identity and the compositional strategy of the Gospel of Mark. The narrative patterns discovered in Mk 14.1-42 and confirmed in Mk 14.43–15.15 must now be tested against the remainder of the passion story.

Chapter 4

MARK 15.16–16.8: THE DEATH OF JESUS

The third major section of the passion account extends from Mk 15.16–16.8. This unit contains four stories: the abuse and mockery (15.16-20), the crucifixion (15.20c-37), interpretive events (15.38-47) and the resurrection promise (16.1-8). Synchronic analysis will focus the internal form and function of each of these units. Subsequently the interaction of each unit within the passion context and within the Gospel context will be considered. Comparative analysis will then set forth a performance field against which to highlight the literary function of these stories. Within this multi-dimensional approach particular attention will be given to the characterization of Jesus which emerges from Mk 15.16–16.8.

Mark 15.16-20: Abuse and Mockery

Following the trial before Pilate Mk 15.16-20 tells of the abuse and mocking of Jesus by Roman soldiers. This account initiates the events of Jesus' death and contributes vital elements to the characterization of Jesus.

Synchronic Analysis
The motifs of Mk 15.16-20 may be plotted in the following manner:

Introduction	
Jesus is led out	15.16a
Narrator informs	15.16b
Cohort assembles	15.16c
Body	
Soldiers clothe	15.17
Soldiers salute	15.18
Soldiers strike	15.19a

Soldiers spit	15.19b
Soldiers bow	15.19c
Soldiers mock	15.20a
Soldiers clothe	15.20b

Conclusion
Jesus is led out   15.20c

Narrative Morphology. The mocking of Jesus is narrated through eleven motifs organized into a rigid, balanced structure. The forced movement of Jesus provides the opening and conclusion for the account. The body of the story centers wholly on the abuse by the soldiers. This central action opens and closes with a dressing scene. Between the changing of garments the soldiers harass and torture Jesus in a variety of ways: saluting, striking, spitting, bowing, mocking. At the center of this abuse stand the images of kingship and the salute of Jesus as a royal spectacle. In stark contrast to the violent mockery of the soldiers stands the passive silence of Jesus. Thus, the form of this account matches its tone—it is solemn and unwavering.

1. Morphologically the scene of mockery provides detailed explication of the reported abuse of Jesus. Earlier analysis suggested that the two trial scenes (14.53-65; 15.1-15) reflect a common foundational report.[1] Various elements from the two scenes support this conclusion.[2] One crucial element operative in both trials is the reported abuse of Jesus (14.65d; 15.15).

1.1. The report of abuse is detailed and focused by each of the trial scenes. The simple report in 14.65d that 'the guards received him with blows' is unfolded through 14.65abc.[3] The simple report of 14.65d is developed through two patterns. (1) Various details of the abuse are noted: spitting, covering the face, striking, mocking. (2) More

---

1. See Chapter 3.
2. Numerous elements suggest that the trial scenes reflect a common foundational report. (1) The naming of the three religious groups and their condemnation of Jesus is cited in both scenes (14.53; 15.1). (2) Both trials highlight the role of the chief priests (14.60; 15.3, 11). (3) A twofold line of questioning is addressed to Jesus (14.60-61; 15.2, 4). (4) A third line of questioning is addressed to the assembled group (14.63-64; 15.9-14). (5) The silence of Jesus is affirmed (14.55-59; 15.10, 14). (6) The interest in the death sentence underlies both accounts (14.55, 64; 15.13, 14). (7) The abuse of Jesus is focused (14.65d; 15.15).
3. Apparently for this reason a few manuscripts (D c K) find 14.65d to be tautological and omit the phrase.

4. *Mark 15.16–16.8: The Death of Jesus*

significantly, the abuse is correlated to the charges presented in the trial (14.64). The soldiers taunt Jesus with the command to prophesy; thus Jesus is mocked and abused as a blasphemous false prophet.

1.2. A similar morphological pattern is seen in Mk 15.16-20. The report of abuse provides a basic element in the trial scene of 15.1-15. This scourging is linked to the handing over to crucifixion and is reported through a single word (φραγελλώσας in 15.15).[1] This terse report of abuse is developed fully in 15.16-20. As in 14.65 the explication of the abuse report follows two patterns. (1) The details of abuse are reported. A Roman cohort is gathered.[2] The soldiers are the subject of each action: they clothe, salute, strike, spit, bow, mock. Jesus is the object of each action. Through this pattern the report of abuse becomes an intense and graphic scene of torture.[3] These details also link the abuse to Mk 14.65, to Mk 10.34 and to various images from the Old Testament. (2) The abuse scene is correlated to the charges which surfaced in the trial. The King of the Jews title is woven throughout the second trial (15.2, 9, 12). The clothing in royal array, the salute and the bowing before Jesus build upon this charge.

---

1. R. Bultmann (*The History of the Synoptic Tradition* [trans. J. Marsh; Oxford: Basil Blackwell, 1963 (1921)], pp. 272, 284, 306) takes the relation between φραγελλώσας and 15.16-20 to its extreme. In Bultmann's view 15.16-20 is a secondary and novelistic legend which arose to explain the scourging. In my opinion reports may also represent a distillation of a scene. The relationship between a terse report and a more fully detailed scene does not require the discrediting of either form.

2. Technically a cohort is one tenth of a Roman legion, or 600 soldiers, though this number sometimes varied. R. Pesch (*Das Markusevangelium* [HTKNT; Freiburg: Herder, 2nd edn, 1980], II, p. 472) views the term as hyperbolic. Most interpreters prefer to see here an unspecified designation.

3. Numerous texts have been proposed as parallels to the abuse and mockery of Jesus. The text favored by most scholars is the incident of Carabas related by Philo (*Flacc.* 36-40). Carabas, who is apparently insane, is crowned with thorns, robed in a mat, given a reed scepter, addressed as lord and given a bodyguard. Various elements prevent this story from being a proper parallel. Most significantly, the mockery is not of Carabas, but is a vicarious derision of Julius Agrippa I. For other possible parallels, see J. Gnilka, *Das Evangelium nach Markus* (EKKNT; Zürich: Benziger Verlag, 1978), II, pp. 308-309; Pesch, *Markusevangelium*, II, pp. 470-71; A. Hermann, 'Farbe', *RAC*, VII, p. 414; E. Schweizer, *The Good News according to Mark* (trans. D.H. Madvig; Atlanta: John Knox, 1970), pp. 340-41. The mocking of the righteous is also an important theme in the Old Testament psalms. See Pss. 109.15; 31.18-24; 39.9; 70.4; and Isa. 50.6.

Jesus is thus abused as a failed pretender to the throne of Israel. In this manner the basic report of abuse is narrated as an explicit and focused scene with crucial ties to its immediate narrative context.

2. The structure of this scene is economical and productive. The scene provides a terse interlude to the cross procession. The intent to crucify Jesus precedes the scene (ἵνα σταυρωθῇ in 15.15) and is taken up at its conclusion (ἐξάγουσιν αὐτὸν ἵνα σταυρώσωσιν αὐτόν in 15.20c). The abuse scene also is framed around a simple but nuanced linguistic pattern. The soldiers are the subject of each deed, with Jesus as the object. This simple structure is applied to some fifteen different verbal forms, producing a lively set of events.

3. Three sets of frames guide the reader to the core of the scene. (1) Externally the story is framed by the procession to the cross (15.15; 15.20c). (2) Jesus is led out at the beginning of the scene (ἀπήγαγον αὐτὸν ἔσω in 15.16) and at its conclusion (ἐξάγουσιν αὐτόν in 15.20c). This movement focuses the stable scene of abuse in 15.17-20b. (3) A further frame encapsulates the actual events of torture. At the beginning of the abuse Jesus is clothed (ἐνδιδύσκουσιν in 15.17) in royal garments. At the end of the scene Jesus is clothed (ἐνέδυσαν in 15.20b) in his own garments.

Thus, three concentric frames encapsulate the abuse story and cast a focused light upon the core of this scene. At the center of this narrative structure stands a graphic scene of torture and a detailed image of Jesus as one rejected and abused.

4. This tightly structured scene has been woven into the fabric of the trial scene in a manner that resists separation of tradition and redaction.[1] Various connections to the surrounding material are assumed. (1) Jesus is never named in this scene, but his identity is clear. (2) The presence and activity of the soldiers is not justified, but is taken as a logical extension of the political trial. (3) The derision of Jesus as the King of the Jews and the act of bowing are unmotivated in 15.16-20 and assume the charges of 15.1-15. (4) The procession to the cross in 15.20c is not explained, but is taken up as an extension of the trial verdict.

---

1. Only the explanatory ὅ ἐστιν πραιτώριον appears separable. Scholars are almost unanimous in this opinion. Even Pesch (*Markusevangelium*, II, p. 471) sees this phrase as secondary. In Pesch's view the earliest community in Jerusalem knew such locations and required no explanation. For Pesch the explanatory phrase comes with the translation of the Aramaic *Urtexte*.

4. Mark 15.16–16.8: The Death of Jesus

Consequently the abuse scene in Mk 15.16-20 provides a carefully developed explication of the abuse report. The detailing of events, the correlation to the trial charges and the careful structuring of the scene create a self-sustained vitality. This vivid scene has been joined to the wider narrative in a way that defies reduction.[1]

5. This morphological constellation likely reflects the unique compositional history and interests behind this account. (1) A conscious pattern of explication is evident. This process moves from a bare report of abuse (15.15) to a fully developed scene of torture. This explication is guided by attention to details, by correlation to the trial charges and by the echo of other texts. This explicatory process reflects anecdotal curiosity and theological interest in the details of Jesus' suffering. At the same time the explication reflects a conscious interest in various characterizations and opinions concerning Jesus. This explicatory process thus reveals a self-conscious interest and involvement in the story of Jesus.[2] (2) A conscious concern for integration is also evident. This scene does not exhibit the qualities of an independent text.[3] At the same time this scene does not provide an artificial, secondary expansion of 15.15.[4] The vivid explanation of the abuse of Jesus has been carefully integrated into the larger account of his trial and death.

The self-conscious and intentional nature of this scene speaks against its deterministic evolution as a self-focused, utilitarian, non-literary text.[5] In contrast the vivid intentionality and careful integration

---

1. Despite this characteristic detailed distinctions have been attempted. See, for example, Gnilka, *Markus*, II, pp. 306-309, who separates the mistreatment motif of 15.19a as secondary. D. Dormeyer, *Die Passion Jesu als Verhaltensmodell: Literarische und theologische Analyse der Traditions- und Redaktionsgeschichte der Markuspassion* (Münster: Aschendorff, 1974), pp. 187-91, finds three distinct layers of material.

2. This self-conscious interest suggests that the text does not evolve primarily through non-directive, utilitarian concerns, as traditional form criticism sometimes implies.

3. Numerous scholars argue that the scene is integral to a pre-Markan passion narrative. See, for example, Pesch, *Markusevangelium*, II, pp. 468-69; Gnilka, *Markus*, II, p. 306; L. Schenke, *Der gekreuzigte Christus: Versuch einer literarkritischen und traditionsgeschichtlichen Bestimmung der vormarkinischen Passionsgeschichte* (Stuttgart: KBW, 1974), p. 60.

4. So Bultmann, *History*, pp. 272, 284, 306.

5. See, for example, the description of the compositional process by

suggest a self-conscious and interconnected literary process. While such processes are generally credited to the authorial design of individual evangelists, the complex patterns of detailing, focus, reflection and interconnection suggest a longer period of reflection and a wider authorial context. Consequently the morphology of Mk 15.16-20 is best explained through a compositional process rooted in the extended reflection of a self-conscious, literary community.

Narrative Syntax. Morphological analysis revealed the intricate structural patterns at work in Mk 15.16-20. Syntactical analysis will focus various narrative dynamics sustained by these patterns.

1. Mk 15.16-20 acts out the abuse report in graphic detail. The transition from a terse report form (15.15) to a detailed and focused scene (15.16-20) sustains a profound literary effect. Within the reader's world the abuse is transformed from the realm of information to the level of experience.

2. The abuse scene is rooted in the contours of the accompanying trial scene. Mk 14.65 presents the abuse of Jesus within a Jewish context. He is condemned by religious authorities, abused by presumably Jewish servants, mocked as a false prophet. In a similar pattern, the abuse of 15.16-20 is rooted in the political trial. Here Jesus is abused by Roman troops in view of political charges. Thus,

---

M. Dibelius, *From Tradition to Gospel* (Philadelphia: Fortress Press, 1983 [1919]). Dibelius (p. 1) describes a compositional process in which 'Many anonymous persons take part in handing down popular tradition. They act, however, not merely as vehicles, but also as creative forces by introducing changes or additions without any single person having a "literary" intent. In such cases the personal peculiarities of the composer or narrator have little significance; much greater importance attaches to the form in which the tradition is cast by practical necessities, by usage, or by origin. The development goes on steadily and independently, subject all the time to certain definite rules, for no creative mind has worked upon the material and impressed it with his own personality.' Dibelius (p. 7) further contends that 'The method of Form-criticism would be completely misjudged if it were regarded as originating in a flirtation with aesthetic standards. In so doing we should be going back to a way of looking at things which has its justification only in literature proper, where individual ability and inclination shape the style, i.e., where the result requires an aesthetic judgment of a personal and creative character. But the popular writings with which we are concerned have no such an individual source. The style which it is our part to observe is a "sociological result".'

4. *Mark 15.16–16.8: The Death of Jesus*

the narrative syntax aligns the scene of abuse to the political context of the second trial.

3. Through these developments the abuse of Jesus is tied precisely to two worlds. (1) The Jewish authorities bind Jesus (15.1), hand him over to Pilate (15.1), raise the charge against him (15.3) and incite the crowd (15.11). These events transport the images of the religious trial (14.53-65) into this scene. (2) Connected to this Jewish (religious) sequence is a Roman (political) sequence. Jesus is tried before a political magistrate, handed over to state execution (15.15) and abused by military personnel (15.16-20). In this manner the narrative links the abuse scene of 15.16-20 to interests both religious and political, both Jewish and Roman.

4. The syntax at work in this story also sustains interest in the characterization of Jesus. This scene no longer speaks of what Jesus does, but of what is done to Jesus; the action of the soldiers controls the plot throughout. Nonetheless this monolithic plot line generates a distinct character study. The identity question is focused by two elements of the narrative: the actions of the soldiers and the passiveness of Jesus. The actions of the soldiers gather around the royal images (robe and crown) and the royal title (King of the Jews). Jesus is thus mocked as a pretended king. At the same time the violence of the soldiers further characterizes Jesus as one despised, rejected and abused. The characterization of Jesus also grows around his passivity: in the face of violence and abuse Jesus suffers in silence. As a result this scene confronts the reader with two graphic and contrasting images of Jesus.

5. Consequently the abuse scene in Mk 15.16-20 sustains a vital narrative effect. Composed as an explication of the abuse report, Mk 15.16-20 provides a carefully crafted scene. The syntax at work in this text imposes upon the reader's experience, aligns itself with the contours of the trial, draws the suffering into a religious and political context and poses anew the question of Jesus' identity.

The Passion Context. The vivid images of the abuse scene are amplified through their interaction with other elements of the passion story. A crucial juncture is reached in the plot line. As earlier scenes in the passion account prepare for the suffering and death of Jesus, a line of tension and expectation develops. The delay in narrative time created by each scene heightens this tension. These various plot expectations and the tension created through the earlier stories begin to unfold with the suffering of Jesus in Mk 15.16-20. The scene of abuse thus culminates an important sequence of plot expectations.

Operating within the passion context the scene of mockery also expands the prophetic aura which surrounds Jesus. Various prophecies from the passion story are fulfilled in the mockery scene. Unknowingly and unwillingly the soldiers bring the words of Jesus to reality. He is taken from his followers as he predicted (Mk 14.7). As he foretold in the Passover meal (Mk 14.22-25), his body is abused and broken. Jesus' linkage of suffering and kingship (Mk 14.25) is played out in ironic fashion. As he predicted, the shepherd of the people is smitten (Mk 14.27; 15.19). The soldiers participate in the 'hour' of which Jesus spoke (Mk 14.35, 41). As he foretold (Mk 14.41), Jesus is handed over to sinners. Thus, the soldiers bring to fulfillment various prophetic images set forth in the passion context.

The passion context also clarifies the ambiguous kingship images of the abuse scene. The soldiers' salute of Jesus as the 'King of the Jews' (Mk 15.18) is open to various interpretations. Do they see Jesus as merely a pretender to the throne?[1] Do they see Jesus as indeed the leader of the Jewish people, then mock him for his lack of royal power and demeanor? Is the salute ironic: is Jesus an incognito king who will ultimately be vindicated?[2] Internally Mk 15.16-20 does not resolve this issue. Within the wider passion context the image of kingship is clarified. Pilate has already attempted to portray Jesus as the innocent leader of the Jewish people (Mk 15.2, 9, 12). The first response of Jesus to Pilate is oblique: 'You say' (Mk 15.2). Further attempts to portray Jesus as king are met by silence (Mk 15.4). Thus, Jesus himself blunts the attempt to label him a king. When seen against this backdrop the royal images of the mockery story become clear. As in the political trial no reply is given to the kingship label. Like the attempts of Pilate, the salute of the soldiers provides an inadequate view of Jesus. Through this wider perspective the kingship imagery is abandoned. Thus, the passion context interacts in definitive ways with the images of Mk 15.16-20.

The Gospel Context. The images of the mockery scene gain their clearest perspective through interaction with the larger narrative

1. So Pesch, *Markusevangelium*, II, pp. 472-73.
2. So Gnilka, *Markus*, II, p. 308.

4. Mark 15.16–16.8: The Death of Jesus

context. Through this engagement the anecdotal elements of Mk 15.16-20 are gathered into a coherent christological focus. The suffering in Mk 15.16-20 is clarified by its relationship with two key themes from the ministry of Jesus: the passion predictions (Mk 8.31; 9.31; 10.32-34) and the parable of the vineyard (Mk 12.1-12).

1. Three passion predictions insert the necessity of suffering into the midst of Jesus' public ministry (Mk 8.31; 9.31; 10.32-34). Most significantly, the first of these predictions is linked precisely to the identity of Jesus as the messiah. Thus, a crucial christological standard is established in the midst of Jesus' teaching and healing with authority: the Son of Man has come to serve and to give his life (Mk 10.45). All confessions of Jesus' messianic identity which avoid his destiny of suffering and death are inadequate.

The abuse presented in 14.65 and in 15.16-20 provides the first realization of this destiny. As he declared, Jesus now suffers much (Mk 8.31) and is handed over to his death (Mk 9.31). In particular the mockery scene realizes the prediction of suffering in Mk 10.32-34. Already Jesus has been handed over to the leaders and condemned to death (Mk 10.33; 14.53-65). Mk 15.16-20 now completes this prophecy. As he predicted, he is handed over to the Gentiles (Mk 10.33). The torture by the Romans matches the prediction in Mk 10.34. The soldiers mock Jesus (ἐμπαίξουσιν in 10.34, ἐνέπαιξαν in 15.20a), they strike him (μαστιγώσουσιν in 10.34, ἔτυπτον in 15.19), they spit upon him (ἐμπτύσουσιν in 10.34, ἐνέπτυον in 15.19), then kill him (ἀποκτενοῦσιν in 10.34, σταυρωσώσιν in 15.20c). Thus, the scene of suffering in Mk 15.16-20 fulfills a key element of the messianic destiny established by Jesus in the midst of his ministry.

2. In a similar manner the abuse and mockery scene is amplified by its relationship to the parable of the vineyard (Mk 12.1-12). The thwarted attempts of the religious authorities (12.12) succeed at last. Jesus no longer departs of his own will to safety (12.12), but is led away to die (15.20c). Thus, the images of violence predicted against the son (12.8) are given stark reality in the abuse of Jesus. Conversely the abused and silent figure presented in Mk 15.16-20 is to be understood by the reader as God's chosen and beloved heir.[1]

---

1. M.A. Tolbert (*Sowing the Gospel: Mark's World in Literary-Critical Perspective* [Minneapolis: Fortress Press, 1989], pp. 271-99) properly connects the death of Jesus to the parable of Mk 12.1-12. She fails, however, to focus the specific links between Mk 12.1-12 and the abuse of Jesus in 15.16-20.

3. This interaction with the larger narrative world amplifies the events of the abuse scene and creates a sharply defined portrait of Jesus. Two images control this portrait. First, Jesus is the authentic prophet from God. Prior to 14.65d the predictions of suffering are unfulfilled and remained in the realm of images and metaphors. The abuse scene turns these images of suffering into graphic reality and fulfills various predictions from Jesus. Earlier predictions of suffering are transformed into prolepses which are now fulfilled in the presence of the reader. These events demonstrate anew the prophetic identity of Jesus: his teaching and his predictions are from God.

The mockery scene also realizes the concept of Jesus as the Suffering Servant. Earlier images of a suffering messiah are brought to painful reality in the abuse scene. The articulation of this messianic image and its subsequent realization in the abuse scene invite the reader to view Jesus in light of the Suffering Servant of the Old Testament (Isa. 42.1-4; 49.1-6; 50.4-11; 52.13–53.12).[1] Various themes from the Servant Songs are fulfilled in Jesus. He does not cry or lift up his voice against those who torment him (Isa. 42.2). He seems to have labored in vain and to have spent his strength for nothing (Isa. 49.4). Like the Servant of old Jesus has given his back to the smiters, and he has not hid his face from shame and spitting (Isa. 50.6). In particular the images of the fourth Servant Song (Isa. 52.13–53.12) are fulfilled in Jesus:

a marred appearance	(Isa. 52.14)
despised and rejected	(Isa. 53.3)
a man of sorrows, acquainted with grief	(Isa. 53.3-4)
stricken, smitten, afflicted, wounded, bruised	(Isa. 53.4-5)
oppressed, afflicted	(Isa. 53.7)
silent in the face of judgment	(Isa. 53.7)
killed	(Isa. 53.8, 9, 12)

The scene of mockery is thus informed by a deep heritage of Suffering Servant images. Drawn from the prophetic tradition of the Old Testament and from the public ministry of Jesus, these images clarify the events of Mk 15.16-20 and draw them into a stark

---

1. Pesch (*Markusevangelium*, II, p. 473) concludes that this scene 'conjures anew the images of the suffering righteous one'. Edward Schweizer finds this connection problematic in view of the absence of παῖς from the passion narrative. For a wider discussion, see the excursus by Schenke, *Der gekreuzigte Christus*, pp. 68-76.

4. Mark 15.16–16.8: The Death of Jesus

christological portrait. Conversely the events of Mk 15.16-20 take the concepts of the Suffering Servant and the servant messiah from the world of information and ideas and make them a concrete reality in the story of Jesus.

4. Consequently the interaction of the abuse scene with the wider narrative context alters its depth and vision. Standing in isolation the unit is largely anecdotal, and its christological images remain ambiguous. Set within the wider narrative world the mockery scene plays a decisive role. Mk 15.16-20 now completes key predictions and interpretations from the larger story. Read in connection with the narrative world which serves as its host, this scene realizes and culminates a clear christological theme: Jesus is the Suffering Servant, the true prophet of God who is despised, abused and rejected.

Comparative Analysis

The abuse and mockery scene also appears in other narrative settings. These various uses of the story provide a comparative field against which to highlight the form and function of Mk 15.16-20.[1]

Pre-Markan Contexts. Various scholars attempt to reconstruct the form and function of the abuse scene prior to its use in the Gospel of Mark. One line of reconstruction views the story as a separate tradition which was subsequently added to the passion account. Rudolf Bultmann took this position, suggesting that the story was a secondary, novelistic legend which arose to explain the scourging (φραγ-ελλώσας) in Mk 15.15b.[2] Vincent Taylor was also attracted to the position that the abuse scene was an expansion upon the passion material. In contrast to Bultmann, Taylor saw this material as primary and as recording historical testimony.[3] In either case such an independent form of the abuse scene would be largely anecdotal and would serve to fill out the details of the trial and death of Jesus.

A second line of reconstruction argues that Mk 15.16-20 forms an intrinsic part of a pre-Markan passion tradition.[4] The narrative ties

---

1. On the use of diachronic analysis as phenomenological description and comparison rather than historical reconstruction, see Chapter 1.
2. Bultmann, *History*, pp. 272, 284, 306.
3. V. Taylor, *The Gospel according to Mark* (London: MacMillan, 1953), pp. 542-43.
4. Pesch, *Markusevangelium*, II, p. 468; Gnilka, *Markus*, II, p. 306;

with other sections of the passion story are taken as supports for this position.[1] These scholars generally argue for the historical value of this tradition. Such a form of the story would interact in various ways with the larger passion tradition, yet its contribution would remain largely anecdotal.

The Gospel of Matthew. Mt. 27.27-31 presents another version of the abuse and mockery scene. Few substantive differences exist between this account and Mk 15.16-20. The kingship imagery is enhanced when the reed is placed in Jesus' right hand as a mock scepter (Mt. 27.29). The various elements of abuse are taken over, as are the undressing and dressing of Jesus. While changes are made in style and in vocabulary, the basic form and function of the story parallel Mk 15.16-20.

The Gospel of Luke. Luke omits the scene of torture by Pilate's soldiers. In its place he reports the abuse of Jesus at the hands of Herod and his troops (Lk. 23.11). Here Jesus is treated with contempt, mocked, then sent back to Pilate in beautiful clothing. It is likely that this transposing of the torture scene reflects Luke's concern to lay the blame for Jesus' death at the feet of the Jewish authorities and to portray the Roman authorities as uninvolved.[2] Luke reports a similar incident, but he does not develop its imagery.

The Gospel of John. The abuse scene has been employed in a distinct form in Jn 19.1-16. Here the abuse of Jesus is intertwined with the story of Pilate's verdict. The torture of Jesus includes scourging, the thorny crown, the purple robe, the salute as King of the Jews and the striking of Jesus (Jn 19.1-3). The remainder of the scene is occupied by Pilate's debate with the crowds and with Jesus. The question of kingship is addressed by the soldiers (Jn 19.3), by Pilate (Jn 19.14, 15) and by the people (Jn 19.12, 15). The innocence of Jesus is confirmed by Pilate (Jn 19.4, 6). The sole response of Jesus confirms his authority, even in his hour of trial (Jn 19.11). The divine control of this situation is asserted, as is the primary guilt of Judas (Jn 19.11). Thus, the Gospel of John has taken over basic elements from the abuse

Schenke, *Der gekreuzigte Christus*, pp. 54-55.
1. See, for example, Gnilka, *Markus*, II, pp. 308-309.
2. See Schweizer, *Mark*, pp. 339-41.

4. Mark 15.16–16.8: The Death of Jesus

scene and employed them in a distinct manner. Within this alternate context the story now supports a distinctly Johannine portrait of Jesus.

Others. The abuse of Jesus is briefly reported in the *Gospel of Peter* (2.5b-3.9), in the *Acts of Pilate* (10.1a), and in the *Historia passionis Domini* manuscript of the *Gospel of the Nazareans* (fragment 34). The *Gospel of the Nazareans* provides an explanation which clarifies the role of the political authorities without absolving the religious leaders: the Jews bribed four soldiers to carry out both the scourging and the crucifixion of Jesus. Significantly, the *Gospel of Peter* uses this report to declare Jesus as the Son of God.

Summary

The story of the abuse and mocking of Jesus has been narrated in a variety of contexts and serves differing narrative functions. In its pre-Markan context the scene perhaps served as an anecdotal account which brought color and detail to the story of Jesus' death. As a part of the pre-Markan passion tradition the story would form a coherent link in the narrative of Jesus' suffering and death. Matthew has taken over Mk 15.16-20 and employed it for similar purposes. In the Gospel of Luke the account has been replaced by a report of abuse before Herod, a Jewish authority. The Gospel of John employs the material as part of the trial before Pilate and uses it to advance a Johannine Christology and a Johannine view of Jesus' death.

Seen over against this comparative field the Gospel of Mark makes distinct use of the abuse scene. Here the reported abuse of Jesus has been explicated in a graphic and nuanced scene of torture. Taken in isolation this story is largely anecdotal and its Christology remains unfocused. When Mk 15.16-20 is read in light of the passion material and in connection with the larger story of Jesus' life, a stark and definitive image of Jesus emerges. The abuse and mockery at the hands of the soldiers fulfills a long line of prophecy. This fulfillment confirms Jesus as the authentic messenger from God. At the same time the Christology of kingship is silenced. In its place emerges the portrait of Jesus as the righteous one who suffers and dies in silence. While this characterization builds upon the elements of the abuse scene, crucial images are drawn from Jesus' ministry (Mk 10.34; 12.8; 14.65d; 15.15) and from Old Testament prophecy (Isa. 42.1-4; 49.1-6; 50.4-11; 52.13–53.12). Consequently Mk 15.16-20 imposes a stark image upon this final procession: Jesus is the true servant and prophet of God, the one rejected, abused and crucified.

Mark 15.20c-37: The Death Scene

The death of Jesus is recorded in Mk 15.20c-37. This account provides the climax to the plot line of the passion story and serves as the focal point for the passion Christology.

Synchronic Analysis
The death scene is composed of a complex series of motifs:

Introduction
Jesus is led out	15.20c
Simon is conscripted	15.21
Jesus is led forth	15.22a
Narrator informs	15.22b

Body
Soldiers offer (wine)	15.23a
Jesus refuses (wine)	15.23b
Jesus is crucified	15.24a
Soldiers divide (garments)	15.24b
Narrator informs	15.25
Narrator informs	15.26
Thieves are crucified	15.27
Passers blaspheme	15.29-30
Leaders mock	15.31-32a
Thieves revile	15.32b
Narrator informs	15.33
Narrator informs	15.34a
Jesus cries	15.34a
Narrator informs	15.34b
Bystanders (mis)interpret	15.35
One offers (vinegar)	15.36
Jesus cries	15.37a

Conclusion
Jesus (Spirit) departs	15.37b

Narrative Morphology. The crucifixion scene contains the most complex morphological presentation found in the Gospel of Mark. This structural density bears witness to its central role in the comprehensive structure of the Gospel and points to its unique dialogue

4. *Mark 15.16–16.8: The Death of Jesus*

between historical and theological interests.[1] More significantly, the complex morphological pattern presented in Mk 15.20c-37 hosts a dynamic, wide-ranging narrative effect. Numerous morphological elements contribute to this account and its significance.

1. The death scene is built around a simple frame of events:

> 22a And they bring him unto the Golgotha place...
> 24a And they crucify him...
> 27a And with him they crucify two thieves...
> 37   But Jesus, having cried out with a great voice, expired.

This structural nucleus presents a concise sequence of Jesus' death and provides the central plot line of this scene.[2] A number of narrative

---

1. It it the relation between historical and theological interests which dominates most critical analyses of this scene. Most interpreters struggle to sift out a collection of historical events from the details of the story. In most instances the less plausible events are taken as key theological interests. In my opinion an arbitrary distinction between history and theology is unnecessary. For examples of intense efforts to identify historical details, see Pesch, *Markusevangelium*, II, pp. 474-503. At the end of each major section Pesch lists historical details isolated from the story (pp. 480, 489-90, 500-502). Concerning the formation of the passion narrative, Pesch concludes that 'The stages of the report appear to be determined by the historical unfolding of reported, consistent events' (p. 476). In a similar manner Gnilka (*Markus*, II, pp. 326-27) follows his analysis with a section called 'Historische Beurteilung'. Gnilka concludes that the theological focus of the passage is to be found in Mark's redactional activity (p. 327). While these concerns are important, narrative analysis is concerned primarily for the effect of interlacing history and theological interests into a narrative gestalt. The reality of the text represents a third level created through the union of interests drawn from historical reality and from theological concerns. The text is ultimately an attempt not merely to record what happened, but to signify the larger relevance of what happened.

2. This frame is a literary phenomenon which undergirds more complex elements of the scene. This literary phenomenon is not to be confused with the attempt by numerous scholars to identify an older, foundational tradition which served as the ground layer upon which subsequent traditions or redactions were developed. A wide-ranging list of 'earliest traditions' has been offered. Bultmann (*History*, pp. 273-74, 279) suggested that 'In Mark's story of the Crucifixion there is a legendary editing of what is manifestly an ancient historical narrative to which we may trace back vv. 20b-24'. Bultmann's proposal was accepted by numerous interpreters, including Schweizer, *Mark*, p. 342. Taylor (*Mark*, pp. 587, 649-51) finds the 'foundation narrative' in 15.21-24, 26, 29-30, 34-37, 39. Gnilka (*Markus*, II, p. 311) finds the 'Grundbericht' in 15.20b-22a. J. Schreiber (*Theologie des Vertrauens: Eine redaktionsgeschichtliche Untersuchung des Markusevangelium*

techniques bring color and detail to this framework.

2. The scene has been organized around a distinct temporal frame. The death scene is narrated in three segments, each of which is marked by the passing of three hours. The first segment begins at the third hour (15.25)[1] and focuses the mocking of Jesus. The second segment begins at the sixth hour and is marked by the darkness which covers the land.[2] The third segment begins at the ninth hour and focuses the final throes of death.[3] This temporal device invokes cosmic (solar) images and provides a clear structural frame for the story.[4]

[Hamburg: Furche Verlag, 1967], pp. 62-66) sees 15.20b-22a, 24, 27 as an ancient cross tradition which is at least as old as 1 Cor. 15.3-5. In sharp contrast to these attempts to base the story in the oldest layer of tradition this analysis contends that 15.22a, 24a, 27a, 37 provides the *structural* base of this text.

1. Reckoned from the dawn (6 a.m.) by Jewish chronology, the third hour would be 9 a.m.

2. Much discussion has centered around this noonday darkness. Astronomically a full moon and an eclipse are mutually exclusive events. Technically Mk 15.33 does not mention an eclipse (Lk. 23.45 does in the stronger manuscript tradition), but rather noonday darkness. Various other natural events (dust storms, cloud cover) have been conjectured. Some discussion has focused on the meaning of ἐφ ὅλην τὴν γῆν. Some argue for darkness over Palestine, while others argue for a cosmic darkness. Beyond the attempts to find an explanation in nature, various parallels from the history of religion have been suggested. The text closest to hand is that of Mk 13.24, where Jesus quotes Joel 2.10 (see also Joel 2.31). A more exact parallel is found in Amos 8.9-10: '"And on that day", says the Lord God, "I will make the sun go down at noon, and darken the earth in broad daylight. I will turn your feasts into mourning, and all your songs into lamentation; I will bring sackcloth upon all loins, and baldness on every head; I will make it like the mourning for an only son, and the end of it like a bitter day".' Various other instances have been cited as explanations. Gnilka (*Markus*, II, p. 321) notes instances in which darkness accompanies the death of famous rabbis or political figures. Such darkness has been interpreted as a sign of sadness or of demonic might (see Gnilka, *Markus*, II, p. 321 for examples). In particular such darkness often accompanies an apocalyptic shift in aeons (Amos 8.9; Joel 2.2, 10, 31; 3.15; Isa. 13.10; 24.23; Mk 13.34; Rev. 6.12-14).

3. In contrast the Gospel of John says that Jesus was condemned at the sixth hour (Jn 19.14).

4. Tolbert (*Sowing the Gospel*, pp. 272-73, 282) notes the presence of this structure, but gives little attention to its narrative effect. Likewise R.A. Culpepper ('The Passion and Resurrection in Mark', *RevExp* 75/4 [1978], p. 584) notes this temporal triad but does not address its effect. Gnilka (*Markus*, II, pp. 312, 317) thinks the designation of the hour of Jesus' death in 15.34 provides the origin for this threefold structure. In Gnilka's analysis the three-hour pattern reflects a

4. Mark 15.16–16.8: The Death of Jesus

3. The scene employs a wide range of actants, many of whom appear for the first (and only) time. Typical actants or groups reappear in this scene: Jesus, religious leaders. Various groups are drawn into the story and used without definition: those who pass by, bystanders, soldiers. Unnamed actants play vital roles: one who offers vinegar, thieves crucified alongside Jesus. The nameless narrator reappears. New characters are introduced in a way that assumes some familiarity: Simon of Cyrene, Rufus, Alexander.[1] Thus, an unusually large and diverse cast inhabits the scene of Jesus' death.

4. The story details the activity around the cross. The list of predicates which sustain this scene is extensive.[2] This impressive collection of verbs chronicles the busy scene which surrounds Jesus' death, yet little attention is given to the process of crucifixion itself.[3]

5. The narrator intrudes into this account to perform various tasks. On two occasions narrative commentary is employed to translate unfamiliar terms. Golgotha is interpreted as 'the place of the skull' in 15.21. The cry of Jesus is also clarified for Greek readers in 15.34. Beyond this the narrator notes the hour (15.25, 33, 34a) and details the content of the inscription (15.26). This relatively frequent use of

---

thoroughly apocalyptic outlook. Various parallels are cited (p. 317 n. 49). Gnilka concludes that the three-hour segmentation reveals this event as God's conclusive judgment and redemption.

1. Of some interest is the discovery in 1941 of a family grave in Kidron Valley. An inscription names one of those buried there as Alexander, Son of Simon. To this name is added קרניח. If a ה were exchanged for the ח this addition would designate an origin in Cyrene. This discovery is reported in N. Avigad, 'A Discovery of Inscribed Ossuaries in the Kidron Valley', *IEJ* 12 (1962), pp. 1-12, and it is discussed in M. Hengel, 'Zwischen Jesus und Paulus', *ZTK* 72 (1975), pp. 183-86.

2. Leading out, crucifying, conscripting, going along, coming, taking up, bringing, interpreting, giving, mixing, receiving, dividing, casting, inscribing, passing by, blaspheming, wagging, saying, destroying, building, saving, coming down, mocking, being able, forsaking, standing by, hearing, calling, running, filling, giving out, expiring.

3. Schweizer (*Mark*, p. 346) sees a theological interest in this approach: 'Since the physical anguish did not constitute Jesus' real suffering, it is not described. His real suffering was caused by his rejection...' Schweizer (*Mark*, p. 354) finds a similar pattern in the simple description of Jesus' death in 15.37: 'Jesus' death is described with stark simplicity. Nothing is glossed over, nor is there any reference to an unshakable inner peace. Of primary significance is the absence of any imposing gestures or statements such as are usually found in Jewish and Christian stories of martyrdom.'

narrative commentary provides important information and becomes a vital element in the world of the story.

6. Various patterns of repetition are employed. Numerous doublets operate within this scene.[1] (1) Jesus is offered something to drink in 15.23 and again in 15.36.[2] (2) The crucifixion is announced in both 15.24 and 15.25. (3) The sarcastic call for Jesus to save himself by coming down from the cross is voiced by two different groups (15.30; 15.31-32b). (4) The loud cry of Jesus is heard in 15.34 and in 15.37.

Mary Ann Tolbert argues for a wider, more complex duality in the framing of this scene. In her analysis each segment of Mk 15.16-39 is paired with a corresponding sequence. This a-a' relationship connects the mocking of 15.16-20 to the confession of 15.39. The sequence in 15.21-24b is paired with a similar sequence in 15.35-38. At the heart of this story 15.25-32 is paired with 15.33-34. In her analysis the scene operates around three sequence pairs which center in the agony of 15.25-34.[3] In Tolbert's view one line (15.16-32 or ABC) shows 'events understood only in the limited, distorted view of this generations's human world' while the second line (15.33-39 or A'B'C') shows 'events directed toward and informed by the cosmic, divine realm'.[4]

In addition to these dualistic patterns, several triads operate in the death scene. The scene is divided into three segments marked by three-hour spans (15.25, 33, 34a). Jesus is mocked by three different groups: passers-by in 15.29-30, chief priests in 15.31, those crucified with Jesus in 15.32.[5]

Thus, various patterns of repetition are employed in the death scene. Consequently the story of Jesus' death resounds with multiple

---

1. Typically scholars interpret these doublets as signs of two different layers of tradition. This theory is supported in various forms by Schreiber, *Theologie*, pp. 62-68; Schenk, *Passionsbericht*, pp. 13-52; Gnilka, *Markus*, II, pp. 311-14; E. Linnemann, *Studien zur Passionsgeschichte* (Göttingen: Vandenhoeck & Ruprecht, 1970), pp. 136-70.

2. Significantly, the drink is rejected in 15.23 but seemingly accepted in 15.36.

3. Tolbert, *Sowing the Gospel*, pp. 271-75, 279-83.

4. Tolbert, *Sowing the Gospel*, p. 279.

5. Culpepper ('Passion and Resurrection', p. 584) sees a larger frame of threes in the death scene. He argues that Mk 15.1-39 develops in three acts (15.1-20; 15.21-32; 15.33-39), each of which contains an event and a response to that event. Culpepper concludes that this structure unveils 'the rich significance Jesus' death had for Mark' (p. 595).

4. *Mark 15.16–16.8: The Death of Jesus*

voices and echoes which enrich its narrative effect.

7. Two distinct patterns of intercalation are employed. This sandwiching technique opens up the story line to further detail and focus.

7.1. At the beginning of the scene the movement of Jesus is separated into his going out (ἐξάγουσιν αὐτόν in 15.20c) and his coming forth (φέρουσιν αὐτὸν ἐπί in 15.22a). Inserted into this opening line of movement is the story of Simon. Various details are provided: Simon is from Cyrene,[1] he is coming from the field,[2] he is the father of Alexander and Rufus.[3] The plot line of this intercalation is simple but poignant: Simon is conscripted to bear the cross of Jesus. Within the scene the symbolic potential of this image is not developed.

7.2. A second intercalation is employed at the end of the death scene. Here the motif of Jesus' loud cry from the cross is opened up (15.34a, 37a).[4] Various images fill the narrative space created by this structure. Within this interlude bystanders debate the meaning of Jesus' cry, and one offers vinegar in an echo of Ps. 69.21. More significantly, the narrator uses the interlude to interpret Jesus' words (15.34b) as the fulfillment of Ps. 22.1. The interlude is further employed to address the expectation of Elijah's return (15.35-36).

Thus, two clear intercalations operate within Mk 15.20c-37. This structural framing brings various aspects of the death scene into sharp focus.

---

1. Cyrene is in North Africa. Acts 6.9 tells of Cyrenians who disputed with Stephen. A connection may exist between the Cyrenians and the synagogue of the Freedmen in Acts 6.9. Many conclude that Simon belongs to diaspora Judaism, though he may live in the area of Jerusalem. Some suggest he is remembered here because of his later conversion to Christianity. Schreiber (*Theologie*, pp. 62-82) ties the entire crucifixion report to a Stephen circle through the connection to Simon of Cyrene and Acts 6.9. He is followed in part by Schenk, *Passionsbericht*, pp. 25-36.

2. It is unlikely that one would return from work in the field at such an early hour. In addition, it is unlikely that such work would be performed on the Passover. Some translations handle this incongruity by suggesting that Simon was returning from 'the country'.

3. Various interpreters suggest that the Rufus greeted in Rom. 16.13 is the son of Simon named here. There is no sufficient evidence to confirm or to reject this identification.

4. Schweizer (*Mark*, pp. 351-54, 359) supports the authenticity of the cry: 'Therefore it is conceivable, at least, that the account of Jesus' dying with a loud cry was handed down to the church and was historically correct...' (p. 354). In Schweizer's view the fact of the cry was developed further: 'the church... used the words of the Psalm to represent the inarticulate cry of Jesus (vs. 37)' (p. 353).

8. Various links are established between the death scene and the Scriptures of Israel. The language of the Old Testament is employed at various places. Ps. 22.18 (22.19 in LXX) is quoted in Mk 15.24. The loud cry in 15.34b cites Ps. 22.1, as does its translation. More indirect allusions are also present. The mingled wine (15.23) and the vinegar (15.36) reflect Ps. 69.21. The crucifixion between two thieves echoes Isa. 53.12. The threefold mocking of Jesus suggests various Old Testament texts (Pss. 22.7; 109.25; Wis. 2.18). The King of Israel title (15.32) is found in Zeph. 3.15. The darkness which accompanies the loss of a son (15.33) is portrayed in Amos 8.9-10. The expectation of Elijah recalls Mal. 4.5. Thus, extensive connections are established between the death of Jesus and the Scriptures of Israel.[1]

9. This complex morphological arrangement most likely reflects the distinct compositional history and interest behind this scene. Various clues suggest the parameters of this compositional process.

9.1. The complex manner in which this scene circulates around a simplistic narrative frame (15.22a, 24a, 27a, 37) suggests a compositional environment familiar with diverse literary forms. The death scene suggests a compositional milieu equally familiar and adept with simple reports as well as complex, integrated narratives.

9.2. This compositional environment exhibits consistent interest in the facts of Jesus' story. This focus on detail and this eye for witnesses suggest a concern to root the death narrative in real events from the life of Jesus. The story, with all of its multiformed creativity, seeks to be a statement about what really happened.

9.3. In a similar manner this compositional milieu exhibits sustained skill and interest in Old Testament texts. A vital concern for correlation with the story of Israel guides the narration of Jesus' death.

9.4. The death scene reflects interest in definition and location of various social groupings. The roles and responsibilities of numerous actants are clarified. Among these are religious leaders, absent disciples, Gentiles, political servants, the common people and various individuals (Simon, Rufus, Alexander, one who offers wine, and later the centurion and the women).

9.5. The story reflects a sustained concern for the identity of Jesus. Various options for understanding Jesus are presented in the scene:

---

1. For detailed analysis of this technique, see A. Suhl, *Die Funktion der alttestamentlichen Zitate und Anspielungen im Markusevangelium* (Gütersloh: Gerd Mohn, 1965), especially pp. 26-66.

4. *Mark 15.16–16.8: The Death of Jesus*

King of the Jews (Israel), thief, false prophet, impotent redeemer, failed messiah, one forsaken, suffering righteous one.

9.6. The composition of the death scene is guided by a reflective intentionality. The details and images of the scene have been aligned with focused interests and biases. These interests have been connected to wider streams of thought and tradition. The result of this process is a carefully crafted story with sharply defined intentions.

The most likely explanation for these traits of composition is to be found in a fully conscious literary community with focused theological interests.[1] This community employed a lectionary hermeneutic of remembrance and reflection. Through this hermeneutic the story of Jesus' death was rooted in various details from his life and in diverse images from the Old Testament.

10. Consequently Mk 15.20c-37 presents the most complex morphological configuration in the Gospel of Mark. This structural constellation provides a scene marked by dramatic detail, powerful images and pointed interests. The narrative effect sustained by this morphology will be focused through syntactical analysis.

Narrative Syntax. Morphological analysis revealed the complex structural constellation present in Mk 15.20c-37. The syntactical interaction of these elements generates a series of vital narrative transactions and effects.

1. Information is transformed into experience. The incidental and anecdotal material gathered into the death story is translated into a dramatic narrative scene. The gathering of this data under decisive syntactical patterns creates a distinct, focused drama with its own gestalt, its own codes and values, its own demands. Consequently this creation confronts the reader not as recorded information, but as a distinct literary experience.

2. The drama is given cosmic and apocalyptic dimensions. The clock which measures the passing of Jesus is cosmic in proportion. Noonday darkness provides a cosmic commentary on the death of

---

1. In my opinion the intentional nature of this text weighs against a deterministic evolution guided by fixed canons of transmission. In addition, the complex interrelationships sustained by this text far exceed the abilities of a single author or a single redaction. The morphology of this account suggests a lengthy community involvement in the production of this text.

Jesus. In this manner a routine execution becomes a cosmic drama which marks the turning of the ages.[1]

3. The narrator's intrusions guide the reader through the scene. The narrator sets the story against the imposing midday darkness (15.33). From the narrator readers learn the meaning of various terms (15.22b, 34b), the content of the inscription (15.26)[2] and the chronology of Jesus' death (15.25, 33, 34a). Beyond this giving of information, the narrator also redirects the Elijah expectation by interpreting Jesus' cry in terms of Psalm 22. Through the intrusions of the narrator the text provides a sense of guidance and companionship for the reading experience.

4. The use of intercalations alters the face of the narrative. The staging technique freezes the temporal line and creates a narrative pause or interlude. Within these interludes crucial information and focus are provided for the death scene.

The first intercalation (15.20c-22a) aids the plotting of the story by creating a sense of time and distance for the journey of Jesus to the cross.[3] Thus, the movement from the scene of abuse to the death scene is given narrative depth. Beyond this the insertion of Simon's experience adds precise detail to the story and sets it within a particular social matrix. This detailing of the story also sustains an aura of authenticity and historicity: the reader is pointed to participants who may verify the account. In addition, the role of Simon as cross-bearer provides a potential image for discipleship.

The opening created by Jesus' cry from the cross (15.34a, 37a) creates a sense of narrative time and extends the last moments of Jesus. Various theological concerns are addressed within this

---

1. Gnilka (*Markus*, II, pp. 317, 321) finds signs of God's cosmic eschatological activity in the enumeration of the hours and in the noonday darkness. Gnilka demonstrates the background of both images in apocalyptic thought.

2. Such inscriptions are known elsewhere in this time period. For a list of parallels, see Pesch, *Markusevangelium*, II, p.484.

3. The use of ἐξάγω in 15.20c may also carry the image of a ban. Such exclusion precedes execution in Lev. 24.14, Num. 15.35-36 and Acts 7.58. The christological and soteriological import of this theme is examined in Heb. 13.11-13.

interlude: the role of the bystanders, the meaning of Jesus' cry,[1] expectations of Elijah.

5. The use of doublets and triads provides emphasis, duration and polyvalence. Some elements are transformed from single images to sequences, thus highlighting their role. The use of repetition stretches the narrative and conveys the passing of time. The presentation of one event from differing perspectives establishes polyvalence and encourages multiple readings of the text.

6. The unusual interest in the actants of this scene sustains a number of effects. A cast of participants—some willing and some not—is presented to the reader. Among these participants are witnesses who may confirm the story of Jesus' death. The role and responsibility of various groups is demonstrated. The stories of individuals—Simon, Rufus, Alexander, one who offers a drink, bystanders, those who pass by—are forever entwined with the story of Jesus' death.

7. The use of details and information roots the death story in a particular historical and social frame. This connection conveys authenticity and provides a primary hermeneutical context within which the reader is to understand the death of Jesus.[2]

8. The death of Jesus is drawn precisely into the stream of Old Testament prophecy. In particular, various lines draw upon the image of the innocent suffering one in the Psalms (15.23 [Ps. 69.21]; 15.24

---

1. Scholars are sharply divided over whether the final cry of Jesus is a cry of abandonment which cites only Ps. 22.1 or whether it is a confident prayer which invokes Ps. 22 in its entirety. Schweizer (*Mark*, p. 353) argues that Jesus' final cry maintains both perspectives: 'The cry of Jesus summarizes in an extraordinarily meaningful way both aspects of what is happening here: it is a radical expression of the loneliness of Jesus' suffering. He has to bear not only the experience of being abandoned by men, but also of being forsaken by God. At the same time, however, it is a radical expression of a devotion to God which endures in every adverse experience—a devotion which continues to claim God as "my" God and will not let him go although he can be experienced only as the absent One who has forsaken the petitioner.'

2. This historical and social connection resists every 'gnosticizing' tendency which might remove the suffering of Jesus from the world of human experience. At the same time rooting the suffering of Jesus in the historical and social context of first-century Palestine resists efforts to overly 'spiritualize' this story as well as overly simplistic efforts to identify present experiences of suffering with the passion of Jesus. This hermeneutical context also stands over against the tendency of the church to view the death of Jesus as an abstract and timeless theological category.

[Ps. 22.18]; 15.29 [Pss. 22.7; 109.25]; 15.34 [Ps. 22.1]; 15.36 [Ps. 69.21]). More significantly, the story of Jesus' suffering and death is shown to be rooted in the story and the actions of God.[1]

9. A solemn portrait of Jesus is presented. The basic frame of the story tells that Jesus died at the hands of the government. These events do little to distinguish the death of Jesus from countless other executions. The use of details and the employment of various narrative techniques extend this outline and clarify the death scene. The abuse and rejection which mark the death of Jesus are demonstrated.[2] At the same time Jesus is portrayed as the innocent sufferer whose heroic death reflects the expectations of the Psalms: 'In various stages this passage expresses the church's discernment of the truth that in Jesus' suffering the path of every righteous sufferer in Israel was fulfilled...'[3]

10. Consequently the local narrative effect of this scene is impressive. Although it is built upon a simplistic literary frame (15.22a, 24a, 27a, 37), Mk 15.20c-37 narrates a complex, multi-faceted death scene. Significantly, little focus is given to the manner of execution,[4] to the physical pain of Jesus, or to his emotional state. The death of Jesus is viewed neither from an internal, psychological perspective nor from the omniscient perspective of divinity. Instead, various details of the

---

1. Schweizer (*Mark*, pp. 350-51) finds the key to the church's understanding of Jesus' death in this connection. He says, 'It is obvious that what moved the church primarily and most impressively was the loneliness of Jesus, which was the real cause of his intense suffering. This is proof of the amazing difference between God's way and everything which men consider their goal or conceive of as being God's way. Gradually this difference was made more prominent as the church discovered the prototype of this suffering in the Psalms of the innocent sufferer. By appropriating these Psalms the church explicitly stated that God's plan of salvation was being fulfilled in this experience.'

2. The reviling of Jesus for his inability to save himself may allude to a wider tradition. Within apocalyptic literature such impotence will designate the Antichrist. Pesch (*Markusevangelium*, II, p. 488) discusses this idea.

3. Schweizer, *Markus*, p. 346. Schweizer refers specifically to 15.20b-26. Pesch (*Markusevangelium*, II, p. 488) attempts to show a common word field between the innocent sufferer of the Psalms and this passage.

4. On the process of crucifixion, see the excursus by Gnilka, *Markus*, II, pp. 318-20. Various physical evidence was gleaned from a family grave near Jerusalem from the first century. The remains of a crucified person were found in this grave, and the findings are reported by N. Haas, 'Anthropological Observations on the Skeletal Remains from Giv' at ha-Mivtar', *IEJ* 20 (1970), pp. 38-59.

4. Mark 15.16–16.8: The Death of Jesus

people and the activity around the cross are configured into a focused presentation in which the reader experiences the tragic drama of Jesus' final hour.

The Passion Context. Mk 15.20c-37 portrays Jesus as the suffering innocent one whose death fulfills Old Testament images. This local portrait of Jesus is expanded and clarified by its interaction with the wider passion narrative. Various connections demonstrate this hermeneutical relationship.

1. Within the wider framework of the passion story the death scene fulfills a long line of plot expectations. The various predictions of suffering and death set forth in the passion story are realized in Mk 15.20c-37. Thus, the death scene provides the climax of the plot line and of plot expectations generated through Mark 14–16.

2. This scene also confirms and fulfills previous expectations about the character of Jesus. This fulfillment of various predictions vindicates the prophetic vision of Jesus. In particular the prophecies of the Passover meal (14.12-26) come to reality. Beyond this the ongoing allusions to Jesus as the Suffering Servant become realized prophecy through the events of his death.

3. In addition, important lines are added to the characterization of Jesus. The offer of wine and vinegar picks up the theme of the suffering righteous one (Ps. 69.21). The refusal of the wine (15.23) picks up the imagery of the trial before Pilate (15.1-15) and the abuse by the soldiers (15.16-20); like the Suffering Servant, Jesus endures his pain in silence. Similarly the dividing of the garments (15.24) picks up the disrobing of Jesus in the abuse scene and advances the Suffering Servant imagery. The focus on Jesus as the King of the Jews (15.26, 32) repeats the theme from Pilate's questioning (15.2, 9, 12) and from the soldiers' abuse (15.17-19). In the death scene Jesus is executed as the thieves are (15.27), and this fulfills the imagery of Mk 14.48. The blasphemy of those who pass by (15.29) recalls the charge of blasphemy by the religious leaders (14.64). The darkness of the hour recalls Jesus' reference to his own 'hour' (14.35, 41).

4. Most importantly, the soteriological significance of the death scene is developed by the passion context. Within Mk 15.20c-37 the saving significance of Jesus' death is not made explicit. Here Jesus, like countless others, is executed at the hands of Rome. The details and the narration of the story show that Jesus dies as an innocent and pious

Jew and that this suffering resonates with Israel's scriptures. Beyond these images the significance of Jesus' death remains veiled in the local context. Only in the larger passion context is the soteriology of this story made clear. In particular the Passover prophecy (14.12-26) provides the key for understanding Jesus' death. His blood is shed as the source of a new covenant for the many (14.24). His death is a sign of and a step toward the coming Kingdom (14.25). Jesus dies in behalf of the people so that he may bring them into God's reign. This image of Jesus is focused around his death but emerges only through the interaction of the death scene with the Passover prophecy.

The Gospel Context. The death scene receives its ultimate value within the larger Gospel context. Elements of the death scene that seem insignificant or anecdotal are transformed into sharp images. The identity of Jesus is given intense focus. The import of the death of Jesus is made explicit. In various ways the Gospel context transforms the focus of the death scene and opens its significance to the reader.[1]

1. The suffering of Jesus is christologized. The local image of Jesus as the suffering innocent one in the death scene is heroic, but not inherently christological. This imagery combines with the Suffering Servant imagery suggested throughout the passion story; Jesus is thus portrayed as the suffering, innocent Servant of God. This characterization provides a heroic image of suffering piety, but even this image is not directly christological. Only through connection to the larger narrative world are the images of the suffering innocent and the Suffering Servant christologized. Through this vital connection to the earlier ministry, Jesus' suffering, service and death are shown to be the keys to his messianic identity.

Three titles confirm this connection. (1) The initial passion prediction (8.31-33) is a response to Peter's use of the Christ title

---

1. Schweizer (*Mark*, p. 354) notes the stark simplicity of this account and the absence of excessive descriptions of Jesus' experience. He concludes that 'Nothing needs to be added to the concise account of the event itself. It acquires its magnificence through all that has been related previously about Jesus.' While stated from a somewhat different critical perspective, Schweizer's conclusion affirms a basic principle of narrative analysis: the primary significance of a text is not to be found in its history of development but rather in the narrative world in which it partakes. A local text is not to be understood primarily through dissection and isolation, but through its integrated relation to its narrative context.

4. Mark 15.16–16.8: The Death of Jesus

(8.27-30). Thus, Jesus himself insists that the key sign of his messianic mission is his suffering, death and resurrection. This definition of the messianic task is renewed in the following passion predictions (9.31; 10.32-34). This call to suffering and service runs counter to the expectations of Jesus' followers (8.32; 9.33-41; 10.35-41). (2) In a similar fashion the mission of the Son of Man is defined in terms of service and death (10.45). (3) Likewise the Beloved Son is destined to suffering and death (Mk 12.1-12). Thus, the dynamics of the larger narrative take events from the death scene which are not explicitly christological and link them directly to the christological portrait of Jesus.

2. The cross is transformed into a concrete symbol of Jesus' messianic identity. Conversely the portrait of Jesus as the suffering, dying messiah is concretized into the image of the crucified messiah. The cross is not employed as a christological symbol in the stories of Mark 1–13.[1] While the suffering and death of Jesus are central to his mission, no explicit reference is made to his death through crucifixion. Conversely the cross event is decisive in the passion story, yet its christological value is not made clear by the local context. While the cross provides the means of Jesus' death in Mark 14–16, it remains largely undeveloped as a messianic symbol. Through the dynamic of the wider narrative the messianic suffering and death of Mark 1–13 are linked precisely to the cross event in Mark 14–16. Images of the crucified Jesus (Mk 14–16) are joined to images of the suffering, dying messiah (Mk 1–13). A decisive characterization emerges for the first time: Jesus is the crucified messiah.

3. The soteriological value of Jesus' death is made explicit. Seen in isolation the events of Mk 15.20c-37 portray the heroic death of a pious, innocent Jew. Through the Passover prophecy (14.22-25) the value of Jesus' death is unveiled. This focus is amplified through the directive of Jesus in Mk 10.45; the Son of Man has come to serve and to die for the many. Here the death of Jesus is interpreted as the act which brings about the reconciliation of the people to God. The Gospel context thus makes explicit the soteriological value of the death scene: this death is somehow God's working 'for us'.

---

1. In Mk 1–13 reference to the cross is found only in 8.34. Here it is not Jesus' cross but the disciple's cross which is mentioned. In Mk 8.34 the cross serves not as a christological symbol but as a sign of discipleship.

4. The informative detail of cross-bearing is transformed into a symbol for discipleship. Within the death scene Simon's bearing of the cross provides a colorful detail.[1] Within the passion narrative no symbolic value is attached to this deed. In the larger Gospel context cross-bearing becomes a sign of discipleship. This transformation is accomplished through a key logion of Jesus: those who wish to follow Jesus must deny themselves and take up their cross (Mk 8.34). Through this process of reciprocal interpretation the unfocused detail of cross-bearing is changed into a decisive image for discipleship.

5. The imagery of the left and right hand of Jesus are linked to discipleship. Within the death story the placement of the thieves appears anecdotal.[2] The larger passion account does not develop this imagery. In contrast the use of this imagery in Mk 10.35-40 creates a stark and ironic narrative focus. The disciples ask to sit at the left and right of Jesus when he comes into his glory; they see these as positions of power and authority. The repetition of this imagery in Mk 15.27 reveals the shallow and misdirected nature of their request. Ultimately the enthronement of Jesus is on a cross, not a throne. Those at his right and left suffer with him in powerlessness. Consequently the theme of the left/right hand is emptied of its royal imagery and transformed into a sign of suffering and dying. Disciples are thus invited to share Jesus' suffering and death—to 'drink the cup which I drink and to be baptized with the baptism with which I am baptized' (10.39).

6. The expectation of Elijah is clarified. The death scene is wholly ambiguous on the reappearance of Elijah. The narrator assures the reader that the cry of Jesus from the cross was misinterpreted. Further, the non-appearance of Elijah leaves this expectation unfulfilled. What value should the reader attach to this expectation? Is it a failed prophecy (Mal. 4.5)? Is the appearance of Elijah forthcoming? Within the context of the death scene the issue is not resolved. No further mention is made of Elijah in the passion account.

Only within the larger narrative world is this issue clarified. Elijah is discussed at various points. Some say that Jesus is the reincarnation of Elijah (8.28). Peter, James and John see Elijah appear in glory with Jesus (9.4). In Mk 9.11 the disciples ask about the prophecy of

---

1. Schweizer (*Mark*, p. 343) traces the gradual loss of this story through subsequent versions of the death scene.
2. Schweizer (*Mark*, pp. 347-48) traces the gradual softening of this scandal in later accounts.

4. Mark 15.16–16.8: The Death of Jesus

Mal. 4.5. The sharp answer of Jesus clarifies the role of Elijah. Jesus confirms that Elijah will come, but he insists that the death of the Son of Man is more crucial (9.12). Jesus then links the reappearance of Elijah to the ministry of John the Baptist: in the Baptist, Elijah has come, he has been killed and the Scriptures are fulfilled (9.13). Through this interpretation by Jesus the Elijah expectation is emptied of its christological value and placed as a past event which points to the cross. Only the operations of the larger narrative world reveal this insight.

7. The reader is reminded of the wondrous power which surrounds the life of Jesus. The midday darkness (15.33) sets the story against a backdrop of power and awe and recalls various wonder stories from Jesus' ministry. The larger narrative world thus provides a familiar backdrop for the epiphanic elements around the cross.

8. The role of the Spirit is focused. The witness to the death of Jesus is simple and direct: 'having cried with a great voice, he expired' (15.37). The term used for Jesus' death (ἐξέπνευσεν) means the emptying of breath. Within the death scene ἐξέπνευσεν has the sense of 'breathing his last breath'. Seen in light of the wider narrative the expiration of Jesus creates a stark irony. The grecophonic reader likely knows that πνεῦμα means both breath and spirit. The beginning of Jesus' ministry was marked by the coming of the Spirit (1.10), and his initial steps are guided by the Spirit (1.12). Jesus is thus shown as the Son of God who teaches and heals in the power of the Spirit (1.22). In this larger context the final expiration receives new perspective. With his death the ministry of Jesus comes to an end and the Spirit departs.

9. Thus, much of what the crucifixion of Jesus signifies is not made explicit in the events of the death scene. The basic elements of the death story make it similar to other executions. The details and narrative techniques which fill out these events show that Jesus is executed as a pious, innocent Jew and that his death fulfills an Old Testament pattern. Read in isolation Mk 15.20c-37 provides no direct, focused Christology or soteriology. The larger passion context widens this perspective by joining the images of innocent sufferer and Suffering Servant and by confirming the role of Jesus as God's prophet. Consequently the passion narrative shows the death of Jesus as the suffering of God's prophet for the people. It is only within the larger context of the story of Jesus' life that the significance of Jesus'

death is made plain. When seen within this wider narrative world Mk 15.20c-37 tells a crucial tale of clear christological and soteriological value. Because of these interconnections the cross scene now presents the death of the Beloved Son—the crucified messiah—who gives his life in behalf of the people.

10. This syntactical interaction of various narrative contexts strongly impacts the focus of the narrative. Two decisive images emerge. First, the narrative generates a vital interpretation of a historical event. The crucifixion of Jesus is shown to be more than a routine execution. This event marks the death of an innocent suffering Jew, of the Suffering Servant, of God's prophet. The crucifixion of Jesus is thus shown to be the death of the messiah, the execution of God's Son. Important links are established between this event and the reconciliation of the people to God. Cross-bearing is established as the mark of Jesus' followers. The cross is thus transformed into a symbol of salvation and a sign of discipleship.

At the same time the narrative generates a vital interpretation of a historical person. Jesus, who was executed at the hands of the Romans, is shown to possess a decisive identity and mission. Jesus is characterized as a pious Jew who suffers innocently. His identity as the Suffering Servant is confirmed. He is shown to be the teacher and prophet of God. In him the teaching and prophecy of the vineyard parable (12.1-12) is realized. The Son, chosen and loved by God, is rejected by his own. Jesus is shown to be God's messiah who suffers and dies for his people.

This decisive characterization of Jesus cannot be generated or sustained in isolation by the events of Mk 15.20c-37. This christological image is instead the product of the systematic interaction of various narrative elements and contexts. This complex image of Jesus does not emerge from a single stage or type of tradition. Neither is this image the sum of several independent portraits of Jesus. This portrait is not the result of one tradition subsuming another or of one message layed over another. Instead, this vital characterization of Jesus is created through the intersection and interaction of the whole story of Jesus. The cross scene thus provides crucial keys for understanding the nature and purpose of the Gospel of Mark. More decisively, the narrative pattern at work in the cross scene culminates the central character study of this Gospel. Through the complex narrative process at work in Mk 15.20c-37 a decisive portrait

4. *Mark 15.16–16.8: The Death of Jesus*

emerges: Jesus is the rejected prophet, the slain Son, the crucified messiah.

Comparative Analysis
The story of Jesus' death appears in various other literary contexts. These alternate uses of the story create diverse narrative images. Comparative analysis will employ these alternate accounts as a performance field against which to read Mk 15.20c-37.[1]

Pre-Markan Contexts. Reconstruction of the history of this tradition has proved difficult and the results varied.[2] Perhaps more so than any other passage, the story of Jesus' death challenges the ability of historical reconstruction. After surveying various attempts at dissection and reconstruction, J. Gnilka notes that, at some point, every single verse has been identified as part of the oldest layer of tradition.[3] His warning to interpreters is timely: 'In view of the...insecurity of the research, reservation is demanded'.[4] R. Pesch is less guarded in his criticism of various dissections of this text:

> The decomposition of the carefully-connected, coherent section of the passion story in older... and recent literature reveals, in the difference and contradiction of the results, only the methodological weakness of a half century of literary-critical work.[5]

Despite such warnings, numerous reconstructions are posed.

Most interpreters see behind the crucifixion a number of layers of tradition. One group of scholars claims that the basic death story has been expanded by various additions and by multiple stages of redaction. Bultmann led in this direction, arguing that the basic story of the crucifixion is found in Mk 15.20b-24, with the possible addition of 15.27, 37. In Bultmann's estimation the remaining material was a legendary reworking of the death scene.[6] Vincent Taylor also gave support to this approach:

1. On the use of diachronic analysis as phenomenological description and comparison of texts, see Chapter 1.
2. For an overview of the history of research, see Gnilka, *Markus*, pp. 310-11.
3. Gnilka, *Markus*, II, p. 311.
4. Gnilka, *Markus*, II, p. 311.
5. Pesch, *Markusevangelium*, II, p. 474.
6. Bultmann, *History*, pp. 273-74, 279.

The narrative consists of short separate scenes strung together in rapid succession. From it one gains the impression of a comparatively brief foundation story, which has attracted to itself various items of tradition, some historical and others legendary, out of which a kind of crucifixion drama has been compiled to meet the religious needs of a Gentile church.[1]

Eduard Schweizer reaches a similar conclusion:

Little by little other statements were added to a brief account telling of Jesus' death with a loud cry, the mockery of the people, and the sympathy of an individual who wanted to alleviate Jesus' suffering with cheap wine.[2]

Various others have supported this pattern of reconstruction.[3]

A second line of reconstruction sees in the death scene the combination of two distinct traditions. This position was put forth by Johannes Schreiber. Schreiber argued that Mk 15.20b-22a, 24, 27 presented one tradition from a theological and apologetic approach. Taking his clue from the mention of Simon and from Acts 6.9, Schreiber links this tradition to a Stephen circle. A second tradition, found in Mk 15.25, 26, 29a, 32c, 33, 34a, 37, 38, narrated the death of Jesus from the standpoint of an Old Testament, Jewish apocalypticism. These two traditions are joined through the editorial activity of Mark.[4] Schreiber's thesis was taken up and expanded by Wolfgang Schenk.[5]

Both lines of reconstruction suggest a pre-Markan passion tradition which is self-standing. In such a form the death story would have little contact with the wider passion or with the ministry of Jesus. It would preserve the details of the crucifixion as a historical report, and its purpose would be largely apologetic. To accomplish this purpose the scandalous death scene would be put into a distinct theological perspective. The death of Jesus is shown to be the heroic suffering which fulfills the Old Testament and accomplishes the will of God.[6]

1. Taylor, *Mark*, p. 587.
2. Schweizer, *Mark*, p. 359.
3. See, for example, Linneman, *Studien*, pp. 168-70; Schenke, *Der gekreuzigte Christus*, pp. 102-10.
4. Schreiber, *Theologie*, pp. 32-49.
5. Schenk, *Passionsbericht*, pp. 13-64.
6. Dibelius (*Tradition*, pp. 183-89, 295-96) saw this emphasis. Dibelius argued that this concern was the catalyst behind the development of the passion story. Dibelius concluded that 'even the earliest record told events from the Passion which only had significance because they were known to be announced by Scripture.

Others argue that the death story is an inseparable part of the pre-Markan passion tradition.[1] In such a form the story would provide the center and the climax of the passion narrative. Within this context the death scene would interact with various other accounts from the passion tradition. This use of the story would develop the christological and soteriological focus to some extent. Missing from this context would be the interpretive depth provided by the story of Jesus' ministry and by his self-definition of his messianic task.

The Gospel of Matthew. The death of Jesus is narrated in Mt. 27.31b-50. This account of Jesus' death takes over the context and the form of Mk 15.20c-37. Typical changes in language and style are present. Various details drop out of this account (Simon's coming from the country, the hour of the crucifixion). The basis of the mocking of Jesus is made clear: he has claimed to be the Son of God (Mt. 27.40, 43). The wording of the cry of Jesus has been altered, as has the translation (Mt. 27.46). Beyond these changes the death scene in Mt. 27.31b-50 differs little from that of Mk 15.20c-37.

The Gospel of Luke. Luke has taken over the framework of the death scene from the Gospel of Mark, but he has reworked its form and outlook. Following the conscription of Simon, Luke adds an extensive dialogue in which Jesus warns the women of Jerusalem of the coming eschatological woes (Lk. 23.27-31). Luke relocates the mention of the two other victims to this point (Lk. 23.32). The offer of wine is omitted, then the mention of the criminals is repeated (Lk. 23.33). A crucial prayer of Jesus is inserted: 'Father, forgive them, for they know not what they do' (Lk. 23.34). Significantly, Luke describes the 'people' (λαός) as innocent bystanders, but he tells of the abuse by the

---

Then everything shameful and dishonouring done to Jesus—arrest, mishandling, dividing of garments, contemptuous treatment, was legitimatized in the Passion story, for it happened according to God's will.' For Dibelius this concern also guided Mark's redactions of this tradition: 'But, as is also quite obviously the purpose of the editing by Mark, it proposes to describe salvation, i.e. the fulfilment of God's will as revealed in the Old Testament' (p. 296).

Schweizer (*Mark*, p. 351) agrees in substance with Dibelius on the purpose of these citations and allusions: 'By appropriating these Psalms the church explicitly stated that God's plan of salvation was being fulfilled in this experience'.

1. See, for example, Pesch, *Markusevangelium*, II, pp. 474-503.

leaders (Lk. 23.35). In the charge of the leaders Jesus is described as the Christ, the Chosen One (Lk. 23.35). Luke relocates the mention of the inscription (Lk. 23.38), then adds an extensive dialogue between the criminals and Jesus (Lk. 23.39-43). This dialogue proclaims the innocence of Jesus and his power to forgive sinners. Luke explains the darkness as an eclipse, then relocates the tearing of the temple curtain to precede Jesus' death (Lk. 23.45). The scandalous cry from Psalm 22 has been replaced in Luke by a prayer: 'Father, into your hands I commit my spirit' (Lk. 23.46). This saying avoids the difficulty of Jesus' cry and makes clear the departure of the Spirit upon Jesus' death.

Luke has thus cast the story of Jesus' death in a distinct form and employed it for his own theological agenda. Various difficulties have been removed. Renewed attention is given to Jesus, who is in control throughout. The words of Jesus show his concern for his followers and his power to forgive. The people observe the events, but the leaders are blamed for Jesus' death. Luke declares Jesus an innocent, yet forgiving victim. This use of the death scene demonstrates a clear alternative to the story in Mk 15.20c-37.

The Gospel of John. Jn 19.17-30 employs the basic elements of the death scene to create a sharply different story. The basic plot elements are present: the journey to Golgotha, fellow victims, the inscription, the dividing of garments, the offer of wine, the expiration. Nonetheless the story has been given a distinct structure and outlook. These events occur on the day of preparation for the Passover (Jn 19.14). Jesus is slain at the hour when the Passover lambs are sacrificed. Jesus bears his cross alone, for Simon is omitted. The mocking of Jesus has been removed. In its place stand the observance by the passers, the objection by the leaders to the title (Jn 19.21) and the division of garments by the soldiers (Jn 19.23-24). The presence of faithful followers is recorded (Jn 19.25-27). This group includes three women named Mary, as well as the Beloved Disciple. Their presence allows an important dialogue in which Jesus gives directions for the future. Various events occur in order to fulfill the Scripture (Jn 19.24, 28). Jesus knows the course of events and is in control throughout (Jn 19.28). His final words are a cry of accomplishment and completion (Jn 19.30). The Spirit is not taken from Jesus, but is given up (Jn 19.30).

4. *Mark 15.16–16.8: The Death of Jesus*

Jn 19.17-30 thus employs the basic elements of the death scene to create a distinct performance. Jesus procedes to his cross in regal fashion; none bears the cross for him, and none mock his procession. Jesus is conscious and in control throughout the scene. No hint of incoherence or anguish marks his words. Jesus fully directs each step of his departure. Faithful followers accompany his journey, and he gives words of encouragement which insure their future. His words and his death fulfill the Old Testament. Jesus dies as a victor in charge of his destiny. Thus, the death scene has been used to narrate the departure of Jesus to the Father and to culminate the Johannine portrait of Jesus.

The Gospel of Peter. The death scene is also recorded in the *Gos. Pet.* 4.10-14 and 5.15-19. Various elements parallel the scene in Mark 15: crucifixion between two malefactors, silent suffering, the inscription, the dividing of the garments, midday darkness, the offer of wine, the final cry. Despite these similarities the *Gospel of Peter* tells a radically different account of Jesus' death. Jesus is portrayed as one who suffers without pain (4.10). One of the crucified proclaims his innocence and acknowledges Jesus as the 'saviour of men' (4.13). The abuse is carried out by the soldiers, who forbid the breaking of Jesus' legs and thus prolong his suffering (5.14). The darkness causes anxiety over a possible violation of Jewish law (5.15). The guilt is laid on the head of the Jewish people (5.17). The people are confused by the darkness (5.18). Significantly, the scandal has been removed from the final cry of Jesus. Acknowledged by the writer as Lord, Jesus cries out, 'My power, O power, thou hast forsaken me' (5.19). With these words Jesus is taken up. Through these arrangements the *Gospel of Peter* gives a distinct direction to the death scene. Central to this account is a carefully guarded Christology: Jesus is the innocent one, the savior who suffers at the hands of Romans and Jews, yet without pain and without scandal.

The Acts of Pilate. The death scene is also narrated in the *Acts Pil.* 10.1-2 and 11.1. This account is an eclectic compilation which draws heavily upon material from the Gospel of Luke and from the Gospel of John. Consequently the story provides a collection of images with no distinct focus.

Summary

Comparative analysis demonstrates wide-ranging possibilities for the story of Jesus' death. Prior to the Gospel of Mark this story may have served as a self-standing apologetic report or as an element in the earliest passion tradition. Matthew's use of the story mimics that of Mk 15.20c-37. In contrast Luke uses the death scene to focus the guilt of the Jewish people and the innocence of Jesus. A dramatic image of Jesus is shown: in charge of his own destiny, Jesus is able to offer forgiveness and to care for his followers. The Gospel of John creates a unique version of the death scene and uses it to crystallize Johannine Christology. Jesus goes to the Father in full control of his destiny. He cares for his own to the end and provides for their future. His last words are a cry of accomplishment and victory. Distinct versions of the scene appear in the *Gospel of Peter* and in the *Acts of Pilate*.

Attention to the various performances of the death scene demonstrate its openness to alternate expressions and outlooks. Most importantly, this comparative analysis demonstrates that the significance of a text is not wholly internal, but draws extensively upon the narrative world which hosts the story.

Seen in comparison with the various performances of the death scene, Mk 15.20c-37 provides a distinct account and generates a unique characterization of Jesus. The basic events of the death scene make it little different from other executions. The details which fill out this account generate a scene of wonder and show Jesus as an innocent sufferer whose pain fulfills Old Testament imagery. Within the wider passion context the suffering of Jesus is joined to the role of the Suffering Servant and to the prophetic mission of Jesus. The saving value of this death first comes into focus through the Passover prophecy. The full christological and soteriological value of Jesus' death is clarified only through the dynamics of the larger narrative world. The portrait of Jesus as the slain Son, the crucified messiah is concretized and made the central image of his story. The cross is transformed into an image of salvation and a sign of discipleship.

Through its intersection with the wider story of Jesus the death scene takes part in an extended process of narrative characterization. Through wide-ranging patterns of reciprocal interpretation the images of Mk 15.20c-37 are crystallized into a vital narrative portrait: Jesus is the rejected prophet, the Son of God who dies. Jesus is the messiah crucified for the people.

4. Mark 15.16–16.8: The Death of Jesus

Mark 15.38-47: Signs of Hope

The events which follow the crucifixion serve a vital plot function. This brief scene helps to interpret the death of Jesus and connects the crucifixion to the empty tomb.

Synchronic Analysis
Mk 15.38-47 exhibits an unusual structure:

> *Introduction*
> —
>
> *Body*
> | | |
> |---|---|
> | Curtain is torn (passive) | 15.38 |
> | Centurion confesses | 15.39 |
> | Women behold | 15.40a |
> | Narrator informs | 15.40b-41 |
> | Narrator informs | 15.42 |
> | Narrator informs | 15.43ab |
> | Joseph requests | 15.43c |
> | Pilate inquires | 15.44 |
> | Pilate consents | 15.45 |
> | Joseph buries | 15.46 |
> | Women behold | 15.47 |
>
> *Conclusion*
> —

Narrative Morphology. Mk 15.38-47 employs eleven motifs to narrate the events which follow Jesus' death. Morphologically this scene presents a distinct configuration.

1. No introduction or conclusion is employed. As a result the story is linked directly to the prior death scene and to the subsequent scene at the tomb.

2. The scene has been framed around four individual segments without extensive interconnections: (1) the rending of the temple veil (15.38); (2) the confession of the centurion (15.39); (3) the experience of the women (15.40-41, 47); (4) the involvement of Joseph of Arimathea (15.42-46). These anecdotal segments present four separate experiences in connection with the death of Jesus.

3. These four segments have been joined into a logical sequence to create an unusual scene. This linkage generates a new narrative

configuration which sustains various narrative effects.

4. The experience of the women has been narrated as two distinct events, creating a type of intercalation.[1] The women observe the crucifixion from a distance in 15.40-41, then observe the place of burial in 15.47.

4.1. The first event is built around their observance of the crucifixion (15.40a). This simple report occasions three further reports on the activity of the women. (1) A specific list of witnesses is given (15.40b).[2] One Mary is described in terms of geographical origin (Magdalene), while the other is defined by familial relationships (James the Less and Josetos).[3] The third witness is named without description (Salome).[4] (2) A definitive description of their activity is provided (15.41a). This retrospective account relates the realm of their activity (Galilee and Jerusalem), as well as the type of their work (following Jesus and serving him). (3) Their activity is shown to be typical for a larger host of women followers (15.41b). Like those named, these unnamed women were with Jesus in Galilee and followed him up to Jerusalem.

4.2. The second event is built around the women's observance of the

---

1. A host of problems is involved in the description of the women. (1) The number of women listed in 15.40 has been disputed, with some arguing for three different women named Mary. (2) The exact relationship to James the Less and to Josetos (or Joses) is unclear. (3) The fact that these women who fulfill key roles in Jesus' ministry are mentioned in retrospect at the end of Jesus' life is enigmatic. (4) The relationship of this list to the names in Mk 6.3 is not certain. (5) The reduction of the list to two witnesses in 15.47 and its relation to 15.40 is problematic. (6) The immediate repetition of the list in 16.1 in a different form raises difficult questions about the relationship of the three lists and the three accounts. (7) The fact that the role of the women concludes in an abrupt flight is troublesome. The women are the sole witnesses to these events, yet they say nothing to anyone (16.8)

2. Pesch (*Markusevangelium*, II, pp. 504-508) argues for the listing of four women in 15.40b—three Marys and Salome. Pesch also gives attention to what may be known of these names from other contexts. Pesch's argument, though rejected by most, is strengthened somewhat by a similar reading in the Syriac translations and in the Syriac *Didaskalia*.

3. Various textual problems accompany this listing. Mary Magdalene is called Mariam in B C W Θ f^1. The second Mary is designated the daughter of James the Less in sy^s. Ἰωσῆτος is read as Ἰωσῆ by ℵ* A C W Ψ 𝔐 sa and translated as 'Joseph' by lat sy^s.

4. Salome is unknown elsewhere in the New Testament, but appears frequently in Gnostic Gospels. See Pesch, *Markusevangelium*, II, p. 506.

4. Mark 15.16–16.8: The Death of Jesus

place of Jesus' burial. As with the first report, a precise list of witnesses is provided. Significantly, only two of the women from 15.40a are present at the tomb (Mary Magdalene and Mary of Josetos).

5. The narrator intrudes on three occasions (15.40b-41; 15.42; 15.43ab) to provide vital information. The first comment (15.40b-41) specifies which women were watching, describes their previous service to Jesus and tells of other women disciples. The second intrusion (15.42) provides temporal references—it is evening of the day of preparation (Friday). The third intrusion (15.43a, b) defines the character of Joseph. Thus, the comments of the narrator lend detail and depth to this scene.

6. The role of Joseph of Arimathea has been specified, and his contribution has been connected to a wider context. Precise information about Joseph's status is provided: he is from Arimathea, a respected citizen, one who awaits the Kingdom of God, one who has courage, one who has access to Pilate. The basic account of Joseph's activity also includes references to the larger time frame (15.42), to the role of Pilate (15.43, 44, 45) and to the role of the centurion (15.44b, 45a).

7. As a result of this morphological configuration the anecdotal lines of Mk 15.38-47 have been joined into a coherent narrative. Two traits characterize this text. (1) The story exhibits an unusual level of concern for description and detail. (2) These rather disparate segments of experience have been integrated into the scene and connected, to some extent, to the larger story of Jesus' death and resurrection.

Narrative Syntax. Morphological analysis revealed the unique configuration presented by Mk 15.38-47. The syntactical strategy which operates upon these motifs sustains various narrative transactions.

1. A series of anecdotal images is transformed into a coherent narrative constellation. By presenting each of these segments within a common framework, this scene now provides interpretive keys to the meaning of Jesus' death.

2. This literary sequence has been used to provide a logical connection between the death scene and the empty tomb. This narrative bridge thus insures the coherence of the narrative.

3. At the same time Mk 15.38-47 creates an interlude between the death of Jesus and the resurrection report. Various information and images are used to fill this narrative gap: the temple curtain is split, a soldier declares Jesus Son of God, Joseph buries Jesus, the women watch. This interlude imitates the passing of time and lends a mimetic sense to the narrative. In particular this passage of time undergirds the prophecy that Jesus will be dead for three days (8.31; 9.31; 10.34).

4. Precise attention is given to historical images. This account uses various elements to sustain a sense of historical grounding: time references, naming of historical figures, detailed descriptions of characters.[1] This imagery confronts the reader with a powerful narrative claim: the story of Jesus is rooted in objective, historical reality.

5. More than any other passage in the Gospel of Mark this scene clarifies the roles and status of individual actants.[2] A host of information is provided. The women are located by geographical and familial origin, and their service to Jesus is rehearsed in location and detail. Joseph is known by geographical origin, reputation, piety,

---

1. From a narrative perspective the text provides the appearance of historicity. Within narratives this type of mimetic presentation is a literary device which may or may not be rooted in an actual history. J.R.R. Tolkien, for example, created in his trilogy a literary world with its own structures, its own genealogy, its own history, its own map, but he denied such a world ever existed in history. The verdict on the world presented in Mk 15.38-47 is quite different. Almost without exception scholars find important pieces of historical data reflected in the literary events of this scene. Bultmann (*History*, pp. 273-74) considers various parts of Mk 15.33-47 as legendary, but he says of the burial scene, 'This is an historical account which creates no impression of being a legend apart from the women who appear again as witnesses in v. 47, and vv. 44, 45 which Matthew and Luke in all probability did not have in their Mark' (p. 274). Gnilka (*Markus*, II, pp. 326-37, 336-37) finds historical reliability in the observation of the women and the burial by Joseph. Schweizer (*Mark*, pp. 369-70) finds historicity in the role of the women, the death on a Friday, the particular piety of Joseph, the burial by Joseph, the details of the burial. Taylor (*Mark*, pp. 599-602) finds strong historicity in the burial account. Pesch (*Markusevangelium*, II, pp. 500-501, 517-18) finds historical detail in the centurion's confession, the presence of the women at the cross, the discipleship of women in Galilee, the extensive number who accompanied Jesus to Jerusalem, the death on Friday, the activity of Joseph.

2. As much or more character information is given in this passage about the women and Joseph as in the scenes in which the disciples are called (1.16-20; 3.13-19).

4. Mark 15.16–16.8: The Death of Jesus

courage and by his actions. This informative approach to characterization is without parallel in the Gospel of Mark.

6. This attention to actants also provides a strong cast of narrative witnesses who may verify this scene. The presence of these witnesses and the character sketches made available to the reader connect the scene not only to the real world which surrounds this story, but also to the real world of subsequent generations. The story of the church is thus verified through a line of known witnesses.

7. The role of the women in the local scene and in the wider story is clarified. The women are shown to be the single connective between the death story and the burial of Jesus. Apart from their presence there is no narrative link between the scenes of Jesus' death, his burial and his resurrection. Beyond this plot function at a most important juncture of the narrative, the precise naming of the women also sets them apart as key participants in the narrative. Typically the Gospel of Mark does not name or describe its characters.[1] This is particularly true of female actants. Prior to Mk 15.40 only the mother of Jesus (6.3; but see 3.31) and Herodias (6.17, 19, 22) are known by name. Although women play key roles throughout this story, they are not named.[2] In light of this narrative trait the naming of the women in 15.40, 47 and in 16.1 is extraordinary. A handful of women are presented by name as witnesses to the death and burial of Jesus.[3] More

---

1. Among the key participants who remain unnamed in the Gospel of Mark are the mother-in-law of Peter (1.29-31), those healed (1.23-26; 2.1-12; 3.1-6; 5.25-34 and others), religious leaders, soldiers, disciples (4.38; 8.28; 9.11; 10.26; 13.1 and others), questioners (10.17; 11.27; 12.13, 18, 28), the two thieves (15.27), the centurion (15.39, 44, 45). The *Acts of Pilate* names one soldier (Longinus) and the two thieves (Dysmas and Gestas).

2. See, for example, the crucial role played by the mother-in-law who serves Jesus as a deacon (διηκόνει in 1.29-31), the woman whose faith saved her (5.25-34), the Syro-Phoenician who debates with Jesus (7.24-30), the widow who gave all she had (12.41-44), the woman who anointed Jesus (14.1-11), those who accompanied Jesus up to Jerusalem (15.41b). While the role of these actants is emphasized, their names are not recalled.

3. In view of the prevailing view of women as witnesses, both inside and outside the early church. this focus on their experience is extraordinary. Consequently numerous scholars find strong evidence of historicity in the witness of the women. For example, Schweizer (*Mark*, p. 361) says of Mk 15.42-47, 'This account, then, is primarily interested in the historical course of events and most likely has reproduced it correctly'.

significantly, their presence at the cross is shown to be indicative of a lengthy service to Jesus.[1] Most significantly, the women of 15.40 are shown as representatives of a host of women followers (15.41b).

Thus, the narrative uses a historical report to provide a retrospective witness to the work of the women. This delayed notice occurs at a crucial stage in the narrative and carves out an undeniable niche for the service of women in the story of Jesus.[2] In addition to its role in the story, this character focus provides a distinct model for the community which reads this Gospel.

8. In the aftermath of Jesus' death signs of hope emerge. A sequence of scattered anecdotes has been shaped into a narrative constellation which offers a new vision of reality.

8.1. A divine sign of hope is present in the rending of the veil. This parting of the veil may be understood as a sign of judgment. If the curtain covers the entrance to the Holy of Holies its rending desecrates the temple and brings sacrificial worship to an end. The rending of the veil may also serve as a positive sign: the temple pattern of exclusion by stages of Gentiles, women, non-priests has been broken. Thus, the barrier which separated individuals from the presence of God has been torn asunder with the death of Jesus. Eduard Schweizer argues that both images are true:

> What is intended here... is not an announcement of future events but the description of a consummation which has come already in the death of Jesus. After what has been said in 11:17; 13:2; 15:29f., vs. 38 must be interpreted as a reference to the end of the temple cult which comes in Jesus' death. More precisely, this is the end of the exclusion from the place of God's presence of all who were not priests, of all who were not Jews...[3]

Beyond this the source of this sign is clear. The notation that the curtain was torn from top to bottom (ἀπ' ἄνωθεν ἕως κάτα) indicates divine action. This action is complete, for the curtain is torn

---

1. As in 1.31 the use of imperfect verbs (ἠκολούθουν, διηκόνουν) displays a durative sense to their service.
2. This issue has been treated systematically by E. and F. Stagg, *Woman in the World of Jesus* (Philadelphia: Westminster Press, 1978), and by E. Schüssler Fiorenza, *In Memory of Her: A Feminist Reconstruction of Christian Origins* (New York: Crossroad, 1983).
3. Schweizer, *Mark*, p. 355. Gnilka (*Markus*, II, p. 324) takes a similar position: 'Both interpretations are to be taken together and present no contradiction'.

4. Mark 15.16–16.8: The Death of Jesus

into two parts (εἰς δύο). The use of the passive confirms the portrayal of this event as a divine sign of hope which accompanies the death of Jesus.[1]

8.2. Three human experiences provide signs of hope. At the moment of Jesus' death a Roman soldier recognizes him as Son of God.[2] Though all other followers have fled, a few women disciples find the courage to watch from a distance. A pious Jew finds the courage to ask for Jesus' body, then provides an honorable burial. The place of his burial is known to two named Mary. The divine sign is thus accompanied by human experiences which sustain subtle images of hope.

9. Consequently this scene generates a new model for the community of faith.[3] The death of Jesus does not negate his mission and minstry, but confirms it. The first human to confess Jesus as Son of God does so in the presence of the cross. Significantly, this first confession is voiced by a Gentile soldier.[4] The burial of Jesus is provided by a respected Jew who awaits the Kingdom of God. The only witnesses and bearers of this tradition are women. The scene thus shapes a new mold for the life of Jesus' followers. The community of faith is not to be destroyed by the death of Jesus, but rather founded upon this event. This new community will be liberated from all structures which hinder the way to God's presence. Jew and Gentile, male and female alike will participate in the fellowship of this new

---

1. The language itself confirms this imagery. The passive of σχίζω presents the work of God in Mk 1.10 and in 15.38. Both passages are accompanied by the designation of Jesus as the Son of God (1.11; 15.39). Thus, Jesus' story opens and closes with a divine witness.

2. Bultmann (*History*, p. 282) notes numerous parallels from martyr literature in which the condemned overcomes or converts the executioner. See also Bultmann, *History*, p. 274 n. 1. Other parallels are cited by Pesch, *Markusevangelium*, II, p. 499 n. 38.

3. Gnilka (*Markus*, II, p. 326) sees a two-part model. The centurion is an example of the proper confession of faith, while the women model the proper lifestyle of discipleship. E. Wendling (*Die Enstehung des Marcus-Evangeliums* [Tübingen: Mohr (Paul Siebeck), 1908], p. 176) finds here models (*Urbilder*) for both Jews (Joseph) and for Gentiles (the centurion) in the early church.

4. The soldier is almost universally presumed to be a Gentile, though the text does not make this specification. See, for example, Gnilka, *Markus*, II, p. 324; Schweizer, *Mark*, p. 355; Pesch, *Markusevangelium*, II, p. 502.

community. Like the parting of the veil, the life of this community will be the work of God.

10. This dynamic scene is intertwined with the larger passion story.[1] The story of Joseph assumes the story of the centurion[2] and the trial before Pilate. Beyond this the role of the women sets the stage for the tomb scene. Most significantly, the description of Joseph connects this theme to the central theme of the Gospel. At the beginning of the ministry Jesus announces the Kingdom of God (1.14-15). At the end of his life Jesus is buried by a pious Jew who awaits the Kingdom of God.

11. The story of Jesus is extended beyond his terminal cry. The execution of Jesus marks the end of his ministry and his last apearance within the story world. His final moments are filled with agony and his last words are marked by desparation. The life of Jesus is thus stamped with the scandal of his death. Because of this ending Mk 15.38-47 plays a crucial role: it extends the story line of the Gospel beyond the point of Jesus' death. Four signs of hope and a handful of witnesses pave the way to a new beginning at the tomb and in Galilee.

12. The significance of this account is left open. The ultimate value of these events is not immediately clear. In particular the christological images of the scene remain implicit and suggestive. The rending of the veil is dramatic, but unfocused. The confession of the centurion is open to various interpretations, as Lk. 23.47 demonstrates ('Surely this man was innocent!').[3] The relationship of Joseph to Jesus is unclear. The women watch but do not act. While the interlude in Mk 15.38-47 employs a variety of images and information to link the death scene to the tomb story and to confront the reader with signs of

---

1. Pesch (*Markusevangelium*, II, pp. 503-19) argues for the indissoluble unity of Mk 15.40-16.8. Gnilka (*Markus*, II, pp. 331-32) contends that 14.42–16.8 was one piece and belonged to the oldest passion report. In contrast Schweizer (*Mark*, p. 361) thinks that 15.42-47 was formerly independent.

2. Gnilka (*Markus*, II, p. 333) notes a parallel connection between the role of the centurion and the death of the Baptist (Mk 6.27-28). In both scenes the executioner reports to the political ruler after the death of the martyr.

3. Gnilka (*Markus*, II, p. 325) incorrectly sees here a full expression of Christian faith. Gnilka does not explain how Luke could miss this meaning! Pesch (*Markusevangelium*, II, p. 500) correctly sees that only the wider narrative context clarifies the status of Jesus as *the* Son of God.

4. Mark 15.16–16.8: The Death of Jesus

hope, the full signficance of these events opens up only in the larger narrative context.[1]

The Passion Context. The passion context sheds more light on the events of Mk 15.38-47. The rending of the temple veil recalls the charge against Jesus as one who claimed to destroy and rebuild the temple (14.58; 15.29). The reader is thus left to wonder if the charge is somehow true. Does the rending of the veil signal the descecration of the sanctuary and the end of worship in the temple? When seen from within the passion context the confession of the centurion provides a stark contrast to the harshness of other soldiers (15.15, 16-20, 24-25). The centurion's confession has its parallel in the confession of Jesus before the high priest (14.61-62). The watching women recall Jesus' command to watch in Gethsemane (14.34, 37, 38). The reference to Pilate (15.43-45) recalls the second trial (15.1-15). The burial by Joseph, particularly the absence of anointing, recalls the anointing for burial in 14.1-11. The concern for Jesus' body recalls the images of 14.8 and 14.22. Thus, the events of Mk 15.38-47 receive interpretive depth through their interaction with the larger passion account.

The Gospel Context. The full significance of Mk 15.38-47 becomes clear only through the larger world of the Gospel. Various images and information that appear anecdotal in the local context are charged with symbolic value through the wider narrative. In this manner the darkness which surrounds the death of Jesus is filled with signs of hope.

1. The role of temple worship is clarified for the followers of Jesus. The rending of the temple veil is joined to a larger thematic line.[2] The conflict with the religious leadership of Israel is prominent throughout

---

1. Despite his thoroughgoing focus on historical concerns, Pesch (*Markusevangelium*, II, p. 502) notes this crucial narrative hermeneutic: 'In the context of the entire Gospel of Mark our scene shifts into a new light'. In a similar manner Pesch notes the impact of the wider narrative context on the understanding of the centurion's confession (p. 500).

2. Schweizer (*Mark*, p. 355) reads the sign in light of the larger narrative: 'After what was said in 11.17; 13.2; and 15.29f., vs. 38 must be interpreted as a reference to the end of the temple cult...' In contrast to narrative analysis Schweizer links this interpretation to the intent of the redactor.

Jesus' ministry (Mk 2.6-7, 16, 24; 3.2-6, 22; 7.1-5; 8.11; 10.2; 11.18, 27-28; 12.12, 13-17). In Mark 14–16 this hostility is focused anew as the backdrop for the passion story. Various literary devices are employed to place Jesus in opposition to the temple: (1) Jesus enters the temple and looks about, a foreboding sign in the Gospel of Mark (11.11); (2) Jesus departs from the temple because the hour is late (11.11); (3) the debates with the religious figures emphasize this conflict (11.28; 12.13, 18); (4) the parable of the vineyard presents a scathing critique (12.1-12); (5) various predictions of the temple destruction are given in Mark 13; (6) narrative opposition is posed between the Mount of Olives and the Temple Mount.[1] Thus, the narrative employs the Mount of Olives to symbolize the future of Jesus' followers over against the temple and its condemned patterns of worship. Within this larger narrative schema of religious conflict the rending of the temple veil is clarified. The failure of temple worship is signaled anew as the sanctuary is laid open. At the same time the parting of the veil signals the presence of God made available to all people.[2] This dramatic imagery confirms and completes the role of temple worship set forth in the larger narrative.

2. The confession of the soldier is clarified.[3] The local confession that Jesus was υἱὸς θεοῦ may be read as a declaration of innocence (Lk. 23.47). The larger context makes clear that Jesus is not simply a son, but the Beloved Son (1.11; 9.7). Nonetheless even this confession does not provide the singular and decisive proclamation that Jesus is messiah and Son of God. Demons know this much (1.24, 34; 3.11; 5.7). Peter declares that Jesus is the Christ (8.29). More significantly, this proclamation has already been made by Jesus himself in the presence of witnesses (14.61-62). Consequently the confession in Mk 14.39 is distinct not because of its content, but because of its

1. I have developed this pattern in 'Which Mountain is "This Mountain"?: A Critical Note on Mark 11.22-25', *Paradigms* 2/1 (1986), pp. 33-38.

2. Schenk (*Passionsbericht*, p. 62) argues that ἀναβαίνειν is a technical cult term drawn from the Old Testament. He concludes that the journey of the women up to Jerusalem points to the founding of a new temple cult upon the death of Jesus.

3. Scholars have long debated the question of whether the confession represents a Hellenistic understanding of Jesus as *a* son of God or a Christian confession of Jesus as *the* Son of God. For a list of scholars on each side of this question, see J. Schreiber, *Der Kreuzigungsbericht des Markusevangeliums Mk 15, 20b-41: Eine traditionsgeschichtliche und methodenkritische Untersuchung nach William Wrede (1859–1906)* (Berlin: de Gruyter, 1986), p. 214 n. 2.

4. Mark 15.16–16.8: The Death of Jesus

context. While the confession of demons is silenced and Peter is rebuked following his confession, the centurion's confession—which stands in the shadow of the cross—is not silenced. The carefully developed Christology unfolds at last: here, in view of his suffering and death, Jesus may be truly seen as the Christ, the Son of God.[1]

3. Faithful women are used to focus the imagery of discipleship. With the mention of the women who witness the death of Jesus (15.40) the narrator recalls their role as disciples of Jesus.[2] They have followed Jesus (ἠκολούθουν) and they have served him (διηκόνουν). Most significantly, they watch with Jesus (14.40, 47). In the Gospel of Mark these are terms for discipleship.[3] Disciples are called to follow (1.16-20; 8.34). Their discipleship is to be marked by service to others (10.43-45). Disciples are called to watch (13.5, 9, 14, 33-37; 14.34, 37-38). The anecdotal reference to the women in Mk 15.40-41 is thus transformed by the larger narrative into a pattern for faithful discipleship.[4]

4. The courage of Joseph of Arimathea provides a further model of discipleship. Within Mk 15.38-47 the heroic actions of Joseph clarify how Jesus is buried in the absence of the Twelve, yet the status of Joseph remains ambiguous. Within the larger narrative the actions of Joseph model faithful discipleship. He awaits the Kingdom whose coming Jesus announced (1.14-15; 15.43). His courage (15.43) demonstrates a trait associated with faith and demanded of disciples (4.40; 6.50). As the followers of the Baptist demonstrate, it is the role of disciples to bury their leader (6.29). Thus, the anecdotal report of Joseph's heroism is transformed by the larger narrative into a pattern for those who would follow Jesus.

5. As these transformations demonstrate, interaction with the larger narrative world realigns the images of Mk 15.38-47. In the dark hour

---

1. A quite different model is suggested by P. Vielhauer, 'Erwägungen zur Christologie des Markusevangeliums', *Aufsätze zum Neuen Testament* (TBü, 31, 65; Munich: Chr. Kaiser Verlag, 1965–79), pp. 199-214.

2. While the watching from a distance has a negative role in Ps. 38.11, this imagery is not developed in this scene. Nonetheless, Pesch (*Markusevangelium*, II, p. 505) finds in the distant watching an element of the innocent sufferer theme.

3. In the wider narrative world these women provide a healthy contrast to the inner three male disciples—Peter, James, John.

4. Consequently, the reader is primed to look for further examples of women disciples. Suggestive accounts may be found in Mk 1.29-31; 3.21, 31-34; 5.25-34; 7.24-30; 12.40-44; 14.1-11; 15.40-41, 47; 16.1-8.

228 Prophet, Son, Messiah

of Jesus' death various local events are transformed into signs of hope. A torn curtain proclaims that the presence of God is available to all. A Gentile soldier is the first to see this light and declares that the crucified one is the Son of God. A respected citizen finds the courage to bury the messiah. Faithful women followers wait and watch.

Comparative Analysis
Various other narratives tell of the events between the cross and the tomb. These alternate uses of this material create a comparative literary field against which to focus the operations of Mk 15.38-47.[1]

Pre-Markan Contexts. Scholars remain divided over the history of this tradition prior to its use in the Gospel of Mark.[2] While many dismiss the validity of the signs in Mk 15.38-39,[3] most scholars see behind the burial story an independent tradition. Bultmann led this line of research, arguing that the mention of the women in three successive stories with differences in the details 'clearly shows that individual stories have been brought together'.[4] For Bultmann the reasons for the survival of this account were simple. He argued that Mk 15.42-47 'is an historical account which creates no impression of being a legend apart from the women who appear again as witnesses in v. 47, and vv. 44, 45'.[5] Taylor confirms this basic description of the burial scene.[6] In the same mode Eduard Schweizer argues that the repetition of the women's names points to an independent story.[7] Along with Bultmann, Schweizer finds the reason for existence in its authenticity: 'This account, then, is primarily interested in the historical course of events and most likely has reproduced it correctly'.[8]

Thus, an important line of scholarship argues for an independent pre-Markan account of the burial. As an isolated story this account would provide information to fill in the gap between the cross and the

1. On the use of diachronic analysis as phenomenological description and comparision of texts, see Chapter 1.
2. For a brief description of this research, see Gnilka, *Markus*, II, p. 331 n. 1.
3. Bultmann, *History*, pp. 282-84.
4. Bultmann, *History*, p. 276.
5. Bultmann, *History*, p. 274.
6. Taylor, *Mark*, p. 599.
7. Schweizer, *Mark*, p. 361; see also Schenk, *Passionsbericht*, pp. 254-58.
8. Schweizer, *Mark*, p. 361.

4. Mark 15.16–16.8: The Death of Jesus

tomb. Such a story would be maintained not because of its theological outlook or function, but because of its role as a historical report.

A second line of reconstruction argues that the burial scene is an intricate part of a fixed pre-Markan passion tradition.[1] In this form the story plays an important role in the wider passion narrative. For Ludger Schenke this burial scene provides the original conclusion to the pre-Markan passion story.[2] For Pesch the story is a historical piece which serves as a bridge between Jesus' death and the empty tomb.[3]

The Gospel of Matthew. Mt. 27.51-61 shares a common framework with Mk 15.38-47, yet this performance of the story is distinct. To the splitting of the temple veil Matthew adds the story of the earthquake and the resurrection of the saints (Mt. 27.51b-53). The confession of Jesus as Son of God is made by a group of soldiers who have 'seen' the earthquake (Mt. 27.54). The language of the story is epiphanic: they 'fear a great fear' (Mt. 27.54). Significantly, Matthew describes Joseph as a disciple of Jesus (Mt. 27.57). As in Mk 15.47, Matthew ends this account with the two Marys, but their watchfulness is not mentioned (Mt. 27.61). Following this scene Matthew has an unparalleled account of the securing of the tomb by Pilate and the religious leaders (Mt. 27.62-66). Matthew thus takes over Mk 15.38-47 but makes internal changes which realign the focus of the story. More significantly, the story now operates in a Matthaean world, exchanging much of the symbolism drawn from the larger context in the Gospel of Mark.

The Gospel of Luke. Lk. 23.47-56 has sharply refocused the events which follow Jesus' death. The rending of the temple veil has been relocated into the life of Jesus (Lk. 23.45). The centurion makes no christological confession; instead, he praises God and declares Jesus innocent (Lk. 23.47). Luke adds the sympathy of the multitudes: the people see these events, then return home beating their breasts (Lk. 23.48). All of Jesus' acquaintances are present with the women (Lk. 23.49). Like Matthew, Luke gives further attention to Joseph of

---

1. Two distinct forms of this theory are held by Schenke, *Der gekreuzigte Christus*, p. 83 and Pesch, *Markusevangelium*, II, pp. 509-19.
2. Schenke, *Der gekreuzigte Christus*, p. 83.
3. Pesch, *Markusevangelium*, II, pp. 509-19.

Arimathea. He is a good and righteous member of the council. Most significantly, he is innocent because he did not consent to the death plot (Lk. 23.51). The women who see the burial go and prepare spices (Lk. 23.56). In accordance with Jewish piety, there is rest on the Sabbath day (Lk. 23.56).

These alterations give the story a new focus. The christological overtones are removed from the centurion's confession. Jesus is declared innocent by a Roman soldier, and Joseph is declared innocent by Luke. The disciples are present, and the people are sympathetic. No unrest occurs on the Jewish Sabbath. Luke thus paints a picture which removes any hint of rebellion and uprising from the activity of Jesus and his followers.

The Gospel of John. Jn 19.31-42 generates an unparalleled account of the events between the cross and the tomb. The story centers around the granting of the body by Pilate (Jn 19.31-37) and the task of burial (Jn 19.38-42). Various Johannine accents shape the story. A distinct awareness of the rules of Jewish piety pervades this account (Jn 19.31, 40, 42). Blood and water, two distinct Johannine metaphors, portray the significance of Jesus' death (Jn 19.34). Explicit references show how the death of Jesus fulfills the Old Testament (Jn 19.36-37). Joseph and Nicodemus are characterized as faithful followers, and their service to Jesus is highlighted (Jn 19.38-42). The true and faithful testimony of an eyewitness supports the faith of later believers (Jn 19.35). The scene in Jn 19.31-42 thus employs a new set of narrative images to generate a Johannine interpretation of Jesus' death.

The Gospel of Peter. The events of Mk 15.38-47 are also recorded in the *Gospel of Peter* (2.3-5a; 5.20; 6.21-24; 7.25-27; 8.28-33; 9.34). This material draws heavily upon the canonical Gospels and presents scattered images of the death of Jesus. Joseph, who is a friend of Pilate, requests the body prior to the crucifixion (2.3-5a). All of the people confess the innocence of Jesus (8.28). An extravagant account of the removal from the cross shows the power of Jesus over both humans and nature (6.21-24). The religious leaders confess their wrongdoing and foresee the end of Jerusalem (7.25). The actions of the disciples are detailed (7.26-27). An extravagant account of the sealing and guarding of the tomb insures its safety (8.28-33). Crowds from the city and from the entire countryside witness the sealed tomb

4. Mark 15.16–16.8: The Death of Jesus

(9.34). Thus, the *Gospel of Peter* presents an eclectic, extravagant vision of the events surrounding Jesus' death.

The Acts of Pilate. The role of the centurion, of the Roman authorities, and of the followers is reported in the *Acts of Pilate* (11.2-3a). The *Acts of Pilate* (11.3) then takes over the burial scene from Lk. 23.50-53. Following this comes an extensive account on the bravery and subsequent imprisonment of Joseph of Arimathea (12.1-2). This story demonstrates the suffering of the followers of Jesus at the hands of the religious leaders.

Other. The *Gospel of the Nazarenes* contains a report of the splitting of the lintel of the temple at the time of Jesus' death. The *Gospel of the Nazarenes* also claims (incorrectly) that Josephus has the same report and adds that awful voices were heard saying 'Let us depart from this abode'.

Summary
The events following the death of Jesus are related in various texts. The use of this material in differing narrative contexts creates distinct images and outlooks. This collection of different performances of this material creates a comparative field against which to focus the narrative form and function of Mk 15.38-47.

When seen over against this divergent use of the material the narrative images and strategy of Mk 15.38-47 are unique. Seen in isolation the events which follow Jesus' death seem anecdotal and ambiguous. Through their intersection and interaction with the larger narrative world of the Gospel of Mark these events are transformed into signs of hope. The rending of the temple veil marks the end of an era and the beginning of a new work of God. The cry of the centurion sets the pattern for the faith of the church. The courage of Joseph provides a model for disciples. The watchfulness of the women confirms their discipleship and provides an open door to the future. These signs indicate that the story is not yet finished and that the mission of the messiah is not yet complete.

Mark 16.1-8: The Resurrection Promise

The final unit of the Gospel of Mark tells of the resurrection promise at the open tomb.[1] This account proves crucial for the plotting

---

1. Mk 16.1-8 is accepted here as the conclusion of the most significant textual tradition. Likely, this ending was intentional, though this question remains open. For a helpful overview of this issue, see J.E. Alsup, *The Post-Resurrection Appearance Stories of the Gospel-Tradition: A History of Analysis with Text-Synopsis* (Stuttgart: Calwer Verlag, 1975), pp. 86-95.

K. Aland ('Bermerkungen zum Schluss des Markusevangeliums', in E. Ellis and M. Wilcox [eds.], *Neotestamentica et Semitica* [Festschrift M. Black; Edinburgh: T. & T. Clark, 1969], pp. 157-80) identifies six lines of tradition for the ending of the Gospel of Mark: (1) texts which end with 16.8; (2) texts which employ 16.1-8 plus the 'shorter ending'; (3) texts with 16.1-8 plus 9-20, but with indications of doubt about the authenticity of 16.9-20; (4) texts with 16.1-8 plus 9-20 as a continuous text; (5) texts with 16.1-8 plus 9-14 plus the Freer Logion (W) plus 15b-20; (6) texts with 16.1-8 plus the 'shorter ending' plus 9-20.

In the pre-critical period 16.9-20 was the unquestioned canonical ending to the Gospel of Mark. Awareness of an important line of manuscripts in which the text ends at 16.8 initiated the modern search for the authentic ending. The confirmation of an ending at 16.8 in two crucial manuscripts from the fourth century (Vaticanus, Sinaiticus), its endurance into the twelfth century (miniscule 304, see also miniscule 2386), its absence from numerous early translations, and the opinion of Eusebius that 16.8 provides the authentic extant ending testify to the validity of this abrupt conclusion. The variety of the supplements to 16.1-8 confirms this position. As a result something of a consensus was reached: the most reliable textual tradition ends the Gospel of Mark at 16.8.

At the same time most scholars concluded that this ending was not intentional. This conclusion was argued from two perspectives. (1) On linguistic grounds various scholars argued that ἐφοβοῦντο γάρ could not end a manuscript—see, for example, the argument of W.L. Knox ('The Ending of St Mark's Gospel', *HTR* 35 [1942], pp. 13-23) that such an ending is without parallel in the Gospel of Mark, the Gospel of John, and in Jewish and Hellenistic literature in general. (2) Others argued on theological grounds that such an ending left the story incomplete and incomprehensible. The appearance traditions in the other Gospels and in 1 Cor. 15.3-5 are cited in support of this position. The conclusion of Schweizer (*Mark*, p. 366) demonstrates this argument: 'the conjecture that the resurrection (of which the church was already aware) is merely alluded to as a mystery—like the Messianic secret—is not very probable. It is necessary to assume that the conclusion of the Gospel has been lost.' Schweizer (*Mark*, p. 373) argues further that 'The resurrected One must open the eyes of the blind once more... The conclusion to the Gospel of Mark, which has been lost, told about this miracle of opening blind eyes which is the first expression of the miracle of Easter morning.'

of the passion story and for the larger narrative characterization of Jesus.

Synchronic Analysis

The resurrection promise in Mk 16.1-8 is structured around nine motifs:

Introduction	
Women come	16.1-2
Body	
Women inquire	16.3
Women behold	16.4a
Narrator informs	16.4b
Women enter	16.5a
Women behold	16.5b
Women fear	16.5c
Messenger speaks	16.6-7
Conclusion	
Women depart	16.8

Narrative Morphology. The resurrection promise is built around a pattern common to the Gospel of Mark: an opening and closing line of movement frame the central elements of the story. Various structural components are brought together to create this final scene.

1. A simple plot line provides the basic framework of the scene. This basic plot is composed of three segments: the women come to the

---

A variety of answers arose to explain this unintended ending. A few conjecture that an appearance from heaven was deliberately suppressed because it became offensive. Others suggest the untimely death of the author. The most popular explanation is an accidental mutilation which separated the original ending from the text.

Recent scholarship has been more receptive to the idea that Mk 16.8 presents the intended ending of the Gospel. Parallel phrases at the end of various texts and manuscripts have been cited—see, for example, the evidence collected by R.H. Lightfoot (*The Gospel Message of St Mark* [Oxford: Clarendon Press, 1950], pp. 80-97), and updated by Lane, *Mark*, p. 583 n. 6. More significantly, the abrupt ending has been seen to support an intentional theological agenda—the failure of the disciples, the immediacy of the parousia or the non-appearance of Jesus. Others have seen here an open-ended text which is part of a reading strategy and have suggested various models for completing this story. On this desire for and creation of narrative closure, see F. Kermode, *The Genesis of Secrecy: On Interpretation of Narrative* (Cambridge, MA: Harvard University Press, 1979), especially pp. 64-65.

tomb, there they receive a message, they flee from the tomb in terror.[1]

2. A host of details fills out this basic plot line. (1) Careful attention is given to temporal markers. The purchase of spices is located at the end of the Sabbath. Strangely, three temporal markers specify the approach to the tomb: it is early, it is the first day after the Sabbath, it is sunrise (16.2).[2] (2) The women are carefully identified (16.1). (3) Clear motivation is provided for the actions of the women (16.1). (4) Various experiences and responses of the women are explained: they question (16.3), they experience amazement (16.5), they flee with trembling, astonishment and fear (16.8).[3] (5) The details of the tomb are clarified: there was a stone (16.3), but this has been rolled away (16.4); the tomb may be entered (16.5); there is room to sit (16.5). (6) The image of the messenger is described (16.5). These numerous details lend depth and complexity to the basic events which sustain this scene.

3. The narrator intrudes to provide further information. Specifically, the concern with the stone is focused through the intrusive comment that 'it was very large' (16.4).

4. The scene has been narrated around a consistent focus on the women. The story is framed by their movement to and from the tomb.

1. The basic unity of this scene has been argued by E. Güttgemanns ('Linguistische Analyse von Mk 16.1-8', *Linguistica Biblica Heft* 11/12 [1972], pp. 13-53) and by Pesch (*Markusevangelium*, II, pp. 519-21). In contrast most scholars see 16.1, 3, 7, 8b as redactional.

2. Various interpreters see theological significance in these temporal markers. Pesch (*Markusevangelium*, II, pp. 530-31) articulates this argument: 'Not only the third day, but especially the early morning, the time of the sunrise, serves as the time of God's help...' These interpretations are based on Old Testament passages such as Pss. 17.15, 143.8, Lam. 3.22-24 and Hos. 6.1-2. See also Gnilka, *Markus*, II, p. 347; K. Lehmann, *Auferweckt am dritten Tag nach der Schrift: Früheste Christologie, Bekenntnisbildung und Schriftauslegung im Lichte von 1 Kor. 15,3-5* (Freiburg: Herder, 1968). For a semiotic view of these elements see Güttgemanns, 'Mk 1.1-8', p. 49, and L. Marin, *Semiotik der Passionsgeschichte: Die Zeichensprache der Ortsangaben und Personennamen* (trans. S. Virgils; Munich: Chr. Kaiser Verlag, 1976).

3. While many see in the response of the women another example of failed discipleship, fear may also represent a positive response to an epiphany. On this question, see Pesch, *Markusevangelium*, II, pp. 532-36. Gnilka (*Markus*, II, p. 344) notes that the response of the women is similar to that in miracle stories (4.41; 5.1, 33, 42). In a similar way Gnilka reads their silence in view of other texts in the Gospel.

4. Mark 15.16–16.8: The Death of Jesus

The women are the subject of seven of the nine motifs. In particular the story is told throughout from the viewpoint of the women: the reader sees what they see, hears what they hear, feels what they feel.

5. Nonetheless the message of the young man[1] provides the central element of the story. More precisely, a saying by Jesus (14.28) stands at the center of this scene.[2] The opening movement climaxes not in the finding of an empty tomb, but in the confrontation with the messenger. The movement away from the tomb demonstrates the response of the women to this message. Consequently the saying by the νεανίσκον stands as the structural center of this scene.[3]

6. Thus, the story of the resurrection promise is structured around a simple frame, but enriched through a host of details. The experience of the women provides a unique human lens through which the reader may view these events. The various lines of plot movement reach their climax in the words of the young man at the tomb who echoes the prophecy of Jesus.[4]

---

1. Almost without exception interpreters identify the νεανίσκον as an angel. For many the parallel descriptions (Mt. 28.2; Jn. 20.12) have simply been read into this passage, transforming the youth into an angel. Others offer more critical support for this position, seeing in the dress and manner of the youth signs of heavenly origin and citing various parallels—so Taylor, *Mark*, pp. 606-607; Pesch, *Markusevangelium*, II, p. 532; Gnilka, *Markus*, II, p. 342.

2. This position is also held by Gnilka (*Markus*, II, pp. 339-40, 342) and by Pesch (*Markusevangelium*, II, p. 535).

3. This form is prevalent in Mk 14–16. A clear example may be seen in 14.1-11, where the saying of Jesus provides the coherent explanation for the surrounding elements. Gnilka (*Markus*, II, p. 342) confirms this structure: 'In the word of the angel the pericope reaches its summit, and a conclusive summit point of the gospel is also given'.

4. Much attention has been given to the question of genre in relation to Mk 16.1-8. Gnilka (*Markus*, II, pp. 339-40) argues that 'the Old Testament angelophany narrative provides the genre model'. Pesch (*Markusevangelium*, II, pp. 522-27) argues for the influence of several models: (1) liberation or door-opening miracles; (2) epiphany or angelophany narratives; (3) narratives which tell of the search for and failure to find a disappeared or raised person. L. Schenke (*Auferstehungsverkündigung und leeres Grab: Eine traditionsgeschichtliche Untersuchung von Mk 16, 1-8* [Stuttgart: Katholisches Bibelwerk, 1968], pp. 56-104) argues for an aetiological cult legend which supports the veneration of the tomb of Jesus in Jerusalem. For a wider discussion of the genre of 16.1-6, see J. Kremer, *Die Osterevangelien—Geschichten um Geschichte* (Stuttgart: Katholisches Bibelwerk, 1977), pp. 41-45. Kremer (p. 44) sees here a type of haggada.

Narrative Syntax. Numerous elements were shown to contribute to the morphological complex presented in Mk 16.1-8. Various syntactical patterns transform these structural components into a focused narrative scene.

1. This scene provides a process of clarification. Numerous narrative elements reach a logical conclusion in this story. Most specifically, the scene confronts the question of what happened to Jesus. This issue is addressed from two directions. (1) The place, manner and details of Jesus' burial are presented to the reader. The absence of Jesus' body is clarified, and a reappearance in Galilee is promised. (2) The role of the women becomes clearer. Their activity at the tomb provides the narrative link which joins the scenes of Jesus' death, his burial and the empty tomb. They provide the sole line of witnesses to this crucial sequence of events. Through their activity Peter and the disciples are (potentially) brought back into the story.

2. At the same time this scene sustains a process of narrative suspension.[1] Various plot elements are left incomplete, and the termination of the plot line means the quest for their significance is suspended.

2.1. The messenger at the tomb remains unfocused. If the messenger is angelic,[2] this is the first appearance of an angel since 1.13, and the identity and the larger role are uncertain. If the messenger is a young human, the ambiguity is more dense.[3] If this is the first among the followers of Jesus to understand the empty tomb, who is this unnamed messenger? If the messenger is neither human nor divine, but a narrative symbol, what is the significance?[4] On these questions the narrative is silent.

2.2. In addition, the role of Galilee is central, but it is largely

---

1. Schweizer (*Mark*, pp. 363-64) notes 'a whole series of riddles' in this scene: (1) the repetition of the name list; (2) the change in the name list; (3) the time of purchase of spices; (4) the entering of a tomb after a day and a half; (5) the failure to consider the stone; (6) the creedal nature of the angel's words; (7) the abrupt ending.

2. On the interpretation of the youth as an angel see p. 232 n. 1 above.

3. Various interpreters seek to identify the young man with a historical figure such as the youth of 14.51-52 or Mark himself.

4. The symbolic value of this character has been discussed by R.A. Culpepper, 'Mark 10.50: Why Mention the Garment?', *JBL* 101 (1982), pp. 131-32; R. Scroggs and K.I. Groff, 'Baptism in Mark: Dying and Rising with Christ', *JBL* 92 (1973), pp. 531-48; Kermode, *Genesis of Secrecy*, pp. 55-63; A. Vanhoye, 'La fuite du jeune homme nu (Mc 14, 1-52)', *Bib* 52 (1971), pp. 401-406.

4. Mark 15.16–16.8: The Death of Jesus

undefined.[1] The followers of Jesus are to meet him in Galilee. Will this be a resurrection appearance similar to those narrated elsewhere? Will the meeting in Galilee bring instead the eschatological days and the parousia of the Son of Man? Is Galilee some future experience, or should the disciples turn again to their past experiences with Jesus as he ministered in Galilee? Mk 16.1-8 does not say.

2.3. The silence of the women creates a profound plot dilemma.[2] They are commanded to tell but say nothing. The plot seems to have reached a dead end.[3] Who, if not the women, will tell the disciples and lead the way to Galilee? Does not their silence mark the end of the narrative voice in the Gospel of Mark? Mk 16.1-8 offers no solution for this dilemma.

2.4. This suspension of meaning at the end of the text creates a sense of shock and denial. Consequently this abrupt termination provokes

---

1. The reference to Galilee has been interpreted in various ways. Three distinct approaches may be identified.

a. Galilee is seen as the place of the resurrection appearances. This widespread interpretation reads in Mk 16.7 a promised resurrection appearance in Galilee. Subsequently this promise is identified with Mt. 28.16-20, Jn 21.1-25 and 1 Cor. 15.3-5.

b. Galilee is seen as the place of an imminent parousia. This view is built upon the observations of E. Lohmeyer, *Galiläa und Jerusalem* (Göttingen: Vandenhoeck & Ruprecht, 1936); R.H. Lightfoot, *Locality and Doctrine* (London: Hodder & Stoughton, 1938); and W. Marxsen, *Mark the Evangelist: Studies on the Redaction History of the Gospel* (trans. J. Boyce, D. Juel, W. Poehlmann; Nashville; Abingdon Press, 1969 [1956]). For subsequent development of this thesis see Culpepper, 'The Passion and Resurrection in Mark', pp. 600 n. 50.

c. Galilee is the place of the Gentile mission of the church. This thesis is represented by G.H. Boobyer, 'Galilee and Galileans in St Mark's Gospel', *BJRL* 35 (1953), pp. 334-48; Schenke, *Grab*, pp. 49-55; M. Karnetzki, 'Die galiläische Redaktion im Markusevangelium', *ZNW* 52 (1961), p. 256; and others.

2. Gnilka (*Markus*, II, pp. 344-45) discusses the women's silence in connection with the commands to silence elsewhere in the Gospel of Mark. Lane (*Mark*, pp. 591-92) sees here a typical response to an epiphany. For Pesch (*Markusevangelium*, II, p. 528) the silence of the women serves a crucial plot function: 'The narrator of the... text uses the silence of the women as a literary device... in order to bring to completion his overlapping narrative cohesiveness'. In Pesch's view the silence of the women allows Mark to emphasize the subsequent appearance to official apostolic (male) witnesses.

3. The impact of this ending on the shape of the narrative has been widely debated. A helpful synopsis may be found in Alsup, *Post-Resurrection Appearances*, pp. 88-89 n. 266.

a variety of responses from the reader.[1]

3. The use of passive verbs at key points in the narrative implies the presence and power of God. (1) The difficulty presented by the closed tomb is confronted in the question of the women: 'Who will roll away the stone for us from the door of the tomb?' (16.3). Thus, three (or four) women cannot move the stone. The additional note that the stone 'was very large' (16.4) confirms this difficulty. In response to this problem the women behold that 'the stone has been rolled away' (ἀποκεκύλισται ὁ λίθος). This pivotal use of the passive implies that God has removed this barrier.[2] (2) More decisively, the resurrection of Jesus is stated in the passive. The absence of Jesus (οὐκ ἔστιν ὧδε) is explained through a single word—'he has been raised' (ἠγέρθη in 16.6). This formulation confirms the prophecy of 14.28 (ἐγερθῆναι). Thus, the hand of God is revealed in the removal of the stone and in the raising of Jesus.[3]

4. An external voice breaks into the world of the narrative. While the intrusions of the narrator represent a type of external voice

---

1. On the need to complete texts, see Kermode, *Genesis of Secrecy*, especially pp. 64-65. Attempts to complete this text fall into three categories.

a. Various interpreters argue that the text is incomplete with its present outlook. Pesch (*Markusevangelium*, II, pp. 540-41) argues that the story points beyond the women to the gathering of official witnesses in Galilee. Lane (*Mark*, pp. 592-93) argues that the astonishment and fear which end the Gospel are typical of the whole narrative and that the 'focus upon human inadequacy, lack of understanding and weakness throws into bold relief the action of God and its meaning'.

b. Various scholars offer texts which complete this Gospel. The addition of 16.9-20, the 'shorter ending', and the Freer Logion represent the first of such attempts. In modern scholarship various scholars attempt to reconstruct the proper ending from other texts. An overview of these efforts may be seen in Alsup, *Post-Resurrection Appearance Stories*, p. 88 n. 265.

c. More recent approaches argue that the abrupt ending calls for a careful re-reading of the Gospel and its images. This strategy of redirection may provide a complete sense for the reader. For examples of this approach, see Crossan, 'Empty Tomb and Absent Lord', pp. 135-42; J.D. Kingsbury, *Conflict in Mark: Jesus, Authorities, Disciples* (Minneapolis: Fortress Press, 1989), pp. 112-15; Tolbert, *Sowing the Gospel*, pp. 288-89.

2. Mt. 28.2 credits an angel and an earthquake with the removal of the stone. Lk. 24.2 simply notes the removal of the stone, though the passive is used. In Jn 20.1 it is the removed stone which Mary Magdalene sees, but she concludes that the body of Jesus has been taken away.

3. In my opinion a similar use of the 'divine passive' may be found in Mk 2.5.

4. Mark 15.16–16.8: The Death of Jesus

(16.4b), the function of this motif is largely informative. In contrast the esoteric, ephemeral youth at the tomb represents a decisive intrusion with a climactic function.

4.1. The intrusion of the external witness serves a key christological function. Jesus is first identified in terms of his human origin: his given name is Jesus and his hometown is Nazareth (16.6). Jesus is then identified as the Crucified One (τὸν ἐσταυρωμένον). This term is titular,[1] and it provides the central image of the scene. Thus, the image of Jesus as the crucified servant of God stands at the center of the tomb story. The remainder of the message tells the fate of the Crucified One: he has been raised and he will go before them into Galilee.[2] In this manner the words of the messenger gather past and future experience with Jesus around a central narrative image: he is the Crucified One.

4.2. In addition, the words of the messenger clarify the task for disicples. They are to leave their fears behind (16.6), and they are to go and to tell the story about the Crucified One (16.7). Their ministry will be founded upon a personal experience of faith: they will see the Risen One. This preaching task is to begin with the women and to be carried on by all the followers of Jesus.

4.3. Most significantly, the divine mandate carried by the external witness is framed and focused through human experience. More precisely, this central message is wrapped in the experience of lowliness and powerlessness.[3] The resurrection promise is born in the experience of women whose discipleship is marked by hesitancy, amazement, fear and trembling.

---

1. For similar use of the substantive participle as a title, see Mk 1.4: John is ὁ βαπτίζων, the Baptist. Gnilka (*Markus*, II, p. 347) denies the presence of a christological title in this scene.

2. In the Gospel of Mark προάγω is used to designate Jesus' leadership in the way of the cross (10.32) and toward a reappearance in Galilee (14.28; 16.7). Thus, προάγω represents Jesus' leadership in the way of discipleship, both past and future. See M. Hengel, *Nachfolge und Charisma: Eine exegetisch-religionsgeschichtliche Studie zu Mt 8.21f. und Jesu Ruf in die Nachfolge* (Berlin: Töpelmann, 1968), pp. 23-24. The term is open to both temporal and local usage.

3. The disregard for women as witnesses in Judaism has been widely discussed. The subsequent development of the Easter traditions shows a similar devaluation of the witness of women in favor of official male witnesses such as those catalogued in 1 Cor. 15.3-7. Origen, *Contra Celsum* 2.55, reports such an attitude in Celsius's ridicule of the gossip of women concerning an empty tomb.

5. These various sytactical maneuvers transform the elements of Mk 16.1-8 into a focused scene which plays a vital role in the story of Jesus. The experience of the women provides a lens through which to focus the resurrection promise. An external witness is brought into this account to announce the central message of the narrative. Through this voice images of Christology and discipleship are crystallized. Jesus is the Crucified One who goes before them into Galilee. Disciples are to go and to tell with courage. This divine message is articulated in the frightful experience of women disciples. These vital processes and images at work in Mk 16.1-8 are amplified through the operations of the larger narrative.

The Passion Context. The resurrection promise was shown to be built upon a complex sequence of narrative components and transactions. The narrative operations at work in Mk 16.1-8 are intensified through their interaction with the wider passion context.[1]

1. In particular the tomb scene completes the image of Jesus as God's prophet. As he predicted, Jesus has been raised (14.27; 16.6). As he pledged earlier, Jesus is going before them into Galilee (14.28; 16.7). This event portends the gathering anew of the scattered disciples (14.27). In the larger passion context the promise of Mk 16.1-8 stands as the fulfillment of Jesus' words and the validation of his identity as the true prophet of God.

2. The passion context also gives some relief to the ruptured plot line. The narrative ends with the story of women who fail to anoint the body of Jesus and of a message shrouded in silence. This disjuncture is given new depth through its connections to the story in Mk 14.1-11. At the beginning of the passion account a woman anoints Jesus for his burial. In stark contrast to the silence which seizes the tomb story, the story of this woman will be told—as a part of the gospel message—throughout the world (14.9). Thus, the story of Jesus' passion is framed by the service of women disciples. This bifocal narrative perspective sustains the hope of an unhindered gospel.

---

1. While many scholars see behind 16.1-8 an independent unit subsequently attached to the passion story, Pesch (*Markusevangelium*, II, p. 520) argues that 'There are no aspects of linguistics, content, narrative, or psychology which speak against the connection of 16.1-8 to the preceeding passion story'.

4. Mark 15.16–16.8: The Death of Jesus

The Gospel Context. The focus of the resurrection promise is starkly realigned through its participation in the larger world of the Gospel.[1] Through this reciprocal connection various images from the tomb scene are amplified into crucial narrative themes.

1. The primary line of prophecy is fulfilled. Earlier in the narrative three passion predictions placed the suffering and death of Jesus at the center of his messianic mission (8.31; 9.31; 10.32-34). Three elements are central to each of these predictions: suffering and rejection, death, resurrection. With its resurrection promise the tomb story puts into place the final element of Jesus' predictions. More specifically, the multiple time references in 16.1-8 may now be used to confirm the prophecy that Jesus will be raised 'after three days' (μετὰ τρεῖς ἡμέρας in 8.31; 9.31; 10.34).[2] This connection thus completes the line of prophecy central to the mission of Jesus. Consequently Mk 16.1-8 plots the ultimate confirmation of Jesus' identity as the authentic prophet of God.

2. An important line of characterization develops around the image of the Nazarene. While this description plays a seemingly minor role in the previous material, the use of the title in 16.6 completes a vital narrative circuit. Jesus is first identified as a Nazarene in the opening scene (1.9). In correlation with this use the divine voice authenticates the identity of Jesus as the Beloved Son (1.11). The second appearance of this term is associated with Jesus' ministry (1.24); here the Nazarene is recognized as the 'Holy One of God' who is able to destroy unclean spirits. In Mk 10.46-52 the Nazarene title is associated with Jesus' healing power and mercy, with Jesus' role as teacher and as Son of David, and with the call to discipleship. The fourth use of the title is found in 14.67; here the servant girl identifies the arrested and abandoned Jesus as the Nazarene. The final use of this title in 16.6 gathers these scattered images into an important line of characterization. Jesus is the Beloved Son, the wondrous teacher, the merciful Son of David, the rejected prophet, but the final key to his identity lies in his death. Jesus the Nazarene is ultimately the Crucified One (16.6). It is precisely this one who has been raised and goes

---

1. This narrative hermeneutic is recognized even by many working from a predominantly diachronic perspective. See, for example, Pesch, *Markusevangelium*, II, p. 540; and Gnilka, *Markus*, II, pp. 344-45.
2. Pesch (*Markusevangelium*, II, p. 530) notes that the time reference becomes symbolic only in the macrocontext.

before them into Galilee (16.6-7). The Nazarene title thus becomes an important device through which to focus the passion Christology.

3. Mk 16.1-8 reverses the earlier commands to silence about the identity of Jesus.[1] The secrecy motif which surrounds the ministry of Jesus in the Gospel of Mark has various expressions. Demons know who Jesus is but are commanded to silence (1.25, 34). Healings are also followed by injunctions to silence (1.44; 7.35; contrast 5.19-20). The disciples are commanded to tell no one who Jesus is (8.30; 9.9). Consequently the command in Mk 16.7 to go and tell that the Crucified One is risen and goes before them reverses this theme of silence. The context of this reversal is crucial. In Mk 9.8 the disciples are to tell no one about the transfiguration experience with the Son of God; this prohibition remains in effect until the resurrection of the Son of Man (9.9). Mk 16.7 thus marks the end of this prohibition and initiates the time of proclamation. This narrative strategy places the christological message in a decisive framework: true insight and proclamation of Jesus' identity is possible only in relation to his death. Jesus is first identified as the Crucified One in the context of Mk 16.1-8, and this identification opens the door to proclamation. Consequently those who would speak of the true identity of Jesus must do so in view of his death on the cross.

4. The meaning of Galilee is refocused through Mk 16.1-8. The promise of a new experience in Galilee completes the anti-temple, anti-Jerusalem motif. Over against the failed worship of Jerusalem and its temple, the followers of Jesus are directed to a new worship and a new future with Jesus in Galilee.[2] Galilee is thus transformed into a symbol for the future of the church. In Galilee the failure and flight of the disciples will be reversed. In Galilee the disciples will see the risen Jesus and will follow him anew.

Galilee also becomes a symbol for their past experiences with Jesus. The command to meet Jesus in Galilee recalls the ministry of Jesus throughout Galilee and the disciples' participation in that ministry. Thus, the days in Galilee provide a memory and a model to

---

1. The pattern of this reversal is complete. Elsewhere those commanded to silence go and tell (1.44-45; 7.36-37); here those commanded to go and tell remain silent.

2. I have traced this motif in 'Which Mountain is "This Mountain"?'. See also W. Kelber, *The Kingdom in Mark: A New Time and a New Place* (Philadelphia: Fortress Press, 1974).

4. Mark 15.16–16.8: The Death of Jesus

which the followers of Jesus are to return.

Galilee may also symbolize the parousia of the Son of Man. Various events narrated in Mark 13 still lie in the future. The promise that some of Jesus' followers will see the Kingdom of God (9.1) remains open. Galilee holds potential for the fulfillment of these promises.[1]

5. An important line of external witnesses comes into focus. The decisive function of the external witness in Mk 16.1-8 alerts the reader to other instances of this narrative technique. A second external witness is found in the transfiguration story (9.2-9). In the presence of Moses and Elijah the heavenly voice declares, 'This is my Beloved Son. Hear him!' (9.7). A third external voice is heard in the baptism story. The heavens are torn asunder, the Spirit descends and a voice declares, 'You are my Beloved Son in whom I am well pleased' (1.10-11).

5.1. A similar narrative pattern is employed in each of these three accounts. The voice is never identified, but its divine aura is clear. Each scene is experienced by a limited number of people. The content of the message provides the most significant element in each account. In each instance the witness advances the characterization of Jesus. At the baptism and the transfiguration Jesus is proclaimed the Beloved Son. At the empty tomb Jesus is declared to be the Crucified One who has been raised and is going before. This use of external witnesses provides a vital and authoritative commentary on the identity of Jesus.

5.2. The external witness technique is also used to articulate the demands of discipleship. Following the baptism come commands to repent, to believe and to follow (1.15, 17, 19). Those present at the transfiguration are commanded to hear and obey Jesus (9.7); the words of Jesus which they are to heed refer to his passion (8.31-9.1). The women at the tomb are to go and tell with courage (16.6-7). Initiated by this authoritative witness and coupled with the identity of Jesus, these demands for discipleship are placed at the center of the narrative world.

5.3. A clear progression may be seen in the use of this narrative technique. In Mark 1 a heavenly voice declares Jesus the Beloved Son. It is likely that this voice is heard by Jesus alone. The demands for discipleship are not addressed explicitly, but emerge in the following

---

1. The promise that 'you will see' (ὄψεσθε) in 16.7 has its only real parallels in 13.26 and in 14.62. Both instances refer to the parousia of the Son of Man. Others see a connection to the 'he was seen' (ὤφθη) of 1 Cor. 15.3-5.

scenes. In Mark 9 a heavenly voice repeats the characterization of Jesus as the Beloved Son. Here the circle of witnesses has been widened to three heavenly figures and three human witnesses. In this instance the demands of discipleship are more explicit: hear the teaching of Jesus about his suffering and death, but tell no one yet of this event. In Mark 16 the witness is given by a human-like figure. The message is heard by women followers. The demands are explicit—go and tell with courage. Through this progression the circle of witnesses is widened, the demands are clarified and the message of the gospel is placed in human hands. Consequently the external voice represents a narrative technique which is used sparingly, but decisively. Through the voice of these external witnesses the identity of Jesus and the demands of discipleship become the central themes of the narrative.

6. The entire Gospel narrative is framed by decisive scenes of presentation and calling. As a consequence Christology and discipleship are focused at the beginning of the narrative (1.1-15) and at its conclusion (16.1-8).

6.1. Close structural ties may be seen between the opening and closing scenes of the Gospel. (1) Both scenes echo with a prophetic voice. The opening lines (1.1-2) recall the words of Isaiah and Malachi, while the closing scene recalls the prophecy of Jesus (14.28; 16.7). (2) Both scenes are told in proximity to Jerusalem (1.5). (3) An unusual messenger is present in both accounts (1.4-8; 16.5-7). In both instances the messenger is described by unusual dress (1.6; 16.5) and by a distinct message (1.7-8; 16.6-7). (4) Both scenes identify Jesus in terms of his journey. The Baptist characterizes Jesus as the one who 'comes after' (1.7), while the youth characterizes Jesus as the one who 'goes before' (16.7). (5) Both accounts focus the role of Galilee in Jesus' mission. In the beginning Jesus comes from Galilee to be baptized (1.9), then begins his ministry by returning to Galilee (1.14). The final scene centers around the promise that Jesus 'is going before you into Galilee' (16.7). (6) An external witness is present in both stories. The voice from heaven dominates the opening scene (1.10-11), while a messenger suggesting heavenly aura stands at the center of the tomb scene (16.5-7). (7) In both stories this external voice provides a distinct christological focus. Jesus is identified at the beginning as the Beloved Son (1.11); at the end he is recognized as the Crucified One (16.6). (8) A call to discipleship issues from both

4. Mark 15.16–16.8: The Death of Jesus

scenes (1.16-20; 16.7). Simon Peter is the focus of both callings.[1] (9) Angelic figures are present in both scenes (1.13; 16.5-7). (10) Both accounts provide a harsh ending. The baptism scene ends with Jesus driven to the desert place, where he is tempted by Satan (1.12-13). The tomb scene ends with the flight of the women, with abrupt grammar and with silence. Consequently the parallel configuration of the opening scene in Mk 1.1-15 and the closing scene in 16.1-8 provides a decisive hermeneutical frame for the Gospel narrative.

6.2. Beyond these structural similarities, both scenes serve a crucial function in framing the world of the narrative. Key images of Christology and discipleship bracket the story of Jesus. In particular the gospel mission is identified throughout with the suffering of God's prophet. The initial proclamation of the gospel is rooted directly in the imprisonment of the Baptist (1.14-15). The renewed proclamation in Galilee is rooted in the identification of Jesus as the Crucified One (16.6). Thus, the way of Jesus is defined throughout as the way of prophetic suffering and death. Consequently the call to discipleship and the proclamation of the gospel are linked precisely to suffering and service. This bridge linking the death of the Baptist and the cross of Jesus has its central support in the proclamation of 8.34: Christology and discipleship center in the way of the cross.

6.3. This configuration of the ideological world confirms the reflective intentionality which guides the composition of this Gospel. The significance of these linked units exceeds their import as isolated traditions controlled by functional interests. This complex narrative configuration cannot be explained by fixed canons of transmission. This narrative pattern conveys an intentional strategy of interconnection guided by clear images of Christology and discipleship. At the same time the complex patterns of interrelationship convey a studied, durative pattern of reflection which far exceeds the authorial intent of a single redaction. The reflective intentionality which undergirds this narrative world is best explained through a lengthy process of focused

---

1. From a narrative perspective the shifting use of Peter's name is crucial. Simon is the name used before his calling (1.16). Peter is a new name given by Jesus and associated with the call to discipleship (3.16). After his resistance to the suffering of the messiah, Jesus addressed him as Satan (8.33). Later Jesus addresses him by his old name, which is associated with his failure (14.37). Significantly, the resurrection promise marks a renewed use of the name Peter (16.7) and may signal a new call to discipleship.

theological reflection within an editorial community.

7. Consequently Mk 16.1-8 plays a decisive role in the larger strategy of the narrative. The story of Jesus, which has come to an apparent end, is suddenly opened up to the future.[1] Because the plot line is broken off and remains unfinished, the story of Jesus is opened up to the reader of the narrative and to further developments in the world of the reader. Stark demands are placed on those who would follow Jesus beyond the pages of this story. Disciples are commanded to hear, to follow, to go and tell with courage. A conclusive christological portrait emerges. In the shadow of the cross and the silence of the tomb the true portrait of Jesus is unveiled: he is the Crucified One who leads the way into God's future.

Comparative Analysis
The resurrection promise to the women is found in various other narrative contexts. These alternate versions of this account provide a comparative field against which to focus the narrative form and function of Mk 16.1-8.[2]

Pre-Markan Contexts. Scholars are divided over the form of this story prior to the Gospel of Mark.[3] Some argue for an independent tradition which was subsequently joined to the passion story. Various

---

1. Pesch (*Markusevangelium*, II, pp. 521, 528) seeks to describe this transition by a distinction between the 'reported narratives' (*berichtende Erzählungen*) which dominate the passion story and the 'constructed narrative' (*konstruierte Erzählung*) in 16.1-8. He further distinguishes the 'narrated world' (*erzälten Welt*) of 15.42-47 from the world of 16.1-8, which cannot be narrated (*nicht erzählbaren*). The speech of the angel 'constructs' (*konstruiert*) the 'announced world' (*besprochen Welt*) of the resurrection of Jesus.

   In my opinion Pesch's distinction is unsatisfactory. Narratives such as Matthew, Luke, John, the *Gospel of Peter* and others made the resurrection and even the risen Christ a part of their narrated world. More importantly, the distinction between reported and constructed worlds is misleading. In narrative terms all texts seek to construct and announce a world. To report or to narrate is to generate a distinct narrative world with its own codes, values, expectations, demands. Pesch's agenda of defining the Gospel of Mark as a passion narrative rooted directly in the historical report of the early Jerusalem community prevents him from seeing the creative strategy which directs the whole presentation of this Gospel.

2. On the comparative use of diachronic analysis, see Chapter 1.

3. For a summary of the research, see Gnilka, *Markus*, II, pp. 337-40.

functions have been offered for this form of the story. Ludger Schenke suggests that the story circulated in the Jerusalem community as an aetiological cult legend which explained their yearly celebration at the tomb in Jerusalem.[1] Dibelius and Bultmann saw an apologetic purpose behind this tradition.[2] Dibelius argued that the story is 'a Legend with a life of its own whose purpose was to demonstrate the resurrection by the fact of the empty grave'.[3]

Others argue that this story cannot be separated from the pre-Markan passion account. Pesch concludes that this material was inherited as part of the extensive passion tradition from the early community in Jerusalem.[4] Gnilka accepts the place of the tomb story in the pre-Markan passion narrative, but he sees here an expansion of 1 Cor. 15.3-5 through the framework of Old Testament angelophanies.[5] In this form the story would complete the events of the passion story and confirm the earlier resurrection predictions.

The Gospel of Matthew. The story of the women at the tomb is narrated in Mt. 28.1-8. Elements such as multiple time references and the pondering of the women are condensed, but other details are added to the account. An earthquake and an angel account for the opening of the tomb (Mt. 28.2). The fear of the soldiers removes them from the story (Mt. 28.4). The announcement to the women is central to the account and parallels Mk 16.6-7, except for the role of Peter. Most significantly, the response of the women has been altered: they go with fear and with great joy, then announce the message to the disciples (Mt. 28.8). Thus, Mt. 28.1-8 provides an alternate performance of the scene at the tomb. Beyond the changes in the details of the story, the realignment of the final lines redirects the entire account. This technique creates a bridge and extends the lines of the narrative. Thus, what was a broken plot line left open to the future and to the world of the reader has been transformed into a continuing narrative.

Mt. 28.9-20 provides a crucial extension to the tomb story. The fleeing women meet the risen Lord, who repeats the call to Galilee (Mt. 28.9-10). Following this a detailed explanation accounts for the

1. Schenke, *Grab*, p. 88.
2. Dibelius, *Tradition*, pp. 190-92; Bultmann, *History*, pp. 284-87.
3. Dibelius, *Tradition*, p. 190.
4. Pesch, *Markusevangelium*, II, pp. 519-21.
5. Gnilka, *Markus*, II, pp. 337-40.

rumor that the disciples stole the body of Jesus (Mt. 28.11-15). Most significantly, the promised appearance in Galilee is narrated in Mt. 28.16-20. The missionary charge of Jesus provides the central focus of this event. Those who have seen the risen Lord are to go to all nations, baptizing and teaching. As they go the risen Lord will go with them.

Thus, the Gospel of Matthew offers a distinct performance of the resurrection story. Building upon the elements of the tomb story, various apologetic concerns are addressed: how was the stone removed, who told the women, how did the disciples learn, why the rumor of a stolen body? Most significantly, this account validates the primary Matthaean themes. Jesus is the teacher in whom God has invested the authority of instruction and interpretation. Followers of Jesus are to go teaching and baptizing all nations. The Christian church lives under the presence and leadership of the risen Lord.

The Gospel of Luke. The Gospel of Luke also builds a resurrection narrative around the tomb story. The basic frame of the promise to the women is taken over in Lk. 24.1-11. Here Jesus is already understood as Lord (Lk. 24.3). Luke tells of two men at the tomb, yet their appearance is angelic (Lk. 24.4). Most significantly, the message to the women contains a different focus. For Luke, Galilee belongs to the past. The messengers declare the raising of Jesus to be a fulfillment of the promises made in Galilee (Lk. 24.6-7). The women respond to this announcement not with fear, but by remembering the words of Jesus. Following this scene the women go and announce these events to the eleven and to the other followers (Lk. 24.8). The message of the women is heard, but it is not believed (Lk. 24.10-11). These alterations realign the narrative in two crucial ways. (1) The Galilean motif is aborted. Galilee is no longer the goal of the story, but simply a past memory and a prophecy completed. (2) While the Galilean journey is halted, the report of the women creates a bridge which extends the story in another direction.

Thus, the performance of this story in the Lukan context demonstrates a clear narrative alternative to Mk 16.1-8. In addition to the internal refocusing of the tomb scene, Lk. 24.12-53 extends the tomb story in a new direction. The priority of Peter surfaces in Lk. 24.12. The appearance on the road to Emmaus incorporates various Lukan themes: appearances in and around Jerusalem, Jesus as the rejected

4. Mark 15.16–16.8: The Death of Jesus

prophet, the suffering of the messiah, the fulfillment of the Old Testament, meal Christology. A second appearance in Jerusalem is narrated in Lk. 24.36-49. Various concerns are addressed in this account: the reality of Jesus' presence, the fulfillment of Scripture, the suffering of the messiah, the movement of the gospel from Jerusalem outward, the promise of the Spirit. A third scene narrates the departure of Jesus (Lk. 24.50-52). In this manner Luke extends and completes the plot line of Jesus' story. Following the departure of Jesus, the disciples return to Jerusalem, initiating a new plot line and new story.

Thus, the Gospel of Luke employs the tomb story as a bridge to a distinctly Lukan version of the resurrection appearances. The Galilean appearance is redirected into a Jerusalem movement. The experience of the women is subsumed by more official appearances to men. The Lukan images of Jesus and of the Christian mission are articulated through the appearances. The story of Jesus is completed and the story of the church is begun.

The Gospel of John. The Gospel of John uses the tomb visit of Mary Magdalene as a bridge to a Johannine resurrection account. The report of Mary's visit is terse: she visits the tomb, discovers the stone removed, then reports the missing body to Peter and the Beloved Disciple (Jn 20.1-2). The second visit of Mary is expanded into a resurrection appearance (Jn 20.11-17). Following this Mary gives the first report of the risen Lord (Jn 20.18). Thus, the Johannine use of the woman at the tomb is unique.

Around this skeleton the Gospel of John builds the official resurrection accounts and uses them to articulate the central themes of the narrative. Peter and the Beloved Disciple lead the community through these events. They run to the tomb, but do not yet believe or understand the fulfillment of the Scriptures (Jn 20.3-10). The role of the whole community of disciples is focused. Jesus appears to the entire group, offering them peace, the gift of the Spirit and the commission to go out with the offer of forgiveness (Jn 20.19-23). A similar appearance eight days later erases the doubts of Thomas (Jn 20.24-29). Significantly, Jesus is addressed as God (Jn 20.28). A summary statement relates the ongoing sequence of appearances and signs (Jn 20.30-31). A subsequent appearance to the disciples focuses the leadership of Peter and the Beloved Disciple in the ongoing life of the community (Jn 21.1-23). These events are confirmed by a closing testimony (Jn 21.24-25).

This distinct arrangement of the resurrection material highlights crucial Johannine themes. Proof of Jesus' resurrection is given, Johannine Christology is focused, the followers of Jesus are empowered to carry on his work, Peter and the Beloved Disciple will lead the community, Jesus remains with his followers at the end of the story.

The Gospel of Peter. The story of the women at the tomb leads to a resurrection account in the *Gospel of Peter.* Mary Magdalene goes with other women to mourn and to anoint the body (12.50–13.57). After deliberating over the stone the women are met by a young man in bright garments. This youth proclaims the resurrection, announcing that Jesus has returned to the place from which he was sent.

This sober account of the women at the tomb is joined to an extravagant narration of the resurrection event (9.35–11.49). Various wonders accompany the raising of Jesus: a loud voice from heaven, two heavenly agents, a stone which removes itself, a cross which follows the angels and a cross which speaks, a resurrection witnessed by many people, a risen Jesus whose stature is higher than the heavens. Various apologetic motifs are focused: witnesses to the resurrection, preaching to the dead, christological confession, innocence and guilt in relation to the death of Jesus, explanation for the silence surrounding the empty tomb. In addition, the story addresses the situation of Peter and the Twelve (15.58-59). Thus, the *Gospel of Peter* employs the tomb scene as part of a larger, quite different narrative strategy. The elements of the tomb story now support a resurrection narrative marked by extravagance and apology.

The Acts of Pilate. The tomb scene is reported by the guards in *Acts of Pilate* (13.1). This account draws its framework from Mt. 28.2-7. Following this scene comes a dispute between the Jews and the Romans (13.2-3). In this dialogue the disappearance of Jesus is paralleled by the disappearance of Joseph. Following this scene comes a reported appearance of Jesus in Galilee (14.1; 16.5); here Jesus gives the commission found in the addendum to the Gospel of Mark (Mk 16.15-18). A further appearance is reported by Joseph of Arimathea (15.6). Various motifs of witness and proof dominate these

4. Mark 15.16–16.8: The Death of Jesus

reports. In particular, the *Acts of Pilate* is concerned to set forth a sharp apologetic for the Christian faith in contrast to its Jewish opposition. Thus, the *Acts of Pilate* employs the tomb scene to support an extended apologetic for the resurrection of Jesus and for the faith of his followers.

Addenda to Mark 16.1-8. Several attempts were made to employ the scene in Mk 16.1-8 as a bridge to resurrection appearances. The most extensive of these attempts appears as an addendum in Mk 16.9-20. Here Mary Magdalene reports the resurrection to other followers, but they do not believe.[1] The Emmaus event is also reported, but not believed. Following this Jesus appears to eleven and chides them for unbelief. A formulaic commission is given to the disciples, the ascension of Jesus is reported, and the mission of the church begins. Thus, the longer ending of the Gospel of Mark takes up the tomb story and joins to it the various traditions of Jesus' appearance and of his commission to the church.

A second addendum to the Gospel of Mark[2] is more to the point. The women complete their task, reporting the empty tomb to Peter and his friends. Following this Jesus himself sends the disciples to the ends of the earth with the message (κήρυγμα) of eternal salvation. Thus, this addition also builds upon the tomb scene to complete the plot line and to spell out the implications of the resurrection.

Early Christian Preaching. While Mk 16.1-8 locates the resurrection message in the narrative of the tomb, the fact of the resurrection has been taken up in other literary forms. The datum of the resurrection becomes a central element in Luke's account of the early Christian proclamation.[3] Typically Jesus is identified in relation to various events:

---

1. The alternate reading in D(*) does not correct this disbelief, but makes it more evident.
2. For the full text of this addition see the critical apparatus in the Nestle-Aland text, 26th edition.
3. For a detailed analysis of the summaries in Acts, see Alsup, *Post-Resurrection Appearance Stories*, pp. 64-85.

1. the past of Israel (Acts 2.16-22, 25-28, 29-31; 3.13, 18, 22, 24-25; 13.17-23);
2. his mighty deeds (Acts 2.22; 10.38);
3. his rejection and crucifixion (Acts 2.23, 36; 3.13-15; 4.10-11; 10.39; 13.27-38);
4. his resurrection at the hands of God (Acts 2.31, 32; 3.15, 26; 4.10; 10.40; 13.30, 33-37);
5. his appearance to witnesses (Acts 2.32; 3.15; 10.40-42; 13.31);
6. his exaltation (Acts 2.33; 10.42);
7. his return (Acts 3.21);
8. a call to repentance and salvation (Acts 2.38; 3.19, 26; 4.12; 10.42-43; 13.23, 26, 38-39).

While this proclamation includes no details of the tomb scene,[1] the fact of the resurrection is presented as a vital element in the early Christian proclamation.

Early Christian Creeds. The fact of the resurrection of Jesus is also taken into the early confessions of faith. In Rom. 1.4 Jesus is designated 'Son of God in power according to the Spirit of holiness by resurrection from the dead'. In Rom. 10.9-13 faith in the resurrection provides the key to salvation. In 1 Thess. 1.9-10 the resurrection is connected to salvation and to the future appearance of Jesus. In 1 Cor. 15.3-5 the fact of the resurrection is one element of early Christian tradition that Christ

> died in behalf of our sins according to the Scriptures
> and that he was buried
> and that he was raised the third day according to the Scriptures
> and that he was seen...

This creedal report, like the preaching summaries, says nothing of the details of the burial and the tomb. Such early creeds were concerned

---

1. In the New Testament the empty tomb tradition plays no role outside of the Gospels. The burial in a tomb is mentioned in Acts 13.29, but no details are narrated and the emptiness of the tomb is not defended. The suggestion by Lane (*Mark*, p. 588) that Acts 2.29 'implies a reference to the empty tomb of Jesus...' is without substance.

4. Mark 15.16–16.8: The Death of Jesus

with the fact of the resurrection, with its soteriological connection, and with the emphasis that the Scriptures are fulfilled in this sequence of events.[1]

1. Almost without exception scholars designate 1 Cor. 15.3-5 as the earliest resurrection tradition. Paul's correspondence with the Corinthians is dated around 55 CE, and he designates this piece as a tradition handed on to him. Scholars speculate that Paul learned this early tradition in Jerusalem or in Antioch.

Consequently most interpreters see Mk 16.1-8 as a later tradition which corresponds to the data of 1 Cor. 15.3-5. Gnilka (*Markus*, II, p. 339) articulates this position. He says of 16.1-8, 'prior to Mark this pericope would announce the resurrection of Jesus as the conclusion of an old passion report. It does so in that it relates back to I Corinthians 15.3-5 and illustrates the message of the resurrection with the help of the empty grave.' In a similar manner Pesch (*Markusevangelium*, II, p. 533) argues that the tomb story is built on the resurrection report, and not the opposite. In his view 'The use of "he was raised" (ἠγέρθη) is a citation of the early Christian kerygma (I Cor 15.4)...'

Others have reached a more radical conclusion: the empty tomb account corresponds to 1 Cor. 15.3-5 because it has been created as narrative expansion of that confession. Bultmann (*History*, p. 287) says of Mk 16.1-8, 'The purpose of the story is without doubt to prove the reality of the resurrection of Jesus by the empty tomb'. For S. Schulz (*Die Stunde der Botschaft: Einführung in die Theologie der vier Evangelisten* [Hamburg: Furche Verlag, 1967], pp. 141-42) the significance of the empty tomb is 'as an apologetic legend which serves to confirm the facts of the resurrection'. In a reversal of this thesis Crossan ('Empty Tomb and Absent Lord', pp. 135-52) sees 16.1-8 as an 'anti-tradition' created by Mark to counter the appearance tradition represented in 1 Cor. 15.3-5.

Consequently scholars are almost unanimous in the assessment that 1 Cor. 15.3-5 is prior to Mk 16.1-8. Alsup (*The Post-Resurrection Appearance Stories*, p. 55) notes how 'the kerygma tradition is recognized throughout the critical discussion as the oldest of the resurrection traditions, not only because it appears in a document written before the composition of the gospels, but also because as formula tradition it goes back to pre-Pauline, Palestinian origins'. In addition, scholars generally consider short creedal formulations such as 1 Cor. 15.3-5 as the foundation for more detailed narratives. C.H. Dodd (*The Apostolic Preaching and its Development* [London: Hodder & Stoughton, 1936]) saw the Gospels as expansions upon the more primitive Christian preaching (kerygma). Dodd's position reflects the earlier contention of Dibelius that the Gospels arose from the worship and missions sermons of the early church. Dodd saw this as particularly true of the earliest Gospel: 'Mark serves as a commentary on the *kerygma*' (p. 48). Specifically, the passion story was shaped by the kerygma: 'Mark then proceeded, according to the formula of the *kerygma* in I Cor. xv, to record how Christ was buried, and rose again on the third day according to the Scriptures' (p. 51). Thus, 1 Cor. 15.3-5 is considered more ancient and more trustworthy on three grounds: (1) temporal, (2) geographical, (3) form-

Summary

As attention to the comparative literature shows, the scene of the women at the tomb has been employed in a variety of narrative contexts to serve radically different functions. This comparative field demonstrates the degree to which a narrative unit draws its ultimate significance from its context rather than from its history of development. At the same time these multiple performances demonstrate the flexibility of narrative units and highlight the unique use of this material in the Gospel of Mark.

In the Gospel of Mark the tomb story completes various plot sequences and marks the end of the text. Through their interaction with the larger story these events play a crucial role in the strategy of the narrative and in its central images. Mk 16.1-8 completes the primary line of prophecy through its portrait of Jesus as the messiah who suffers, dies and is raised. Various images of the Nazarene are consummated in the portrait of the Crucified One. The silence which surrounds Jesus' messianic identity is shattered by the command at the tomb. Galilee is transformed into a polyphonic symbol of hope which throws the narrative open to the future and to the choices of the reader. A crucial line of external witnesses steps forward to proclaim the identity of Jesus and the demands upon those who would follow him. The entire Gospel is framed with insistent images of Christology and discipleship. Consequently the final voice of the narrative sounds with unblemished clarity. Jesus is the Crucified One—true prophet, rejected messiah, Beloved Son. Disciples are to go with courage and tell his story.

Conclusion

The four scenes in Mk 15.16–16.8 provide the central structural elements of the passion account. Through these events decisive contributions are made to the plotting of the death story, to the characterization of Jesus, and to the identity of the Gospel.

Plotting

By initiating the passive suffering of Jesus the scene of abuse (15.16-20) confirms a long line of plot expectation. Through this torture a

critical. In my opinion a critical reassessment of this presupposition and its consequences is in order.

4. Mark 15.16–16.8: The Death of Jesus

sequence of fulfillment is begun. The crucifixion scene (15.20c-37) employs complex narrative techniques to portray the death of Jesus. This production realizes an extended line of plot expectations concerning the destiny of Jesus and provides the summit of the plot line. Mk 15.38-47 serves a crucial plot role by bridging the death scene to the scene at the tomb. This technique generates a narrative interlude which provides a sense of reality and a window of hope. The tomb scene (16.1-8) plots the experience of the women in order to focus the external witness of the young messenger. This technique completes various parts of the plot line, but leaves other elements unfinished.

Thus, the stories in Mk 15.16–16.8 participate in a complex, extended plot strategy. The stories of Mk 14.1-42 employ prediction and symbol to initiate the story line of the passion. The scenes in Mk 14.43–15.15 build upon this prophetic Christology and narrative symbolism through a series of interpretive images which prepare for the death of Jesus. The stories in Mk 15.16–16.8 complete the prophetic characterization and provide the ultimate realization of the passion Christology. Thus, the four scenes of Mk 15.16–16.8 map the culmination of the plot line of this narrative.

In addition, the closing scenes provide a guide for reading this narrative. The concluding image of Jesus is decisive: he is the Crucified One—true prophet, rejected messiah, Beloved Son; disciples are to go with courage and tell his story. At the same time the story line remains open: the women are to go and announce the promise, the disciples are to go to Galilee, Jesus is to appear at some point in the future. This open-ended text falls into the lap of the reader as a demanding, unfinished story. Within the text reside various options for completing this account. Competing opinions of Jesus are offered through the narrative, and various responses to Jesus are modeled. Faithful models of discipleship exist alongside tales of cowardice, faithlessness and failure. At the end of this narrative the reader is left with an unfulfilled command and a gospel not yet proclaimed.

Thus, the closing images of this story provide for initiation of a new story. Luke narrates this story for his audience in a second volume; the Gospel of Mark leaves that task to the reader. At the center of this new account will be the renewed experience with the Crucified One, the demands of discipleship and the ongoing story of the gospel message. Having encircled the reader with its promise and its demands, the narrative gives its concluding focus to the potential of a new beginning—the beginning of the Gospel of Jesus Christ...

Characterization

The four scenes in Mk 15.16–16.8 also provide conclusive elements in the characterization of Jesus. Both the content and the process of this character study prove decisive.

1. Through the scene of abuse (15.16-20) the model of passive suffering is established. This innocent suffering gives substance to the prophetic images of the passion narrative. In connection with this pattern the kingship imagery is abandoned as an inadequate model for Jesus. In conjunction with this prophetic Christology the scene of abuse also brings the passion Christology to reality. Through this connection Jesus is shown to be the authentic prophet who suffers in righteousness.

This initial realization of the union of prophetic identity and passion Christology draws upon and informs the larger world of the narrative. From the beginning of the Gospel a key link is established between Jesus' ministry of proclamation and his death. In the passion story the powerful words and wondrous deeds which characterize the teaching of Jesus are linked to prophetic images. This connection between Jesus' prophetic ministry and his death is taken up in a new way in Mk 15.16–16.8. Beginning with the abuse scene the passion prophecies become Jesus' realized destiny.

2. The death scene (15.20c-37) brings this passion Christology to reality. This scene fills out the images of Jesus as the Suffering Servant and condemned prophet. The Psalms are invoked to describe Jesus as the innocent sufferer. The death of Jesus is pronounced.

This concrete realization of the passion Christology reverberates against a larger world of images. In the scene of Jesus' death scattered echoes from the Old Testament and the building cadence of the Gospel are joined in a climactic chorus. Through this blending of voices the soteriological depth of Jesus' death emerges.

3. The interlude in Mk 15.38-47 extends the story line and surrounds the death of Jesus with signs of hope. The larger narrative focuses the centurion's confession and gives attention to its context. In the moment of his suffering and death the true identity of Jesus comes into view.

4. Subsequently the tomb scene (16.1-8) provides a climactic focus on Jesus as the Crucified One. This title provides the hinge which

4. Mark 15.16–16.8: The Death of Jesus

connects past and future experiences with Jesus. Consequently the promise at the tomb provides the ultimate prophetic fulfillment within the narrative and confirms the identity of the crucified Jesus as the true prophet of God. In addition, this resurrection promise extends the characterization of Jesus into the future.

5. Thus, the final scenes of the Gospel play a culminative role in the characterization of Jesus. The prophetic Christology is fulfilled in the events which end Jesus' life. The passion Christology is realized in a climactic scene, a poignant confession and a focused title. At the same time the portrait of Jesus remains open to the vision of the future.

Identity

The four scenes in Mk 15.16–16.8 were analyzed in terms of morphological construction, syntactical relationships and narrative effect. This formalistic analysis revealed important internal transformations and decisive external connections in each of these scenes. These narrative processes were shown to support vital patterns of plotting and characterization. Most significantly, this analysis reveals the complex christological strategy sustained within this narrative world.

This formalistic analysis sheds further light on the fundamental strategy of the Gospel of Mark. Analysis of Mk 14.1-42 demonstrated the vital connection between the story of Jesus' life and the narrative of his death. This symbiotic relationship was deepened in the stories of Mk 14.43–15.15. The key patterns discovered in 14.1-42 and confirmed in 14.43–15.15 are consummated in the final stories of the Gospel. The arrest of Jesus is a response to his prophetic teaching. The death of Jesus fulfills the prophecies at the heart of his ministry. Concluding christological images and signs of hope draw their perspective from Jesus' ministry. Mk 15.16–16.8 thus generates a dramatic climax and a focused characterization by drawing upon the full wealth of Jesus' story.

These complex patterns of reciprocity and realignment which circulate throughout the world of this narrative provide important evidence about the identity of this Gospel. In light of these patterns the oft-repeated suggestion of Martin Kähler—the Gospels are passion narratives with extensive introductions—appears shallow and stereotypical. The 'extended introduction' proves to be the seedbed for various images and themes which come to fruition in the passion story. A coherent logic of mission and rejection guides the Gospel from its inception. The final scene of Christology and commission has its closest parallel in the opening lines of the Gospel. The pattern becomes undeniable: the passion narrative serves as one component in a complicated narrative universe and a complex strategy of presentation.

In a similar manner the proposal of Theodore Weeden—that the passion narrative provides a singular corrective for other characterizations of Jesus—proves inadequate. The interchange between passion Christology and other images provides an extensive, reciprocal realignment. While various images of Jesus are focused around his suffering, the passion Christology is also realigned by other christological interests. Chief among these is the complex image of Jesus as one who proclaims with wondrous power and insight. Consequently the processes of realignment operative in the Gospel are multi-dimensional and multi-directional, sustaining a complex interchange of images.

These complex interpretive patterns unveiled through formalistic analysis demonstrate the interlaced coherence presented by the Gospel of Mark in its language, its structure and its thought. This literary trait points to the reflective intentionality which guides the composition of this Gospel. Theories of composition which fail to account for the intentional nature present in the structure and Christology of this Gospel must be rejected. Hence, the presupposition of a functional evolution guided by rigid rules of transmission proves an insufficient explanation. Likewise, theories which do not explain the complex and reflective staging of these scenes through internal transformations and external connections are inadequate. References to a final editor or evangelist may explain the intentional nature of this text but provide inadequate explanation for the reflective depth and interconnection of narrative scenes and images.

Thus, formalistic analysis of Mark 14–16 reveals various inadequacies in current descriptions of the Gospel of Mark and demonstrates the general failure of traditional theories of composition to account for the intricate design of this Gospel. The complex narrative universe focused through formalistic analysis of the passion narrative insists upon a new understanding of the basic identity, the narrative intent and the compositional origin of the Gospel of Mark.

Chapter 5

CONCLUSION

This analysis has investigated the narrative function of Mark 14–16. A type of formalistic analysis has been employed to focus the unique role played by the passion story in the strategy of the Gospel of Mark and in its characterization of Jesus. Within this text an unexpected image of Jesus emerges through a distinct process of characterization. This chapter will delineate the form and process which sustain this narrative image. Following a description of the characterization of Jesus in Mark 14–16, various implications of this narrative portrait will be considered. The characterization of Jesus in the passion narrative will be used to determine the relationship between Mark 14–16 and the rest of the narrative. The identity and purpose of the Gospel of Mark will be reconsidered in light of these findings and possible implications for the composition history will be focused. In light of this study the viability of narrative analysis will be considered.

Narrative Form and Function in Mark 14–16

Mark 14–16 provides a central component in the narrative world of this Gospel. This story of Jesus' death is built upon distinct narrative structures and strategies.

Narrative Structures
A rich variety of narrative elements are employed in the stories of Mark 14–16. These morphological components provide the structural frame of these texts.

Actions. Various types of action guide the plotting of the death story. Among these are:

conspiring	grieving	torturing	saluting	being torn
anointing	praying	identifying	spitting	(passive)
complaining	informing	denying	bowing	confessing
responding	betraying	crowing	mocking	requesting
questioning	seizing	remembering	conscripting	inquiring
instructing	striking	condemning	offering	consenting
coming	fleeing	being amazed	refusing	burying
prophesying	seeking	(passive)	crucifying	beholding
distributing	testifying	demanding	dividing	entering
interpreting	being silent	inciting	blaspheming	fearing
drinking	(passive)	leading	reviling	speaking
departing	answering	assembling	crying	
commanding	judging	clothing		

Agents. The various types of action are connected to an unusual collection of actants. Among these actants are found diverse categories of both roles and characters.

1. Most of the actants in the passion story are nameless figures. These agents serve in roles and are not developed into full characters. Among these groups which surround Jesus are:

some	witnesses	cohort	passers
all	chief priests	soldiers	women
crowd	bystanders	thieves	

Various individuals emerge from these groupings, yet remain nameless:

a woman	a servant	the youth (14.51-52)
the chief priest	the centurion	

Other roles are filled by isolated figures, but without character traits. Among these are the narrator and the messenger at the tomb.

2. A small collection of actants are developed into more rounded figures. Three types of characters inhabit the passion narrative.

2.1. Two examples of collective characterization are present. The religious authorities take on a full character role as the opponents of Jesus. The disciples are characterized as the privileged companions who ultimately abandon Jesus.

2.2. A few actants serve as flat characters with limited tasks. Among these are Pilate, Joseph, Judas, Barrabbas, Simon of Cyrene.

5. Conclusion

2.3. Two actants are given deeper character traits. Simon Peter is presented in terms of companionship (14.33, 54), debate (14.29, 31), failure (14.33, 66-70). Significantly, Peter is also singled out in the resurrection promise (16.7).

Jesus stands alone as the one full character in the passion story. Each scene of Mark 14–16 circulates around his mission and his identity.[1]

3. Thus, the passion narrative places Jesus at the center of its story world. He is surrounded by a host of individuals and groups who play brief, functional roles. He is accompanied by Simon Peter, who serves as both companion and counterpart to Jesus' mission. The story also surrounds Jesus with lesser characters who create a world of contrast and contradiction. The effect of this configuration is crucial: Mark 14–16 sustains a profound and extended character study based on the mission and destiny of Jesus.

Motifs. These various agents and actions are combined to create a host of narrative motifs.[2] Each scene is composed around a limited selection of these motifs.[3] These motifs provide the primary compositional material for the scenes of the passion narrative.

Genre. The twelve scenes in Mark 14–16 belong to no fixed genre. This unusual composition has led scholars to focus instead on the passion narrative as a whole. Thus, many have argued that the passion account is a unified piece of literature, somewhat akin to a genre.[4] In

---

1. Significantly, this character study is far removed from modern interests in psychological insight and motivation. Mk 14–16 views the story of Jesus largely from outside and provides a character study marked by action and identification rather than introspection.

2. For example, the role of the women is presented through seven different motifs: a woman anoints, women behold, women come, women inquire, women enter, women fear, women depart.

3. For a full listing of motifs see the synchronic analysis of each scene.

4. Thus, R. Bultmann (*The History of the Synoptic Tradition* [trans. J. Marsh; Oxford: Basil Blackwell, 1963 (1948)]) divides the synoptic material into apophthegms, dominical sayings, miracle stories and a category labeled as historical stories and legends, among which he places the passion narrative. In a similar manner M. Dibelius (*From Tradition to Gospel* [trans. B.L. Woolf; New York: Charles Scribner's Sons, 1966 (1919)]) catalogues the synoptic material under sermons, paradigms, tales, legends, analogies and the passion story. R. Pesch (*Das*

contrast formalistic analysis reveals two basic forms employed in the scenes of Mark 14–16: pronouncement scenes and report scenes.

1. A common structure undergirds the majority of scenes in the passion narrative. This pattern gathers various reported elements around a central pronouncement or cluster of sayings. This pattern dominates all the scenes of the passion story, with the exception of Mk 15.16-20 and 15.38-47.

1.1. This central sayings cluster provides the most dramatic element and the interpretive key to these scenes. Three examples will demonstrate this normative pattern.

1.1.1. The scene in Mk 14.12-26 is framed as a typical celebration of the Passover. A central group of sayings transforms the scene and introduces images of Christology and soteriology. Through the words of Jesus (14.18, 22b, 24, 25) the Passover becomes a symbol of Jesus' rejection, suffering and death as well as a sign of the coming Kingdom.

1.1.2. A similar pattern is present in the Gethsemane scene (14.32-42). The basic frame of the story provides a scene of departure. At the center of this story is a trilogy of sayings which reshapes the scene with images of Christology and discipleship. Jesus prays to the Father for deliverance, but he offers obedience as well (14.35-36). He then questions the sleeping disciples (14.37). Jesus finally commands his followers to watchfulness (14.38). The narrative develops this sayings cluster into three separate incidents.

1.1.3. The same pattern controls the trial before the high priests. Various attempts to convict Jesus come to naught. The seeking by the leaders (14.55), two lines of testimony (14.56-59) and the questions of the chief priest (14.60) do not incriminate Jesus. Only the pronouncement by Jesus himself (14.62) accomplishes this. Subsequently the confession by Jesus serves as the basis for judgment (14.63-64) and as the grounds for his torture (14.65).

1.2. Various alterations of this basic pattern are employed. When seen as variations upon an expected norm, these scenes take on new

Markusevangelium [HTKNT; Freiburg: Herder, 2nd edn, 1980]), argues for a fixed, coherent, unified passion tradition to which Mark has made no significant alterations. From the opposite perspective, other scholars see the passion narrative as one coherent piece created wholly by Mark. Thus, the question of genre has been connected to the identity of the entire passion account rather than to its individual stories.

5. Conclusion

significance. Such variations are found in Mk 14.26-32a, 14.66-72, 15.1-15, 15.20c-37 and 16.1-8.

1.2.1. At the center of Mk 14.26-32a stands Jesus' prophecy of betrayal (14.27-28, 30). In a creative extension of this pattern, a counter-proclamation is presented in Peter's rebuke (14.29, 31a). Thus, sayings elements are used to provide a decisive flow/counter-flow at the center of this story.

1.2.2. A stark variation of the pronouncement pattern may be seen in 14.66-72. Jesus is absent from the scene, and the proclamation is provided instead by Peter. Significantly, Peter pronounces a threefold denial of Jesus. This pronouncement stands as a counter tradition to the confession of Jesus in 14.62. In addition, the words of Jesus are focused through the remembrance by Peter (14.72).

1.2.3. While numerous scenes circulate around sayings of Jesus, the trial scene in Mk 15.1-15 centers around his silence (15.5a). This non-pronouncement is the source of Pilate's amazement (15.5b) and provides a crucial image of Jesus: like the Suffering Servant and the innocent sufferer, Jesus endures injustice with silent pain.

1.2.4. An unusual extension of the pronouncement pattern is found in the cross scene (15.20c-37). A chorus of pronouncements surround the death of Jesus. A silent inscription pronounces Jesus the King of the Jews (15.26). Those passing by pronounce Jesus a failed prophet (15.29-30). The chief priests mock Jesus as an impotent messianic and royal pretender (15.31-32). Even the thieves crucified with Jesus revile him (15.32). This chorus of misunderstanding and rejection leads to the central cry of Jesus from the cross (15.33), but even this word is misunderstood. Ultimately Jesus dies with a loud cry (15.37). Thus, the pronouncement pattern has been extended into a chorus of misunderstanding, abuse and rejection.

1.2.5. A final variant is found in Mk 16.1-8. Through the use of a messenger the words of Jesus are placed at the center of this scene. Thus, even in his absence the command of Jesus remains authoritative for his followers.

1.3. The sequence of pronouncements found in ten of the final scenes embodies the basic plot of the passion story.[1] It is likely that this connection plays a key role in the formation and transmission of the passion account. By recalling the words of Jesus or their absence,

1. See the Appendix.

one would recall the story and the significance of his death.

2. A second form is found in two report scenes (15.16-20; 15.38-47). These scenes describe the events which follow Jesus' condemnation (15.16-20) and his crucifixion (15.38-47). This report form serves primarily in the plotting of the narrative, but christological images are also present. Significantly, both scenes have been impacted by pronouncements, and both pronouncements present ambiguous christological titles. The account of the soldiers' abuse (15.16-20) notes the greeting of the soldiers: 'Hail, King of the Jews' (15.18). This greeting embodies the aura of the scene by attaching to Jesus a title already abandoned. In a similar manner a pronouncement is one of the signs of hope in 15.38-47. The confession of the centurion gives human articulation to the hope embodied in this scene. Mk 15.16-20 and 15.38-47 thus present report scenes which have been shaped by the use of pronouncements.

3. Consequently the stories of the passion narrative exhibit an ordered framework. Reports which center in pronouncements by Jesus provide the normative pattern. Alterations upon this pattern provide creative variations with distinct interpretive significance. This primary pattern provides the backbone of the passion narrative. A second, though related, pattern is found in report scenes which carry pronouncements by others about Jesus as a secondary element. Thus, the passion story is framed around a simple formal pattern which has been developed in diverse and creative ways. Genre descriptions of Mark 14–16 must reflect this formal pattern.

Narrative Strategies
The diverse field of morphological components is taken up into a focused syntactical strategy. This strategy operates in four areas: syntactical divisions, syntactical functions, syntactical foci, syntactical patterns.

Syntactical Divisions. The twelve scenes of the passion narrative operate around a simple three-part frame: introduction, body, conclusion. Typically the introduction and conclusion contain elements of transition which connect the scene to its context. In addition, any temporal and geographical markers usually occur in the opening or closing lines. The body of the story contains the central focus of the scene, most often in a saying by Jesus.

5. Conclusion

Variations upon this pattern prove significant for interpretation. The absence of a conclusion in the first trial (14.53-65) is followed by a missing introduction to Peter's denial (14.66-72). This deviation from the established norm links the trial of Jesus and the trial of Peter in an interpretive bond.

In a similar manner the absence of both introduction and conclusion in Mk 15.38-47 is significant. This variation marks an interim scene and provides a bridge between the cross scene (15.20c-37) and the resurrection promise (16.1-8).

Syntactical Functions. The syntactical strategy of the passion narrative operates in four functional fields: setting, narration, plot, characterization. (1) Setting is largely optional in the scenes of the passion narrative. Temporal and geographical markers are used in some stories, but absent from others. If present these markers usually occur in the opening or closing phrases. The primary exception to this pattern is the careful timing of the death scene (15.20c-37). Consequently the setting of the passion narrative is limited to a single week in and around Jerusalem. (2) The narrating function is mostly unobtrusive. The exception is the occasional use of an intrusive motif—'the narrator informs'—to provide information vital to the reading of the narrative. (3) Plotting is carried out along a sequential, rather than circular, pattern. In contrast to the limited use of motifs in setting and narration, the plotting of the narrative draws upon the full range of narrative elements. (4) Character studies are marked by great reserve and limited descriptions. Inner motivations and psychological profiles are missing. This indirect approach weaves the characterization function into the larger pattern of the narrative.

Syntactical Foci. Setting, narration, plotting and characterization combine to create three distinct foci: the characterization of Jesus, the role of discipleship, opposition to Jesus. (1) From the beginning Jesus is shown in faithful obedience to God (1.1-20). This image is taken up and consummated in the story of Jesus' death (14.32-42). Thus, the passion account focuses Jesus as the Beloved Son who is obedient to God. (2) The counter-image to the obedience of Jesus is formed around the religious authorities. Their opposition to Jesus begins early (2.6-7; 3.6) and culminates in his death (14.63-64; 15.11). (3) The disciples vacillate between these two poles. These companions of Jesus exhibit a faltering discipleship marked by faith and by failure. At the end of the narrative their fate remains open. Consequently the passion narrative uses these three focal points to map the landscape of faith. All the characters of the story move along this continuum of failure and faithfulness.

Syntactical Patterns. The strategy of the passion narrative operates around two primary patterns. This configuration proves crucial in the framing of narrative significance.

1. The first pattern is seen in the plotting strategy. The plot line of the passion story is focused upon the death of Jesus and patterned around prophecy and fulfillment. Beginning with the preparation for burial in Mk 14.1-11, a sequential line leads to the death of Jesus (15.20c-37) and his announcement as the Crucified One (16.1-8). This plot line moves forward upon a pattern of prophetic fulfillment. This strategy operates in concentric circles. Prophecies given within the passion story are fulfilled (14.8/15.46; 14.18/14.44-45; 14.27/14.50; 14.30/14.66-70). Predictions from the ministry of Jesus are fulfilled (8.31; 9.31; 10.32-34). Images from the Old Testament are completed (14.12-26; 14.27, 34; 15.5, 16-20, 24, 29, 33). Other prophecies expect future fulfillment (14.28, 62; 16.7).

This plotting pattern generates a crucial narrative effect. The focus of the plot sequence on the death of Jesus produces a pointed passion Christology. The sustaining of the plot line through prophecy/ fulfillment produces a strong prophetic Christology. Consequently the plotting strategy of the passion narrative unites prophetic Christology and passion Christology in a decisive portrait of Jesus.

2. The second primary pattern operates in the field of characterization. Throughout Mark 14–16 the content of Jesus' character is filled out with images of suffering and death. These images are drawn from the events of the passion, from the ministry of Jesus and from the Old Testament. Because the content of the characterization centers on Jesus as one who suffers and dies in obedience to God, the passion Christology is established.

The structural frame of this characterization proves crucial. The passion narrative is built around a typical pattern of report scenes which center in a saying by Jesus. This configuration places the words of Jesus at the center of the passion story and establishes a prophetic Christology. Consequently the syntactical pattern employed in the

5. Conclusion

characterization of Jesus also unites prophetic Christology and passion Christology.

Summary
Formalistic analysis provides an orderly description of the narrative components and moves at work in Mark 14–16. Various regions of narrative structure and narrative strategy may be identified. Various agents and actions combine to provide a wide range of narrative motifs. Selected motifs are configured into an unusual collection of pronouncement reports which provide the stock of the passion account. These elements serve as components in an effective narrative strategy. This syntactical strategy focuses the image of Jesus and confronts the reader with a continuum of faith and failure. Most significantly, patterns of plotting and characterization merge in a decisive christological strategy which unites prophetic Christology with passion Christology. Consequently the characterization of Jesus provides the key element in the passion narrative and in its strategy of presentation.

The Characterization of Jesus in Mark 14–16

Attention to narrative form and function in Mark 14–16 reveals a complex narrative world focused on the image of Jesus. Generated through an intricate textual strategy, this portrait provides the interpretive key to this Gospel.

The Content of the Characterization
Mark 14–16 has been typically understood as a death story with a monolithic focus on passion Christology and on the soteriological value of Jesus' death. In contrast to this view narrative analysis reveals a complex series of christological images which are related in various ways to the death of Jesus.

Jesus the Prophet. Mark 14–16 employs the death story to give surprising focus to the role of Jesus as the true prophet of God. Through this process the passion story highlights an image of Jesus missing from other traditions of his death.[1] The prophetic Christology

---

1. See the traditions of Jesus' death in Acts 2.14-36; 4.8-12; 10.34-43; 13.16-41; 17.22-31; 26.22-23; 1 Thess. 4.13-18; Rom. 1.1-6; Gal. 6.14; Phil. 2.5-11;

in Mark 14–16 is developed around three distinct roles: instruction, prediction, and suffering.

1. The prophetic activity of Jesus provides instruction for his disciples. His words guide, correct and encourage his followers through the events of his passion. He serves for his disciples as teacher (14.14, 49) and rabbi (14.45). Through his words Jesus interprets his own identity: he is the messiah (14.6-8, 61-62), the bringer of a new covenant (14.24), the Son of Man (14.21, 41, 62), the Son of God (14.36, 61), the shepherd of God's flock (14.27), the fulfillment of the Old Testament (14.49). Jesus further instructs the disciples about his destiny: he will die and be buried (14.8); he will be betrayed (14.18-21, 41); his blood will be shed and his body broken (14.22-25); he will be abandoned by his own (14.27, 30); he will be raised and go to Galilee (14.28). Jesus also interprets for his disciples various events and symbols which surround his passion: the woman has anointed him for burial (14.8); the bread and cup of Passover portray the death of Jesus (14.22-25); the relation of Jesus' arrest and death to the Scriptures is shown (14.49; 15.34). Thus, the passion scenes implicitly portray Jesus as the teaching prophet who guides his followers through his final days.

2. An extended line of predictions confirms the image of Jesus as the prophet of God. Various predictions have immediate fulfillment: the Passover preparation (14.13-16), the coming of the betrayer (14.41-42). The narrative thus places a paradigm of prediction/ fulfillment at the beginning of the passion and surrounds the words of Jesus with an aura of certainty. Other predictions are fulfilled in the subsequent events of the narrative: the disciples fall away (14.27, 50); Peter denies Jesus (14.30, 66-72); Jesus is betrayed by one of the Twelve (14.18, 43-46); the Scriptures are fulfilled (14.21, 27, 49; 15.34); Jesus is struck down, killed, buried. These transactions extend the prediction/fulfillment schema and confirm the identity of Jesus as the authentic prophet of God. Various other predictions remain unfulfilled within the narrative, but the reader is encouraged to see these as authentic prophecy: Jesus will go before them into Galilee (14.28; 16.7); the gospel will be preached throughout the world (14.9); the Son of Man will come with the clouds of heaven (14.62);

1 Cor. 15.3-7; 2 Tim. 1.8-10; Tit. 2.11-14; Eph. 1.3-14; Col. 1.13-23; Heb. 10.1-25; 1 Pet. 1.3-5; 1 Jn 1.5-10; 5.6; Rev. 1.4-7; 5.1-14; the prophetic image is mentioned but not developed in Lk. 24.19-27; Acts 3.22; 7.37.

5. Conclusion

Jesus will celebrate anew in the Kingdom (14.25). Thus, Jesus' predictions characterize him as the true prophetic voice sent from God.

3. The passion narrative also characterizes Jesus as the suffering prophet. The theme of Jesus' instruction is his destiny of suffering and death (14.8, 18-21, 22-25, 27, 28, 30, 41, 49). Jesus' predictions center on his passion (14.18, 27, 30). In addition, various texts draw upon the prophetic image of the Suffering Servant (14.53-65; 15.1-15, 16-20, 20c-37). This portrayal of Jesus as the suffering and rejected prophet is made explicit in the scene of abuse: 'And some began to spit upon him and to cover his face and to strike him and to say to him, "Prophesy!" And the guards received him with blows' (Mk 14.65).

4. Consequently the passion narrative generates a dynamic prophetic Christology. The passion account employs instruction, prediction and suffering to show Jesus as the true messenger of God. This portrait wraps Jesus in the garments of the Old Testament prophets.[1] At the same time the role of suffering is heightened beyond its prophetic norm in the portrait of Jesus: this prophet dies for the people (10.45; 14.21-26).

Jesus the Messiah. Mark 14–16 makes clear the identity of Jesus as the messiah of Israel. The passion narrative opens with a symbol of Jesus' identity: he is the anointed one of God (14.3-9). This implicit identity of Jesus as messiah is made explicit before the religious authorities. Jesus responds to the question 'Are you the Christ?' with a stark allusion to the name of Yahweh: 'I am' (14.62). Thus, the clearest confirmation of the messianic identity is found on the lips of Jesus as a public witness: he is the anointed messiah sent from God. The contours of this messianic identity are developed through the larger strategy of the narrative.

Jesus the Son of God. Various elements of the passion narrative characterize Jesus as Son of God. The first witness is a private one, given by Jesus in Gethsemane. Here Jesus addresses God as Abba and

---

1. See, for example, the combination of instruction, prediction and suffering present in Moses, Elijah, Hosea and Jeremiah. For a thorough treatment of the suffering of the prophets, see O.H. Steck, *Israel und das gewaltsame Geschick der Propheten: Untersuchungen zur Überlieferung des deuteronomistischen Geschichtsbildes im Alten Testament, Spätjudentum und Urchristentum* (WMANT; Neukirchen–Vluyn: Neukirchener Verlag, 1967).

as Father, then responds to God in faithfulness and obedience (14.36). The second witness is a public testimony. The question is placed bluntly by the high priest: 'Are you the messiah, the son of the Blessed One?' The answer of Jesus employs the name of God to confirm his identity: 'I am' (14.62). The third witness to Jesus' sonship occurs in the shadow of the cross. Here a centurion sees the manner of Jesus' death and declares publicly that 'this man was Son of God' (15.39).

Jesus the Son of Man. The passion story generates a clear image of Jesus as the Son of Man. Two traits guide this imagery: suffering and coming in power. The Son of Man suffers and is betrayed unto death (14.21, 41). In contrast the Son of Man will be seen at the right hand of power, and he will come with the clouds of heaven (14.62). Thus, 'Son of Man' is used to sustain a complex union of suffering and power.

Jesus the Suffering One. Various passages employ Old Testament images to characterize Jesus. Through his own words Jesus is characterized as the smitten shepherd of Zechariah (Mk 14.27). The agony of Jesus in Gethsemane (14.32-42) draws upon images of Psalms 42 and 43. The arrest of Jesus fulfills the Scriptures (14.49). The trial before the religious leaders (14.53-65), the trial before Pilate (15.1-15) and the scene of mockery (15.16-20) characterize Jesus in terms of the Suffering Servant from Isaiah. The death scene (15.20c-37) portrays Jesus as the innocent sufferer from the Psalms. Through these various images the passion account shows Jesus as one whose suffering and death find their meaning in the Scriptures of Israel. Subsequently the suffering and death which pervade the passion story are solidified into a title at the tomb (16.6). The words of the messenger gather these various images into a decisive new description of Jesus: he is the Crucified One.

Summary. The passion account generates a characterization of Jesus with surprising complexity and depth. The content of this portrait is diverse, and its lines of development are extensive. Consequently no monolithic image of Jesus emerges from the passion story. The characterization of Jesus is built instead around a complex of images. He is the true prophet and messiah, the Son of God. He is the suffering

5. Conclusion

Son of Man who will come in power and glory. He is innocent and righteous, the Suffering Servant, the Crucified One.

The Process of the Characterization

This complex portrait of Jesus is generated by a unique narrative strategy. Two elements guide this design: narrative focus and narrative depth.

Narrative Focus. The first element in this strategy is the narrative focus provided by the death of Jesus. The multiple images used to characterize Jesus are gathered around a singular event: the crucifixion.

1. The prophetic task of Jesus is linked directly to his passion. His instructions to his followers point to his suffering and death: he will die and be buried (14.8); he will be betrayed (14.18-21, 41); his blood will be shed and his body broken (14.22-25); he will be abandoned by his own (14.27, 30). The passion of Jesus also provides the subject for his predictions: the disciples will fall away (14.27); Peter will deny Jesus (14.30); Jesus will be betrayed by one of the Twelve (14.18); the Scriptures are fulfilled by his suffering (14.21, 27, 49); Jesus' body will be broken and his blood poured out (14.22-24). Thus, the prophetic activity of Jesus is focused around his suffering and death.

2. Various other christological images are focused around the crucifixion. The messiah is anointed unto burial (14.8). The messianic identity is made public only in the context of the trial and the death sentence (14.62). The portrait of Jesus as Son of God is built around the agony in Gethsemane (14.36), the trial and death sentence (14.62) and the scene of execution (15.39). The Son of Man is characterized through suffering and death (14.21, 41). Jesus goes to his death as the innocent and righteous one, the Suffering Servant of God. Thus, the passion story unites diverse and contrasting images around a singular narrative event. This technique gathers the scattered images of Jesus into a sharp narrative focus—he is the Crucified One.

Narrative Depth. Through a second literary technique the local characterization of Jesus is given narrative depth by its interaction with the wider story of Jesus. Consequently the portrait of Jesus in Mark 14–16 does not represent a stark realignment or corrective of previous images. Instead, the portrait of Jesus in the passion story shows extensive connections and interactions with the earlier characterization.

1. Several character elements in Mark 14–16 are placed before the reader with little or no definition. This bare positing of titles and images requires the reader to fill out the content of these claims from the earlier narrative. (1) Jesus' role as the shepherd (14.27) is defined by the feeding stories (6.30-44; 6.34; 8.1-10). (2) In the passion account Jesus is named as the teacher (14.14, 45, 49) and various scenes of instruction are narrated (14.6-9, 13-15, 18-21, 22-25, 27-31). Apart from references to his death the content of Jesus' teaching is largely missing from this portrait. The full image of Jesus as one who teaches with authority and announces the Kingdom of God is developed in the earlier narrative and undergirds the teaching of Jesus in his final days. (3) Two scenes from the passion story confirm that Jesus is messiah (14.6-9, 60-62), but the parameters of this identity are not specific. In contrast the earlier narrative gives sharper definition to the messianic task. Subsequently the passion story builds upon this definition for its portrait of Jesus as messiah. (4) In particular, the passion narrative uses the Son of God title without definition. Jesus confirms the title (14.62), but his unique claim to the name of God may be interpreted as blasphemy (14.63). The centurion also affirms the title (15.39), but his confession may be interpreted as a judgment of innocence (Lk. 23.47). Within the passion context the Son of God title remains largely undefined. This use points to an extensive undergirding of the title in the previous narrative (1.1, 11; 3.11; 5.7; 9.7; 12.6; 13.32).

2. Other images carry a more full definition within the passion context. Nonetheless these images also sustain a dialogical relationship with the images of Mark 1–13. In some instances the passion portrait is given extensive confirmation in the wider narrative. The coming of the Son of Man mentioned in the passion context (14.62) is detailed in Mark 13. Other images from the passion narrative are amplified through earlier scenes. The suffering of Jesus is realized in the passion context, but only in the earlier narrative is this suffering shown as a definitive messianic task (8.31; see also 9.31; 10.32-34).

Summary. The characterization of Jesus is established through intensive lines of narrative focus and extensive lines of narrative depth. Thus, images from the passion story reshape and are themselves reshaped by images from Mark 1–13. Consequently the process of characterization employed is one of reciprocal interchange. The image of Jesus which

5. Conclusion

emerges is intricate and complex, both in its development and in its content. As the following section demonstrates, this narrative process and this christological constellation provide key insights for understanding the role of the passion narrative in the larger strategy of this Gospel.

The Role of the Passion Story in the Gospel of Mark

Critical scholarship has acknowledged from the beginning the key relationship between passion story and Gospel story. This relationship has been variously defined. Martin Kähler and a host of followers have understood the passion story as the definitive element in the Gospel tradition. Other descriptions were, as Werner Kelber notes, 'based on the assumption that the Gospel of Mark divides conceptually into two separate parts'.[1] This conceptual division contrasts the power and the passion of Jesus. Theodore Weeden proposes a collision of rival Christologies in which the passion narrative renders all other images obsolete. Others propose a more moderate combination in which Mark uses the passion narrative as the corrective to traditional images of power. Thus, the passion narrative has been understood as the definitive focus of the Gospel story or as the dominating element in a collision or collusion of conceptual images.

Narrative analysis suggests a different role for the passion narrative in the Gospel of Mark. Laying aside for the moment attempts to reconstruct the prior history of segments of tradition and bracketing the question of what an author intended, narrative analysis challenges both the description by Kähler and the suggestion of a conceptual division in the structure and strategy of the literary text. Narrative analysis reveals a critical interrelationship between the forms and images circulating in this Gospel. This interactive relationship calls for a renewed understanding of the role of the passion story in the Gospel of Mark.

Comparable Images

Martin Kähler's description gave singular focus to the influence of the passion story. Weeden's thesis posed passion Christology against

---

1. W. Kelber, 'From Passion Narrative to Gospel Narrative', in W. Kelber (ed.), *The Passion in Mark: Studies on Mark 14–16* (Philadelphia: Fortress Press, 1976), p. 178.

Christologies of power. Eventually Weeden saw this conceptual conflict embodied in the very structure of the narrative. Weeden argued that the earlier sections of the Gospel of Mark contained a *theologia gloriae* dominated by the wonders of Jesus and by the immediate sense of presence provided by the sayings traditions. This early image of Jesus was then corrected by the *theologia crucis* generated in the second half of the Gospel. Both the monolithic view of Kähler and the rival Christology of Weeden see the Gospel under the stark domination of passion images. Their views would prove difficult to maintain if contrasting images of power and passion[1] were shown to circulate throughout the Gospel.[2]

Passion Elements. The portrait of Jesus as wonder worker is prevalent throughout Mark 1–13, yet this image is not exclusive. A significant number of passion elements occur within Mark 1–13, prior to the formal passion account. Significantly, several of these passion elements are imbedded within formal miracle stories. (1) The charge of blasphemy which supports the death sentence against Jesus originates in a miracle story (2.7). (2) Likewise the death plot against Jesus grows out of a controversial healing (3.1-7a). Subsequently the charge of blasphemy and the death plot prove decisive in the passion story (14.1-2, 10-11, 64). (3) The transfiguration story (9.2-14a) presents a wondrous scene of epiphany. Significantly, this epiphanic miracle uses the Son of Man imagery and the Elijah expectation to point uniquely to the suffering and death of Jesus.

Throughout his ministry the wondrous teaching of Jesus is linked to his passion. While the authority of Jesus' teaching is demonstrated through miracles (1.21-39), the effect of Jesus' teaching is demonstrated through the hostility which it generates (2.6-7, 16, 24; 3.2-6, 22; 7.1-5; 8.11; 10.2; 11.18, 27-28; 12.12, 13-17). Significantly, the death plot is a response by the religious leaders to the wondrous teaching of Jesus (3.6). The content of Jesus' teaching is demonstrated

---

1. I have developed this relationship from the viewpoint of the miracle stories in *Teaching with Authority: Miracles and Christology in the Gospel of Mark* (Sheffield: JSOT Press, 1992).

2. This demonstration would not, however, discount the corrective Christology which sees Mark's contribution in the combination of various Christologies under the central passion focus. A reciprocal pattern of realignment would, however, render suspect a one-directional Christology.

5. Conclusion

through three passion predictions (8.31; 9.31; 10.32-34): he is the Son of Man who will suffer and die. A further teaching in Mk 10.45 points to the death of Jesus: the Son of Man has come to serve and to give his life. Consequently the narrative links miracle, teaching and passion in its early portrait of Jesus. This model is transported to Jerusalem through the cursing of the fig tree (11.12-27). This final miracle story is linked to Jesus' teaching on the temple (11.15-16) and on true worship (11.17, 22-27a). The response to this scene is explicit: the religious leaders plot the death of Jesus (11.18).

Thus, the narrative creates an early and extensive paradigm around the teaching of Jesus. The authority of his teaching is demonstrated in wonders. The response to his teaching is demonstrated in the hostility and the death plot of religious leaders. The content of his teaching is demonstrated through the passion predictions. Thus, Mark 1–13 provides no exclusive, monolithic Christology of wonder and glory. Jesus' wonders are not self-serving, but participate in a larger, more complex strategy. From the beginning suffering and death are crucial elements in the characterization of Jesus. Consequently the passion Christology participates in the power and wonder of Jesus' ministry.

Miracle Elements. Various scholars see in the absence of miracle stories in Mark 14–16 a conscious suppression of the miracle traditions in favor of the passion Christology. In contrast narrative analysis shows that there is no effective line separating wonders and passion in the Gospel of Mark.[1] While Mk 14.1–16.8 contains no formal miracle stories, important wonders pervade the death story. These miracle elements cluster around three events: preparation, crucifixion and resurrection.

1. The miracle elements which surround the preparation scenes demonstrate the miraculous foreknowledge of Jesus. Significantly, each of these miracle elements is linked to the suffering and death of Jesus. In 14.8-9 Jesus foretells his death and the future of the gospel. The miraculous insight in 14.12-16 leads to the celebration of the Passover as a sign of Jesus' death. The foreknowledge of Jesus in 14.17-21 points to the one who will hand him over to die. Jesus knows beforehand that the disciples will abandon him at the time of his passion (14.27-31). While this concentration of miraculous insight

---

1. See Broadhead, *Teaching with Authority*, especially pp. 180-87.

generates no formal miracle stories, its impact is significant. This wondrous foreknowledge demonstrates the authority of Jesus, it focuses the central role of Jesus' suffering and it shows that the death of Jesus was no accident.

2. A second cluster of miracle elements is found around the scene of crucifixion. The darkness of 15.33 and the torn veil of 15.38 provide epiphanic events, though no formal miracle story is narrated. Other elements provide the potential for miracle stories: the demand for a sign (15.29-32), the search for Elijah (15.34-37). Thus, the cross scene provides ample opportunity for narration of a miracle story, but none is narrated. Nonetheless miracle elements around the cross demonstrate the power and presence of God in the death of Jesus.

3. The third cluster of miracle elements surrounds the resurrection. The removal of the stone is unexplained (16.4). The messenger at the tomb resembles an angel (16.5). The tomb is empty (16.6). The appearance of Jesus is promised (16.7). Although no formal miracle story is generated from these events, these miracle elements are integral to the resurrection promise.

4. While Mark 14–16 demonstrates a clear tendency to suppress formal miracle stories, it nonetheless supports the presence of miracle elements. These miracle elements play an important role in the story of Jesus' suffering, death and resurrection. Thus, the passion narrative and its portrait of Jesus have been carefully wrapped in images of power and wonder. A stark union of power and passion is presented. Jesus' wondrous teaching leads to his suffering and death; Jesus' passion is marked by the wondrous power and presence of God.

Other Elements. Various other images resist efforts to define the Gospel and its Christology solely in terms of the passion story. Throughout the narrative Jesus is the messiah whose suffering and death provide the defining trait of his messianic identity (1.1, 34; 8.29; 9.41; 14.61; 15.32; son of David in 10.47, 48; 12.35, 37). Through the entirety of the story Jesus is the teacher (4.38; 5.35; 9.17, 38; 10.17, 20, 35; 12.14, 32; 13.1; 14.14; rabbi in 9.5; 10.51; 11.21; 14.45). From beginning to end Jesus is the Son of God (1.1, 11; 3.11; 5.7; 9.7; 12.6; 13.32; 14.61-62; 15.39). The Son of Man imagery is operative throughout the text (2.10, 28; 8.31, 38; 9.9, 12, 31; 10.33, 45; 13.26; 14.21, 62). The prophetic image central to the passion narrative emerges from the ministry of Jesus (6.4; see also

5. Conclusion

6.15; 8.28). The Old Testament is fulfilled by Jesus' words and deeds as well as by his suffering and death (1.2-3; 4.12, 32; 6.34; 7.6-7; 8.18; 9.11-13, 48; 10.5-9; 10.19-20; 11.9-10, 17; 12.10-11, 26-27, 29-34, 35-37; 13.14, 24-25, 26; 14.27, 34, 62; 15.24, 33). A stark external witness clarifies Jesus' identity at the beginning (1.9-11), the middle (9.2-8) and the conclusion (16.1-7) of the narrative. Thus, the narrative employs a common stock of images to characterize both the ministry of Jesus and his passion. This widespread use of contrasting images in both halves of the Gospel resists the definitions proposed by Kähler and by Weeden.

Mutual Interpretation
The circulation of contrasting images of Jesus throughout the Gospel of Mark resists viewing the passion narrative as the sole bearer of authentic Christology. A second literary trait challenges not only Kähler and Weeden, but also those who argue that a Christology of wonder has been reshaped by the singular corrective of the cross. Narrative analysis demonstrates not only that contrasting images of Jesus may be found throughout the narrative, but also that these images participate in a process of mutual interpretation and correction. Each image of Jesus participates, through reciprocal interchange, within a wider interpretive world. Various images from the life of Jesus are indeed focused through the death story; at the same time, however, the death story is filled out by the images of Jesus' life and ministry. To whatever degree a process of critical reinterpretation is present, that process is reciprocal. This mutual interchange creates a strategy of clarification and amplification which generates an extended and complex characterization of Jesus. This process and its effect may be demonstrated in different images of Jesus.

Teacher and Prophet. The image of Jesus as the rejected teacher and prophet emerges only through this complex interaction within the wider narrative. Mark 1–13 paints a broad portrait of Jesus as the authoritative preacher/teacher who meets hostility and rejection. Significantly, all three elements of the final prophetic focus—instruction, prediction, suffering—are already present in the passion teachings in the midst of Jesus' ministry (8.31; 9.31; 10.32-34). Conversely the passion narrative takes up the teaching task as an element in the prophetic identity. Thus, Jesus' teaching activity is expanded into an intricate portrait composed of diverse images: wondrous power, hostility, prediction, suffering and rejection, death. This cluster of images has its parallel in various Old Testament prophets of God who serve, speak and suffer for the sake of Israel. Through a wide-ranging process of mutual interaction the proclamation of Jesus is gathered into a complex, multi-faceted image: he is the wondrous teacher and prophet of God who gives his life for the people.

The Cross. The christological and soteriological value of the cross is made explicit only through this broad interaction of various images of Jesus. Through his ministry Jesus is identified as the messiah who will suffer and die for the people. No element from Jesus' ministry links this suffering to crucifixion. In contrast the cross scene (15.20c-37) does not surround the death of Jesus with explicit messianic images.[1] Read in isolation the death scene presents the execution of a righteous and pious Jew. Only through the critical interaction of these two narrative strategies is the image completed: the messiah suffers and dies on a cross, and the crucified Jesus is revealed as God's anointed. This central characterization is not made explicit by an isolated reading of either the life story or the death story. Only through the mutual intersection and realignment of images from the ministry and from the passion is the christological import of the cross made clear.

In the same manner the soteriological value of the cross is made explicit only through the interaction of various narrative elements. Mk 14.38-47 presents the death of Jesus as the fulfillment of the Scriptures, but does not spell out its saving significance. In contrast the story of Jesus' ministry makes plain his death in behalf of the people (10.45), and this relationship is clarified in the Passover scene (14.22-25). Still, neither of these passages links the death of Jesus to the cross. Thus, the soteriological value of the cross is not explicit in either tradition alone, but emerges only through the narrative linkage of these two images of Jesus.

Son of God. The role of the Son of God is clarified only through this wider, reciprocal process of characterization. In the passion account two confessions declare Jesus as the Son of God (14.61; 15.39). These

---

1. In my analysis the narrative strategy abandons the King of the Jews title (15.26) as inappropriate.

5. Conclusion

claims are explicit, yet open to misunderstanding. The leaders reject the claim of Jesus as blasphemy and sentence him to death (14.63-64). Luke understands the confession of the centurion as a sign of innocence (Lk. 23.47). Thus, the passion narrative confirms the Son of God title but does not clarify its meaning. In contrast Mark 1–13 provides a broad portrait of the Son of God. Moving forward from the opening designation of Jesus as God's Son (1.1), the narrative traces the mission of the Son. He pleases God with his work (1.11), demons bow before him and worship him (3.11; 5.7), the heavenly voice confirms that disciples are to obey his commands (9.7), the Son knows less than the Father (13.32). Mark 1–13 fills out the role of the Son of God, but does so without explicit reference to his suffering and death. This destiny is foreshadowed in parabolic form (12.6), but it is made clear only through the passion account. Thus, the passion narrative draws upon a well-established image, then culminates the mission of the Son of God around the cross event. Such linkage refocuses and realigns both traditions. This strategy of interconnection produces a complex and paradoxical portrait which neither tradition sustains in isolation. The one who dies is the wondrous Son who does the work of the Father; the Son who pleases God is put to death at the hands of sinners.

Son of Man. The union of power and suffering in the Son of Man imagery is built upon this wider strategy of narrative characterization. In Mark 1–13 the service, suffering and death of the Son of Man (8.31; 9.12, 31; 10.32-34, 45) are narrated alongside images of wonder and power. The Son of Man has authority to forgive sins and is lord over the Sabbath (2.10, 20). He will rise from the dead (9.9) and he will come in the power and glory of the Father (8.38; 13.26). Such images tend to overshadow the predictions of suffering and to whet the appetite of disciples for power and glory (10.37). Elements of power and wonder associated with the Son of Man imagery leave it open to an overly enthusiastic Christology of success. This danger is already countered by the sober predictions of service, suffering and death. Within the passion context the equilibrium between suffering and power is reconfirmed: the Son of Man is betrayed unto death, yet he will come with power and glory. Within the shadow of the cross the union of power and suffering in the Son of Man becomes inescapable. This delicate balance is held most effectively through the intermingling of Jesus' life story with the story of his death.

Crucified One. The decisive christological title—the Crucified One—gains true perspective only through the critical interaction of narrative elements and images. Reference to crucifixion and use of the title Crucified One are reserved for the closing sections of the narrative. This strategy provides a dramatic culmination for the process of characterization. Read in isolation this concluding imagery is sharply focused, but flat and undeveloped. The scrolls of Jewish and Roman history are filled with crucified ones, and two others were crucified with Jesus. The designation of Jesus as the Crucified One in 16.6 gains interpretive depth only through the wider transactions of the narrative (1.9, 24; 14.67). The image of the Crucified One is linked to the larger story of Jesus, the Nazarene (16.6). Through this process the image of the Crucified One is transformed into a broad and complex portrait. The Crucified One is the wondrous teacher from Galilee; he is the Beloved Son and the mysterious Son of Man; he is the ultimate prophet; he is the Suffering Servant and the righteous suffering one; he is the shepherd of God's people; he is David's son and David's Lord; he is the messiah of Israel. The image of the Crucified One is thus undergirded by the whole energy of the narrative and by its intricate, paradoxical portrait of Jesus. At the same time the conclusive image of Jesus as the Crucified One casts its shadow across every characterization of Jesus. Various christological images are true, but none which draws back from the final destiny of Jesus is adequate. Jesus' suffering and death culminates the story of his life; the whole of his life story undergirds his identity as the Crucified One.

Summary

Narrative analysis demonstrates two literary traits which challenge efforts to see in the passion narrative the sole image of Jesus or the exclusive corrective of all other images. First, varied and contrasting images of Jesus circulate throughout the story. Secondly, these images engage in a mutual interpretive exchange which ultimately corrects and realigns all images of Jesus. Consequently the intricate and paradoxical characterization of Jesus in the Gospel of Mark emerges from a complex narrative strategy of reciprocity. Through a process of mutual interaction the passion story partakes of the wider interpretive world of the narrative. Through this intratextual process the passion account both shapes and is shaped by the larger portrait of

5. Conclusion

Jesus. All lines of characterization remain effective, with none consumed and none unchanged.

Martin Kähler saw the passion narrative as part of a reflexive strategy: it recasts the entire narrative in its own image. Moderate proposals of corrective Christology also envision a reflexive strategy: Mark's use of his traditions has combined all christological images under the corrective influence of the passion. In contrast to this reflexive strategy, Theodore Weeden suggests a repressive pattern: Mark uses the passion narrative in the second half of his Gospel to obliterate the power Christology of the first half. Both the reflexive strategy and the repressive strategy identify the Gospel story with the passion story.[1] Narrative analysis suggests a different role for the passion narrative: it is one component in an intricate, extensive, paradoxical portrait of Jesus created through a complex intratextual strategy of reciprocity. This reciprocal strategy of characterization unveiled through narrative analysis carries decisive implications for the nature and purpose of the Gospel of Mark.

The Nature and Purpose of the Gospel of Mark

The role of the passion narrative has proven a central question in each stage of critical research in the Gospels: source criticism, linguistic studies, form criticism, redaction criticism. Particular attention has been given to the relation between passion story and Gospel story. Various reconstructions of the history of the traditions and the intent of the redactors have undergirded this process. Building upon this history of research, narrative analysis attempts to re-evaluate the role of the passion story in the Gospel tradition through a critical analysis of the textual strategy operating within the Gospel of Mark. As this section will show, the reciprocal pattern of characterization unveiled through narrative analysis provides definitive keys to the form, content and purpose of the Gospel of Mark.

Form

Formally the Gospel of Mark presents a coherent, unified narrative. An extensive line of linguistic investigations demonstrates the coher-

---

1. Thus, Kähler's description is repeated widely among proponents of corrective Christology. Kelber ('From Passion Narrative to Gospel', p. 177) associates Weeden's thesis with Kähler's dictum.

ence of language and style which pervades the entire Gospel.¹ Consequently the narrative cannot be divided into competing camps along linguistic lines. This linguistic analysis is supported by the findings of narrative analysis. Two central traits demonstrated the unity of the narrative strategy. First, an ideological coherence surrounds the portrait of Jesus throughout the narrative. From beginning to end Jesus is the wondrous teacher and prophet, Son of God, Son of Man, the suffering messiah. Secondly, this extensive portrait of Jesus is constructed through the intersection and mutual interpretation of various narrative images. The passion story and its Christology have infiltrated and influenced the life story; Jesus' life story and its images undergird and amplify the passion story.

Consequently the Gospel of Mark presents itself as an irreducible literary whole. Whatever historical development or authorial intention underlies this production, the result is a coherent narrative which can best be understood as a unity. Dissection of the narrative into constituent elements or evolutionary stages tends to destroy the narrative framework and to constitute a different text. While this dissection may aid the search for historical settings or authors, such deconstruction and reformulation tends to obscure the nature and purpose of the text. The Gospel of Mark presents itself as an 'autosemantic language form' and generates a framework with significance greater than the sum of its parts.² Because the Gospel form itself provides the context of expectation for interpretation of the constituent parts, each Gospel must be read as a whole.³ The Gospel of Mark constitutes a 'literary, theological unity', and 'it must be understood by the cohesion of the whole rather than by collision or combination of its parts'.⁴ Narrative analysis of Mark 14–16 confirms the formal identity of the Gospel of Mark as a unified narrative text.

---

1. See Chapter 1.
2. E. Güttgemanns, *Candid Questions concerning Gospel Form Criticism: A Methodological Sketch of the Fundamental Problematics of Form and Redaction Criticism* (trans. W. Doty; Pittsburgh: Pickwick Press, 1979 [1970]), pp. 287-92, 307.
3. R. Guelich, 'The Gospel Genre', in P. Stuhlmacher (ed.), *Das Evangelium und die Evangelien* (Tübingen: Mohr, 1983), p. 219.
4. Kelber, 'From Passion Narrative to Gospel', p. 178.

Content

The content of the Gospel of Mark centers on its characterization of Jesus. Various narrative strategies confirm this central focus. The narrative is identified in its opening lines as the story of Jesus, the messiah and Son of God (1.1).[1] The controversy over Jesus' identity and mission guides much of the plot line. The trial before the religious leaders (14.53-65) culminates this plot sequence by focusing the identity of Jesus as messiah, Son of God, Son of Man. The death scene culminates in the confession of Jesus as Son of God (15.39).[2] The identity of Jesus is focused through a variety of other materials. Titles serve to highlight different christological images (messiah, Son of God, teacher, prophet, Crucified One and others). Various miracle stories are structured around the characterization of Jesus (1.24, 27; 4.38, 41; 5.7, 35; 10.48; 11.21).[3] The sayings of Jesus are used to focus his identity (8.31; 9.31; 10.32-34; 12.35-37), as are parables (12.1-12). The passion narrative focuses the identity of Jesus through various techniques: symbol (14.1-9, 22-25), allusion to the Old Testament (14.27, 32-42, 53-65; 15.1-15, 16-20, 21-37), confession (14.62; 15.39).

Consequently the central focus of the narrative is not historical recollection or doctrinal formulation, but christological presentation. Concern for characterization guides the narrative strategy; the portrait of Jesus is the primary narrative product. The content of the Gospel of Mark centers in the story of Jesus' identity and mission as messiah.

Purpose

This christological narrative may be employed for a variety of tasks: historical data, apologetic, polemics, justification of community existence and practice, catechetical instruction, paranesis. Nonetheless the form and content of the Gospel of Mark suggest a kerygmatic function which holds priority over all others. The Gospel of Mark is presented as a proclamation. The entire work is a message about Jesus

---

1. The υἱοῦ θεοῦ title is omitted by ℵ* Θ (28) *pc* sa^{ms}; Or but included by ℵ¹ B D L W *pc* (*sed* του θεου A $f^{1.13}$ 𝔐) latt sy co; Ir^{lat}.

2. On the absence of the article in this title in 15.39, see Schweizer, *The Good News according to Mark* (trans. D. Madvig; Atlanta: John Knox, 1970), p. 355.

3. For extensive development of this function see Broadhead, *Teaching with Authority*.

(1.1). The central task of Jesus is proclamation (1.14-16, 22-23, 39). Disciples are to go and tell what they have seen and heard (3.13-14; 5.20; 6.7-13; 13.10; 14.9; 16.7). The Gospel of Mark posits a central demand for those who act within the story and for those upon whom this story acts: go and tell the story of God's work in Jesus.

Summary

Narrative analysis unveils in the Gospel of Mark an intricate portrait of Jesus generated through an extensive process of narrative interaction and reciprocity. This narrative strategy provides crucial keys to the nature and purpose of the Gospel of Mark. Formally the Gospel presents itself as a unified narrative text which must be interpreted in the context of its own distinct gestalt. Materially the content of this narrative is christological, centering on the identity and mission of Jesus as the messiah. Functionally the narrative defines proclamation as the central, comprehensive task. Thus, narrative analysis shows that the Gospel of Mark is a narrative account of Jesus' messianic life, death, resurrection shaped by and for the task of proclamation.

This definitive model focused through narrative analysis confirms the recent scholarship which sees in the Gospel of Mark a literary and theological unity. The model of the Gospel of Mark as solely a passion narrative proves inadequate, as do various models of corrective Christology. Seen from the perspective of the whole work, the passion story proves to be the culmination of an extensive, reciprocal, paradoxical strategy of characterization. The Gospel of Mark is a narrative prism with many facets, angles, images, but only one center. The Gospel of Mark is a complex, intricate, ironic narrative centered on Jesus the Nazarene, the Crucified One. This description of the Gospel of Mark offered by narrative analysis also provides a foundational model for definition of the Gospel genre.

The Gospel Genre

The attempt to define the parameters of the Gospel genre has proved elusive. Various definitions are offered on the basis of services provided by the Gospels. They have been described alternately as histories of Jesus, as reflections of church struggles, as reflections of the Evangelists' personalities, as legal or cultic guides, as doctrinal formulations, as apologetic, as polemic. While each of these elements

5. Conclusion

may be drawn from the Gospels, no one element or combination of elements is definitive for the Gospel genre.

More organized attempts at definition of the Gospel genre draw upon parallels from Jewish or Hellenistic contexts. The Gospels have been alternately defined as apocalyptic, as biography, as some Old Testament form, as aretalogies.[1] Other descriptions see the Gospel genre as without parallel and search for its meaning in the process of development. Numerous scholars were convinced of the connected nature and primary importance of the passion narrative and argued that the Gospels were simply expansions and extensions of the death story.[2]

A more enduring description saw the Gospels as extensions of the kerygma of the early church. Rooted in the work of Schmidt, Dibelius and Bultmann, this theory argued for the evolution of Christian tradition from scattered independent units to the Gospel framework.[3] This evolution was spurred by the expectation of an imminent parousia, by the mission of the church and by the primitive kerygma of Jesus' death and resurrection. In this view the passion story provided the groundstock from which the Gospels emerged through expansion and accretion. This process was defined in more intentional terms by C.H. Dodd.[4] Dodd separated the teaching of the church from its proclamation (kerygma), then found a common kerygma in Paul, Acts and the Gospel of Mark. For Dodd the Gospel genre emerges from Mark's explication of this common Christian kerygma. In Dodd's view Mark fills out the content of this apostolic preaching by writing 'a commentary on the kerygma'—a Gospel.[5]

With the advent and development of redaction criticism, the role of the Evangelist in this process was given increasing focus.

---

1. The Gospels are seen as apocalyptic by Perrin, Kelber and Kee. The biography category is supported by D. Lührmann, C. Votaw, C. Talbert and P. Schuler. Old Testament parallels are suggested by E. Schweizer. Aretalogy is posited by M. Smith and countered by the proponents of corrective Christology. For a coherent overview of this work, see Guelich, 'The Gospel Genre', pp. 185-204.

2. This line of research is traced in Chapter 1.

3. For a summary of this process, see R. Guelich, 'The Gospel Genre', pp. 196-201.

4. See C.H. Dodd, *The Apostolic Preaching and its Developments* (London: Hodder & Stoughton, 1936). A concise sketch of Dodd's work is found in Guelich, 'The Gospel Genre', pp. 201-204.

5. Dodd, *Apostolic Preaching*, pp. 48-49.

Consequently the Gospel of Mark has been defined in terms of Mark's literary and theological intentions. With this approach the Gospel genre is built on traditional elements, but gains its shape through authorial intent.[1] While each of these approaches draws upon some element inherent in the Gospel narratives, none of these categories or processes provides an adequate description of the form, content and function which distinguishes the Gospels as a literary genre.

The Gospel of Mark represents the first known attempt to write a Gospel, and it subsequently provided a model for the Gospel of Matthew and the Gospel of Luke (and perhaps the Gospel of John). Because of this primary position, the form, content and function of the Gospel of Mark provide definitive elements for genre description. Consequently narrative analysis makes a decisive contribution to the definition of the Gospel genre. Formally the Gospel of Mark was shown to be a unified narrative text which creates its own framework and environment. Materially the Gospel of Mark was shown to center on the characterization of Jesus as the messiah. Functionally the Gospel of Mark was shown to center in the task of proclamation. Taking these cues from the Gospel of Mark, an initial description of the Gospel genre may be set forth: a Gospel is a narrative account of Jesus' messianic life, death and resurrection shaped by and for the task of proclamation.

This delineation of the Gospel genre is drawn not from reconstructed history or from personality composites of the Evangelists, but from formal narrative structures and strategies. This description of the Gospel genre provides suggestive images about the compositional process which underlies the Gospel of Mark and the Gospel tradition.

The Composition of the Gospel Tradition

Narrative analysis unveils the strategy which guides the story of Jesus in the Gospel of Mark. This strategy provides suggestive images of the composition history which generates this text. The narrative casts a shadow and echoes with a voice suggestive of its place and process of origin. These reflected images will be gathered as cues offering guidance in the search for the Gospel tradition. These suggestive cues are

---

1. This position is amply represented from contrasting sides by T.J. Weeden, *Mark—Traditions in Conflict* (Philadelphia: Fortress Press, 1971), and by W. Lane, *The Gospel according to Mark* (NICNT; Grand Rapids: Eerdmans, 1974).

5. Conclusion

posited as a preliminary hypothesis worthy of further investigation. This hypothesis marks the beginning of an attempt to create a bridge from narrative characteristics to the historical events and processes which best account for these narrative traits.[1]

Cue 1

Undergirding the Gospel of Mark is a coherent structured account containing the primary scenes of Jesus' life, death and resurrection. The unified, interlaced form of the Gospel of Mark points to an underlying framework in which the basic elements of Jesus' story are already present in connected form. The idea of a fixed, dominant, pre-Markan passion narrative presents a tenuous hypothesis. It is more likely that passion story and Gospel story were inextricably linked from the inception of the Gospel tradition.

Cue 2

The christological content of the Gospel of Mark reflects a central preoccupation with the identity and mission of Jesus of Nazareth.[2] This preoccupation signals the need to clarify the experience with Jesus, both as a past event and as an ongoing event. Made in the presence of Jewish hearers, the claim that the messiah of Israel was crucified required clarification about the identity and work of Jesus. The presence of Roman authority likewise required explanation of claims to follow an executed peasant wrapped in messianic images. Thus, the identity and mission of Jesus posed the central question behind the Gospel tradition.

Cue 3

The functional focus of the Gospel of Mark on the kerygmatic (preaching) task points to a preoccupation with the event (but not the details) of Jesus' proclamation.[3] Behind the Gospel tradition lies a

---

1. I hope to fully develop this hypothesis and to consider its implications in a subsequent study.

2. Numerous Christologies have been presented in the history of the church with little or no substantive interest in the life and works of Jesus of Nazareth. Even Paul's concerted focus on the crucified and risen Lord draws little from the story of Jesus' ministry.

3. In comparison with Matthew and Luke, the content of Jesus' teaching is scarce in the Gospel of Mark. The question of whether the sayings document (Q) is

central concern with the larger focus of what Jesus proclaimed and with what should be proclaimed about Jesus.

Cue 4

In view of the form, content and function of the Gospel of Mark, the functional evolution of scattered traditions under fixed canons of transmission[1] provides an inadequate explanation for the formation of

known to the Gospel of Mark remains open. More typical in the Gospel of Mark is a summary focus on Jesus as one who proclaims the Kingdom of God with authority (1.14-15, 22, 28) and sends his followers to do likewise (6.7-13). Dibelius (*Tradition*, pp. 233-65) saw in the sayings tradition a different process of transmission only distantly related to Mark's pattern. He thus reversed the usual question of why Mark would omit so many sayings. Dibelius (*Tradition*, p. 260) concluded, 'The combination of the two webs of tradition was therefore not so inevitable as it appears to us to-day. The fact that Mark does not give the material which we find in the Q sections of Matthew and Luke is not at all strange. Rather the question could be asked why Mark gives any saying of Jesus in a form already in various passages arranged in little speeches.' For Dibelius, Mark includes sayings as a part of narrative patterns, not as isolated units: 'The conception is not far off that Mark included also sections of the heritage of the actual words either because they were already transformed into narratives or because he could so transform them' (*Tradition*, p. 260).

1. Two different forms of this pattern are offered by Bultmann, *History*, and by Dibelius, *Tradition*. Employing what he calls a 'constructive method', Dibelius sought to reconstruct the history of the synoptic material in view of the needs of the early Christian community. Dibelius (*Tradition*, p. 1) said of this material, 'In such cases the personal peculiarities of the composer or narrator have little significance; much greater importance attaches to the form in which the tradition is cast by practical necessities, by usage or by origin. The development goes on steadily and independently, subject all the time to certain definite rules, for no creative mind has worked upon the material and impressed it with his own personality.' Thus, Dibelius envisioned a process lacking aesthetic quality and authorial design. The guiding factors for this evolution are functional need (worship and missions) and the fixed rules of transmission. For Dibelius this process led to Mark's gathering of various materials under the theory of the Messianic Secret. Thus, Mark 'put not only the miracles but the whole activity of Jesus under the standpoint of a secret epiphany' (*Tradition*, p. 297), though Dibelius saw Matthew as the first Gospel in the strictest sense.

Rudolf Bultmann saw himself working in the opposite direction from Dibelius. Rather than moving from the needs of the community, Bultmann sought to 'proceed from the analysis of the particular elements of the tradition' (*History*, p. 5). He saw the two approaches as compatible: 'we are not opposed to each other, but rather engaged in mutually complementary and corrective work' (*History*, p. 5). Bultmann's investigation has its central concern with 'the one chief problem of

5. Conclusion

the Gospels. Isolated examples of sayings, titles, controversies, lessons and sermons do not provide an adequate groundstock or a sufficient Christology by which to explain the formation of this narrative. The 'kerygmatic' material isolated in instances such as 1 Cor. 15.3-5 and Acts 10.34-43 does not sufficiently account for the emergence of the Gospel narratives. Various interests and needs of the church provide inadequate means and processes for transforming such material into a coherent and christological narrative of Jesus' life and death. Even an extended passion story does not provide the proper framework or outlook for evolution into a Gospel. Indeed, the use of independent traditions in the life of the church and the formulation of kerygmatic creeds and sermons is best explained over against an established, structured narrative of Jesus' entire story. These independent traditions likely represent not the preconditions for the Gospels, but rather a subsequent distillation of the gospel story into functional units of creedal, paranetic and sermonic material.

Thus, evolution of separate bits of tradition through collection and expansion into a coherent Gospel narrative seems unlikely. The

---

primitive Christianity, the relationship of the primitive Palestinian and Hellenistic Christianity' (*History*, p. 5). Bultmann found this problem engrained in the New Testament material: 'I do not believe it is possible to state sufficiently sharply the contrast in the NT Canon with the Synoptic Gospels on the one hand and the Pauline letters and later literature on the other' (*History*, p. 303). Bultmann also reckoned with controlling canons of transmission: 'what we have done was essentially to recognize a certain tradition-law as going right back to the earliest possible form of the material...' (*History*, p. 321). Bultmann then described the stages in this ordered collection of material: (1) the collection of the spoken material and the composition of speeches; (2) the insertion of the speech material into the narratives; (3) the editing of the narrative material and the compositions of the Gospels. For Bultmann, Mark writes the first Gospel, and his accomplishment is significant: 'This in fact marks the purpose of the author: *the union of the Hellenistic kerygma about Christ*, whose essential content consists of the Christ myth as we learn of it in Paul (esp. Phil. 2.6ff.; Rom. 3.24) with the *tradition of the story of Jesus*' (*History*, p. 34).

Several elements are common to the descriptions offered by Dibelius and Bultmann. For both the tradition has a weight which overshadows the contribution of the individual Evangelists. For both the evolution of the tradition is motivated by specific needs of the Christian community (worship and missions for Dibelius; union of the Palestinian and Hellenistic traditions for Bultmann). For both this evolution is guided by fixed canons of transmission which guide oral and literary productions. Both agree that the Gospel of Mark provides a decisive stage in this process.

consistent use of images, the extensive interaction of elements and the intricate equilibrium of the narrative process in the Gospel of Mark suggest a more complex, more conscious origin and development for the Gospel tradition.

Cue 5

The theory which posits Mark as a creative genius who controls the formation of the Gospel tradition is more plausible, yet still problematic. The Gospel of Mark suggests extensive reworking, reinterpretation and critical interchange between various elements. The image of a single writer composing a finished Gospel is shaped by modern literary conventions and is too simplistic to account for this narrative texture and depth. More complex theories which describe multiple stages and redactors create a conflict of interest and tend to further obscure the process of development. While the theory of a singular composer accounts for the unity of the narrative—particularly the relationship of the passion story to the life of Jesus—it does not adequately account for its complexity and depth.

Cue 6

The form, content and function of the Gospel of Mark are best explained as the work of a larger community operating over a longer period of time. The Gospel tradition is most likely generated in and by a discipleship community focused on instruction and proclamation.

Cue 7

The text of this community likely existed as a stable, structured narrative account of Jesus' life, death and resurrection. Whether memory or manuscript—oral or written—the form of this text was stable, consistent and reproducible. This narrative was primarily an insider tradition—the kerygma as taught, preserved and transmitted within the framework of a self-critical community of disciples.

Cue 8

This text provided the basis for and sustained the preaching activity of the community. This external proclamation was marked by more flexible forms, more spontaneity and more wondrous demonstrations of power. It is likely that this preached kerygma was practiced by wandering proclaimers. Drawing upon the extensive insider tradition,

5. Conclusion

all or part of the kerygma might be preached. Through this preaching segments of the larger narrative might be circulated as isolated traditions or as sermonic distillations of the Gospel kerygma.

Cue 9

The enthusiastic preaching was based on the stability of the taught kerygma; this preaching in turn provided decisive influence and shaping for the ongoing development of the Gospel tradition. This continuing recirculation of the kerygma through inside instruction and external proclamation provided a process of presentation and renewal. This process maintained the Gospel in stable form while preserving its living voice. This circulation also accounts for various narrative traits: two versions of the feeding story (Mk 6.33-45; 8.1-10), other doublets, cycles of three.

Cue 10

This critical process of circulation and renewal was guided by a lectionary hermeneutic of remembrance. First, a careful reading of the Old Testament provided the framework for Jesus' work as the messenger of God, clarified various events in the life of Jesus and highlighted the prophetic quality of his life. Secondly, a careful reading (or hearing) of the taught kerygma stirred other memories and other stories. Summary statements about Jesus healing and teaching were filled out by further examples, and various stories stirred images of similar scenes. Through this careful process of reading and remembering, the story of Jesus was shaped and preserved in the teaching of his followers.

Cue 11

Because this kerygma was the message of Jesus lived in and through the community of his followers, the Gospel was not attached to any one person (such as Peter) or to any one group (such as the Twelve). Only subsequently was apostolic authority attached to the Gospel tradition. In the time of its generation and earliest circulation the kerygma was learned and proclaimed as the Gospel of Jesus, the messiah.

Cue 12

The narrative known to history as the Gospel of Mark represents one stage (not neccesarily the final one) in this process of composition and circulation. Three subsequent Gospels take up the task and circulate distinct narratives of Jesus. At least two of these begin their work with a fixed narrative kerygma (the Gospel of Mark), then recirculate this story in a new form and setting. The narratives credited to Matthew, Luke and John each bear witness that the task of instruction and proclamation is not unilateral, and it is not yet complete.

Theses

Attention to the form and function of Mark 14–16 reveals a complex narrative strategy which centers around the image of Jesus. An intricate and paradoxical portrait of Jesus is generated through a reciprocal pattern of realignment. This narrative strategy and its christological portrait offer programmatic clues to the nature and function of the Gospel of Mark and to the development of the Gospel tradition. The findings of this analysis may be focused through twelve theses.

Thesis 1

The characterization of Jesus stands at the center of the narrative strategy of Mark 14–16.

Thesis 2

Narrative analysis unveils in Mark 14–16 a multi-faceted portrait of Jesus. This portrait represents neither a monolithic passion Christology nor a dialectical synthesis of power versus passion. Instead, the characterization of Jesus in Mark 14–16 represents a paradoxical cohesion of numerous images: he is wondrous teacher and prophet, Son of God, Son of Man, Suffering Servant, righteous one, crucified messiah.

Thesis 3

This polyphonic image of Jesus is clarified and amplified through a reciprocal relationship with narrative images in Mark 1–13.

5. Conclusion

Thesis 4
The characterization of Jesus which emerges from the Gospel of Mark is polyphonic and complex, but also coherent and consistent. Central to this characterization is the intricate union of prophetic Christology and passion Christology.

Thesis 5
The pattern of extensive interaction found in christological images is true of various other narrative themes. Among these are discipleship failure, rejection by the religious authorities, temple critique, fulfillment of Scriptures, messianic secret, eschatology, Galilee, the gospel theme.

Thesis 6
This strategy of characterization provides important clues concerning the nature and purpose of the Gospel of Mark. Formally the Gospel of Mark is a unified narrative whole which generates its own interpretive world. Materially the focus of this narrative is christological. Functionally the Gospel of Mark is a kerygmatic text.

Thesis 7
The identity of the Gospel of Mark provides definitive keys for description of the Gospel genre. Seen through the structures and strategies of the Gospel of Mark, a Gospel is a coherent narrative account of Jesus' messianic life, death and resurrection shaped by and for proclamation.

Thesis 8
The images focused through narrative analysis provide suggestive clues concerning the compositional process undergirding the Gospel tradition. The entirety of the narrative reflects one complex pattern of redaction. The evolution of isolated traditions provides an inadequate explanation for this unity. The common linguistic and redactional patterns exhibited throughout the narrative speak against a fixed pre-Markan passion tradition which guides the compositional process. The complexity and depth of the narrative strategy weighs against a single redaction by a single author. The historical process which best explains the literary characteristics of this narrative is the hypothesis of a consistent shaping of the entire text by a wider community over

Thesis 9
The narrative process and product seen in the Gospel of Mark provides an exemplar of the kerygma. It is likely that the more stable teaching of the kerygma served as the base for widespread spontaneous, enthusiastic preaching of the kerygma, yet this teaching was in turn shaped by the preaching mission. Thus, the stable narrative exemplar of the kerygma likely undergirds the formation and use of didactic, creedal and sermonic forms of the kerygma in oral proclamation.

Thesis 10
The kerygmatic identity focused through narrative analysis is a literary product with historical framing. This decisive proclamation emerges from a history of faith and discipleship, and it aims to create a new history of faith and discipleship.

Thesis 11
The kerygmatic identity clarified through narrative analysis carries profound soteriological implications. In view of this analysis any valid understanding of salvation must be shaped by the full story of Jesus. Theologies, critical or popular, which reduce soteriological dimensions to a three-day passion play prove inadequate. While the death of Jesus remains central to soteriological formulations, the key to Jesus' death lies in the full story of his words and deeds.

Thesis 12
The kerygmatic identity clarified through narrative analysis provides a fundamental model for Christian proclamation. Both the content and the process of proclamation must be wholistic. Proclamation which reduces the story of Jesus to creeds or theories of atonement proves inadequate. The task of preaching the gospel demands the preaching of the Gospels—the full stories of the life, ministry and death of Jesus as God's messiah.

5. Conclusion

Concluding Thoughts

Narrative analysis makes a vital and refreshing contribution to the ongoing investigation of the Gospels. This descriptive approach provides productive means for focusing the narrative world which confronts the reader of the Gospel of Mark. This Gospel narrative creates a closed, self-referential literary environment. Within this world narrative elements and voices generate distinct points of reference and create a concerted world-view. The Gospel of Mark places before the reader this world of strategies and portraits, of persuasion and polemic. This world is not neutral, but engages the reader with seductive persuasion and powerful sanction.

The use of narrative analysis also presents various liabilities. At the end of this process the interpreter may be left with textual phenomena without historical setting or purpose. As in other approaches, zealous interpreters may read into the text their own strategies, images, concerns. Readers may create unity and coherence where none exists. The gospel message may be gnosticized into spiritual images with no relation to human reality.

Various steps have been employed to avoid these pitfalls. First, a carefully controlled strategy of analysis was developed on the basis of the underlying linguistic grammar. This analysis was applied inductively to provide a descriptive blueprint of each text. Speculation about generative bases and philosophical substructures was avoided. Secondly, narrative traits were traced through wider readings of the Gospel of Mark and through comparative analysis with other textual traditions. Thirdly, this analysis ends with an attempt to bridge the world of the narrative to the reality of writers and readers—to the world of history and hermeneutics.

The bridge which opens the Gospel of Mark to the wider world is its central kerygmatic function. This intrinsic identity provides the most certain level of historicity—the narrative is kerygma for some time, some place, some people. Building on the clues offered by the narrative, various images of this community come into focus. This kerygmatic identity likewise opens the Gospel of Mark to the world of hermeneutics. This narrative presents itself throughout as a kerygmatic word from God, about God. This demand may be accepted or rejected by the reader, but it may not be displaced. The kerygmatic demands of the Gospel of Mark provide the cues and the codes by which the narrative is to be unleashed in the world of readers.

Attention to Mark 14–16 revealed a paradoxical christological complex built upon an intricate narrative strategy and a crucial interrelationship with the larger narrative. In light of this narrative model a decisive understanding of the Gospel of Mark was focused. In view of these findings the Gospel of Mark must no longer be seen as a vehicle for or expansion of the kerygma. In contrast this narrative is the kerygma—the full story of God's work in Jesus. This kerygma provides both the soteriological foundation of Christian faith and the pattern for its proclamation. This kerygma is a literary production, yet it carries within its world the shadows and the echoes of history. This kerygmatic narrative echoes the voice of a prior history of faith and discipleship which undergirds the life of the Gospel. At the same time this kerygmatic narrative insists upon a subsequent history of faith and discipleship. Consequently narrative analysis invites the interpreter to encounter this kerygma as a text deeply rooted within the history of faith and salvation. At the same time narrative analysis invites the interpreter to re-encounter this kerygma as a living voice in the world of its hearers. This kerygma offers, both in its prior history and in its subsequent history, a new beginning—the beginning of the Gospel of Jesus the messiah.

Appendix

SAYINGS TRADITIONS IN THE PASSION NARRATIVE

1. *Mark 14.1-11: The Anointing Scene*

'Leave her alone. Why do you cause her trouble? She has worked a good work in relation to me. For always you have the poor with you and whenever you choose you are able to do good for them, but you do not always have me. She has done what she had. She has taken up beforehand to anoint my body unto burial. Amen, I say to you, wherever the gospel should be preached in all the world, also what she did shall be spoken of in remembrance of her.'

2. *Mark 14.12-26: The Passover Meal*

'Amen, I say to you that one of you will betray me—one eating with me. One of the Twelve, one dipping with me in the vessel. Because the Son of Man indeed goes up even as it stands written concerning him, but woe to that person through whom the Son of Man is betrayed. It is better for him if that person had not been born.'

'Take, this is my body. This is my blood of the covenant which is poured out in behalf of the many. Amen, I say to you that I will in no way drink of the fruit of the vine until that day when I shall drink it new in the Kingdom of God.'

3. *Mark 14.26-32a: The Prophecy of Betrayal*

'All will be scandalized, because it stands written: "I will strike the shepherd and the sheep will be scattered." But after I am raised, I will go before you into Galilee.'

'Amen, I say to you that today, in this night, before the second cockcrow, you will deny me three times.'

4. *Mark 14.32-42 Gethsemane*

'My soul is troubled unto death. Remain here and watch.'

'Abba, Father, all things are possible to you. Take this cup from me. But not what I wish but what you (wish).'

'Simon, are you sleeping? Are you not able one hour to watch? Watch and pray so that you might not enter into temptation. The spirit is indeed willing, but the flesh is weak.'

'Sleep on and take your rest. It is enough. The hour has come. Behold the Son of Man is betrayed into the hands of sinners. Arise, let us go. Behold the one betraying me is near.'

5. Mark 14.43-53a: Betrayal, Arrest, Abandonment

'As upon a thief you have come out with swords and staves to arrest me. Daily I was with you in the temple teaching and you did not seize me. But in order that the Scriptures should be fulfilled—'

6. Mark 14.53-65: The First Trial

'I am, and you shall see the Son of Man seated at the right hand of power and coming with the clouds of heaven.'

7. Mark 14.66-72: The Trial of Peter

(Peter): 'I neither know nor understand what you are saying.'
(Peter): 'I do not know this person about whom you speak.'
(Peter remembers the words of Jesus): 'Before the rooster crows twice, you will deny me three times.'

8. Mark 15.1-15: The Trial Before Pilate

Silence

9. Mark 15.16-20: The Scene of Mockery

Exception

10. Mark 15.20c-37: The Death Scene

'Eloi, eloi, lema sabachthani.' (My God, my God, why have you forsaken me?)
The loud cry (15.37).

11. Mark 15.38-47: Signs of Hope

Exception

12. Mark 16.1-8: The Resurrection Promise

(Messenger): 'Fear not. You are seeking Jesus the Nazarene, the Crucified One. He has been raised. He is not here. Behold the place where they laid him. But go up, say to his disciples and to Peter that he is going before you into Galilee. There you will see him, even as he said to you.'

BIBLIOGRAPHY

Aarne, A., and S. Thompson, *The Types of the Folk-tale: Annti Aarne's Verzeichnis der Märchentypen Translated and Enlarged* (Folklore Fellows Communications, 74; Helsinki, 1928 [1910]).
Abrams, M.H., *A Glossary of Literary Terms* (New York: Harcourt Brace Jovanovich, 6th edn, 1993).
Achtemeier, P.J. *Invitation to Mark* (Garden City, NY: Image Books, 1978).
—*Mark* (Proclamation Commentaries; Philadelphia: Fortress Press, 1975).
—'The Origin and Function of the Pre-Marcan Miracle Catenae', *JBL* 91 (1972), pp. 198-221.
Aland, K., 'Bermerkungen zum Schluss des Markusevangeliums', in E. Ellis and M. Wilcox (eds.), *Neotestamentica et Semitica* (Festschrift M. Black; Edinburgh: T. & T. Clark, 1969).
Alsup, J., *The Post-Resurrection Appearance Stories of the Gospel-Tradition: A History of Analysis with Text-Synopsis* (Stuttgart: Calwer Verlag, 1975).
Aristotle's Poetics (trans. L. Golden; commentary by O.B. Hardison, Jr; Englewood Cliffs, NJ: Prentice-Hall, 1968).
Aristotle, *De Poetica* (trans. I. Bywater), in *Introduction to Aristotle* (ed. R. McKeon; New York: The Modern Library, 1947).
Auerbach, E., *Mimesis: The Representation of Reality in Western Literature* (trans. W. Trask; Princeton, NJ: Princeton University Press, 1953 [1946]).
Avigad, N., 'A Discovery of Inscribed Ossuaries in the Kidron Valley', *IEJ* 12 (1962), pp. 1-12.
Barthes, R., *S/Z* (trans. R. Howard; New York: Hill & Wang, 1974).
Bauer, W., W. Arndt, and F. Gingrich, *A Greek–English Lexicon of the New Testament and other Early Christian Literature* (ed. F. Gingrich and F. Danker; Chicago: University of Chicago Press, 2nd rev. edn, 1979).
Beardslee, W., *Literary Criticism of the New Testament* (Philadelphia: Fortress Press, 1970).
Belo, F., *A Materialist Reading of the Gospel of Mark* (Markyknoll, NY: Orbis Books, 1981).
Best, E., *The Temptation and the Passion: The Markan Soteriology* (Cambridge: Cambridge University Press, 1965).
Betz, O., 'The Concept of the so-called "Divine Man" in Mark's Christology', in *Studies in the New Testament and Early Christian Literature* (Festschrift A.P. Wikgren; NTSup, 33; Leiden: Brill, 1972).
Bieler, L., ΘΕΙΟΣ ΑΝΗΡ: *Das Bild des 'göttlichen Menschen' in Spätantike und Frühchristentum* (Darmstadt: Wissenschaftliche Buchgesellschaft, 1967).

Bird, C.H., 'Some γάρ clauses in St Mark's Gospel', *JTS*, NS 4 (1953), pp. 121-87.
Black, C., *The Disciples according to Mark: Markan Redaction in Current Debate* (Sheffield: JSOT Press, 1989).
Blanche, R., *Structures intellectuelles* (Paris: Vrin, 2nd edn, 1969).
Blinzler, J., *The Trial of Jesus* (trans. I. McHugh and F. McHugh; Westminster, MD: Newman, 1959).
Boff, L., *Jesus Christ Liberator: A Critical Christology for our Times* (Maryknoll, NY: Orbis Books, 1978).
Boobyer, G., 'Galilee and Galileans in St Mark's Gospel', *BJRL* 35 (1953), pp. 334-48.
Bornkamm, G., *Jesus of Nazareth* (trans. I. McLusky and F. McLusky; London: Hodder & Stoughton, 1960 [1956]).
Branscomb, H., *The Gospel of Mark* (London: Hodder & Stoughton, 1937).
Broadhead, E.K., 'Mark 14.1-9: A Gospel within a Gospel', *Paradigms* 1/1 (1985), pp. 32-41.
—*Teaching with Authority: Miracles and Christology in the Gospel of Mark* (Sheffield: JSOT Press, 1992).
—'Which Mountain is "This Mountain"?: A Critical Note on Mark 11.22-25', *Paradigms* 2 (1986), pp. 33-38.
Büchsel, F., 'κεῖμαι', *TDNT*, III, p. 655.
Bultmann, R., *The History of the Synoptic Tradition* (trans. J. Marsh; Oxford: Basil Blackwell, 1963 [1921]).
—*Theology of the New Testament* (trans. K. Grobel; New York: Charles Scribners' Sons, 1951 [1948]).
Burkhill, T.A., *Mysterious Revelation* (Ithaca, NY: Cornell University Press, 1963).
Carrington, P., *According to Mark* (Cambridge: Cambridge University Press, 1960).
Chatman, S., *Story and Discourse* (Ithaca, NY: Cornell University Press, 1978).
Chomsky, N., *Aspects of the Theory of Syntax* (Cambridge, MA: The MIT Press, 1965).
—*Syntactic Structures* (The Hague: Mouton, 1957).
Clevenot, M., *Materialist Approaches to the Bible* (Maryknoll, NY: Orbis Books, 1985).
Conzelmann, H., 'Historie und Theologie in den synoptischen Passionsberichten', in F. Viering (ed.), *Zur Bedeutung des Todes Jesu: Exegetische Beiträge* (Gütersloh: Gerd Mohn, 2nd edn, 1967).
Cranfield, C.E.B., *The Gospel according to St Mark* (Cambridge: Cambridge University Press, 1959).
Croatto, S., *Exodus: A Hermeneutics of Freedom* (Maryknoll, NY: Orbis Books, 1981).
Crossan, J.D., 'Empty Tomb and Absent Lord', in Kelber (ed), *The Passion in Mark*, pp. 135-52.
Culler, J., *Structuralist Poetics* (Ithaca, NY: Cornell University Press, 1975).
Culpepper, A., *Anatomy of the Fourth Gospel* (Philadelphia: Fortress Press, 1983).
—'Mark 10.50: Why Mention the Garment?', *JBL* 101 (1982), pp. 131-32.
—'The Passion and the Resurrection in Mark', *RevExp* 75/4 (1978), pp. 583-600.
Dabrowski, E., 'The Trial of Jesus in Recent Research', *SE* 4/1 (1968), pp. 21-27.
Dewey, K., 'Peter's Curse and Cursed Peter', in Kelber (ed.), *The Passion in Mark*, pp. 96-114.
Dibelius, M., *From Tradition to Gospel* (trans. B. Woolf; New York: Charles Scribners' Sons, 1966 [1919]).

Dijk, T. van, 'On the Foundation of Poetics: Methodological Prolegomena to a Generative Grammar of Texts', *Poetics* 5 (1972), p. 90.

Dodd, C.H., *The Apostolic Preaching and its Developments* (London: Hodder & Stoughton, 1936).

Donahue, J., 'Temple, Trial, and Royal Christology', in Kelber (ed.), *The Passion in Mark*, pp. 61-79.

Dormeyer, D., *Die Passion Jesu als Verhaltensmodell: Literarische und theologische Analyse der Traditions- und Redaktionsgeschichte der Markuspassion* (Münster: Aschendorff, 1974).

Doudna, J.C., *The Greek of the Gospel of Mark* (JBLMS, 12; Philadelphia: Society of Biblical Literature, 1961).

Dschulnigg, P., *Sprache, Redaktion und Intention des Markus-Evangeliums: Eigentümlichkeiten der Sprache des Markus-Evangeliums und ihre Bedeutung für die Redaktionskritik* (SBB; Stuttgart: Katholisches Bibelwerk, 1986).

Dundes, A., 'From Etic to Emic Units in the Structural Study of Folktales', *Journal of American Folklore* 75 (1962), pp. 95-99.

Eagleton, T., *Literary Theory* (Minneapolis: University of Minnesota Press, 1983).

Evans, C.F., 'I will go before you into Galilee', *JTS* 5 (1954), pp. 3-18.

Frege, G., 'On Sense and Reference', in *Translations from the Philosophical Writings of Gottlob Frege* (trans. M. Black; ed. P. Geach and M. Black; Oxford: Basil Blackwell, 1970).

Frye, N., *Anatomy of Criticism* (Princeton, NJ: Princeton University Press, 1957).

Gadamer, H.-G., *Truth and Method* (trans. and ed. G. Barden and J. Cumming; London: Sheed & Ward, 1975 [1960]).

Genette, G., *Narrative Discourse: An Essay in Method* (trans. J. Lewin; Ithaca, NY: Cornell University Press, 1980).

Georgi, D., *The Opponents of Paul in Second Corinthians* (Philadelphia: Fortress Press, 1986 [1964]).

Gnilka, J., *Das Evangelium nach Markus* (EKKNT; Zürich: Benziger Verlag, 1978).

Gould, E., *The Gospel according to St Mark* (New York: Charles Scribners' Sons, 1896).

Grant, F.C., *Interpreter's Bible* (New York: Abingdon Press, 1951), VII.

Grundmann, W., *Das Evangelium nach Markus* (Berlin: Evangelische Verlagsanstalt, 1959).

Guelich, R., 'The Gospel Genre', in *Das Evangelium und die Evangelien* (ed. P. Stuhlmacher; Tübingen: Mohr, 1983).

Gunkel, H., *Einleitung in die Psalmen: Die Gattungen der religiösen Lyrick Israels* (Göttingen: Vandenhoeck & Ruprecht, 1933).

Gutierrez, G., *A Theology of Liberation* (Markyknoll, NY: Orbis Books, 1973).

Güttgemanns, E., *Candid Questions concerning Gospel Form Criticism: A Methodological Sketch of the Fundamental Problematics of Form and Redaction Criticism* (trans. W. Doty; Pittsburgh: Pickwick Press, 1979 [1970]).

—'Linguistische Analyse von Mk 16:1-8', *Linguistica Biblica Heft* 11/12 (1972), pp. 13-53.

Haas, N., 'Anthropological Observations on the Skeletal Remains from Giv' at ha-Mivtar', *IEJ* 20 (1970), pp. 38-59.

Haenchen, E., *Der Weg Jesu: Eine Erklärung des Markus-Evangeliums und der kanonischen Parallelen* (Berlin: Töpelmann, 1966).

Hahn, F., *The Titles of Jesus in Christology: Their History in early Christianity* (London: Lutterworth Press, 1969 [1963]).
Hanse, H., 'ἔχω', *TDNT*, II, p. 828.
Hauck, F., 'βάλλω', *TDNT*, I, pp. 528-29.
Hawkins, J.C., *Horae Synopticae: Contributions to the Study of the Synoptic Problem* (Oxford: Clarendon Press, 1899).
Hengel, M., *Nachfolge und Charisma: Eine exegetisch-religionsgeschichtliche Studie zu Mt 8:21f. und Jesu Ruf in die Nachfolge* (Berlin: Töpelmann, 1968).
—*Studies in the Gospel of Mark* (trans. J. Bowden; London: SCM Press, 1985).
—*The Zealots: Investigations into the Jewish Freedom Movement in the Period from Herod I until 70 AD* (trans. D. Smith; Edinburgh: T. & T. Clark, 1989 [1961]).
—'Zwischen Jesus und Paulus', *ZTK* 72 (1975), pp. 183-86.
Hermann, A., 'Farbe', *RAC*, VII, p. 414.
Hirsch, E.D., *The Aims of Interpretation* (Chicago: University of Chicago Press, 1976).
—*Validity in Interpretation* (New Haven: Yale University Press, 1967).
Hjelmslev, L., *Prolegomena to a Theory of Language* (trans. F. Whitfield; Madison: The University of Wisconsin Press, 1961).
Jeremias, J., *Die Abendmahlsworte Jesu* (Göttingen: Vandenhoeck & Ruprecht, 4th edn, 1967).
—'Die Salbungsgeschichte Mc 14,3-9', *ZNW* 35 (1936), pp. 77-81.
—'Mc 14,9', *ZNW* 44 (1952/53), pp. 103-107.
—'πάσχα', *TDNT*, V, pp. 896-904.
Kähler, M., *The So-Called Historical Jesus and the Historic, Biblical Christ* (trans. and ed. C.E. Braaten; Philadelphia: Fortress Press, 1964 [1892]).
Karnetzki, M., 'Die galiläaische Redaktion im Markusevangelium', *ZNW* 52 (1961), pp. 238-72.
Keck, L., 'Mark 3.7-12 and Mark's Christology', *JBL* 84 (1965), pp. 341-48.
Kee, H.C., *Community of the New Age: Studies in Mark's Gospel* (Philadelphia: Westminster Press, 1977).
Kelber, W., 'From Passion Narrative to Gospel', in Kelber (ed.), *The Passion in Mark*, pp. 156-57.
—'Mark 14.32-42: Gethsemane', *ZNW* 63 (1972), pp. 166-87.
—*Mark's Story of Jesus* (Philadelphia: Fortress Press, 1979).
—'Markus und die mündliche Tradition', *LB* 45 (1979), pp. 5-58.
—'The Hour of the Son of Man and the Temptation of the Disciples', in Kelber (ed.), *The Passion in Mark*, pp. 41-60.
—*The Kingdom in Mark: A New Place and a New Time* (Philadelphia: Fortress Press, 1974).
—*The Oral and the Written Gospel: The Hermeneutics of Speaking and Writing in the Synoptic Tradition, Mark, Paul, and Q* (Philadelphia: Fortress Press, 1983).
Kelber, W. (ed.), *The Passion in Mark: Studies on Mark 14–16* (Philadelphia: Fortress Press, 1976).
Kermode, F., *The Genesis of Secrecy* (Cambridge, MA: Harvard University Press, 1979).
Kertelge, K., *Die Wunder Jesu im Markusevangelium: Eine redaktionsgeschichtliche Untersuchung* (SANT; Munich: Kösel, 1970).
Kingsbury, J.D., *Conflict in Mark: Jesus, Authorities, Disciples* (Minneapolis: Fortress Press, 1989).
—*The Christology of Mark's Gospel* (Philadelphia: Fortress Press, 1983).

Klostermann, A., *Das Markus-Evangelium nach seines Quellenwert für die evangelische Geschichte* (Göttingen, 1867).

Knox, W.L., 'The Ending of St Mark's Gospel', *HTR* 35 (1942), pp. 13-23.

Koch, D.-A., *Die Bedeutung der Wundererzählungen für die Christologie des Markusevangeliums* (Berlin: de Gruyter, 1975).

Koester, H., 'One Jesus and Four Primitive Gospels', in *Trajectories through Early Christianity* (with J.M. Robinson; Philadelphia: Fortress Press, 1971).

Kremer, J., *Die Osterevangelien—Geschichten um Geschichte* (Stuttgart: Katholisches Bibelwerk, 1977).

Kuhn, H.G., 'Jesus in Gethsemane', *EvT* 12 (1952/53), pp. 260-85.

Lagrange, M.-J., *Evangile selon Saint Marc* (Paris: Gabalda, 1974).

Lai, Pham hu'u, 'Production du sens par la foi: Autorités religieuses contestées/ fondées. Analysis structurale de Matthieu 27,57–28,20', *RSR* 61 (1973), pp. 85, 87-89.

Lane, W., *The Gospel according to Mark: The English Text with Introduction, Exposition and Notes* (NICNT; Grand Rapids: Eerdmans, 1974).

Lehmann, K., *Auferweckt am dritten Tag nach der Schrift: Früheste Christologie, Bekenntnisbildung und Schriftauslegung im Lichte von 1 Kor. 15,3-5* (Freiburg: Herder, 1968).

Lentricchia, F., *After the New Criticism* (Chicago: University of Chicago Press, 1980).

Lepschy, G., *A Survey of Structural Linguistics* (London: Andre Deutsch, 1982).

Lévi-Strauss, C., *The Raw and the Cooked* (New York: Harper & Row, 1969).

Lightfoot, R.H., *Locality and Doctrine* (London: Hodder & Stoughton, 1938).

Linnemann, E., *Studien zur Passionsgeschichte* (Göttingen: Vandenhoeck & Ruprecht, 1970).

Lohmeyer, E., *Das Evangelium nach Markus* (Göttingen: Vandenhoeck & Ruprecht, 10th edn, 1937).

—*Galiläa und Jerusalem* (Göttingen: Vandenhoeck & Ruprecht, 1936).

Lohse, E., *History of the Suffering and Death of Jesus Christ* (trans. M. Dietrich; Philadelphia: Fortress Press, 1967 [1964]).

—'συνέδριον', *TDNT*, VII, pp. 867-68.

Luz, U., 'Das Geheimnismotiv und die markinische Christologie', *ZNW* 56 (1965), pp. 9-30.

—'Das Jesusbild der vormk Tradition', in G. Strecker (ed.), *Jesus Christus in Historie und Theologie* (Festschrift H. Conzelmann; Tübingen: Mohr, 1975).

—'Markusforschung in der Sackgasse?', *TLZ* 105 (1980), pp. 641-45.

—'Theologia crucis als Mitte der Theologie im NT', *EvT* 34 (1974), pp. 131-39.

Mack, B., *A Myth of Innocence: Mark and Christian Origins* (Philadelphia: Fortress Press, 1988).

McKnight, E., *Meaning in Texts: The Historical Shaping of a Narrative Hermeneutics* (Philadelphia: Fortress Press, 1978).

Marin, L., *Semiotik der Passionsgeschichte: Die Zeichensprache der Ortsangaben und Personennamen* (trans. S. Virgils; Munich: Chr. Kaiser Verlag, 1976).

Martitz, W. von, 'υἱός', *TDNT*, VIII, pp. 334-40.

Marxsen, W., *Introduction to the New Testament: An Approach to its Problems* (trans. G. Buswell; Philadelphia: Fortress Press, 1968 [1963]).

—*Mark the Evangelist: Studies on the Redaction History of the Gospel* (trans. J. Boyce, D. Juel and W. Poehlmann; Nashville: Abingdon Press, 1969 [1956]).

Merkel, H., 'Peter's Curse', in *The Trial of Jesus: Cambridge Studies in Honour of C.F.D. Moule* (ed. E. Bammel; London: SCM Press, 1970).
Mohr, T.A., *Markus- und Johannespassion: Redaktions- und traditionsgeschichtliche Untersuchung der Markinischen und Johanneischen Passionstradition* (ATANT; Zürich: Theologischer Verlag, 1982).
Montefiore, C.G., *The Synoptic Gospels* (London: MacMillan, 1927).
Mowinckel, S., *The Psalms in Israel's Worship* (trans. D. Ap-Thomas; Nashville: Abingdon Press, 1962).
Neirynck, F., *Duality in Mark: Contributions to the Study of the Markan Redaction* (ETL, 31; Leuven: Leuven University Press, 1972).
Nineham, D.E., *The Gospel of St Mark* (Baltimore: Penguin Books, 1963).
Paul, H., *Principles of the History of the Language* (trans. H. Strong; New York: MacMillan, 1889).
Perrin, N., *A Modern Pilgrimage in New Testament Christology* (Philadelphia: Fortress Press, 1974).
—'The High Priest's Question and Jesus' Answer', in Kelber (ed.), *The Passion in Mark*, pp. 80-95.
—'The Literary Gattung 'Gospel'—Some Observations', *ExpT* 82 (1970), pp. 4-7.
—'Towards an Interpretation of the Gospel of Mark', in *Christology and a Modern Pilgrimage: A Discussion with Norman Perrin* (ed. H.D. Betz; Missoula, MT: Scholars Press, rev. edn, 1974).
Pesch, R., *Das Markusevangelium* (HTKNT; Freiburg: Herder, 2nd edn, 1980).
—*Der Prozess Jesu geht weiter* (Freiburg: Herder, 1988).
Petersen, N., *Literary Criticism for New Testament Critics* (Philadelphia: Fortress Press, 1974).
—'The Composition of Mark 4.1–8.26', *HTR* 73 (1980), pp. 192-93.
Priebe, D., 'The Woman Who Anoints Jesus: Mark 14.3-9' (unpublished paper presented to the Society of Biblical Literature, November, 1989).
Propp, V., *Morphology of the Folktale* (ed. L. Wagner; Austin: University of Texas Press, 2nd edn, 1968 [1928]).
Pryke, E.J., *Redactional Style in the Marcan Gospel: A Study of Syntax and Vocabulary as Guides to Redaction in Mark* (Cambridge: Cambridge University Press, 1978).
Rawlinson, A., *St Mark* (London: Methuen, 1925).
Reynolds, L., 'Materialist Reading as a Hermeneutical Approach to Christian Proclamation' (unpublished Th.M. thesis, The Southern Baptist Theological Seminary, 1988).
Rhoads, D., and D. Michie, *Mark as Story: An Introduction to the Narrative of a Gospel* (Philadelphia: Fortress Press, 1982).
Ricoeur, P. *Interpretation Theory: Discourse and the Surplus of Meaning* (Fort Worth: Texas Christian University, 1976).
—'Structure, Word, Event', *Philosophy Today* 12 (1968), pp. 114-29.
Robbins, V., 'Last Meal: Preparation, Betrayal, and Absence', in Kelber (ed.), *The Passion in Mark*, pp. 21-40.
Robertson, A.T., *A Grammar of the Greek New Testament in the Light of Historical Research* (Nashville: Broadman Press, 4th edn, 1923).
Russell, B., *An Inquiry into Meaning and Truth* (London: George Allen & Unwin, 1940).

Saussure, F. de, *Course in General Linguistics* (ed. C. Bally and A. Sechehaye in collaboration with A. Reidlinger; trans. W. Baskin; New York: Philosophical Library, 1959 [1916]).
Schenk, W., *Der Passionsbericht nach Markus: Untersuchung zur Überlieferungsgeschichte der Passionstraditionen* (Gütersloh: Gerd Mohn, 1974).
Schenke, L., *Auferstehungsverkündigung und leeres Grab: Eine traditionsgeschichtliche Untersuchung von Mk 16,1-8* (Stuttgart: Katholisches Bibelwerk, 1968).
—*Der gekreuzigte Christus: Versuch einer literarkritischen und traditionsgeschichtlichen Bestimmung der vormarkinischen Passionsgeschichte* (Stuttgart: KBW, 1974).
—*Die Wundererzählungen des Markusevangeliums* (SBB; Stuttgart: Katholisches Bibelwerk, 1974).
—*Studien zur Passionsgeschichte des Markus: Tradition und Redaktion in Markus 14:1-42* (Würzburg: Echter Verlag, 1971).
Schille, G., 'Das Leiden des Herrn', *ZTK* 52 (1955), pp. 161-205.
—*Die urchristliche Wundertradition: Ein Beitrag zur Frage nach dem irdischen Jesus* (Stuttgart: Calwer Verlag, 1967).
Schmidt, K.L., *Der Rahmen der Geschichte Jesu: Literarkritische Untersuchungen zur ältesten Jesusüberlieferung* (Darmstadt: Wissenschaftliche Buchgesellschaft, 1964 [1919]).
Schmithals, W., *Das Evangelium nach Markus* (OTNT; Gütersloh: Gerd Mohn, 1979).
Schnackenburg, R., *The Gospel according to St Mark* (trans. W. Kruppe; New York: Crossroad, 1981).
Schneider, G., *Die Passion Jesu nach den drei älteren Evangelien* (Munich: Kösel, 1973).
—'Gab es eine vorsynoptische Szene "Jesus vor dem Sanhedrium"?', *NovT* 12 (1970), 22-39.
—'Jesus vor dem Sanhedrium', *BL* 11 (1970), pp. 1-15.
Schreiber, J., *Der Kreuzigungsbericht des Markusevangeliums Mk 15,20b-41: Eine traditionsgeschichtliche und methodenkritische Untersuchung nach William Wrede (1859–1906)* (Berlin: de Gruyter, 1986).
—'Die Christologie des Markusevangeliums', *ZTK* 58 (1961), pp. 158-59.
—*Die Markuspassion: Wege zur Erforschung der Leidensgeschichte Jesu* (Hamburg: Furche Verlag, 1969).
—*Theologie des Vertrauens: Eine redaktionsgeschichtliche Untersuchung des Markusevangeliums* (Hamburg: Furche Verlag, 1967).
Schulz, S., *Die Stunde der Botschaft: Einführung in die Theologie der vier Evangelisten* (Hamburg: Furche-Verlag, 1967).
Schüssler Fiorenza, E., *In Memory of her: A Feminist Reconstruction of Christian Origins* (New York: Crossroad, 1983).
Schweitzer, A., *The Quest of the Historical Jesus: A Critical Study of its Progress from Reimarus to Wrede* (London: A. & C. Black, 1948 [1906]).
Schweizer, E., 'Die theologische Leistung des Markus', *EvT* 24 (1964), p. 340.
—'Neuere Markus-Forschung in USA', *EvT* 33 (1973), pp. 533-37.
—*Neues Testament und Christologie im Werden* (Göttingen: Vandenhoeck & Ruprecht, 1982).
—*The Good News according to Mark* (trans. D. Madvig; Atlanta: John Knox, 1970).
—'υἱός', *TDNT*, VIII, pp. 363-92.

Scroggs, R., and K. Groff, 'Baptism in Mark: Dying and Rising with Christ', *JBL* 92 (1973), pp. 531-48.
Segundo, J., *The Liberation of Theology* (Maryknoll, NY: Orbis Books, 1976).
Sobrino, J., *Christology at the Crossroads* (Maryknoll, NY: Orbis Books, 1980).
Stagg, E., and F. Stagg, *Woman in the World of Jesus* (Philadelphia: Westminster Press, 1978).
Stählin, G., 'σκάνδαλον', TDNT, VII, pp. 339-58.
Steck, O.H., *Israel und das gewaltsame Geschick der Propheten: Untersuchungen zur Überlieferung des deuteronomistischen Geschichtsbildes im Alten Testament, Spätjudentum und Urchristentum* (WMANT; Neukirchen–Vluyn: Neukirchener Verlag, 1967).
Sternberg, M., *Expositional Modes and Temporal Ordering in Fiction* (Baltimore: The Johns Hopkins University Press, 1978).
Strack, H., and P. Billerbeck, *Kommentar zum Neuen Testament aus Talmud und Midrasch* (Munich: Beck, 1928).
Suhl, A., *Die Funktion der alttestamentlichen Zitate und Anspielungen im Markusevangelium* (Gütersloh: Gerd Mohn, 1965).
Tannehill, R., 'The Disciples in Mark: The Function of a Narrative Role', *JR* 57 (1977), pp. 398-400.
Taylor, V., *The Formation of the Gospel Tradition* (London: MacMillan, 1933).
—*The Gospel according to Mark* (London: MacMillan, 1953).
Theissen, G., *The Miracle Stories of the Early Christian Tradition* (trans. F. McDonagh; Philadelphia: Fortress Press, 1983 [1974]).
Tolbert, M.A., *Sowing the Gospel: Mark's World in Literary-Historical Perspective* (Minneapolis: Fortress Press, 1989).
Trocmé, E., *The Formation of the Gospel according to Mark* (trans. P. Gaughan; London: SPCK, 1975 [1963]).
Turner, C.H., 'Marcan Usage: Notes, Critical and Exegetical, on the Second Gospel', *JTS* 25–29 (1923–28).
Vanhoye, A., 'La fuite du jeune homme nu (Mc 14,1-52)', *Bib* 52 (1971), pp. 401-406.
Vielhauer, P., 'Erwägungen zur Christologie des Markusevangeliums', in *Aufsätze zum Neuen Testament* (TBü, 31, 65, Munich: Chr. Kaiser Verlag, 1965–79), pp. 199-214.
Weder, H., *Neutestamentliche Hermeneutik* (Zürich: Theologischer Verlag, 1986).
Weeden, T.J., *Mark—Traditions in Conflict* (Philadelphia: Fortress Press, 1971).
—'The Cross as Power in Weakness', in Kelber (ed.), *The Passion in Mark*, pp. 115-34.
—'The Heresy that Necessitated Mark's Gospel', *ZNW* 59 (1968), pp. 145-58.
Weiss, B., *Das Markusevangelium* (Berlin: Hertz, 1872).
Wendling, E., *Die Entstehung des Marcus-Evangeliums* (Tübingen: Mohr [Paul Siebeck], 1908).
Wink, W., *The Bible in Human Transformation* (Philadelphia: Fortress Press, 1973).
Winter, P., 'Mark 14,53b.55-64 ein Gebilde des Evangelisten', *ZNW* 53 (1962), pp. 260-63.
—'The Trial of Jesus and the Competence of the Sanhedrin', *NTS* 10 (1963–64), pp. 494-99.
Wrede, W., *The Messianic Secret* (trans. J.C.G. Greig; Cambridge: James Clark, 1971 [1901]).

Wright, G.A., 'Markan Intercalations: A Study in the Plot of a Gospel' (unpublished PhD dissertation, The Southern Baptist Theological Seminary, 1985).

Zerwick, M. *Untersuchungen zum Markus-Stil: Ein Beitrag zur stilistischen Durcharbeitung des Neuen Testaments* (SPIB; Rome: Pontifical Biblical Institute, 1937).

INDEXES

INDEX OF REFERENCES

OLD TESTAMENT

Genesis		1 Samuel		22.1	199, 200,
22.5	97	9.9	52		203, 204
27.26-27	114	10.1-10	52, 53	22.7	200, 204
40.19	116	10.1	37	22.18	200, 204
				22.19	200
Exodus		2 Samuel		23	64
3.5-6	137	15.5	114	23.5	37
3.13-14	137	20.9-10	114	27	134
16.2-3	119	20.9	114	31	134
18.13-27	135			31.18-24	183
19.3	97	1 Kings		34	134
19.25	97	13.11-32	136	35	134
24.9-11	58	17.8-16	52, 53	37.14	117
33.11-23	97	18.15-16	37	38	134
		18.17-40	136	38.11	169
Leviticus		19.4	92, 98	38.12	169
13–14	40	19.9-10	97	38.13	169
24.14	202	19.10	119	39	134
24.16	136	19.14	97, 119	39.9	183
		22.13-38	136	40	134
Numbers				41	134
12.1-8	119	2 Kings		41.10	55
15.35-36	202	1.1-17	52, 53	42	134, 271
27.17	82	9.6	37	42.5	92
35.30	134	17.15	53	42.6	92
		17.19-20	53	42.11	92
Deuteronomy		17.23	53	43	134, 271
1.12-18	135	18.37	136	43.5	92
13.1-5	136	19.1	136	54	134
16.18-20	135			55	134
18.15-22	136	Esther		69	134
19.15	134	5.14	116	69.21	199, 200,
21.23	116				203-205
		Psalms		70.4	183
Joshua		17.15	234	71	134
10.26	116	22	134, 202,	71.11	117
10.27	116		203	86	134

Index of References

88	134	55.1	64	2.31	196
109	134	61	42	3.15	196
109.15	183	65.13	64		
109.25	200, 204			*Amos*	
110.1	131, 136	*Jeremiah*		2.16	115, 119
118	134	2.8-9	136	8.9-10	196, 200
133.2	37	5.12-13	136	8.9	196
141.5	37	5.30-31	136		
143.8	234	6.13-14	136	*Obadiah*	
		7.1-15	119	1.5	116
Proverbs		7.11	122		
7.13	114	8.10-11	136	*Jonah*	
27.6	114	14.13-16	136	4.1-11	97
		15.15-18	97	4.9	92, 98
Isaiah		23.9-40	136		
13.10	196	26.8-9	119	*Micah*	
24.23	196	26.8	117, 119	2.6-11	136
25.6	64	27–28	136	3.5-8	136
42.1-4	190, 193	27.8-22	136	3.11	136
42.2	190	28.1-17	136	16.6	280
49.1-6	190, 193	37.13-15	117		
49.4	190			*Zechariah*	
50	134	*Lamentations*		13.7	76, 78, 84,
50.4-11	190, 193	3.22-24	234		117, 119
50.6	183, 190			13.8-9	76, 78
52.13–		*Ezekiel*			
53.12	190, 193	22.9	116	*Malachi*	
52.14	190			3.1	117, 119
52.15	169	*Daniel*		4.5	200, 208,
53	57, 134, 169	7.13	97, 131, 136		209
53.3-4	190	11.40	97		
53.3	190	11.45	97	*Wisdom of Solomon*	
53.4-6	169			2.18	200
53.4-5	190	*Hosea*			
53.5-6	169	4.4-6	136	*Sirach*	
53.7-9	170	6.1-2	234	29.5	114
53.7	131, 190	7.1	116		
53.8	169, 190			*Baruch*	
53.9	190	*Joel*		29.8	64
53.12	119, 190,	2.2	196		
	200	2.10	196		

NEW TESTAMENT

Matthew		5.34	34	6.10	106
5–15	53	5.39	34	6.16	96
5–7	85	5.44	34	7.21	106
5.22	34	6.2	96	8.11-12	64
5.26	34	6.5	96	10.1	53
5.28	34	6.9-13	106	14.24	96
5.32	34	6.9	91, 106	14.28	78

14.66-72	159	26.75	159			272, 276,
15.1-15	174	27.1-26	174			279, 283,
15.8	96	27.3-10	174			284
17.20	92	27.11	174	1.2-3		76, 81, 277
20.2	37	27.14	174	1.2		52
20.22	92	27.15	174	1.3		52
20.23	92	27.17	174	1.4-8		244
22.1-14	64	27.19	174	1.4		52, 239
24.36-50	92	27.21	174	1.5		244
25.1-13	64	27.22	174	1.6		52, 244
25.31-46	45	27.24-25	174	1.7-8		244
26.1-16	45, 46	27.25	174	1.7		244
26.1-5	45	27.27-31	192	1.9-13		37, 100, 105
26.2	45	27.29	192	1.9-11		277
26.8	31, 45	27.31-50	213	1.9		82, 241, 280
26.13	45	27.40	213	1.10-11		243, 244
26.14-16	46	27.43	213	1.10		209, 223
26.17-30	68, 69	27.46	213	1.11		100, 141,
26.17-25	69	27.51-61	229			223, 226,
26.17-20	69, 72	27.51-53	229			241, 244,
26.20	69	27.54	229			272, 276,
26.22	69	27.57	229			279
26.23	69	27.61	229	1.12-13		100, 141,
26.25	69	27.62-66	229			245
26.27	92	28.1-8	247	1.12		209
26.28	69	28.2-7	250	1.13		236, 245
26.29	58, 69, 106	28.2	235, 238,	1.14-16		284
26.30-36	85		247	1.14-15		25, 41, 42,
26.35	159	28.4	247			58, 81, 96,
26.36-46	106	28.8-20	79			224, 227,
26.39	106	28.8	247			245, 288
26.42	106	28.9-20	247	1.14		42, 172, 244
26.44	106	28.9-10	247	1.15		25, 42, 96,
26.47-57	125	28.11-15	248			243
26.50	125, 147	28.16-20	237, 248	1.16–8.30		39
26.52-54	125			1.16-20		26, 41, 80,
26.52	125	*Mark*				155, 156,
26.53-54	125	1–13	15, 45, 62,			220, 227,
26.55-56	125		63, 66, 68,			245
26.56	125		80, 81, 85,			
26.57-68	143, 144		99, 100,	1.17		243
26.57	144		105, 207,	1.19		243
26.60-62	144		272, 274,	1.21-39		274
26.63	144		275, 277,	1.22		81, 123,
26.64	144		279, 292			141, 173,
26.68	144	1.1-20	265	1.23-39		209, 288
26.69-75	158, 159	1.1-15	39, 244, 245	1.23-39		81
26.69	158	1.1-3	56	1.23-26		221
26.71	158	1.1-2	121, 244	1.24-25		140
26.72	158	1.1	25, 41, 42,	1.24		140, 141,
26.73	158		81, 141,			226, 241,
26.74-75	159		142, 146,	1.25		280, 283
						242

Index of References

1.26	172	3.13-19	80, 100,	5.21-37	283
1.27	283		156, 220	5.21-31	93
1.28	288	3.13-14	284	5.21-24	41
1.29-31	221, 227	3.13	100	5.25-34	40, 41, 221,
1.31	40, 222	3.14	148		227
1.34	140, 226,	3.16	245	5.29	222
	242, 276	3.17	91	5.30-32	80, 121, 155
1.37	31	3.19	172	5.31	99
1.39	40, 82, 284	3.21	227	5.33	234
1.40-45	41	3.22	31, 40, 45,	5.34	56
1.40-42	40		81, 226, 274	5.35-43	41, 93
1.44-45	242	3.23-28	33	5.35	114, 276,
1.44	140, 242	3.26	277		283
2.1-12	221	3.31-34	227	5.38-47	264
2.5	238	3.31	221	5.38	92
2.6-7	40, 45, 81,	3.32	31	5.40	53, 93
	226, 265,	3.34-35	40	5.41	91
	274	3.38	34	5.42	234
2.6	31	3.41	33	5.43	40
2.7	274	4.3-20	83	6	64
2.10	65, 276, 279	4.11-12	140	6.3	74, 218, 221
2.14-17	40	4.11	80	6.4	119, 233,
2.14	41	4.12	121, 277		276
2.15-17	41	4.13	80, 99, 121,	6.5	234
2.15	40, 53		154	6.6	40, 171
2.16	40, 45, 81,	4.16	83	6.7-31	150
	226, 274	4.17	74, 83	6.7-30	166
2.18-22	40, 58	4.26-29	66	6.7-13	156, 284,
2.18-20	41	4.29	172		288
2.20	58, 279	4.30-32	66	6.8-11	53
2.22	58	4.32	277	6.11	34
2.23-28	40, 150	4.35-41	156, 157	6.15	277
2.24	40, 45, 81,	4.38	114, 221,	6.17	221
	226, 274		276, 283	6.19	221
2.28	276	4.40-41	80, 99, 121,	6.22	221
3.1-7	274		155	6.26	53
3.1-6	33, 42, 221	4.40	227	6.27-28	224
3.2-6	40, 81, 226,	4.41	234, 283	6.29	41, 227
	274	4.60	153	6.30-44	272
3.2	45, 171	5.1-20	40	6.30	156
3.4	33	5.1-15	263	6.31	32
3.6	33, 45, 81,	5.1	234	6.32-46	64, 65, 110
	99, 121,	5.5	167, 172	6.33-45	291
	134, 140,	5.6	163	6.34	64, 65, 82,
	163, 168,	5.7	141, 172,		83, 272, 277
	171-73, 265		226, 272,	6.35-44	156, 157
3.10	40		276, 279,	6.35-37	80, 121, 155
3.11-18	81		283	6.36	99
3.11-12	140	5.17	184	6.39	64
3.11	141, 172,	5.18	148	6.42	64
	226, 272,	5.19-20	242	6.45-52	156, 157
	276, 279	5.20	41, 171, 284	6.49-52	80, 121, 155

6.50	137, 227	8.32	99, 155,	9.31	54-56, 62,
7.1-5	40, 45, 81,		157, 207		63, 82, 99,
	226, 274	8.33	101, 245		100, 121,
7.1	31	8.34	168, 207,		140, 141,
7.5	31		208, 227,		156, 172,
7.6-7	121, 277		245		189, 207,
7.6	31, 96	8.35	41, 42		220, 241,
7.11	91	8.38	155, 276,		266, 272,
7.13	172		279		275-77,
7.14-16	40	9	104, 105,		279, 283
7.24-30	41, 221, 227		244	9.32	99, 157
7.32	40	9.1	34, 62, 63,	9.33-41	207
7.34	91		66, 243	9.33-37	80, 121
7.35	242	9.2-14	274	9.34	99
7.36-37	242	9.2-13	104, 110	9.38-41	81, 121, 155
7.36	41, 140	9.2-10	101, 155	9.38	114, 276
8.1-10	64, 65, 110,	9.2-9	243	9.41	34, 276
	156, 157,	9.2-8	93, 277	9.42-48	74
	272, 291	9.2	93, 101	9.42	74
8.1-9	40	9.4	208	9.43	74
8.4	80, 99, 121,	9.5-6	141, 154	9.45	74
	155	9.5	101, 114,	9.47	74
8.11	31, 40, 45,		276	9.48	277
	81, 226, 274	9.6	80, 99, 101,	10.1	40
8.12	13, 31, 34		121, 155	10.2	40, 45, 81,
8.14-21	156, 157	9.7	101, 141,		226, 274
8.18	121, 277		226, 243,	10.5-9	277
8.22	40, 92		272, 276,	10.15	34
8.26	140		279	10.17	114, 221,
8.27-38	42, 140	9.8	242		276
8.27-30	80, 121,	9.9-10	80, 121, 155	10.19-20	277
	155, 207	9.9	101, 140,	10.20	114, 276
8.28	208, 221,		242, 276,	10.21	41
	277		279	10.23-27	81, 121, 155
8.29	155, 276	9.10	99	10.24	99
8.30	140, 242	9.11-13	80, 121,	10.26	221
8.31–10.52	39		155, 277	10.28	155
8.31–9.1	243	9.11	92, 208, 221	10.29-30	34
8.31-33	80, 81, 121,	9.12	56, 100,	10.29	34, 41, 42
	155, 206		101, 141,	10.32-45	81, 99
8.31-32	99		209, 276,	10.32-42	155
8.31	62, 63, 82,		279	10.32-34	62, 63, 82,
	99, 100,	9.13	34, 209		99, 100,
	113, 119,	9.14-28	80, 121, 155		121, 140,
	121, 140,	9.14	31		141, 156,
	141, 156,	9.16	31		189, 207,
	189, 220,	9.17	114, 276		241, 266,
		9.18	99, 101		272, 275,
	241, 266,	9.24	172		277, 279,
	272, 275-	9.26	172		283
	77, 279, 283	9.30-32	80, 121, 155	10.32	81, 99, 121,
8.32-33	154	9.31-32	81, 99		155, 239

Index of References

10.33-34	100		140, 156,	12.18	123, 221,
10.33	54, 55, 56,		163, 172,		226
	172, 189,		173, 226,	12.19	114
	276		274, 275	12.26-27	277
10.34	183, 189,	11.19	121	12.27-40	117
	193, 220,	11.20-26	156	12.28-34	41
	241	11.20-25	102	12.28	31, 123, 221
10.35-45	81, 121, 155	11.21	114, 154,	12.29-34	277
10.35-41	207		156, 276,	12.32	114, 276
10.35-40	100, 208		283	12.34	123
10.35-37	99, 157	11.22-27	275	12.35-37	123, 277,
10.35	100, 114,	11.22-26	92		283
	276	11.22-25	58	12.35	123, 276
10.37	279	11.23	34	12.36	121
10.38	92, 100	11.25	91	12.37	276
10.39	92, 100, 208	11.27–		12.40-44	227
10.43-45	227	12.44	123	12.41-44	41, 221
10.45	57, 155,	11.27-28	40, 45, 81,	12.43	34
	169, 189,		121, 140,	13	101-105,
	207, 269,		226, 274		109, 141,
	275, 276,	11.27	31, 92, 113,		155, 226,
	278, 279		123, 156,		243, 272
10.46-52	40, 41, 241		221	13.1-37	62, 104
10.46	92, 166	11.28	122, 123,	13.1-3	82
10.47	172, 276		226	13.1-2	156
10.48	172, 276,	11.32	31	13.1	102, 114,
	283	11.36	123		221, 276
10.50-52	155	12.1-12	119, 122-	13.2	63, 102,
10.51	114, 276		24, 141,		103, 222,
11	122		178, 189,		225
11.1–16.8	82		207, 210,	13.3-37	82
11.1–13.37	39		226	13.3	82, 101, 102
11.1-6	51, 52, 62	12.1	122	13.5	103, 227
11.1	52, 82	12.6	123, 272,	13.6	63
11.9-10	121, 168,		276, 279	13.8	63
	277	12.8	189, 193	13.9-11	102
11.11	121, 156,	12.9	123	13.9	101, 103,
	226	12.10-11	121, 277		155, 172,
11.12-27	275	12.12-13	121, 140		227
11.12-14	102, 156	12.12	31, 40, 81,	13.10	42, 63, 102,
11.14	156		122, 134,		284
11.15-19	121-24,		163, 172,	13.11	102, 103,
	156, 178		173, 189,		172
11.15-18	121		226, 274	13.12	102, 103,
11.15-16	275	12.13-17	40, 81, 226,		172
11.15	92		274	13.13	63, 102,
11.17	121, 122,	12.13-14	45, 124, 178		103, 155
	222, 225,	12.13	123, 173,	13.14-20	115
	275, 277		221, 226	13.14	103, 227,
11.18	31, 40, 45,	12.14	114, 124,		277
	81, 121,		276	13.16	102
	122, 134,			13.18	102

13.19-20	63		36, 38, 40,	14.13-16	268
13.22	63, 102		45, 60, 61,	14.13-15	50, 51, 59,
13.23	104		81, 99, 120,		60, 272
13.24-25	63, 102, 277		121, 134,	14.13	52, 54, 56
13.24	196		140, 274	14.14	52-54, 60,
13.26-27	100	14.1	30-32, 44,		65, 114,
13.26	56, 63, 65,		63, 80, 114,		268, 272,
	66, 102,		133, 163		276
	110, 276,	14.2	32, 59, 172	14.16	51, 52, 54,
	279	14.3-9	30-33, 35,		57, 59
13.27	63		38, 44, 45,	14.17-26	51
13.28	102		269	14.17-21	51-57, 275
13.30	34	14.3	32, 37, 42,	14.17-18	53
13.32	56, 91, 102-		45, 118	14.17	32, 50, 54,
	104, 272,		32		55, 57, 121
	276, 279	14.4-9	29, 31, 32,	14.18-21	269, 271,
13.33-37	227	14.4-5	40, 44		272
13.33	103, 155	14.4	45	14.18-20	99
13.34	102, 103,	14.5	38	14.18	34, 50, 54-
	196	14.6-9	29, 37, 272		56, 60, 61,
13.35	95, 102, 103	14.6-8	37, 268		63, 80, 99,
13.36	102, 103,	14.6	33, 44		119, 172,
	155	14.7-8	33, 42		262, 266,
13.37	34, 95, 102,	14.7	33, 41, 44,		268, 269
	103, 155		188	14.19	50, 51, 55,
14–16	11, 15, 23,	14.8-9	32, 44, 275		56, 75, 93
	27, 28, 45,	14.8	33, 38, 138,	14.20-21	50, 59, 80
	63, 80, 205,		225, 266,	14.20	54-56, 60,
	207, 226,		268, 269,		61, 63, 99,
	235, 258,		271		102, 120
	259, 261,	14.9	33, 34, 38,	14.21-26	269
	262, 264,		42, 43, 102,	14.21-23	284
	266-69,		240, 268,	14.21	54-56, 66,
	271, 272,		284		80, 99, 100,
	275, 276,	14.10-11	30-33, 35,		119, 120,
	282, 292,		36, 38, 40,		139, 141,
	296		44, 60, 61,		172, 268,
14	52, 57		80, 99, 121,		270, 271,
14.1–16.8	275		140, 155,		276
14.1-52	138, 139		274	14.22-26	51, 52, 54,
14.1-42	29, 109-	14.10	32, 36, 102,		57, 58
	112, 120,		120, 172	14.22-25	67, 99, 188,
	177, 180,	14.11	31, 36, 38,		207, 268,
	255, 257		120, 172		269, 271,
14.1-11	29, 33, 36,	14.12-26	29, 50-54,		272, 278,
	38, 39, 40-		57-68, 70-		283
	50, 59, 109,		73, 103,	14.22-24	271
	110, 138,		109, 205,	14.22	50, 54, 57,
	221, 225,		206, 262,		59, 225, 262
	227, 235,		266, 275	14.23-24	80, 99
	240, 266	14.12	51, 54, 57,	14.23	50, 51, 58,
14.1-2	29-32, 35,		59, 133		61, 75, 92

Index of References

14.24	50, 57-60, 79, 206, 262		120, 154, 155, 261, 263	14.38-40 14.38	88 88, 89, 93, 94, 95, 102, 103, 225, 262
14.25	34, 50, 58, 60, 61, 188, 206, 262, 269	14.32-42	29, 88-96, 98-104, 106-108, 110, 121,	14.39	88, 89, 98, 226
14.26-32	73, 74, 76, 77, 79-85, 87, 89, 98, 109, 263		141, 149, 154-57, 262, 265, 270, 283	14.40-42 14.40	90, 105 88, 89, 93, 95, 100-103, 106, 227
14.26-31	84, 85, 154	14.32-41	104		
14.26	50, 58, 69, 73, 74, 77, 82, 91, 101, 102	14.32-38 14.32	88 53, 73, 74, 77, 88-90, 92, 94, 95, 97, 98, 105	14.41-44 14.41-42 14.41	33 90, 96, 100, 268 55, 56, 88-90, 93, 95-103, 138, 139, 141, 172, 188, 205, 268-71
14.27-31	121, 125, 155, 158, 161, 272, 275	14.33-38 14.33-37	88 155		
14.27-28	73, 76-78, 99, 117, 263	14.33-34 14.33	90, 105 88, 93, 94, 100, 101, 261	14.42–16.8 14.42	224 55, 80, 88, 93, 96, 102, 103, 119, 172
14.27	58, 61, 74-76, 78, 83, 84, 86, 93, 98, 99, 117, 119-21, 188, 240, 266, 268-72, 277, 283	14.34-36 14.34	100 88, 90, 92-95, 97, 98, 99, 102, 103, 121, 225, 227, 266, 277	14.43– 15.15	177, 179, 180, 255, 257
14.28	74, 76-78, 80, 82, 84, 87, 99, 139, 235, 238, 239, 240, 244, 266, 268, 269	14.35-36 14.35	88, 89, 92, 94, 95, 97, 106, 262 88-90, 92, 95, 96, 102, 103, 105, 188, 205	14.43-53 14.43-52 14.43-47 14.43-46 14.43	112, 113, 117, 118, 120-28, 177 32 113-19 61, 114, 268 31, 32, 102, 112, 116, 118-24
14.29-31	76, 80, 83, 84, 154	14.36-38 14.36	90, 105 89-92, 99, 100, 101, 104, 268, 270, 271		
14.29	73-76, 84, 86, 98, 120, 154, 155, 261, 263			14.44-46 14.44-45 14.44	124 80, 266 55, 112, 114, 119, 120, 125, 172
14.30-31	75	14.37-42 14.37-41 14.37-38 14.37	61 93, 94 154, 227 88, 89, 95, 96, 100-103, 147, 225, 245, 262		
14.30	34, 73, 86, 93, 98, 99, 102, 148, 149, 263, 266, 268, 269, 271			14.45	112, 121, 122, 155, 268, 272, 276
14.31-32	78			14.46	112, 120, 147
14.31	58, 61, 73, 74, 75, 98,	14.38-47	278	14.47	112, 118,

	124, 227	14.55-65	148, 150, 153		182, 262, 265, 279
14.48-49	113, 116-19	14.55-59	163, 182	14.63	31, 128, 130-33, 153, 272
14.48	113, 116, 117, 121, 122, 124, 138, 172, 205	14.55-56 14.55	129, 132 31, 128-34, 163, 171, 182, 262	14.64	129-34, 163, 182, 183, 205, 274
14.49	113, 117, 120-22, 124, 268-72	14.56-59 14.56	133, 262 128, 130, 132, 133, 153	14.65-68 14.65	147 12-34, 136, 163, 171, 182, 183, 186, 189, 190, 193, 262, 269
14.50-53	113-16, 118, 119	14.57-61	133		
14.50-52	61, 63, 80, 117, 118, 120, 121, 124, 154	14.57-59 14.57 14.58	128, 129, 132, 153 130, 132 122, 130, 132, 133, 136, 225		
14.50	58, 61, 75, 80, 113, 114, 155, 266, 268	14.59 14.60-62	134 129, 130, 131, 272	14.66-72	61, 80, 112, 130, 131, 146, 147, 149, 150, 153-56, 157-61, 166, 167, 170, 178, 263, 265, 268
14.51-52	113-15, 118, 236	14.60-61	130, 132, 134, 163, 165, 182		
14.53-15.37	120				
14.53-72	159				
14.53-65	102, 112, 128, 129, 131-35, 137-39, 142, 143, 145, 146, 153, 163, 165, 166, 170, 182, 187, 189, 265, 269, 270, 283	14.60 14.61-62 14.61	31, 128, 130-32, 163, 182, 262 130, 135, 142, 225, 226, 268, 276 31, 128, 131-34, 137, 153, 163, 268, 276, 278	14.66-70 14.66-68 14.66-67 14.66 14.67 14.68	266 147 148, 153 146, 147, 153, 156 146, 148, 153, 241, 280 102, 146-49, 153-55
14.53-59	129, 131			14.69	146, 153
14.53-56	40, 130	14.62	56, 61, 66, 128, 130-33, 135-42, 146, 153, 163, 165, 180, 262, 263, 266, 268-72, 276, 277, 283	14.70-72	147
14.53-54	129, 147			14.70	146, 149, 153, 154
14.53	113-16, 119, 120, 128-33, 148, 150, 153, 163, 168, 182			14.71 14.72	146, 153, 154, 156, 171 102, 146, 147, 149, 153, 155, 156, 263
14.54-55	149				
14.54	61, 128, 130, 131, 133, 146-49, 153, 154, 261	14.63-65 14.63-64	129, 131, 132 130, 133, 137, 139, 156, 163,	15.1-20 15.1-15	102, 154, 198 112, 130, 132, 156, 161, 162,

	165, 166, 168-73, 176, 178, 182-84, 205, 225, 269, 270, 283	15.13-14 15.13	168 162, 163, 168, 172, 182	15.21-39 15.21-32 15.21-24 15.21 15.22	156 198 195, 198 41, 194, 197 91, 194-96, 199, 200, 202, 204
15.1	40, 81, 114, 132-34, 162, 163, 165, 167, 171, 172, 182, 187	15.14-15 15.14 15.15	171 134, 162, 163, 166, 168, 172, 182 134, 162-64, 167, 168, 171, 172, 182-87, 191, 193, 225	15.23 15.24-25 15.24	198, 200, 203, 205 225 194-96, 198, 200, 203-205, 212, 266, 277
15.2-5	165				
15.2-4	130				
15.2-3	134	15.16-16.8	177, 181, 254, 255, 256, 257	15.25-34	198
15.2	162-65, 167, 170, 175, 182, 183, 188, 205	15.25-32	198
15.16-39	198	15.25	194, 196-98, 202, 212
15.16-32	198
15.16-20	181, 183-93, 198, 205, 225, 254, 256, 262, 264, 266, 269, 270, 283	15.26	195, 197, 205, 212, 263, 278
15.3-5	162
15.3	162-65, 171, 182, 187	15.27	194-96, 200, 204, 205, 208, 211, 212, 221
15.4-5	167
15.4	162-64, 171, 182, 188	15.16 15.17-20 15.17-19 15.17 15.18 15.19 15.20-37	181, 184 184 205 181 181, 264 181, 182, 188, 189 170, 181, 194, 195, 199, 201, 204, 205, 207, 209-11, 213, 214, 216, 256, 263, 265, 266, 269, 270, 278	15.29-32 15.29-30 15.29	276 194, 195, 198, 263 122, 204, 205, 212, 225, 266
15.5	134, 162-64, 263, 266
15.6-14	164
15.6-7	162
15.7	163, 166	15.30 15.31-32 15.31 15.32	198 194, 198, 263 31, 198 194, 198, 200, 205, 212, 263, 276
15.8-14	167
15.8	162
15.9-14	182
15.9	162, 167, 170, 183, 188, 205
15.10	162, 163, 166, 170, 172, 182	15.33-39 15.33-34 15.33	198 198 194, 196-98, 200, 202, 209, 212, 263, 266, 276, 277
15.11-39	198
15.11	31, 40, 81, 162, 163, 165, 171, 182, 187, 265	15.20-26 15.20-24 15.20-22 15.20	204 195, 211 195, 196, 202, 212 182, 184, 189, 194, 199, 202
15.12	162, 167, 170, 183, 188, 205	15.34-37 15.34	195, 276 91, 194, 196-200,

	202, 204,		233, 235-	7.36-50	46, 47
	212, 268		37, 240,	7.36-40	38
15.35-38	198		242-46,	7.40	46
15.35-36	199		248, 251,	7.41-42	46
15.35	194		253-56,	7.43	46
15.36	194, 198,		263, 265,	7.44-47	46
	200, 204		266	7.48	46
15.37	194-200,	16.1-7	277	7.49	46
	202, 204,	16.1-6	235	7.50	46
	209, 211,	16.1-2	233	8.1-3	47
	212, 263	16.1	218, 221,	9.1-6	53
15.38-47	181, 217,		234	11.2	91, 107
	219, 220,	16.2	234	12.40	92
	224, 225,	16.3	233, 234,	15	47
	227-31,		238	15.8	96
	255, 256,	16.4	233, 234,	15.20	96
	262, 264,		238, 239,	17.6	92
	265		276	22.7-39	69, 70, 72
15.38	212, 217,	16.5-7	244, 245	22.7-23	70
	223, 225,	16.5	233, 244,	22.7-16	69
	276		276	22.8	69
15.39	41, 195,	16.6-7	233, 242-	22.15-16	69
	198, 217,		44, 247	22.17-18	70
	221, 223,	16.6	14, 31, 168,	22.17	92
	270-72,		238-41,	22.19	70
	276, 278,		244, 245,	22.20	70, 92
	283		270, 276,	22.24-38	70
15.40–16.8	224		280	22.24-27	70
15.40-41	217-19, 227	16.7	61, 80, 82,	22.27	53
15.40	217-19,		84, 101,	22.28-30	70
	221, 222,		139, 155,	22.29	70
	227		234, 237,	22.30	70
15.41	41, 218,		239, 240,	22.31-34	70, 85, 86
	221, 222		242-45,	22.31-32	85
15.42-47	221, 224,		261, 266,	22.31	85
	228, 246		268, 276,	22.32	85, 86
15.42-46	41, 217		284	22.33	85
15.42	217, 219	16.8	61, 80, 232-	22.34	85
15.43-45	225		34	22.35-38	70
15.43	217, 219,	16.9-20	232, 251	22.37	97
	227	16.9-14	232	22.39-46	106, 107
15.44	171, 217,	16.15-20	232	22.39	85, 107
	219-21, 228	17–21	57	22.40-46	85
15.45	41, 217,	24.8	57	22.40	106, 107
	219-21, 228			22.42	92, 107
15.46	217, 266	*Luke*		22.43-44	107
15.47	217, 218,	4.16-20	37	22.45	106, 107
	220, 221,	6.24	97	22.46	107
	227-29	6.27	34	22.47-54	125, 126
16.1-8	39, 41, 49,	7.6	96	22.48	125
	63, 181,	7.34-35	47	22.49	126
	227, 232,	7.34	46	22.50	126

Index of References

319

22.51	126	24.10-11	248	16.32	86	
22.52-53	126	24.12-53	248	17.1	92, 107	
22.52	126	24.12	248	18.1	86, 91	
22.53	126	24.13	96	18.2-12	126, 127	
22.54-71	144	24.19-27	268	18.2-11	86	
22.54-62	159	24.36-49	249	18.3	126	
22.55-63	144	24.50-52	249	18.4	126	
22.57	159			18.5	126	
22.58	159	*John*		18.6	126	
22.60	159	1.9-11	145	18.7	126, 175	
22.61	144, 159	2.4	107	18.8	126	
22.63-65	144	7.30	107	18.9	126	
22.66	144	8.20	107	18.10	126	
22.68	144	11.1-44	48	18.11	92, 126, 160	
22.69	144	11.5	48	18.12	126	
22.70	144, 159	11.21	48	18.13-24	144, 145	
22.71	144	11.25-26	48	18.13-14	176	
23.1-25	174, 175	11.27	48	18.13	144	
23.2	174	11.28	48	18.14	144	
23.4	174	11.32	48	18.15-27	130	
23.5	174	11.39	48	18.15-18	150, 159,	
23.6-12	174	11.49-53	47		160	
23.11	192	11.55	47	18.15-16	144	
23.14	174	11.56	47	18.15	160	
23.15	174	11.57	47	18.17-18	144	
23.20	174	12.1-8	47, 48	18.19-24	160	
23.22	174	12.2	53	18.19	145	
23.27-31	213	12.4-5	31	18.20-21	145	
23.32	213	12.7	48	18.20	127	
23.33	213	12.8	48	18.22	145	
23.34	213	12.9-11	47	18.23	145	
23.35	214	12.23	107	18.25-27	150, 159,	
23.39-43	214	12.27-28	107		160	
23.45	196, 214, 229	12.27	92, 107	18.25	160	
		13.1-31	70-72	18.26	160	
23.46	214	13.1	71, 107	18.27	160	
23.47-56	229	13.9	152	18.28–		
23.47	224, 226, 229, 272, 279	13.14	71	19.17	175, 176	
		13.22-25	71	18.28	175	
		13.31	71	18.29-32	175	
23.48	229	13.36-38	86	18.31-32	175	
23.49	229	13.37	86	18.33	175	
23.50-53	231	13.38	86, 160	18.34-37	175	
23.51	230	14.30	151, 152	18.36	175	
23.56	230	14.53-65	151	18.37-38	175	
24.1-11	248	14.67-68	151	18.38	175	
24.2	238	14.68	152	18.39	175	
24.3	248	14.69-70	151	18.40	116, 175	
24.4	248	14.70-72	151	19.1-16	192	
24.6-7	248	14.70	151, 152	19.1-3	192	
24.6	79	14.71	152	19.3	192	
24.8	248	14.72	151, 152	19.4	175, 192	

19.6	175, 192	2.32	252	10.16	92
19.7	175	2.33	252	10.21	92
19.10	175	2.36	252	11	72
19.11	192	2.38	252	11.17-22	71
19.12	176, 192	3.13-15	252	11.20	71
19.14	192, 196, 214	3.13	252	11.23-26	62, 71
		3.15	252	11.23	71
19.15	176, 192	3.18	252	11.24-25	71
19.16	176	3.19	252	11.24	71
19.17-30	214, 215	3.21	252	11.26	71, 72
19.17	160	3.22	252, 268	11.27-33	71
19.21	214	3.24-25	252	11.27	72
19.23-24	214	3.26	252	11.32	72
19.24	214	4.3	147	13.2	92
19.25-27	214	4.8-12	267	15.3-7	239, 268
19.28	214	4.10-11	252	15.3-5	11, 196, 232, 237, 243, 247, 252, 253, 289
19.30	214	4.10	252		
19.31-42	230	4.12	252		
19.31-37	230	5.18	147		
19.31	230	5.30	116		
19.34	230	6.9	199, 212	15.3	169
19.35	230	7.37	268	15.4	253
19.36-37	230	7.58	202		
19.38-42	230	10.34-43	267, 289	*Galatians*	
19.41	230	10.38	252	3.13	116
19.42	230	10.39	116, 252	4.6	91
20.1-2	249	10.40-42	252	6.14	267
20.1	238	10.40	252		
20.3-10	249	10.42-43	252	*Ephesians*	
20.11-29	79	10.42	252	1.3-14	268
20.11-17	249	13.16-41	267		
20.12	235	13.17-23	252	*Philippians*	
20.18	249	13.23	252	2.5-11	267
20.19-23	249	13.26	252	2.6	289
20.24-29	249	13.27-38	252	4.8	97
20.28	249	13.29	116, 252		
20.30-31	249	13.30	252	*Colossians*	
21.1-25	237	13.31	252	1.13-23	268
21.1-23	79, 250	13.33-37	252		
21.15-19	86	13.38-39	252	*1 Thessalonians*	
21.20-23	86	17.22-31	267	1.9-10	252
21.24-25	250	26.22-23	267	4.3	96
				4.13-18	267
Acts		*Romans*		5.22	96
2.14-36	267	1.1-6	267		
2.16-22	252	1.4	252	*1 Timothy*	
2.22	252	3.24	289	4.3	96
2.23	252	8.15	91		
2.25-28	252	10.9-13	252	*2 Timothy*	
2.29-31	252			1.8-10	268
2.29	252	*1 Corinthians*			
2.31	252	7.35	147		

Titus		*1 Peter*		*Revelation*	
2.11-14	268	1.3-5	268	1.4-7	268
		2.11	96	5.1-14	268
Philemon		2.24	116	6.12-14	196
15	97			6.15-17	115
		1 John			
		1.5-10	268		
Hebrews		5.6	268		
10.1-25	268				
13.11-13	202				

EARLY CHRISTIAN WRITINGS

Acts of Pilate		*Gospel of Peter*		9.34	230, 231
3.2	176	2.3-5	230	9.35–11.49	250
4.4-5	176	2.5–3.9	193	12.50–	
9.4-5	176	3.9	145	13.57	250
10.1-2	215	4.10-14	215	15.58-59	250
10.1	193	4.10	215	15.59-60	79
11.1	215	4.13	215		
11.3	231	5.14	215	*Gospel of Thomas*	
12.1-2	231	5.15-19	215	71	145
13.1	250	5.15	215		
13.2-3	250	5.17	215	*Gospel of the Nazareans*	
14.1	250	5.18	215	frag. 34	193
15.6	250	5.19	215		
16.5	250	5.20	230	Justin, *Apology*	
		6.21-24	230	1.31.6	152
Didache		7.25-27	230	1.66.3	72
9.1-5	72	7.25	230		
		7.26-27	230	Origen, *Contra Celsum*	
Gospel of the Ebionites		8.28-33	230	2.55	239
7	72	8.28	230		

OTHER ANCIENT WRITINGS

1 Enoch		7.5	133	Josephus, *War*	
62.10	115	11.2	133	2.254	116
62.14	64				
		Pirke Abot		Pliny, *Epistles*	
m. Sanhedrin		3.20	64	10.96.3	152
4.1	133				

INDEX OF AUTHORS

Achtemeier, P.J. 13, 14, 67
Aland, K. 232
Alsup, J. 232, 237, 238, 251, 253
Arndt, W. 97, 114, 147
Auerbach, E. 150

Barthes, R. 17
Bauer, W. 97, 114, 147
Belo, F. 26
Billerbeck, P. 52
Bird, C.H., 93
Blinzler, J., 133, 134
Boff, L., 26
Boobyer, G. 79, 237
Bornkamm, G. 12
Branscomb, H. 115
Bremond, C. 17
Broadhead, E.K. 15-17, 64, 81, 82, 91, 173, 275, 283
Bultmann, R. 12, 33, 35, 44, 51, 54, 67, 90, 91, 104, 116, 124, 132, 143, 157, 158, 173, 183, 185, 191, 195, 211, 220, 223, 228, 247, 253, 261, 285, 288, 289
Burkhill, T.A. 156
Büchsel, F. 53

Carrington, P. 115
Chatman, S. 17, 23
Chomsky, N. 16, 17
Clevenot, M. 26
Conzelmann, H. 12
Cranfield, C.E.B. 115
Croatto, S. 26
Crossan, J.D. 79, 238, 253
Culpepper, A. 17, 23, 60, 196, 198, 236, 237

Dabrowski, E. 129
Dewey, K. 147-49, 159
Dibelius, M. 12, 35, 43, 44, 67, 84, 105, 132, 133, 158, 186, 212, 213, 247, 261, 285, 288, 289
Dodd, C.H. 253, 285
Donahue, J. 132-34
Dormeyer, D. 14, 45, 55, 67, 132, 143, 149, 156, 162, 173, 185
Doudna, J.C. 14
Dschulnigg, P. 14

Evans, C.F. 79

Frege, G. 20

Gadamer, H.-G. 20
Genette, G. 17, 23, 60
Gingrich, F. 97, 114, 147
Gnilka, J. 30, 31, 37, 38, 52, 67, 76, 84, 85, 93, 96, 97, 106, 116, 124, 129, 132, 143, 149, 150, 152, 163, 164, 166, 168, 173, 174, 183, 185, 188, 191, 192, 195-98, 202, 204, 211, 220, 222-24, 228, 234, 235, 237, 239, 241, 246, 247, 253
Gould, E. 115
Grant, F.C. 115
Greimas, A. 17
Groff, K. 115, 236
Grundmann, W. 104
Guelich, R. 282, 285
Gutierrez, G. 26
Güttgemanns, E. 17, 234, 282

Haas, N. 204
Haenchen, E. 67, 115
Hahn, F. 132, 162

Index of Authors

Hanse, H. 97
Hauck, F. 147
Hawkins, J.C. 14, 92
Hengel, M. 116, 152, 197, 239
Hermann, A. 183
Hirsch, E.D. 20
Hjelmslev, L. 16

Jakobson, R. 16
Jeremias, J. 30, 33, 34, 54

Kähler, M. 12, 13, 111, 179, 257, 273, 274, 277, 281
Karnetzki, M. 237
Keck, L. 13
Kee, H.C. 14, 285
Kelber, W. 13, 66, 79, 84, 89, 91, 93, 100, 106, 242, 273, 281, 282, 285
Kermode, F. 233, 236, 238
Kertelge, K. 13
Kingsbury, J.D. 13, 238
Klostermann, A. 132
Knox, W.L. 232
Koch, D.-A. 13
Kremer, J. 235
Kuhn, H.G. 89, 90, 94, 105

Lane, W. 134, 233, 238, 252, 286
Lehmann, K. 234
Lightfoot, R.H. 233, 237
Linnemann, E. 14, 90, 118, 124, 132, 143, 198, 212
Lohmeyer, E. 90, 91, 105, 114, 115, 164, 237
Lohse, E. 33, 67, 133, 134
Loisy, A. 147
Luz, U. 13, 140
Lührmann, D. 285
Lévi-Strauss, C. 16

Mack, B. 13, 14
Malbon, E. 17
Marin, L. 17, 234
Marxsen, W. 12, 76, 79, 84, 237
Merkel, H. 152
Michie, D. 156
Mohr, T.A. 68
Montefiore, C.G. 115

Neirynck, F. 14, 156
Nineham, D.E. 156

Patte, D. 17
Peirce, C. 17
Perrin, N. 13, 66, 79, 133, 135, 139, 142, 285
Pesch, R. 13, 30, 40, 45, 51-57, 68, 74, 79, 85, 90, 91, 93, 105, 114, 116, 124, 130, 134, 139, 143, 147, 149, 156, 158, 163, 164, 166, 183-85, 188, 190, 191, 195, 202, 204, 211, 213, 218, 220, 223-25, 227, 229, 234, 235, 237, 238, 240, 241, 246, 247, 253, 261
Petersen, N. 17, 156
Priebe, D. 41
Propp, V. 16
Pryke, E.J. 14

Rawlinson, A. 115
Reynolds, L. 26
Rhoads, D. 156
Ricoeur, P. 20
Robbins, V. 65
Robertson, A.T. 90
Russell, B. 20

Saussure, F. de 16, 17, 20
Schenk, W. 14, 67, 76, 90, 94, 106, 132, 143, 149, 198, 199, 212, 226
Schenke, L. 14, 54, 57, 64, 65, 67, 90, 96, 105, 132, 143, 185, 190, 192, 229, 235, 237, 247
Schmidt, K.L. 12, 30, 43, 285
Schnackenburg, R. 164
Schneider, G. 132
Schreiber, J. 13, 14, 64, 147, 195, 198, 199, 212, 226
Schulz, S. 132, 253
Schüssler Fiorenza, E. 222
Schweitzer, A. 64, 65
Schweizer, E. 13, 33, 40, 42, 44, 51, 53, 58, 64, 67, 76, 84, 90, 93, 96, 106, 113-18, 124, 129, 133, 163, 164, 165, 168, 171, 183, 190, 192, 195, 197, 199, 203, 204, 206, 208, 212, 213, 220, 221-25, 228, 232, 236, 283, 285
Scroggs, R. 115, 236
Segundo, J. 26
Smith, M. 285
Sobrino, J. 26
Stagg, E. 222
Stagg, F. 222

Stählin, G. 74, 114
Steck, O.H. 119, 269
Strack, H. 52
Suhl, A. 134, 200

Talbert, C. 285
Tannehill, R. 17, 156
Taylor, V. 12, 35, 52, 64, 67, 79, 115, 116, 124, 147, 148, 158, 163, 173, 191, 195, 212, 220, 228, 235
Todorov, T. 17
Tolbert, M.A. 17, 189, 196, 198, 238
Tolkien, J.R.R. 220
Trocmé, E. 13, 14
Turner, C.H. 14, 92, 93

Vanhoye, A. 236
Via, D.O. 17
Vielhauer, P. 227
Votaw, C. 285

Weder, H. 27
Weeden, T.J. 13, 111, 179, 258, 273, 274, 277, 281, 286
Weiss, B. 115
Wendling, E. 223
Winter, P. 129, 132
Wrede, W. 93, 140
Wright, G.A. 130

Zerwick, M. 14

JOURNAL FOR THE STUDY OF THE NEW TESTAMENT

Supplement Series

1. THE BARREN TEMPLE AND THE WITHERED TREE
    William R. Telford
2. STUDIA BIBLICA 1978
    II. PAPERS ON THE GOSPELS
    Edited by E.A. Livingstone
3. STUDIA BIBLICA 1978
    III. PAPERS ON PAUL AND OTHER NEW TESTAMENT AUTHORS
    Edited by E.A. Livingstone
4. FOLLOWING JESUS:
    DISCIPLESHIP IN THE GOSPEL OF MARK
    Ernest Best
5. THE PEOPLE OF GOD
    Markus Barth
6. PERSECUTION AND MARTYRDOM IN THE THEOLOGY OF PAUL
    John S. Pobee
7. SYNOPTIC STUDIES:
    THE AMPLEFORTH CONFERENCES OF
    1982 AND 1983
    Edited by C.M. Tuckett
8. JESUS ON THE MOUNTAIN:
    A STUDY IN MATTHEAN THEOLOGY
    Terence L. Donaldson
9. THE HYMNS OF LUKE'S INFANCY NARRATIVES:
    THEIR ORIGIN, MEANING AND SIGNIFICANCE
    Stephen Farris
10. CHRIST THE END OF THE LAW:
    ROMANS 10.4 IN PAULINE PERSPECTIVE
    Robert Badenas
11. THE LETTERS TO THE SEVEN CHURCHES OF ASIA IN THEIR LOCAL
    SETTING
    Colin J. Hemer
12. PROCLAMATION FROM PROPHECY AND PATTERN:
    LUCAN OLD TESTAMENT CHRISTOLOGY
    Darrell L. Bock
13. JESUS AND THE LAWS OF PURITY:
    TRADITION HISTORY AND LEGAL HISTORY IN MARK 7
    Roger P. Booth
14. THE PASSION ACCORDING TO LUKE:
    THE SPECIAL MATERIAL OF LUKE 22
    Marion L. Soards

15 HOSTILITY TO WEALTH IN THE SYNOPTIC GOSPELS
    Thomas E. Schmidt
16 MATTHEW'S COMMUNITY:
    THE EVIDENCE OF HIS SPECIAL SAYINGS MATERIAL
    Stephenson H. Brooks
17 THE PARADOX OF THE CROSS IN THE THOUGHT OF ST PAUL
    Anthony Tyrrell Hanson
18 HIDDEN WISDOM AND THE EASY YOKE:
    WISDOM, TORAH AND DISCIPLESHIP IN MATTHEW 11.25-30
    Celia Deutsch
19 JESUS AND GOD IN PAUL'S ESCHATOLOGY
    L. Joseph Kreitzer
20 LUKE
    A NEW PARADIGM (2 Volumes)
    Michael D. Goulder
21 THE DEPARTURE OF JESUS IN LUKE–ACTS:
    THE ASCENSION NARRATIVES IN CONTEXT
    Mikeal C. Parsons
22 THE DEFEAT OF DEATH:
    APOCALYPTIC ESCHATOLOGY IN 1 CORINTHIANS 15 AND ROMANS 5
    Martinus C. de Boer
23 PAUL THE LETTER-WRITER
    AND THE SECOND LETTER TO TIMOTHY
    Michael Prior
24 APOCALYPTIC AND THE NEW TESTAMENT:
    ESSAYS IN HONOR OF J. LOUIS MARTYN
    Edited by Joel Marcus & Marion L. Soards
25 THE UNDERSTANDING SCRIBE:
    MATTHEW AND THE APOCALYPTIC IDEAL
    David E. Orton
26 WATCHWORDS:
    MARK 13 IN MARKAN ESCHATOLOGY
    Timothy J. Geddert
27 THE DISCIPLES ACCORDING TO MARK:
    MARKAN REDACTION IN CURRENT DEBATE
    C. Clifton Black
28 THE NOBLE DEATH:
    GRAECO-ROMAN MARTYROLOGY
    AND PAUL'S CONCEPT OF SALVATION
    David Seeley
29 ABRAHAM IN GALATIANS:
    EPISTOLARY AND RHETORICAL CONTEXTS
    G. Walter Hansen
30 EARLY CHRISTIAN RHETORIC AND 2 THESSALONIANS
    Frank Witt Hughes

31 THE STRUCTURE OF MATTHEW'S GOSPEL:
   A STUDY IN LITERARY DESIGN
   David R. Bauer
32 PETER AND THE BELOVED DISCIPLE:
   FIGURES FOR A COMMUNITY IN CRISIS
   Kevin Quast
33 MARK'S AUDIENCE:
   THE LITERARY AND SOCIAL SETTING OF MARK 4.11-12
   Mary Ann Beavis
34 THE GOAL OF OUR INSTRUCTION:
   THE STRUCTURE OF THEOLOGY AND ETHICS
   IN THE PASTORAL EPISTLES
   Philip H. Towner
35 THE PROVERBS OF JESUS:
   ISSUES OF HISTORY AND RHETORIC
   Alan P. Winton
36 THE STORY OF CHRIST IN THE ETHICS OF PAUL:
   AN ANALYSIS OF THE FUNCTION OF THE HYMNIC MATERIAL
   IN THE PAULINE CORPUS
   Stephen E. Fowl
37 PAUL AND JESUS:
   COLLECTED ESSAYS
   Edited by A.J.M. Wedderburn
38 MATTHEW'S MISSIONARY DISCOURSE:
   A LITERARY CRITICAL ANALYSIS
   Dorothy Jean Weaver
39 FAITH AND OBEDIENCE IN ROMANS:
   A STUDY IN ROMANS 1-4
   Glenn N. Davies
40 IDENTIFYING PAUL'S OPPONENTS:
   THE QUESTION OF METHOD IN 2 CORINTHIANS
   Jerry L. Sumney
41 HUMAN AGENTS OF COSMIC POWER:
   IN HELLENISTIC JUDAISM AND THE SYNOPTIC TRADITION
   Mary E. Mills
42 MATTHEW'S INCLUSIVE STORY:
   A STUDY IN THE NARRATIVE RHETORIC OF THE FIRST GOSPEL
   David B. Howell
43 JESUS, PAUL AND TORAH:
   COLLECTED ESSAYS
   Heikki Räisänen
44 THE NEW COVENANT IN HEBREWS
   Susanne Lehne

45 THE RHETORIC OF ROMANS:
    ARGUMENTATIVE CONSTRAINT AND STRATEGY AND PAUL'S
    DIALOGUE WITH JUDAISM
    Neil Elliott
46 THE LAST SHALL BE FIRST:
    THE RHETORIC OF REVERSAL IN LUKE
    John O. York
47 JAMES AND THE Q SAYINGS OF JESUS
    Patrick J. Hartin
48 TEMPLUM AMICITIAE:
    ESSAYS ON THE SECOND TEMPLE PRESENTED TO ERNST BAMMEL
    Edited by William Horbury
49 PROLEPTIC PRIESTS:
    PRIESTHOOD IN THE EPISTLE TO THE HEBREWS
    John M. Scholer
50 PERSUASIVE ARTISTRY:
    STUDIES IN NEW TESTAMENT RHETORIC
    IN HONOR OF GEORGE A. KENNEDY
    Edited by Duane F. Watson
51 THE AGENCY OF THE APOSTLE: A DRAMATISTIC ANALYSIS OF PAUL'S
    RESPONSES TO CONFLICT IN 2 CORINTHIANS
    Jeffrey A. Crafton
52 REFLECTIONS OF GLORY:
    PAUL'S POLEMICAL USE OF THE MOSES–DOXA TRADITION IN
    2 CORINTHIANS 3.12-18
    Linda L. Belleville
53 REVELATION AND REDEMPTION AT COLOSSAE
    Thomas J. Sappington
54 THE DEVELOPMENT OF EARLY CHRISTIAN PNEUMATOLOGY
    WITH SPECIAL REFERENCE TO LUKE–ACTS
    Robert P. Menzies
55 THE PURPOSE OF ROMANS:
    A COMPARATIVE LETTER STRUCTURE INVESTIGATION
    L. Ann Jervis
56 THE SON OF THE MAN IN THE GOSPEL OF JOHN
    Delbert Burkett
57 ESCHATOLOGY AND THE COVENANT:
    A COMPARISON OF 4 EZRA AND ROMANS 1–11
    Bruce W. Longenecker
58 NONE BUT THE SINNERS:
    RELIGIOUS CATEGORIES IN THE GOSPEL OF LUKE
    David A. Neale
59 CLOTHED WITH CHRIST:
    THE EXAMPLE AND TEACHING OF JESUS IN ROMANS 12.1–15.13
    Michael Thompson

60 THE LANGUAGE OF THE NEW TESTAMENT:
    CLASSIC ESSAYS
    Edited by Stanley E. Porter
61 FOOTWASHING IN JOHN 13 AND THE JOHANNINE COMMUNITY
    John Christopher Thomas
62 JOHN THE BAPTIZER AND PROPHET:
    A SOCIO-HISTORICAL STUDY
    Robert L. Webb
63 POWER AND POLITICS IN PALESTINE:
    THE JEWS AND THE GOVERNING OF THEIR LAND 100 BC–AD 70
    James S. McLaren
64 JESUS AND THE ORAL GOSPEL TRADITION
    Edited by Henry Wansbrough
65 THE RHETORIC OF RIGHTEOUSNESS IN ROMANS 3.21-26
    Douglas A. Campbell
66 PAUL, ANTIOCH AND JERUSALEM:
    A STUDY IN RELATIONSHIPS AND AUTHORITY IN EARLIEST CHRISTIANITY
    Nicholas Taylor
67 THE PORTRAIT OF PHILIP IN ACTS:
    A STUDY OF ROLES AND RELATIONS
    F. Scott Spencer
68 JEREMIAH IN MATTHEW'S GOSPEL:
    THE REJECTED-PROPHET MOTIF IN MATTHAEAN REDACTION
    Michael P. Knowles
69 RHETORIC AND REFERENCE IN THE FOURTH GOSPEL
    Margaret Davies
70 AFTER THE THOUSAND YEARS:
    RESURRECTION AND JUDGMENT IN REVELATION 20
    J. Webb Mealy
71 SOPHIA AND THE JOHANNINE JESUS
    Martin Scott
72 NARRATIVE ASIDES IN LUKE–ACTS
    Steven M. Sheeley
73 SACRED SPACE:
    AN APPROACH TO THE THEOLOGY OF THE EPISTLE TO THE HEBREWS
    Marie E. Isaacs
74 TEACHING WITH AUTHORITY:
    MIRACLES AND CHRISTOLOGY IN THE GOSPEL OF MARK
    Edwin K. Broadhead
75 PATRONAGE AND POWER:
    A STUDY OF SOCIAL NETWORKS IN CORINTH
    John Kin-Man Chow
76 THE NEW TESTAMENT AS CANON:
    A READER IN CANONICAL CRITICISM
    Robert Wall and Eugene Lemcio

77 REDEMPTIVE ALMSGIVING IN EARLY CHRISTIANITY
    Roman Garrison
78 THE FUNCTION OF SUFFERING IN PHILIPPIANS
    L. Gregory Bloomquist
79 THE THEME OF RECOMPENSE IN MATTHEW'S GOSPEL
    Blaine Charette
80 BIBLICAL GREEK LANGUAGE AND LINGUISTICS: OPEN QUESTIONS IN
    CURRENT RESEARCH
    Stanley E. Porter and D.A. Carson
81 THE LAW IN GALATIANS
    In-Gyu Hong
82 ORAL TRADITION AND THE GOSPELS: THE PROBLEM OF MARK 4
    Barry W. Henaut
83 PAUL AND THE SCRIPTURES OF ISRAEL
    Craig A. Evans and James A. Sanders
84 FROM JESUS TO JOHN: ESSAYS ON JESUS AND NEW TESTAMENT
    CHRISTOLOGY IN HONOUR OF MARINUS DE JONGE
    Edited by Martinus C. De Boer
85 RETURNING HOME: NEW COVENANT AND SECOND EXODUS AS THE
    CONTEXT FOR 2 CORINTHIANS 6.14–7.1
    William J. Webb
86 ORIGINS AND METHOD: TOWARDS A NEW UNDERSTANDING OF JUDAISM
    AND CHRISTIANITY—ESSAYS IN HONOUR OF JOHN C. HURD
    Edited by Bradley H. McLean
87 WORSHIP, THEOLOGY AND MINISTRY IN THE EARLY CHURCH: ESSAYS IN
    HONOUR OF RALPH P. MARTIN
    Edited by Michael Wilkins and Terence Paige
88 THE BIRTH OF THE LUKAN NARRATIVE
    M. Coleridge
89 WORD AND GLORY: ON THE EXEGETICAL AND THEOLOGICAL
    BACKGROUND OF JOHN'S PROLOGUE
    Craig A. Evans
90 RHETORIC IN THE NEW TESTAMENT:
    ESSAYS FROM THE 1992 HEIDELBERG CONFERENCE
    Edited by Stanley E. Porter and Thomas H. Olbricht
91 MATTHEW'S NARRATIVE WEB: OVER AND OVER AND OVER AGAIN
    J.C. Anderson
92 LUKE: INTERPRETER OF PAUL, CRITIC OF MATTHEW
    E. Franklin
93 ISAIAH AND PROPHETIC TRADITION IN THE BOOK OF REVELATION
    J. Fekkes III
94 JESUS' EXPOSITION OF THE OLD TESTAMENT IN LUKE'S GOSPEL
    C.A. Kimball
95 THE SYMBOLIC NARRATIVES OF THE FOURTH GOSPEL
    D.A. Lee

96 THE COLOSSIAN CONTROVERSY: WISDOM IN DISPUTE AT COLOSSAE
R.E. DeMaris
97 PROPHET, SON, MESSIAH: NARRATIVE FORM AND FUNCTION
IN MARK 14–16
Edwin K. Broadhead